C000258053

# High Integrity Ada

## *The SPARK Approach*

# High Integrity Ada

## *The SPARK Approach*


John Barnes

*with Praxis Critical Systems Limited*

ADDISON-WESLEY

Harlow, England • Reading, Massachusetts • Menlo Park, California
New York • Don Mills, Ontario • Amsterdam • Bonn • Sydney
Singapore • Tokyo • Madrid • San Juan • Milan • Mexico City • Taipei

Addison Wesley Longman Limited
Edinburgh Gate
Harlow
Essex CM20 2JE
England

and Associated Companies throughout the World.



Cover designed by odB Design & Communication, Reading, UK
Illustrations and typesetting by the author
Printed and bound in Great Britain by Biddles Ltd., Guildford and King's Lynn

First printed 1997. Reprinted with revisions 2000.

ISBN 0–201–17517–7

**British Library Cataloguing-in-Publication Data**

A catalogue record for this book is available from the British Library

*There are two ways of constructing a software design. One way is to make it so simple that there are* ***obviously*** *no deficiencies. And the other way is to make it so complicated that there are no* ***obvious*** *deficiencies.*

Professor C. A. R. Hoare
the 1980 Turing award lecture

# Foreword

To the participants, the early years of SPARK were more than just exciting... The first challenge was to produce, rather rapidly, a formally-based computational model and analysis tools, for a core of Ada large enough to be considered a usable language. At the time, even compilation of Ada was still regarded as a major undertaking, and few people believed rigorous static-analysis methods could ever 'scale up' to industrial proportions; bringing the two together was seen as a rather wild enterprise. The idea was nevertheless brought to fruition, through the imaginative talent and determination of the youthful SPARK team at PVL (Program Validation Limited) that I was so privileged to lead at that time. There were too many of them to name here, but a number of their works are cited in the Bibliography. The success of this first phase of the development of SPARK also owed much to the confidence and sympathetic help of the early users of SPARK, guiding us in the right direction.

SPARK is more than a programming language – it is a way of conceiving programs. To use it to advantage, in concert with one's other preferred software development paradigms, requires a very good understanding of what it offers. The second important phase in the development of SPARK – this time as a support for the software design and development process – required direct involvement in high integrity Ada projects on a much larger scale than PVL could undertake. Crucial to this was the vision of Praxis Critical Systems (in which PVL is now incorporated), in recognizing the potential of the technology, and fielding it judiciously in large projects to great advantage. It has been pleasing to see the change in SPARK users' perception of software verification, from a retrospectively-applied purgative, inflicting on the developer a level of pain matching the integrity level required – to an integral part of a software development process aimed at getting it right first time. It should not really be surprising that techniques that help to produce the right product can also be economically beneficial; and indeed, our gradual absorption into a cultural movement towards Correctness by Construction has been very good news.

It is said that most of the best books never get written. For some time we had agonized over the need to inform the wider programming community of what SPARK can accomplish; although there were many successful applications, it remained very difficult to discover enough about SPARK to use it well. Yet it seemed that a good exposition of the subject would remain a dream forever. What a joy and a relief that John Barnes, having developed an interest in SPARK over a number of years, and having experienced the need for a book, should write it for us! And better, so much better, than we could have done ourselves!

Obviously John shares our belief in the importance of language, in shaping and implementing one's ideas in software. But his healthy scepticism of the usefulness of formalization, his energetic questioning of every aspect of SPARK, took us on a new voyage of discovery, casting an interesting new light on the language. And when it came to the adaptation to Ada 95 (on which John is an expert, being the principal author of the official Ada 95 Rationale), the decisions on how SPARK should be extended at this time were rather obvious to him.

The reader will enjoy John Barnes' lively guidance through SPARK. With panache, he combines rigorous clarity and a great sense of fun.

*Bernard Carré*
Southampton, England
April 1997

# Preface

This book is about programming in SPARK – a language highly suited for writing programs that need to be reliable.

SPARK is sometimes regarded as being just a subset of Ada with a few annotations that you have to write as Ada comments. This is mechanically correct but is not at all the proper view to take.

SPARK should be seen as a distinct language in its own right which has just those features required for writing reliable software: not so austere as to be a real pain, but not so rich as to make program analysis or proof out of the question. But, for convenience, it is sensible to share compiler technology with some other standard language and it so happens that Ada has a better framework than many other languages. It should also be observed that many of the application areas which are concerned about reliability (such as avionics) use Ada anyway.

So for pragmatic reasons, I expect that many readers will be familiar with Ada. Nevertheless, the principles of writing reliable software should be clear whatever the reader's background and I have tried to ensure that a knowledge of Ada is not required in order to appreciate the discussion.

I have always been interested in techniques for writing reliable software if only (presumably like most programmers) because I would like my programs to work without spending ages debugging the wretched things.

Perhaps my first realization that the tools used really mattered came with my experience of using Algol 60 when I was a programmer in the chemical industry. It was a delight to use a compiler that stopped me violating the bounds of arrays; it seemed such an advance over Fortran and other even more primitive languages which allowed the program to violate itself in an arbitrary manner.

On the other hand I have always been slightly doubtful of the practicality of the formal theorists who like to define everything in some turgid specification language before contemplating the process known as programming. It has always seemed to me that formal specifications were pretty obscure to all but a few and might perhaps even make a program less reliable in a global sense by increasing the problem of communication between client and programmer.

Nevertheless, I have often felt that underlying mathematical foundations can provide us with better tools even if the mathematical nature is somewhat hidden by a more practical façade. For example, enumeration types are really about sets but a deep understanding of set theory is not necessary in order to obtain the benefits of strong typing by realizing that a set of apples is not the same as a set of oranges.

SPARK has this flavour of practical helpfulness underpinned by solid mathematical foundations. You don't have to understand the theorems of Böhm and Jacopini in order to obtain the benefits of good flow structure. Equally, SPARK does not require esoteric annotations of a formal kind but quite simple affirmations of access and visibility which enable the SPARK Examiner to effectively 'look over your shoulder' and identify inconsistencies between what you said you were going to do in the annotations and what you actually did in the code.

One of the advantages of SPARK is that it may be used at various levels. At the simplest level, the annotations ensure that problems of mistaken identity do not arise, that undefined values are not used and other similar flow errors are trapped. The next level gives additional assurance regarding the inter-dependence between variables and can highlight unexpected relationships indicative of poorly organized data.

For certain applications, formal proof may be useful and SPARK provides a third level in which formal preconditions, postconditions and other assertions enable proofs to be established with the aid of the SPARK tools.

However, formal proof is easily oversold; the effort involved in developing a proof is high and in many cases might well be spent more effectively on other aspects of ensuring that a program is fit for its purpose. So the ability to apply SPARK at various levels according to the application is extremely valuable.

All three levels might even be mixed in a single program. The fine detail of key algorithms might be formally proved, higher organizational parts might benefit from the middle level whereas the overall driving routines could well need only the simplest level of annotation.

The language described in this book is based on the 1995 Ada standard and is consequently referred to as SPARK 95 when it is necessary to distinguish it from previous versions based on Ada 83.

SPARK 95 is a significant advance on SPARK 83 for a number of reasons. One of the most important is the introduction of the lowest level of annotation which enables the benefits of most aspects of flow analysis to be obtained without the burden of the so-called derives annotations. Interestingly enough, the feasibility of permitting this stems largely from the ability in Ada 95 to read **out** parameters. That such a small change should permit such benefits reveals the importance of getting the underlying concepts correct.

The parameter mechanism of Ada 83 was flawed although the flaw seemed but a minor irritant to most – but I do recall one programmer in a Southern State exclaiming 'Hallelujah, Praise the Lord!' when being told of this improvement in Ada 95. Whether he saw the fundamental nature of the change or the practical benefit I do not know, but I certainly felt in close agreement.

Existing SPARK users will find many other benefits in SPARK 95 as well, such as decomposition using child packages, use type clauses rather than operator renaming, and the elimination of the rules on the order of declarations.

Equally, I hope that those unfamiliar with SPARK will learn something of its benefits and will find it useful for their own applications whether they be in overtly safety critical areas such as avionics, automotive control or medical systems or more general application areas which too would benefit from correct programs.

Perhaps I might be permitted to say a little about the background to this book. I first encountered the foundation work done by Bob Phillips at Malvern when a consultant to the British Government and tasked with monitoring the usefulness of various research activities. I remember feeling that the flow analysis he was investigating was potentially good stuff but needed practical user interfaces.

That was twenty years ago. The current language and tools reflect the enormous energy put into the topic since then by Bernard Carré and his colleagues, first at Southampton University, then at Program Validation Limited and now at Praxis Critical Systems. The original approach was for the analysis of existing programs but now the emphasis is much more on writing the programs correctly in the first place.

However, it always seemed to me that although the tools and techniques were gaining steady acceptance, nevertheless both the tools and indeed the world of programmers deserved a more accessible description than that found in conference papers and user manuals.

A big impetus to actually do something was when my daughter Janet and I were invited by Program Validation Limited to join in a review of the formal definition of SPARK and its potential transition to Ada 95. This resulted in a report familiarly known as *Janet and John go a-Sparking* (non-British readers should note that there is a series of children's books concerning the activities of Janet and John).

Being involved in the review strengthened my feeling that a book would be very appropriate particularly with the transition to Ada 95. The book then followed thanks to Praxis for whose support I am deeply grateful.

I must also thank all others who have helped in many different ways. The external reviewers included Alan Burns, John Dawes, Bob Duff, Fred Long, Pat Rogers, Jim Sutton, Tucker Taft and Phil Thornley; their comments were extremely valuable in reshaping the focus of certain aspects of the book as well as eliminating a number of errors. Many of the staff of Praxis Critical Systems seem to have been involved at various stages and I am almost reluctant to mention them by name in case I have forgotten someone. The following made major contributions: Mike Ainsworth, Peter Amey, Janet Barnes, Stephen Bull, Rod Chapman, Denton Clutterbuck, Gavin Finnie, Jonathan Hammond, Adrian Hilton, David Jackson, Mel Jackson, Robin Messer, Ian O'Neill, Paul Wand, Will Ward, Michael Worsley and of course Bernard Carré.

Finally, many thanks to my wife Barbara for her help in typesetting and proof-reading, to friends at Addison-Wesley for their continued guidance and to Sheila Chatten for her help in the final stages of production.

*John Barnes*
Caversham, England
April 1997

PS See over for notes on enhancements in this revised printing =>

## Enhancements in this revised printing

This printing is essentially based on Release 5.0 of the SPARK Examiner. The main changes from the first printing are:

- Flow analysis on records is now in terms of individual components rather than entire variables; that on arrays, of course, remains the same.
- There are some minor changes regarding when the name of a child unit has to be given in full.
- String literals are now unambiguously of the type String and no longer have to be qualified.
- Quantification using **for all** and **for some** is now allowed in proof contexts such as preconditions, postconditions and assert annotations.
- Proof types have been introduced. These enable an abstract own variable to be given an abstract type. An important consequence is that proof can be performed in conjunction with refinement.

The CD in the back of this book contains Release 5.0 of the Examiner within the same GUI interface as in the first printing. This release also contains two options which are not available through that GUI interface and so are not discussed in this book; they are the ability to generate HTML report files for ease of browsing and to set a specific annotation character. These options are available through other interfaces as explained in the documentation on the CD. As well as the material described in Appendix 4, the CD also contains additional documentation such as the manual for Generation of Verification Conditions; this contains a fuller description of new features such as proof with refinement than is provided in the body of this book.

Another improvement in Release 5.0 is that all error messages now include an error number as well as the text of the message. This number refers to the explanation in the user manual. In order to avoid clutter these error numbers are omitted from the sample messages in the book except for the report in Section 9.5.

Further information including the very latest release of the tools may be found at www.sparkada.com.

# Contents

# Part 1

# An Overview



This first part comprises three chapters which cover the background to SPARK and provide a broad overview of the main features of the language and its associated tools.

Chapter 1 starts with a brief account of the categories of software, the need for reliable software and the origins of SPARK. It then discusses the key requirements of a language for high integrity systems and explains how the features of Ada incorporated into SPARK together with various annotations meet those requirements. There is then a very brief introduction to the main SPARK tools which comprise the Examiner, Simplifier and Proof Checker and this is followed by a couple of simple examples.

Chapter 2 discusses the general principles of decomposition through abstraction and the concepts of Abstract State Machines and Abstract Data Types. It then illustrates the major features of the SPARK language through a number of examples of these abstractions. The chapter concludes with an introduction to the important topics of refinement and program composition. In a sense this chapter provides an overview of the second part of the book which discusses the SPARK core language in detail.

Chapter 3 introduces the various SPARK tools and the process of proof which form the topics of the third part of the book. It starts with some philosophical remarks on correctness and then introduces the use of the Examiner for flow analysis. It concludes with an outline of the use of path functions and the generation and proof of verification conditions.

---

# Introduction



SPARK is a high level programming language designed for writing software for high integrity applications. In this introductory chapter we briefly outline the development of SPARK, its main objectives and the overall structure of the rest of this book.

It is perhaps difficult to give a rigid definition of high integrity applications other than to say that they are applications where it is beneficial for the program to be well written. High integrity applications include safety critical applications which are usually defined to be those where life and limb or the environment are at risk if the program is in error. But clearly any application benefits from being written correctly and the merit of SPARK is that it enables errors to be detected in a more predictable manner.

## 1.1 Background

Software pervades all aspects of our modern society. Banking systems, transport systems, medical systems, industrial control systems and office systems all depend upon the correct functioning of software. As a consequence the safety of many human lives and much property now depends upon the reliability of software.

Software takes many forms and there are many styles of application. At one extreme is the casual calculation on a pocket calculator or similar machine. Speed of programming and immediacy of answer are key considerations.

Then there are office programs such as spreadsheets, word processors and presentation graphics. These highly interactive programs are the subject of much attention and market driven development. They tend not to be critical. If incorrect, a word processor may crash and lose data but disaster does not strike (except perhaps that the user may get angry and suffer a heart attack). The specification of such programs is not given; they do what they do and the user learns by experience.

And finally there are serious programs that, if incorrect, cause real difficulties. These range from small programs such as engine controllers to larger programs such as telecommunications systems. Such programs have definite specifications against which their behaviour can be judged. For small critical systems the problem of getting them correct may not be too large but the consequence of any error can be loss of life, property or damage to the environment. For larger programs the problems are usually those of integration and the definition of correct interfaces between parts of a total system written by teams of programmers. The consequences of error may be catastrophic but are more likely to be economic embarrassment through delays in commissioning.

It is these serious programs that SPARK addresses. SPARK encourages the development of programs in an orderly manner with the general intention that the program should be correct by the nature of the techniques used in its construction. There is strong evidence from a number of years of use of SPARK in application areas such as avionics and railway signalling that indeed not only is the program more likely to be correct but the overall cost of development is actually less in total after all the testing and integration phases are taken into account.

SPARK has its technical origins in work carried out in the 1970s at the then Royal Signals and Radar Establishment (RSRE) by the late Bob Phillips. (RSRE at Great Malvern in the UK is now part of the Defence Research Agency (DRA).) Phillips was interested in understanding and analysing the behaviour of existing programs and developed tools to perform such analysis. However, it was soon realized that analysis would be easier if the programs were written in a sensible language in the first place. There was also growing awareness of the importance of the correctness of software for safety critical applications such as the control of aircraft.

A group at Southampton University led by Bernard Carré doing research in the field of graph theory then became closely involved; the group developed tools for a subset of Pascal called SPADE – or more grandly the Southampton Program Analysis Development Environment. It was of course realized that Pascal was an inadequate base because it did not address separate compilation and information hiding. An alternative foundation language was hence sought.

There were two obvious possibilities at the time, Modula-2 (whose industrial future was already in doubt) and Ada (which would need simplifying because it had facilities not relevant for high integrity software). C was dismissed on the grounds of the lack of an international standard and the general permissiveness of the language. Ada on the other hand was an international standard, was strongly supported among those application areas interested in high integrity software and moreover was eminently readable with clean syntax amenable to both human and machine analysis.

Accordingly, Ada was chosen as the foundation for future work. It was of course necessary to exclude certain features of Ada from programs that were to be analysed by the SPADE tools and this resulted in the SPADE Ada Kernel or SPARK. However, SPARK is not just a subset of Ada but also requires embedded annotations giving extra information about the program; these annotations take the form of Ada comments so that the program is still strictly an Ada program.

SPARK was originally defined informally by Bernard Carré and Trevor Jennings of Southampton University in a document entitled *SPARK – The SPADE Ada Kernel* [Carré and Jennings, 1988]. This Specification described SPARK as a variation on Ada 83 using the usual syntax together with informal semantics. A good knowledge of Ada was necessary in order to understand this Specification document. It has subsequently been reissued several times, as SPARK has evolved [Finnie, 1997].

SPARK was also defined formally in *The Formal Semantics of SPARK* which comprises two main parts addressing the static and dynamic semantics respectively [Marsh and O'Neill, 1994]. This formal definition uses a variant of Z and by its very nature is difficult to understand without considerable experience of that notation as well perhaps as a background in Ada.

In 1995, the Ada standard itself was revised resulting in Ada 95. Although the changes to Ada were very largely outside the subset on which SPARK is based, nevertheless some small changes to the core of Ada are quite fundamental and very relevant to SPARK. As a consequence SPARK has been updated and it is this new version that forms the subject of this book. Whenever it is necessary to distinguish the two versions they are referred to as SPARK 83 and SPARK 95 respectively.

A recent publication in the standards area is the *Guide for the Use of the Ada Programming Language in High Integrity Systems* [ISO, 2000]. This contains excellent general background material on the whole topic and in particular gives guidance on which features of Ada are appropriate for use with various verification techniques.

## 1.2 The rationale for SPARK

The general goal of SPARK is to provide a language which increases the likelihood of the program behaving as intended and thereby reduces to an acceptable level the risks of disaster arising as a result of an error in the program. The following paragraphs illustrate the range of factors considered in the design of SPARK.

### *Logical soundness*

For the behaviour of a program to be completely predictable, it is vital that the language in which it is written be precise. For example, most languages (including Ada) permit a statement such as

```
Y := F(X) + G(X);
```

but do not define the order of evaluation. As a consequence, if the functions F and G have side effects (by making assignments to X for example) then it is possible for the result assigned to Y to depend upon whether F or G is called first. This potential ambiguity does not arise in SPARK because functions cannot have side effects; functions are true mathematical functions which may observe the state of some part of the system but cannot change that state.

It is interesting to observe that the absence of ambiguity is achieved by preventing side effects and not by prescribing the order of the evaluations. In turn, the absence of side effects is not prescribed directly but, as we shall see, is a consequence of the interaction between a number of more fundamental rules.

### *Simplicity of language definition*

Simplicity is generally considered to be good since it reduces the risk of a program actually meaning something different from what it appears to mean. Indeed, experience shows that parts of a language which cause complexity in any formal definition of the language are likely to be sources of problems. A good example of this is the definition of variant records in Pascal. These cause complexity in the formal definition of Pascal and are indeed the source of difficulties in the use of Pascal because of the effective loophole in the type checking system. Another advantage of a simple formal definition is that writing such a definition is likely to be a fruitful exercise and not merely an academic marathon whose correctness is suspect.

Generally we can expect that simplicity of definition means simplicity of reasoning which implies simplicity of supporting tools and simplicity of testing. If tools are simpler then they are more likely to be reliable so that risks are reduced.

### *Expressive power*

On the other hand the language must not be so simple as to be trivial and not able to provide the key benefits of a modern language and its concepts of abstraction. Thus languages such as Basic, Pascal and C do not have enough expressive power largely because they do not have adequate facilities for hiding implementation details.

Another aspect is the need to be able to make stronger assertions about the values of variables and their relationships than is traditional in imperative programming languages. Such assertions clearly increase the expressive capability of the language.

### *Security and integrity*

A language must be secure in the sense that it should not have rules that cannot be checked with reasonable effort (technically within polynomial time). Moreover the behaviour of any program must lie within certain well defined bounds. This is achieved by ensuring that the program does not stray outside a well defined computational model. In particular, a program must not be able to 'run wild' by jumping or writing to arbitrary locations.

For example, an Ada program is not permitted to read or write outside the bounds of an array. Ada thus provides a good starting point and all such possibilities for violating the abstract model of the language are prevented in SPARK.

### Verifiability

Safety critical programs have to be shown to be correct. In order to do this it is necessary that the language constructions are such that a program can be subjected to rigorous mathematical analysis. For example it can be shown that goto statements impede analysis by making the decomposition of the flow of control intractable in the general case. It has been shown that it is highly desirable that every fragment of code has a single entry point and limited exit points. Thus the goto statement and arbitrary internal exits from loops and subprograms must be prevented.

It is also important to be able to analyse fragments of program on their own. This impacts on many aspects of the language such as the control of visibility. For example, inheritance (currently so popular as part of Object Oriented Programming (OOP)) creates difficulties because properties are inherited remotely and thus not visible where they are used.

### Bounded space and time requirements

In order to prove that a program is able to function satisfactorily it is necessary to be able to predict the amount of storage space that it requires. So it must be possible to calculate the maximum amount of space required prior to execution, that is statically. General dynamic storage allocation is thus prohibited; in language terms this means that recursion, the declaration of arrays with arbitrary bounds and especially access types and the use of heap storage have to be forbidden. It is interesting to note that recursion is not forbidden explicitly but cannot occur as a consequence of other rules in much the same way that side effects cannot occur as discussed above. The absence of recursion (direct and mutual) means that the depth of calls and hence the amount of stack space is bounded and can be computed statically.

Bounding time is more difficult. A real-time program that does not meet its deadlines is incorrect just as much as a numerical program that gives the wrong answer. SPARK itself offers little direct support in this area; however, the language is such that some analysis of loops is possible thereby giving warnings of certain non-terminating situations.

### Correspondence with Ada

There are benefits in sharing technology and general resources with an existing standard language. However these benefits can only be obtained if the special language truly is a subset of the parent language in the sense that compilers (and other tools) for the parent language can also be used for the special language. SPARK is indeed a true subset of Ada in this sense since any legal SPARK program is also a legal Ada program and always executes with exactly the same meaning.

Note that SPARK does not impose additional requirements on the Ada compiler itself. Even though Ada permits an Ada program to mean different things using different implementations (that is, using different compilers) because of phenomena such as side effects, nevertheless the rules of SPARK are such that those Ada programs are not legal SPARK programs anyway.

### *Verifiability of compiled code*

In an ideal world we would like to be assured that the compiled code does properly correspond to the source code written by the programmer. There would seem little point in carefully writing and verifying a program at the source level if bugs in the compiler mean that the object code does not exactly correspond to the source code. Thus we would like in turn to be assured that there are no bugs in the compiler. This seems to be outside our present abilities. In principle it would seem easier to develop a correct compiler for a smaller language such as SPARK rather than for full Ada. However, such a compiler would be expensive to develop relative to the number of applications. There is also evidence that it is more reliable to use the well trodden parts of a widely used compiler for a larger language than to write and use a special compiler for an intrinsically simpler language.

An alternative approach is to prove the correspondence between the source code and the object code by inspection. For this to be feasible, the compiler must be able to produce straightforward code. The Ada 95 Safety and Security Annex prescribes facilities to request this. Of course, a possible disadvantage of this approach is that various desirable optimizations may not be possible with the result that the program is too slow for critical real-time applications.

### *Complexity of run time system*

The final system delivered in an operational environment will typically comprise two parts, the code corresponding to that written by the programmer and a run time system written by the compiler developer which supports language features that cannot be sensibly implemented by inline code. The run time system is thus an integral part of the operational system and has to be shown to be correct (certified) just as much as the specific code for the application. Therefore the run time system must itself be simple and capable of analysis; this in turn imposes restrictions on the complexity of the source language.

In practice it may not always be possible to use a simplified run time system because, although it may be possible to write most of the program in a simple language, nevertheless there may be some (less critical) parts that need more general facilities.

## 1.3 SPARK language features

The SPARK language comprises a kernel which is a subset of Ada 95 plus additional features added as annotations in the form of Ada comments. These

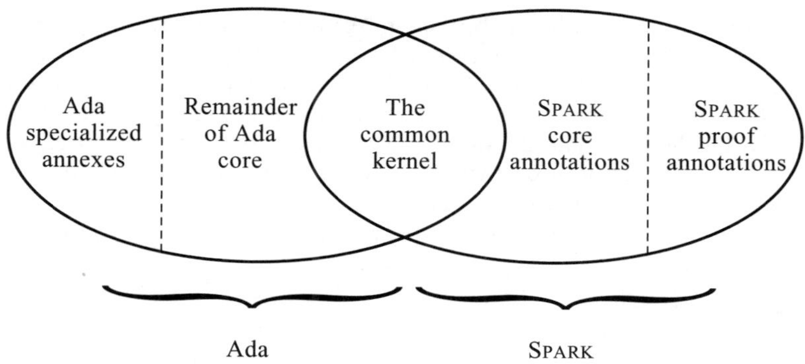


**Figure 1.1** Relationship between SPARK and Ada.

annotations are thus ignored by an Ada compiler and so a SPARK program can be compiled by a standard compiler.

The annotations are in two categories. The first category concerns flow analysis and visibility control and the second category concerns formal proof. The kernel plus the first category of annotations comprises the SPARK core language and the corresponding annotations are called the core annotations. The additional annotations concerning proof are referred to as the proof annotations. Thus SPARK comprises a core language plus optional features concerning proof. There is an interesting parallel with Ada which comprises a core language plus optional specialized annexes (the Safety and Security Annex was mentioned above).

The relationship between SPARK and Ada is represented diagrammatically in Figure 1.1. This shows both languages comprising a core plus additional features. The overlap between them is the kernel. An important point is that SPARK should not be perceived as just a subset of Ada with a few bits tacked on in comments. SPARK should be seen as a language in its own right with just those facilities necessary for writing high integrity programs and permitting analysis and proof according to the needs of the application. For convenience SPARK and Ada overlap in terms of the compilable kernel for the very good reason of wishing to share compiler technology. Indeed it is clear that SPARK is not a subset of Ada at all since SPARK imposes additional requirements through the annotations. Nevertheless, for pedagogic purposes and especially bearing in mind that many readers will be familiar with Ada, it is convenient at times to discuss the SPARK kernel in terms of the corresponding features of full Ada.

(Incidentally, the term full Ada is sometimes used for emphasis in the sense of 'as opposed to the kernel subset' and has nothing to do with the specialized annexes of Ada.)

Although the kernel language necessarily omits many features of full Ada it is nevertheless a rich language in its own right. It includes

- packages, private types, library units,
- unconstrained array types, functions returning composite types.

Thus SPARK contains a full capability for defining Abstract Data Types. This is not possible in Pascal which does not have private types and does not allow functions to return composite types. SPARK also has facilities for separate compilation in the same way as Ada. Another advantage over Pascal as originally defined is that unconstrained array types are permitted and so subprograms can be written which will operate upon arrays of any size (although local arrays must have static size).

On the other hand, the kernel excludes the following features of full Ada

- tasks, exceptions, generics,
- access types, goto statements, use package clauses.

These are omitted largely on the grounds that they create difficulties in proving that a program is correct. (But note that use type clauses are allowed.)

The core annotations take various forms. There are two important annotations regarding subprograms and these add further information to that provided by the specification in the Ada sense which simply gives the types and modes of the formal parameters.

- Global definitions – declare the use of global variables by subprograms.
- Dependency relations of procedures – specify the information flow between their imports and exports via both parameters and global variables.

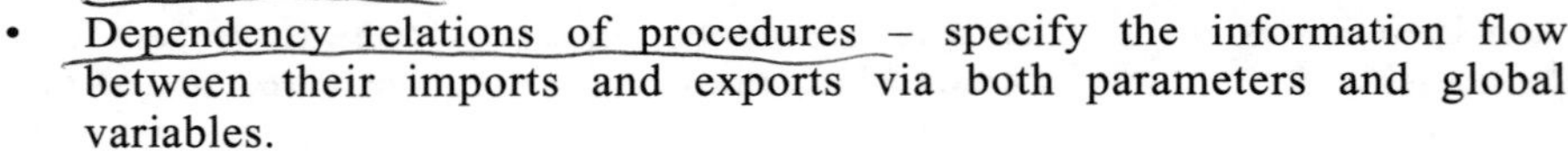

These annotations should be seen as part of the specification and should be written at the design stage before coding is commenced. Of course, the information provided by these annotations just completes the static semantic description of the interface that the subprogram presents to the rest of the program. When the code of the subprogram body is written the SPARK Examiner can be used to check that the code is consistent with the annotations.

On the other hand, once the code of the subprogram body is written, the annotations might be seen as simply providing an alternative view of information also existing in the subprogram body. This essential redundancy thereby gives confidence that the program is correct. There is an analogy with hardware redundancy where physical replication of measurements gives confidence if they are consistent.

SPARK permits flow analysis at two levels: data flow analysis which just concerns the direction of data flow, and information flow analysis which also considers the coupling between variables. The dependency relation (familiarly known as the derives annotation) can be omitted if information flow analysis is not required but the global annotation is always necessary whenever global variables are used.

Other important core annotations relate to the access of variables in packages. The visibility rules of full Ada are complex and permit access to variables in a fairly liberal manner. Thus at times it is not obvious from looking at an Ada text just where variables are declared. The main difficulty is so-called use package clauses and these are forbidden in SPARK so that a variable V in a package P has to be referred to as P.V and can never be abbreviated to just V when used outside the package. In addition, SPARK requires annotations to ensure that certain uses of variables in packages are made more explicit.

- Inherit clauses – control the visibility of package names.
- Own variable clauses – control access to package variables.
- Initialization annotations – indicate initialization of own variables.

Note that an own variable is one declared inside a package and thus contains state preserved between calls of subprograms in the package.

A general guideline in the design of the fine detail of SPARK was to ensure that a SPARK program is as explicit as reasonably possible and that all potential ambiguities (whether in the mind of the compiler or the human reader) are eliminated wherever possible. This overall guideline is reflected in the following principles

- overloading should be avoided as far as possible;
- scope and visibility rules should be such that each entity has a unique name at a given place;
- operations on complete arrays should be explicit wherever possible, implicit operations such as sliding should be avoided;
- all subtypes should be named and all constraints should be static.

These principles are not followed exactly in every instance. For example, although the user cannot declare overloading of subprograms and enumeration literals, nevertheless the integer and floating types really have to use overloading for the predefined operations such as "+". Another example is that loop parameters do not in general have a named subtype and their range need not be static. However, the general observance of these principles does facilitate the rigorous analysis of SPARK programs.

A number of further features of Ada are omitted on the grounds that they can create complexity in the mind of the reader by introducing effects at a distance (that is the effect on the program is at a place remote from where the feature is used). These include such things as derived types (and hence type extension, class wide types and dispatching), default parameters and default record components. Other features omitted are discriminants (and hence variant parts) and block statements.

Intrinsically unreliable features such as unchecked conversion are also prohibited in SPARK. However, where absolutely essential, they (and indeed any feature of full Ada) can be used in parts of a program covered by the special hide directive which tells the Examiner that a part of a program is not to be examined.

Those familiar with the evolution of Ada 83 into Ada 95 will note that many of the facilities added in Ada 95 are not available in SPARK. This is almost inevitable because most of the new facilities in Ada 95 were added in order to increase dynamic flexibility – that is to give more flexibility at run time. But this is precisely what SPARK is not about; in order to prove that a program is correct, it is necessary that dynamic flexibility be kept to a

minimum. However, a number of changes to Ada which were made to ease the static burden on the programmer have also been made to SPARK. The most obvious of these is the introduction of child packages. Other changes include the introduction of the use type clause, the ability to read out parameters, the clarification of the rules for conformance, and the removal of the petty restriction on the order of declarations. Perhaps surprisingly, the ability to read out parameters had far reaching effects; it permitted the introduction of global annotations with mode information and this in turn allowed greater flexibility in flow analysis by enabling it to be performed at two different levels.

## 1.4 Tool support

The main SPARK tool, the Examiner, is vital to the use of SPARK. It has two basic functions

- It checks conformance of the code to the rules of the kernel language.
- It checks consistency between the code and the embedded annotations by control, data and information flow analysis.

The Examiner is itself written in SPARK and has been applied to itself. There is therefore considerable confidence in the correctness of the Examiner.

The SPARK language with its core annotations ensures that a program cannot have certain errors but does not address the issue of dynamic behaviour. In order to do this a number of proof annotations can be inserted which enable dynamic behaviour to be analysed prior to execution. The general idea is that these annotations enable the Examiner to generate theorems which then have to be proved in order to verify that the program is correct with respect to the annotations. These proof annotations address

- pre- and postconditions of subprograms,
- assertions such as loop invariants,
- declarations of proof functions.

The generated theorems are known as verification conditions. These can then be verified by human reasoning, which is usually tedious and unreliable, or by using other tools such as the SPADE Automatic Simplifier (usually referred to as just the Simplifier) and the Proof Checker.

Even without proof annotations, the Examiner can generate theorems corresponding to the run-time checks of Ada such as range checks. The proof of these theorems shows that the checks would not be violated and therefore that the program is free of run-time errors that would raise exceptions in full Ada.

The Examiner can also generate path functions for analysis; these show the effect of traversing the various paths in part of a program.

It should be noted that there are a number of advantages in using a distinct tool such as the Examiner rather than simply a front-end processor which then passes its output to a compiler. One general advantage is that it encourages the early use of a V & V (Verification and Validation) approach. Thus it is possible to write pieces of SPARK complete with annotations and to have them processed by the Examiner even before they can be compiled. For example, a package specification can be examined even though its private part might not yet be written; such an incomplete package specification cannot of course be compiled.

There is a temptation to take an existing piece of Ada code and then to add the annotations (often referred to as 'Sparking the Ada'). This is to be discouraged because it typically leads to extensive annotations indicative of an unnecessarily complex structure. Although in principle it might then be possible to rearrange the code to reduce the complexity, it is often the case that such good intentions are overridden by the desire to preserve as much as possible of the existing code.

The proper approach is to treat the annotations as part of the design process and to use them to assist in arriving at a design which minimizes complexity before the effort of detailed coding takes one down an irreversible path. This is discussed further in Chapter 12.

## 1.5 Examples

We conclude this introductory discussion with two small examples which illustrate a number of aspects of SPARK.

The first example shows how the SPARK annotations increase the level of information concerning abstraction. An important aspect of decomposing a program into components is the definition of the interfaces between the components. Such interfaces provide an abstract view of each component. Ideally an abstraction should hide all irrelevant detail but expose all relevant detail. Alternatively we might say that an abstraction should be both complete and correct.

The analysis performed by the SPARK Examiner is based largely on the analysis of the interfaces between components and ensuring that the details on either side do indeed conform to the specifications of the interfaces. The interfaces are of course the specifications of packages and subprograms and the SPARK annotations say more about these interfaces and thereby improve the quality of the abstraction as we shall now see.

Consider the information given by the following Ada procedure specification

```
procedure Add(X: in Integer);
```

Frankly, it tells us very little. It just says that there is a procedure called Add and that it takes a single parameter of type Integer whose formal name is X. But it says nothing about what the procedure does. It might do anything at all. It certainly doesn't have to add anything nor does it have to use the value of X. It could for example subtract two unrelated global variables and print the result to some file. But now consider what happens when we add the lowest level of SPARK annotation. The specification might become

```
procedure Add(X: in Integer);
--# global in out Total;
```

This states that the only global variable that the procedure can access is that called Total. Moreover the mode information tells us that the initial value of Total must be used (**in**) and that a new value will be produced (**out**). The SPARK rules also say more about the parameter X. Although in Ada a parameter need not be used at all, nevertheless an **in** parameter must be used in SPARK.

So now we know rather a lot. We know that a call of Add will produce a new value of Total and that it will use the initial value of Total and the value of X. We also know that Add cannot affect anything else. It certainly cannot print anything or have any other malevolent side effect.

The next level of annotation gives the detailed dependency relations so that the specification becomes

```
procedure Add(X: in Integer);
--# global in out Total;
--# derives Total from Total, X;
```

In this particularly simple example, this adds no further information. We already knew that we had to use X and the initial value of Total and produce a new value of Total and this is precisely what this derives annotation says.

Finally we can add the third level of annotation which concerns proof and obtain

```
procedure Add(X: in Integer);
--# global in out Total;
--# derives Total from Total, X;
--# post Total = Total~ + X;
```

The postcondition explicitly says that the final value of Total is the result of adding its initial value (distinguished by ~) to that of X. So now the specification is complete.

As a second example, consider the following procedure to multiply two matrices X and Y giving the result in Z.

```
type Matrix_Index is range 0 .. 9;
type Matrix is array (Matrix_Index, Matrix_Index) of Integer;
...
procedure Multiply(X, Y: in Matrix; Z: out Matrix)
--# derives Z from X, Y;
is
begin
```

```
      for I in Matrix_Index loop
         for J in Matrix_Index loop
            Z(I, J) := 0;
         end loop;
      end loop;
      for I in Matrix_Index loop
         for J in Matrix_Index loop
            for K in Matrix_Index loop
               Z(I, J) := Z(I, J) + X(I, K) * Y(K, J);
            end loop;
         end loop;
      end loop;
   end Multiply;
```

Using the above, the procedure call

```
Multiply(A, A, A);
```

intended to replace a matrix A by its square will instead nullify A if the arrays are passed by reference rather than by copy. However, in SPARK this procedure call is illegal because an actual parameter cannot correspond to both an imported parameter (such as X) and an exported parameter (such as Z).

When the Examiner examines the call of Multiply it reports

```
***          Semantic Error    : This parameter is overlapped
             by another one which is exported.
```

for the first two parameters and so the program is rejected. Note that the Examiner detects such aliasing errors whatever level of flow analysis is used.

It is interesting to note that SPARK does not require parameter passing to be by reference or by copy; it just imposes other restrictions that ensure that they give the same result so that it does not matter. (Just imposing a restriction on the parameter mechanism itself would actually violate the goal of the SPARK kernel being a subset of Ada because it would mean that a particular program well-defined in SPARK might have a different meaning in Ada.)

We conclude by emphasizing that the global and derives annotations are part of the procedure specification. (In the case of distinct specification and body, the annotations are not repeated in the body; if there is no distinct specification then they occur in the body before the reserved word **is**.) The annotations separate the interaction between the caller and the specification from that between the specification and the implementation just as the Ada parameter profile specifies enough for the subprogram to be called without regard to the details of the body. Hence the Examiner carries out two sets of checks; it checks that the annotations are consistent with the procedure body (which they are – but see Exercise 6.6(**2**)) and it also checks that the annotations are consistent with the call (which they are not in this example).

Other points to be noted from the array example are that all arrays must have static bounds and that index subtypes must be named in SPARK. Note also that we have used the ability to read an **out** parameter; this was not permitted in Ada 83 but SPARK permits this useful extension added in Ada 95.

## 1.6 Structure of this book

The purpose of this book is to provide an overall description of the use of SPARK for writing reliable software. Knowledge of Ada is not really required since almost all features are described in reasonable detail. Certainly the general principles should be clear even though some of the details such as interfacing to hardware using representation clauses might not. However, some knowledge of Ada would certainly be helpful in understanding the comparative remarks between SPARK and full Ada which have been included largely because it is expected that many readers will indeed have a working knowledge of Ada. A good introduction to those parts of Ada relating to SPARK would be obtained by reading Chapters 1 to 9, 11, 12 and 15 of *Programming in Ada 95* by the author [Barnes, 1998]. The ultimate reference for Ada is of course the Ada Reference Manual [ISO, 1995]; this is generally referred to as the *ARM*.

The description of SPARK as a language is (intended to be) complete apart from a few features such as fixed point arithmetic. However, the discussion of the use of the SPARK tools for proof is simply an introduction. There are many matters of detail which are not included partly because they would occupy a great deal of space and also because they are best learnt through practical interactive tuition and experience. Thus only the general principles of proof are described and the interactive use of the Proof Checker is barely covered.

The CD accompanying this book contains additional documentation as well as demonstration versions of the Examiner and Simplifier plus all necessary installation information and user guides. The Proof Checker is not included on the CD but is available with professional versions of the other tools from Praxis Critical Systems.

This book is in three main parts. The first part, Chapters 1 to 3, is an overview of the topic and introduces the reader to most of the features of SPARK and its associated tools in an informal manner and illustrates the language and the tools with some small examples.

The second part, Chapters 4 to 8, comprises a thorough description of the SPARK core language including its relationship with Ada 95. The syntax notation is widely used because it enables a precise description to be given in a compact and clear manner. It is anticipated that this part of the book will be found most useful as reference material.

The third part, Chapters 9 to 13, covers in more detail the use of the various associated tools and also describes their theoretical background. It is written in a more tutorial style and contains many examples including some case studies of complete programs.

The book concludes with a number of appendices covering such matters as lists of reserved words and attributes, a complete syntax and a summary of the differences between SPARK 83 and SPARK 95.

Most chapters have a few exercises; the reader should at least attempt these and consult the answers because they cover a number of quite notable points and are sometimes referred to in later material. The CD contains the text of all the major examples and exercises and the reader might find it instructive to apply the Examiner and (where appropriate) the Simplifier to them. Further details will be found in Appendix 4.

# 2 Language Principles



This chapter provides an overview of the key ideas of the SPARK language and shows how the core annotations are used. We start with some ruminations on design and the overall importance of the ideas of abstraction and information hiding.

The next chapter provides an overview of the associated SPARK tools and the use of the proof annotations. Later chapters then address the various topics in more detail.

## 2.1 Decomposition and abstraction

The solution of a large programming problem requires its decomposition into subproblems which can then be solved separately by independent functional units; this is often known as 'divide and conquer'. An important concept in enabling this to be done effectively is abstraction.

According to the *Oxford English Dictionary*, abstraction is 'the process of stripping an idea of its concrete accompaniments'. The general idea is that the problem is simplified if irrelevant detail is removed or hidden. Abstraction allows decomposition to be performed effectively, by changing the level of detail to be considered at various stages.

Decomposition allows us to conceive of a program in terms of components that can then be combined to solve the original problem. By identifying the essence of a problem, abstraction can help us to make a good choice of components; that is ones that are easy to specify, easy to build, and easy to use in combination.

The design process typically involves alternation between decomposition and abstraction, until the original problem is reduced to a set of problems that we already know how to solve or can solve readily.

The evolution of programming languages has very largely been driven by a deeper understanding and use of abstraction. There are two important kinds of abstraction which in a sense are complementary

- abstraction by parameterization,
- abstraction by specification.

In abstraction by parameterization we choose to ignore the identity of the actual data being used. The abstraction is defined in terms of formal parameters to which actual data objects are bound when the abstraction is used. The identity of the actual parameters is irrelevant to the 'refinement' or development of the abstraction – though their presence, number and types remain important.

Parameterization of subprograms has been the most familiar form of abstraction since the early days of Fortran II and Algol 60. Such parameterization increases the generality of program components, making them useful in more situations. It can therefore reduce the amount of code to be written and maintained. This kind of abstraction thus looks at the situation from within the subprogram and enables the developer to ignore the details of the actual external data.

Thus we might have a function to take the square root of some number. We write

```
function Sqrt(X: Float) return Float is
   Result: Float;
begin
   ...  -- compute the result in the variable Result
   return Result;
end Sqrt;
```

and the important point is that we write the code in such a way that it works (generally) without considering the location and value of the actual parameter.

In abstraction by specification on the other hand, we decide to ignore the details of the computations to be performed in a component of the program, and we reason instead in terms of the required overall effect of the component. Thus we focus on what the component is intended to accomplish, rather than on how it is to meet its requirements. This kind of abstraction therefore looks at the situation from outside and enables the user to ignore the hidden workings of the component.

We can look at the Sqrt function in this way as well; from the point of view of the user, the details of the method used to actually find the square root are irrelevant provided they meet general criteria such as those concerned with accuracy and time.

These two abstractions are thus really just two different views of the same concept; the hiding of irrelevant detail. One view is from the inside and one view is from the outside. It is the recognition of the importance of the external view of abstraction that has led to the enthusiasm for Object Oriented Programming.

In order to be useful, abstractions must be given precise definitions. We define them by means of specifications written in a specification language which can be either formal or informal. Formal specifications (such as in Z or VDM) are more precise, but they may be harder to write and to understand and thus may not be accessible to a sufficiently large number of programmers. There is also the risk that if they are hard to understand, then although they may be precise, they may nevertheless be misinterpreted by the human reader and thus used incorrectly. Program Design Languages (PDLs) and programming languages themselves impose varying levels of formality of specification.

The design of a program through abstraction, with careful construction of the (formal or informal) specifications of its various components, greatly simplifies its detailed implementation and subsequent maintenance. There are two main reasons for this

- The implementation of one abstraction can be written and understood without it being necessary to examine the implementation of any other abstraction. In order to write a component that uses an abstraction, a programmer need only understand its behaviour, not the details of its implementation.
- The effects of program modifications are bounded. If the implementation of an abstraction is changed, but its specification remains the same, the rest of the program should not be affected by the change.

This ideal situation whereby the different parts of a program are logically separate and cannot interfere with each other can only be completely achieved (and demonstrated to have been achieved) if the abstractions are described fully and accurately in the first place.

## 2.2 Language support for abstraction

All programming languages provide some mechanisms that allow programmers to construct their own abstractions as needed. The most common of these is the facility to employ subprograms (procedures and functions), allowing separation of their definition and invocation. As mentioned above, this concept has been around since the earliest days of programming.

In a sense, the use of subprograms allows us to extend the virtual machine represented by a programming language by adding new and higher-level operations to it.

This kind of extension is most useful in dealing with a problem that is conveniently decomposed in terms of independent functional units. Often, however, it is more fruitful to think of adding new kinds of data objects to the virtual machine, with operations to create such objects, to obtain information from them, and to modify them in meaningful ways. This is of course the basis for OOP. For example, it can be useful to introduce a stack type, with 'push' and 'pop' operations.

An Abstract Data Type (ADT) defines a set of objects, with a set of operations that characterize the behaviour of those objects. In some programming languages one can define abstract data types, hiding their implementation details, by means of 'packages' or 'modules' or 'classes'. In Ada, this is done with the concept of a package containing the declaration of a private type and operations on objects of the type.

We will look at the Ada implementation of a stack in order to illustrate the ideas of abstraction. (This will also provide a brief survey of some features of Ada for those readers who may not be so familiar with the language.) Packages in Ada typically come in two parts, a specification describing the external interface and a body providing the implementation details. Thus we might declare an Ada package whose specification is

```
package Stacks is

   type Stack is private;

   procedure Clear(S: out Stack);
   procedure Push(S: in out Stack; X: in Integer);
   procedure Pop(S: in out Stack; X: out Integer);

private
   ...
end Stacks;
```

In this example we have an abstract data type Stack plus the operations Clear, Push and Pop acting on objects of that type. The package specification declares the type Stack and indicates that it is private (which means that the details are logically hidden from the user) and then gives the details of the specification of the three procedures that can operate upon objects of the type Stack.

The procedure specifications give the names of the procedures and the types and modes of their formal parameters. The modes **in** and **out** indicate the direction of flow of information on the procedure call. Thus the parameter X of Push is an **in** parameter because it provides information going in giving the value to be pushed onto the stack whereas the parameter X of Pop is an **out** parameter because the value being popped comes out. An **in out** parameter transfers information in both directions. Thus the parameter S of Push is used for both the original value of the stack and the final value and so is accessed in both directions. On the other hand, the parameter S of Clear need only be an **out** parameter because the initial value of S is irrelevant.

Various items of lexical detail will be obvious, note the use of **is** in the declaration of the package and the type Stack. Words such as **is** and **type** are reserved and cannot be used for any other purpose; we show them in bold for clarity. Note that the various identifiers such as Stack can be written in either case, thus stack, Stack and STACK all mean exactly the same in Ada. Finally note the use of semicolons to terminate the various constructions and how the name of the package is repeated after its final **end**.

The private part starting **private** gives the full details of the type Stack and the package body gives the full details of the implementation of the three procedures. We will return to these in Section 2.6.

In order to use a stack we must first declare a stack object and we can then operate upon it. Thus we might write a main subprogram which in outline might be

```
with Stacks;
procedure Main is
   My_Stack: Stacks.Stack;
   A: Integer;
begin
   Stacks.Clear(My_Stack);
   ...
   Stacks.Push(My_Stack, 55);
   ...
   Stacks.Pop(My_Stack, A);
   ...
end Main;
```

The procedure starts with a context clause consisting of **with** followed by the name of the package Stacks. This indicates to both the compiler and reader that this main subprogram is making use of the facilities to be found in the package Stacks. We then declare our stack and also an integer variable A. Declarations go between the **is** and **begin** and then the various executable statements go between **begin** and the final **end**.

Note how we have to give the package name Stacks followed by a dot as a prefix to the names of the various items declared in the package. This makes it easy to see where the items are declared and is especially important if several packages are 'withed'. Those familiar with full Ada will recall that the prefix can be omitted if we insert a use package clause naming the package. Use package clauses are forbidden in SPARK on the grounds that their omission can obscure the origin of entities.

An Abstract State Machine (ASM) is a related concept and is implemented in much the same way. The major difference is that whereas an abstract data type package gives the ability to declare objects and then to operate upon them, an abstract state machine package declares just one object for us and the operations upon it. The package is then itself essentially the object and has internal 'state' or 'memory' containing the current value of the object. Internal variables holding such state are often referred to as 'own' variables of the package.

The specification of an Ada package giving an abstract state machine for a single stack might be

```
package The_Stack is

   procedure Clear;
   procedure Push(X: in Integer);
   procedure Pop(X: out Integer);

end The_Stack;
```

and the user would then write

```
with The_Stack;
procedure Main is
   A: Integer;
begin
   The_Stack.Clear;
   ...
   The_Stack.Push(55);
   ...
   The_Stack.Pop(A);
   ...
end Main;
```

Note that Clear now has no parameters and both the specification and the call then omit the parentheses.

It is interesting to observe that the abstract state package is really just an extension of a single variable. If it is only to be used by the procedure Main then we can declare the whole package locally to Main thus

```
procedure Main is

   package The_Stack is
      ...
   end The_Stack;

   package body The_Stack is
      ...
   end The_Stack;

   A: Integer;
begin
   The_Stack.Clear;
   ...
   The_Stack.Push(55);
   ...
   The_Stack.Pop(A);
   ...
end Main;
```

Thus a package at the outermost level (known as a library package) corresponds to a global variable whereas a locally declared package corresponds to a local variable.

## 2.3 Program units

A SPARK program is composed of one or more program units. Program units are subprograms or packages. They can be declared at the outermost level (sometimes called the top level) and can then be compiled separately as illustrated by Main and Stacks of the previous section; program units at the outermost level are referred to as library units. Program units can also be nested inside each other as for example the package The_Stack was nested inside Main in the last example.

A subprogram expresses a sequence of actions and its execution is invoked by a subprogram call. There are two kinds of subprograms – procedures and functions. A procedure call is a statement standing alone, whereas a function call always occurs in an expression and returns a value as part of the expression.

A package on the other hand provides a means of grouping various entities together within a common framework; the entities might be data types, data objects, subprograms and even other packages. Packages also provide hiding properties; the details of the private part and the body are not visible to the external user of the package. A package can also have an initialization part as we shall see in a moment.

In general, a SPARK program unit (package or subprogram) has a two-part structure, consisting of a specification and a body. The specification of a program unit gives the information needed by a user of that unit; it defines the interface between the unit and the remainder of the program. The body of a program unit contains the details of its implementation and this is logically hidden from the users (although of course they may be able to read the printed text of the body).

In order to facilitate program design and development, the specification and body of a library package may be written and compiled separately. The various library units are held in a program library which ensures that they are consistent. A library package may also have child packages and these may also be compiled separately from their parent. (Child units are discussed in more detail in Section 4.2.) A complete program is then formed by linking together appropriate units from the library while nominating one of the subprograms as the main subprogram whose execution constitutes the execution of the program as a whole.

Note that in SPARK a program can only have one library subprogram which is of course the main subprogram. All other library units must be packages. Moreover the library subprogram is always compiled as a single unit and never as separate specification and body as it can be in full Ada.

The compilation rules of Ada state essentially that a unit can only be compiled after all the units it depends upon are in the program library. There are three main dependency rules

- A unit depends upon the specification of all units mentioned in its with clauses.
- A package body depends upon the corresponding specification.
- A child package depends upon the specification of its parent.

So a package body can only be compiled after its specification has been entered into the library. And similarly a main subprogram such as Main of the previous section can only be compiled after the specification of The_Stack has been entered into the library. But it is important to note that there is no Ada dependency between the body of The_Stack and the main subprogram.

These Ada rules equally apply to SPARK but in addition there are other relationships indicated by inherit clauses as discussed in Section 2.9.

Similar rules apply to changes. If we change and thus recompile a unit then all others which depend upon it will also have to be recompiled. So this means that the body of The_Stack can be changed and recompiled without impacting upon the main subprogram provided that the specification of The_Stack remains unchanged. But if we change the specification of The_Stack then both its body and the main subprogram will have to be recompiled.

These rules ensure that the entire program is always consistent and yet minimize the impact of change to just those other units directly affected.

## 2.4 Declarations and objects

Before embarking on a survey of the main properties of SPARK subprograms, it will be helpful to establish some terminology regarding declarations and objects.

Objects are either variables or constants. As their name implies, constants have the same value throughout their life and cannot be assigned to; a corollary is that they have to be given an initial value when they are declared. Variables on the other hand can have new values assigned to them and need not be given an initial value when declared. Parameters of subprograms are also treated as objects and get any initial values from the corresponding actual parameters.

The reading and updating of objects is defined to reflect that objects may themselves be part of larger objects. Thus an array component is part of an array and a component of a record is part of the enclosing whole record object. The idea of whole or *entire* variables which are not part of other variables is important as we shall see in a moment.

- The value of an object (variable or constant) is *read* when the value of any part of the object is evaluated or when the value of an enclosing object is evaluated.
- The value of an object (which is necessarily a variable) is *updated* when an assignment is performed to any part of the object or when an assignment is performed to an enclosing object.

Thus if we have a record type and some objects such as

```
type Complex is
  record
    Real: Float;
    Imag: Float;
  end record;
```

```
Z, W: Complex;
```

then an assignment

```
Z.Imag := 3.5;
```

is said to update the record object Z as a whole as well as to update the component Z.Imag. Similarly the assignment

```
W := Z;
```

is said to read both the object Z and its components Z.Real and Z.Imag. Thus Z and W are entire variables but their individual components are not. Note that assignment in Ada uses colon equals (:=).

Objects may also be read and updated via subprogram parameters. Parameters of scalar types (such as Integer) are always passed by copy. Parameters of array and record types may be passed by copy or by reference (this is according to the choice of the implementation and is not under the control of the programmer). When a parameter is passed by copy, the formal parameter denotes a separate object from the actual parameter, and any information transfer occurs only before and after executing the subprogram. When a parameter is passed by reference, the formal parameter denotes (a view of) the object denoted by the actual parameter; reads and updates of the formal parameter directly reference the actual parameter object. Passing by reference is typically implemented by passing the address of the object to the subprogram and then all references access the actual parameter via its address.

Another important concept is that of a declarative region associated with program units. A declarative region is a portion of program text in which entities can be declared. A single declarative region is formed by the text of the declaration of a subprogram or a package specification, together with the corresponding body, if any. Thus the subprogram Main forms a declarative region and the specification and body of the package Stacks together form a single declarative region.

We say that an entity is local to a declarative region if its declaration occurs immediately within the declarative region. On the other hand, we say that an entity is global to a declarative region if its declaration occurs immediately within another declarative region that encloses the declarative region.

Thus we can declare one procedure inside another

```
procedure Outer is
   I, L: Integer;

   procedure Inner(K: in Integer) is
      J: Integer;
   begin
      J := K + I;
      I := J + 2;
   end Inner;
```

```
begin
   I := 4;
   L := 2;
   Inner(L);
end Outer;
```

and then I and L are local to Outer and global to Inner whereas J is local to Inner. Note that we can reference global variables such as I directly.

The identifier of a variable can be reused in an inner region. Thus we could declare I inside Inner with a totally different meaning and then this declaration would hide the one in Outer so that it could not be directly accessed from Inner. As we shall see in the next section any potential ambiguity in the mind of the reader is overcome in SPARK through the use of global annotations which prevent an accidental hole in the scope of an outer variable.

## 2.5 Subprograms

As mentioned above, subprograms take two forms – procedures and functions. We will look first at procedures and then at functions.

The purpose of any procedure P is to perform an updating action of some kind; this will involve the computation of values and the assignment of the values to variables which are external to the procedure. It can do this either by updating a global variable directly or alternatively by updating one of its formal parameters (in this latter case the actual parameter will be the external variable – this might be global to the procedure P but might also be a local variable of a calling procedure Q and not global to P). In either case we can consider the procedure call as returning values to the calling environment.

The global variables and formal parameters used to convey its results to its calling environment are called the *exported variables* of P. In order to *derive* its results the procedure P may need to read values previously existing in its calling environment. The global variables and formal parameters used to convey these values are called the *imported variables* of P. A variable may be both imported and exported.

(Note that the term 'derives' is used here in the sense of obtaining the value of something and not in the sense of inheritance and derived types of Ada; these concepts are not part of SPARK.)

These ideas are illustrated in Figure 2.1 which shows the imports and exports of the procedure Inner of the previous section. The parameter K is imported and the global variable I is both imported and exported.

It is important to note that an imported variable is not just one that is read by the procedure; it is also necessary that the original value existing in the variable before the procedure call influence the final values of exported variables. Thus if it were always overwritten before being read then it could not influence the outcome and would not be considered an import.

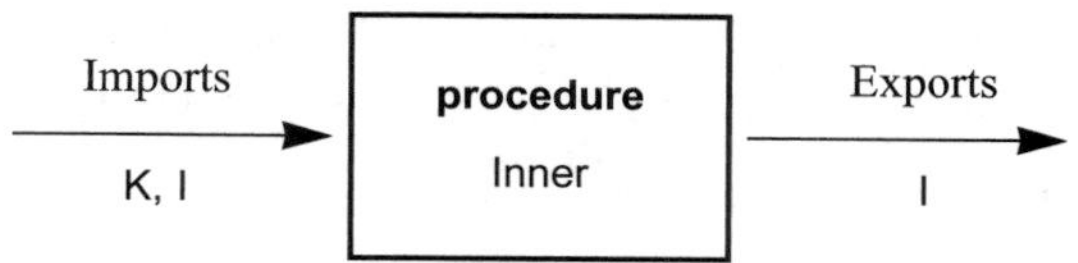


**Figure 2.1** Imports and exports of Inner.

The general idea is that in the early stages of the design of a procedure one chooses its exported variables, and determines which (initial values of) imported variables may be required by the procedure in order to derive (the final value of) each exported variable. This information is given with the procedure specification in the form of a dependency relation. Dependency relations are specified in terms of entire variables, that is variables that are not subcomponents of composite variables (arrays and records).

The consistency between the dependency relation of a procedure and its eventual code implementation, and also between the dependency relation and the various calls of the procedure are checked by the SPARK Examiner.

As a simple example consider

```
procedure Exchange(X, Y: in out Float)
--# derives X from Y &                    -- dependency relation
--#         Y from X;
is
   T: Float;
begin
   T := X;  X := Y;  Y := T;
end Exchange;
```

The dependency is given by the derives annotation which like other annotations takes the form of an Ada comment. It is thus not processed by the compiler but is processed by the SPARK Examiner. The annotation states that the final value of X depends upon the initial value of Y and vice versa. Note that the final value of X does not depend upon the initial value of X.

The parameters X and Y have mode **in out**. This enables them to be both read and updated as required. As mentioned above there are three parameter modes in SPARK as in Ada. Their behaviour can be summarized as follows.

**in** The formal parameter is a constant initialized by the value of the associated actual parameter.

**in out** The formal parameter is a variable initialized by the actual parameter; it permits both reading and updating of the value of the associated actual parameter.

**out** The formal parameter is an uninitialized variable; it permits updating of the value of the associated actual parameter.

In Chapter 1, we stated that SPARK is based on Ada 95. A minor but important difference between Ada 95 and Ada 83 is that an **out** parameter can be read in Ada 95 whereas it could not in Ada 83; earlier versions of SPARK were based on Ada 83 and so were different in this respect. An **out** parameter in Ada 95 is just like a variable that does not have an initial value whereas an **out** parameter in Ada 83 was rather bizarre.

The value of an **out** scalar parameter that is not updated by the call is undefined upon return; the same holds for the value of a scalar subcomponent. As a consequence the actual parameter becomes undefined. The Examiner produces messages regarding such undefined values.

Scalar parameters are always implemented by copy. At the start of each call, if the mode is **in** or **in out** the value of the actual parameter is copied into the associated formal parameter; then, after normal completion of the subprogram body, if the mode is **in out** or **out** the value of the formal parameter is copied back into the associated actual parameter.

For a parameter whose type is an array or record, an implementation may also use this copy technique just as for scalar types. Alternatively, an implementation may pass an array or record parameter by reference, that is, by arranging that every use of the formal parameter (to read or to update its value) be treated as a use of the actual parameter. The Ada language does not define which of these two mechanisms is to be adopted for parameter passing, nor whether different calls to the same procedure are to use the same mechanism.

In full Ada, the behaviour of a program can depend upon whether a parameter is passed by copy or by reference. However, SPARK has a number of rules (which ensure, for example, that functions cannot have side effects and that aliasing is forbidden) and these have the consequence that the behaviour is the same whichever mechanism is used.

If an imported or exported variable is a formal parameter, the mode of this parameter must be compatible with its use

- imported parameters must be of mode **in** or **in out**,
- exported parameters must be of mode **in out** or **out**.

The reverse also holds, thus every **in out** parameter must be both imported and exported.

These different modes and appropriate derives annotations are illustrated by the following example of a stack abstract data type.

```
package Stacks is

   type Stack is private;

   function Is_Empty(S: Stack) return Boolean;
   function Is_Full(S: Stack) return Boolean;

   procedure Clear(S: out Stack);
   --# derives S from ;

   procedure Push(S: in out Stack; X: in Integer);
   --# derives S from S, X;
```

```
    procedure Pop(S: in out Stack; X: out Integer);
    --# derives S, X from S;

private
    --# hide Stacks;
end Stacks;
```

This shows a package specification containing the private type Stack and the specification of various subprograms operating upon an object of the type Stack. The private part and the body are not shown. The hide annotation in the private part makes it possible to defer examination of the implementation of the Stack type during the preliminary design. Thus although the above text cannot be compiled because the private part is not complete, nevertheless it can be processed by the Examiner in order to check the consistency of the annotations.

Observe that Clear has a null list of imports for deriving the value of S; this is because the new value does not depend upon any parameter. Also note that Push and Pop both show S as depending upon S; this is because the final value of S does indeed depend upon its original value.

Imported and exported variables do not have to be parameters; they can also be global variables which are updated and read directly (or through the call of another subprogram that accesses them directly and so on). The names of such global variables must be given in a *global definition*, which is another annotation in the procedure specification. This annotation also gives the modes of access – **in**, **out** or **in out** – just as for parameters (these modes can be omitted in certain circumstances as discussed in the next chapter). Global variables named here must be entire variables as in derives annotations; they cannot for instance be an individual component of an array or record.

(In the case of an array it is natural that the array has to be treated as an entire variable because we may not know which components are being read or updated since the index values might be dynamic expressions. This argument does not apply to components of records because they are always identified by name; nevertheless it turns out to be sensible to treat records in the same way for the description of interfaces. However, flow analysis within subprograms is done in terms of individual components for records but not for arrays.)

A simple example of a global variable is provided by a classical random number generator

```
package Random_Numbers
--# own Seed;
--# initializes Seed;
is
    procedure Random(X: out Float);
    --# global in out Seed;
    --# derives X, Seed from Seed;

end Random_Numbers;

package body Random_Numbers is
    Seed: Integer;
    Seed_Max: constant Integer := ... ;
```

```
    procedure Random(X: out Float) is
    begin
       Seed := ... ;
       X := Float(Seed) / Float(Seed_Max);
    end Random;
begin                              -- initialization part
    Seed := 12345;
end Random_Numbers;
```

This example shows the package body containing the declaration of a variable Seed and the body of the subprogram Random. Each call of Random updates the value of Seed using some pseudo-random algorithm and then updates X by dividing by the constant Seed_Max. Note that all constants have to be initialized with a value known at compile time. Each successive value of Seed depends upon the previous value and is preserved between calls of Random. The variable Seed is initialized in the initialization part of the package body.

This example also illustrates a number of other annotations. The variable Seed has to be mentioned in both an own annotation and an initialization annotation of the package specification. The own annotation makes it visible to other annotations and the initializes annotation indicates that it will be initialized. The procedure Random contains a global annotation for Seed as well as a derives annotation.

The initializes annotation can also be satisfied by initializing Seed in its declaration thus

```
Seed: Integer := 12345;
```

An alternative approach might be to declare some procedure Start in the package Random_Numbers (to be called from outside) whose purpose is to assign a first value to Seed like the procedure Clear in the case of the stacks in Section 2.2. In this case an initializes annotation would not be required and for reasons that will become apparent later it is best not to consider this as initialization in any formal sense.

It is important to observe that from the Ada point of view the variable Seed is not declared until the body and is thus not known to the compiler at the point of the specification of the subprogram Random. However, Seed is an imported and exported global variable of Random from the point of view of SPARK and thus must be mentioned in the annotation for Random so that flow through Random may be tracked; the own annotation ensures that Seed is known to the Examiner at the specification of Random.

The derives annotation shows that each call of Random produces a number X derived from Seed and also modifies Seed. The variable Seed is protected from users of the procedure Random (by being declared within the body of the Random_Numbers package).

When the body of a procedure has been implemented, the Examiner will check that all reading and updating of global variables – directly, and through calls of other subprograms – is consistent with the procedure annotation.

The scope of program objects should always be as restricted as possible. The rules of SPARK discourage the use of a global variable simply as a 'temporary store'. Thus we might try to redefine the procedure Exchange so that the temporary T is global by writing

```
procedure Exchange(X, Y: in out Float)
--# global T;
--# derives X from Y &
--#         Y from X;
is
begin
  T := X;  X := Y;  Y := T;
end Exchange;
```

But this is illegal because it violates one of several rules of completeness which we will encounter later (in Section 6.6). The one that is violated here is that every variable mentioned in a global definition must be used somewhere in the dependency relation. (We have omitted the mode of T for the moment.) Of course we could add T to the derives annotation thus

```
--# derives X from Y &    -- dependency relation
--#         Y from X &
--#         T from X;
```

but this forces us to admit that we actually change T. Moreover, flow analysis of a call of Exchange will reveal the use of T. Indeed the Examiner will probably complain that the value assigned to T is then not used; this will certainly apply if another call of Exchange promptly overwrites the previous value of T. (This is discussed in more detail in Section 12.3.)

Some texts on high integrity programming suggest that all variables to be read or updated by a procedure be passed as parameters, in the interests of (1) generality, (2) clarity, and (3) safety. Using SPARK, some of the usual arguments under (2) and (3) no longer apply; the dependency relation of a procedure describes its data transactions with its environment more precisely than does its Ada formal parameter specification and the Examiner checks both. In effect we can think of globals as simply parameters in which the actual and formal parameter are always the same.

We now turn to a consideration of functions. A function is a subprogram that returns a value (the result of the function call). Whereas a procedure is designed to update variables in its calling environment, in SPARK the execution of a function is not allowed to have any side effects at all, that is its execution shall not cause any global variables to be updated. In our terminology, a function cannot have any exported variables and so all parameters of functions have mode **in**. Thus we could not make the procedure Random into a function as it stands because it has a side effect by updating the value of Seed.

Incidentally, the mode of a parameter can be omitted and is taken to be **in** by default; this applies to both procedures and functions. We generally use the convention of always giving the mode for procedures and omitting it for functions.

A function may have imported variables other than its formal parameters, that is it may read some global variables directly – in which case the function specification must include a global definition naming all those variables. We could for example split the procedure Random into two parts, a procedure that updates the value of Seed and then a function which returns the corresponding random number. The annotations would then be

```
procedure Update;
--# global in out Seed;
--# derives Seed from Seed;

function Random return Float;
--# global Seed;
```

Note that since the data flow between a function and its calling environment is completely prescribed by its formal part and global definition, the specification of a function does not need a derives annotation. Thus in the package Stacks above the functions Is_Empty and Is_Full do not need any annotations. Also note that global annotations on functions never have an explicit mode because they are naturally always of mode **in**.

We conclude this discussion of subprograms by briefly summarizing some of the key differences between the philosophy used in SPARK and more general languages.

SPARK imposes the use of annotations – in particular global definitions and dependency relations – to make the data transactions between a subprogram and its calling environment more explicit.

These annotations prevent language insecurities, such as the risk of aliasing. (As mentioned above, whether parameter passing is implemented by copy or by reference, a SPARK program always gives the same results.)

The subprogram annotations also provide the principal defence against corruption of global variables as we saw in the attempt to use a global variable in the procedure Exchange. As well as helping to achieve integrity, this enables the programmer to choose the means of data transfer (that is through global variables or alternatively through parameters) that is more efficient.

In SPARK, a function cannot have side effects and behaves like a pure mathematical function. An important consequence is that function calls within expressions can be safely reordered.

---

**EXERCISE 2.5**

1. Write the procedure Inner of Section 2.4 in SPARK by adding appropriate global and derives annotations.
2. Write an appropriate procedure Start for the package Random_Numbers.
3. If we foolishly persist in writing the procedure Exchange with a global temporary T, then what should be the mode of T in the global annotation?

---

## 2.6 Abstract data types

As we have seen, abstract data types are constructed using packages with private types. We will now look at this technique in more detail.

A package implementing an abstract data type always consists of two separate components – a specification and a body. The specification defines the type and the operations acting upon objects of the type. The body, containing implementation details, is hidden from users of the package. (As we shall see later some packages do not have a body.)

The specification may itself have two parts, a visible part and a private part. The visible part declares the various entities that may be used outside the package (such as types, constants and subprograms). The package is said to export these entities.

The private part, which is introduced by the reserved word **private** and appears at the end of the package specification, cannot be referenced outside the package (other than from a child package). The private part is in the specification rather than the body (where it might be considered to belong from the point of view of abstraction) in order to support separate compilation. Although the private part is not part of the logical interface it does provide information about the physical interface and that is needed by the compiler.

In the visible part a type can be declared to be private, in which case the full details of its construction are given in the private part.

The only operations that can be applied (outside the package) to objects of a private type are those declared in the visible part, plus the assignment operator and tests for equality and inequality. A private type may also be marked as limited and then even assignment and the predefined tests for equality and inequality are not available outside the package.

As an illustration we show the full details of the package Stacks introduced earlier, also giving the various annotations.

```
package Stacks is

   type Stack is private;

   function Is_Empty(S: Stack) return Boolean;
   function Is_Full(S: Stack) return Boolean;

   procedure Clear(S: out Stack);
   --# derives S from ;

   procedure Push(S: in out Stack; X: in Integer);
   --# derives S from S, X;

   procedure Pop(S: in out Stack; X: out Integer);
   --# derives S, X from S;

private
   Stack_Size: constant := 100;
   type Pointer_Range is range 0 .. Stack_Size;
   subtype Index_Range is Pointer_Range range 1 .. Stack_Size;
   type Vector is array (Index_Range) of Integer;
```

```
      type Stack is
         record
            Stack_Vector: Vector;
            Stack_Pointer: Pointer_Range;
         end record;
   end Stacks;

   package body Stacks is
      function Is_Empty(S: Stack) return Boolean is
      begin
         return S.Stack_Pointer = 0;
      end Is_Empty;

      function Is_Full(S: Stack) return Boolean is
      begin
         return S.Stack_Pointer = Stack_Size;
      end Is_Full;

      procedure Clear(S: out Stack) is
      begin
         S.Stack_Pointer := 0;
      end Clear;

      procedure Push(S: in out Stack; X: in Integer) is
      begin
         S.Stack_Pointer := S.Stack_Pointer + 1;
         S.Stack_Vector(S.Stack_Pointer) := X;
      end Push;

      procedure Pop(S: in out Stack; X: out Integer) is
      begin
         X := S.Stack_Vector(S.Stack_Pointer);
         S.Stack_Pointer := S.Stack_Pointer - 1;
      end Pop;
   end Stacks;
```

The private part gives the full type for Stack and also illustrates the declarations of types, subtypes and arrays in SPARK. First of all we have the declaration of the named number Stack_Size; this is simply a convenient shorthand for the integer literal 100 and can be used in any context where such a literal is permitted.

The declaration of the type Pointer_Range indicates that it is an integer type with values constrained to lie within the range given; that is, greater than or equal to 0 and less than or equal to Stack_Size. The type Pointer_Range has similar properties to the predefined type Integer but is a distinct type; the advantage of introducing a distinct type is that errors of confusion between it and other integer types are detected at compile time. The subtype Index_Range is a subtype of Pointer_Range and objects of this subtype are constrained with a lower bound of one.

The type Vector is an array type and the declaration indicates that arrays of this type have a component for each possible value of the subtype Index_Range and that the components themselves are of the type Integer. Thus every array of the type Vector has 100 components since 100 is the value of Stack_Size. Such an array type is known as a constrained array type because all arrays of the type are constrained to be the same size (we will meet unconstrained array types later).

Finally, the private part gives the full declaration of the type Stack which is a record with two components; one is an array Stack_Vector of type Vector and the other is Stack_Pointer of type Pointer_Range.

The bodies of the subprograms are then given in the package body. These are much as might be expected. Note that components of records are accessed by following the record name by a dot and then the component name whereas components of arrays are given by following the array name by an index expression in parentheses.

Observe that the annotations which appear after the procedure specifications are not repeated in the procedure bodies. However, if a subprogram does not have a distinct specification and body then the annotation goes in the body as in the procedure Exchange.

Those familiar with full Ada will note some of the simplifications to the type model in SPARK. For example, the array type Vector cannot be declared as

```
type Vector is array (Pointer_Range range 1 .. Stack_Size) of Integer;
```

as it can in Ada because the syntax of SPARK requires that the index subtype has to be given by just a subtype name (a subtype mark to use the proper jargon) and not the more general subtype indication (subtype mark plus constraint) as allowed in full Ada. This accords with the general SPARK principle that all types and subtypes should have names in the interests of clarity. The names are also especially valuable when it comes to proving correctness.

## 2.7 Abstract state machines

An abstract state machine is an entity which has well defined states plus a set of operations which cause state transitions. Properties of the state can be observed by calling appropriate functions.

Many computing processes can conveniently be viewed as abstract state machines. A large example is provided by a database manager, with procedures for inserting, modifying and removing records (which change the state of the database), and functions for answering queries. At the other extreme we have the random number generator discussed above.

An abstract state machine can conveniently be represented by a package, with variables which record its state declared in its body. Procedures that act on the machine and functions that observe its state are specified in the visible part of the package specification. All other details are hidden in the package body. The package body may conclude with a statement part to initialize the state variables.

The following shows the full details of a single stack treated as an abstract state machine rather than as a variable of an abstract data type. In contrast to the example in Section 2.5, the state is initialized automatically.

```
package The_Stack
--# own S, Pointer;
--# initializes Pointer;
is
   procedure Push(X: in Integer);
   --# global in out S, Pointer;
   --# derives S       from S, Pointer, X &
   --#         Pointer from Pointer;

   procedure Pop(X: out Integer);
   --# global in S; in out Pointer;
   --# derives Pointer from Pointer &
   --#         X       from S, Pointer;
end The_Stack;

package body The_Stack is
   Stack_Size: constant := 100;
   type Pointer_Range is range 0 .. Stack_Size;
   subtype Index_Range is Pointer_Range range 1 .. Stack_Size;
   type Vector is array (Index_Range) of Integer;
   S: Vector;
   Pointer: Pointer_Range;

   procedure Push(X: in Integer) is
   begin
      Pointer := Pointer + 1;
      S(Pointer) := X;
   end Push;

   procedure Pop(X: out Integer) is
   begin
      X := S(Pointer);
      Pointer := Pointer - 1;
   end Pop;
begin                              -- initialization
   Pointer := 0;
end The_Stack;
```

The stack state variables S and Pointer are declared in the body of the package and Pointer is initialized. These internal variables are not directly accessible to users of the stack object. However, their existence and the existence of the initialization of Pointer are made visible to the Examiner for the purpose of analysis by the **own** and **initializes** annotations in the package specification just as the variable Seed of the package Random was made visible.

However, the reader will realize that the above technique is not terribly satisfactory since we have made visible considerable detail of the internal representation of the state of the machine, namely the existence of the individual variables S and Pointer. If at some later stage we need to change the implementation then there is a high risk that the specification will need to be changed because of the SPARK rules even though it would not need to be changed by the Ada rules. This would in turn give rise to tiresome dependencies and recompilations since it would require all the calls to be recompiled and reexamined.

## 2.8 Refinement

The problems of unnecessary dependencies introduced in the previous section can be overcome by using abstract own variables to provide what is known as refinement. An abstract own variable does not correspond to a concrete Ada variable at all but instead represents a set of variables used in the implementation.

As a consequence, an abstract own variable occurs in two annotations, the own variable clause in the package specification and then also in a refinement definition in the body giving the set onto which it is mapped.

The stack example could then be rewritten as

```
package The_Stack
--# own State;                                -- abstract variable
--# initializes State;
is
   procedure Push(X: in Integer);
   --# global in out State;
   --# derives State from State, X;

   procedure Pop(X: out Integer);
   --# global in out State;
   --# derives State, X from State;
end The_Stack;

package body The_Stack
--# own State is S, Pointer;                  -- refinement definition
is
   Stack_Size: constant := 100;
   type Pointer_Range is range 0 .. Stack_Size;
   subtype Index_Range is Pointer_Range range 1 .. Stack_Size;
   type Vector is array (Index_Range) of Integer;
   S: Vector;
   Pointer: Pointer_Range;

   procedure Push(X: in Integer)
   --# global in out S, Pointer;
   --# derives S        from S, Pointer, X &
   --#         Pointer from Pointer;
   is
```

```
    begin
       Pointer := Pointer + 1;
       S(Pointer) := X;
    end Push;

    procedure Pop(X: out Integer)
    --# global in S; in out Pointer;
    --# derives Pointer from Pointer &
    --#         X       from S, Pointer;
    is
    begin
       X := S(Pointer);
       Pointer := Pointer - 1;
    end Pop;
begin                              -- initialization
    Pointer := 0;
    S := Vector'(Index_Range => 0);
end The_Stack;
```

This essentially enables the more abstract specification to be linked with the concrete body. The refinement acts as the link and says that the abstract own variable State is implemented by the two concrete variables S and Pointer.

Note moreover that the subprogram bodies have to have a refined version of their global definition and dependency clause written in terms of the concrete variables. This is only necessary if the global definition of the subprogram specification mentions an abstract own variable such as State.

One consequence of the refinement is that both Pointer and S have to be initialized because we have promised that the abstract variable State will be initialized. The initial value for S uses a form known as a qualified aggregate and indicates that all the components are to be set to zero. Of course we know that the dynamic behaviour is such that the initialization of S is unnecessary and we could omit it in practice and ignore the consequential message from the Examiner. (A similar remark applies to the procedure Clear of Section 2.6; this is discussed further in Section 6.6.)

The various constituents of the refinement must either be variables declared immediately within the package body (such as S and Pointer) or they could be own variables of private child packages or of embedded packages declared immediately within the body.

The process of refinement can be repeated since an own variable in the constituent list might itself be an abstract own variable of the child or embedded package.

We conclude by summarizing some key points regarding the visibility of state variables of abstract state machines.

- The **own** annotation of an abstract state machine makes the existence of its state visible wherever the machine is visible.
- Annotations of subprograms external to a machine which (indirectly) read or update its state (by executing subprograms of the machine) must indicate their import or export of the machine state.

- Only the existence of the machine state (and its reading or updating) is significant in this context. The details can still be hidden by refinement.

The second point is important and illustrates that annotations have to be explicitly transitive. Thus if we had some procedure that called Push and Pop then it too would have to be annotated to indicate that it changes the state of the stack.

```
procedure Use_Stack
--# global in out The_Stack.State;
--# derives The_Stack.State from The_Stack.State;
is
begin
   ...
   The_Stack.Push( ... );
   ...
   The_Stack.Pop( ... );
   ...
end Use_Stack;
```

Finally note that one abstract state machine could be implemented using another abstract state machine embedded within it. Thus if a machine B is to be embedded in a machine A, this can be done by embedding the package representing B in the body of the package representing A. The state of B can then be represented as an item in the refinement. Alternatively the package representing B could be a private child of the package representing A as we shall see in Section 7.3.

Refinement of course relates to top-down design and provides a natural way of implementing such a design. It is especially important that refinement can be cascaded; this avoids a combinatorial explosion of visible data items which might otherwise occur especially in large programs.

## 2.9 Program composition

In Section 2.3 we mentioned that a complete program comprised a number of packages plus a main subprogram. These program units can be compiled separately and are then linked together. We also noted that a unit must start with a with clause naming all other units it references. Thus the main subprogram Main of Section 2.2 has a with clause for the package The_Stack.

The rules in Ada permit a with clause to appear on either a package body or on a package specification. It often happens that it is only the package body that uses the facilities of some other package and putting the with clause on the specification would cause an unnecessary dependency. For example suppose that the procedure Use_Stack of the previous section was in an intermediate package. Ignoring the SPARK annotations for the moment the Ada might be

```
package The_Stack is
   procedure Push(X: in Integer);
   procedure Pop(X: out Integer);
end The_Stack;

package body The_Stack is
   ...
end The_Stack;

package Go_Between is
   procedure Use_Stack;
end Go_Between;

with The_Stack;
package body Go_Between is

   procedure Use_Stack is
   begin
      ...
      The_Stack.Push( ... );
      ...
      The_Stack.Pop( ... );
      ...
   end Use_Stack;

end Go_Between;

with Go_Between;
procedure Main is
begin
   ...
   Go_Between.Use_Stack;
   ...
end Main;
```

The important things to note are the with clauses on the main subprogram Main and the package body Go_Between. The specification of Go_Between does not need a with clause for The_Stack because it is only the body that directly uses it. This means that we could change and recompile the specification of The_Stack without impacting on the specification of Go_Between and consequently on the main subprogram. The key point is that the specification of Go_Between does not need to be aware of the existence of The_Stack at all – at least not in Ada terms.

Now when we come to add the SPARK annotations we note that the specification of the procedure Use_Stack declared in the specification of Go_Between needs to mention The_Stack.State. So now the specification of Go_Between does need to be aware of The_Stack – not for the purposes of Ada but so that the SPARK annotations can be written correctly and so be processed by the Examiner.

This information is provided by prefixing the specification of Go_Between by an inherit clause which is another form of core annotation. Including all annotations the program now becomes

```
package The_Stack
--# own State;
--# initializes State;
is
   procedure Push(X: in Integer);
   --# global in out State;
   --# derives State from State, X;

   procedure Pop(X: out Integer);
   --# global in out State;
   --# derives State, X from State;
end The_Stack;

--# inherit The_Stack;
package Go_Between is

   procedure Use_Stack;
   --# global in out The_Stack.State;
   --# derives The_Stack.State from The_Stack.State;

end Go_Between;

with The_Stack;
package body Go_Between is

   procedure Use_Stack is
   begin
      ...
      The_Stack.Push( ... );
      ...
      The_Stack.Pop( ... );
      ...
   end Use_Stack;

end Go_Between;

with Go_Between;
--# inherit The_Stack, Go_Between;
--# main_program;
procedure Main
--# global in out The_Stack.State;
--# derives The_Stack.State from The_Stack.State;
is
begin
   ...
   Go_Between.Use_Stack;
   ...
end Main;
```

where the body of The_Stack is omitted.

An inherit clause is also necessary on the subprogram Main because it refers to The_Stack in annotations and to Go_Between in the code. Note also the **main_program** annotation on the main subprogram.

The reader might feel that having to place the inherit clause on the specification somehow violates the privacy of the body and breaks down the Ada separation of dependency. Although it is true that the specification of Go_Between and indeed also of Main does now reveal the use of The_Stack, it should be remembered that because of refinement it is only the abstract own variable State that is being mentioned. We can still change the body of The_Stack without having to reexamine the specification of Go_Between and Main so the dependency is not really changed provided that refinement is used (and of course that the pattern of information flow remains the same).

In a strategic sense it is important that Main does mention The_Stack.State because otherwise we would have no warning that calling Main does indeed have the effect of changing the state of some other package. Inherit clauses thus draw to our attention the potential global impact that one unit has on other units even if the effect is indirect.

We have now covered the main concepts of the core of SPARK and introduced all the core annotations. These annotations essentially concern the flow and visibility of information; they have a significant impact on the style of program design using SPARK as we shall see in more detail in Chapter 12. Meanwhile, in the next chapter we will introduce the proof annotations and the various analysis tools which enable us to prove that programs are correct.

---

**EXERCISE 2.9**

1 Rewrite the program of this section using the abstract data type package Stacks of Section 2.6 and declare an object of the type Stack inside Go_Between.

---

# 3 SPARK Analysis Tools



This chapter provides an overview of the program analysis tools used in conjunction with SPARK. The individual tools and some of the mathematics behind their use are described in more detail in the third part of this book.

## 3.1 Program correctness

As mentioned in the previous chapter, the evolution of programming languages has largely been concerned with abstraction. Programs designed around the concepts of abstraction and information hiding are easier to develop and maintain because irrelevant detail is hidden and many typical errors possible with primitive techniques are detected at compile time.

For example an advantage of any high level language over an assembly language is that the detail of the hardware registers is hidden. The compiler does not make typical hand coding errors such as reading register 4 when the data was in register 5. Thus suppose we wish to compute

```
X := A * B;
```

using integer arithmetic (we assume that the answer will not overflow). As an illustration we will consider the use of the IBM 370 which has an interesting architecture; we might write

```
L       4, A          -- load A
M       4, B          -- double length product in 4, 5
ST      4, X          -- store result
```

but this is incorrect because A has to be loaded into register 5 and the final answer is also in register 5 even though the multiply instruction correctly refers to register 4. This sort of error is impossible using a high level language assuming that the compiler is correct. Of course the compiler might not be correct but the risk that it is incorrect in such a fundamental matter is very low compared with the risk of making such human errors in assembler programming. Perfection is never achievable; the goal is simply to reduce risks to an acceptable level.

It is of course preferable to detect errors at compile time rather than at run time. The compiler typically gives a message pointing directly to the source of the difficulty whereas run-time errors involve the unpredictable process known as debugging (good fun perhaps but not the essence of disciplined engineering development).

Abstraction makes it easier to find errors at compile time. A simple example is given by strong typing. Thus in Ada we might declare

```
type Signal is (Clear, Caution, Danger);
```

for some railroad application and we can then manipulate signals just in terms of the three possible literal values, Clear, Caution and Danger. Of course in machine terms the three values are probably represented as 0, 1 and 2. Nevertheless the compiler prevents us from assigning an integer value to a signal.

```
S: Signal := Danger;          -- initial value is Danger
...
S := 2;                       -- illegal
```

The assignment is illegal because the enumeration type Signal is treated as a distinct type from the type Integer. Weaker languages such as C do not make such a distinction and it is possible to make ludicrous errors such as assigning 4 to a signal.

Other aspects of Ada which help to detect errors at compile time are the visibility control provided by packages and private types and the ability to declare objects as constants so that they cannot be inadvertently changed.

But even in Ada a number of errors inevitably remain until run time. However, violation of the Ada structure is prevented by run-time checks which cause an exception to be raised in various circumstances. Thus if we have an array with bounds 1 and 5 such as

```
A: array (1 .. 5) of Float;
```

and attempt to assign to the eighth element by

```
I := Eight;                   -- some expression which evaluates to 8
A(I) := 0.0;
```

then the automatically compiled check prevents the assignment from taking place and instead the exception Constraint_Error is raised. In full Ada the programmer can look out for this exception and then take remedial action, or if this is not done then the program will simply terminate with the run-time system typically giving a message saying what went wrong.

Languages such as C do not afford such protection and the assignment will take place and overwrite some other data or maybe even some code thereby completely destroying the program and perhaps causing the system to crash.

This is why typical commercial software such as word processors crash from time to time; they have residual errors and the code does not protect against them. So that rather than getting some helpful diagnostic which you can send to the vendor with a complaint that the system is not fit-for-purpose, all you can do is curse and start again.

The Ada approach is obviously better. But for critical applications it is not realistic to have such run-time checks raising exceptions. The pilot coming in to land will not be happy with a message saying

Constraint_Error raised by task Landing_Control
in procedure Lower_Undercarriage.

So critical software just has to be correct. Or at least the risks associated with it being incorrect must be reduced to an acceptable level such as less than the risk of the wings falling off if the plane hits a duck.

The approach taken with SPARK therefore is that we should ideally prove that the program is correct. This is really just the final stage in moving the detection of errors from run time to compile time – they all have to be found statically, that is before run time (we can hardly say at compile time because the analysis is not done by the compiler but by other tools).

Another point regarding exceptions is that it is usually harder to prove that any code handling the exception is correct than it is to ensure that the exception is not raised in the first place. As a consequence, exceptions are not catered for in SPARK because hopefully they will not be raised – this is discussed further in Section 6.2.

It is interesting to consider the four predefined exceptions of Ada and to note why they do not arise in a proven SPARK program.

Constraint_Error cannot arise if analysis shows that the program cannot violate ranges such as array bounds and does not cause arithmetic overflow or attempt to divide by zero.

Storage_Error cannot arise since the storage requirements can be determined at compile time (recursion and dynamic arrays are forbidden in SPARK) and suitable hardware can therefore be provided.

Program_Error cannot arise because the conditions leading to it such as running into the end of a function can never arise in SPARK.

Tasking_Error cannot arise because SPARK does not support tasks and protected objects and the communication between them.

(Note that Numeric_Error is just another name for Constraint_Error in Ada 95.)

Proving that a program is correct is not easy. It is similar in some ways to proving that a mathematical theorem is correct. We have to understand what the statement of the theorem really means and then we have to be convinced of the validity of the arguments in each step of the proof. Typical mathematical proofs are never that rigorous but rely upon the understanding in the mind of the reader of the objectives of the author; to complete every fine detail would be too much of a burden and mathematicians rely heavily on previously proved lemmata and often resort to phrases such as 'it follows that', or 'clearly', or the hopeful 'without loss of generality', or even 'it is left to the reader to show that'. Important mathematical proofs are also widely published and subjected to much scrutiny.

Analysing programs by walkthroughs and arguing about the consequences of the program logic are much like mathematical proofs in that they rely upon human understanding and agreed prior conditions such as possible values of data. The problem with programs is that they are typically very long and detailed and so analysis is tedious and repetitive and very prone to errors arising from jumping to conclusions. Moreover, they are usually not widely published and so are reviewed by only a small number of people.

The SPARK approach relies upon a number of tools to help us. This relieves much of the tedium of analysis and prevents one from jumping to conclusions; it also draws the attention of the programmer to the consequences of initial data conditions that might not have been foreseen.

## 3.2 The Examiner

In practice, formal rigorous proof is not appropriate for every safety related program. We always have to balance the costs of developing such a proof against the consequences of an error. Programs vary in the degree of reliability needed, errors in some might cause serious loss of life whereas in others they might be merely a nuisance.

Programs controlling an inherently unstable system such as certain modern aircraft are clearly very critical. Errors in some programs might be prevented from causing a disaster by additional systems; thus a train passing a red signal might be stopped by some mechanical trackside device which cuts off the power (as on the London Underground). An error in a program which thereby allowed a train to pass a red signal is highly undesirable because the trackside system itself might fail but of itself is not an immediate calamity. Such systems give safety in depth.

Other examples are provided by automobile systems. The software controlling the brakes is obviously very critical. The software controlling an anti-theft protection system is not so critical. Software controlling the entertainment system might be considered quite harmless – but one might argue otherwise if by suddenly playing *The Ride of the Valkyries* at full volume it made the driver jump and steer into a ditch!

The key SPARK tool is the Examiner. It enables programs to be subjected to three different levels of analysis according to their criticality.

The lowest level is called data flow analysis. Not only does it check that the usage of parameters and global variables corresponds to their modes but it also checks that variables are not read before being given a value, that values are not overwritten without being used, that all imported variables are used somewhere and so on. However, it does not check the interdependencies between variables as expressed in the derives annotation and accordingly the derives annotation is not required and, if provided, is ignored.

The next level is called information flow analysis. This requires derives annotations. As well as carrying out data flow analysis it also checks that the modes of parameters and global variables and their usage in the code of the body correctly match the detailed interdependencies given in the derives annotation. This level of analysis is sometimes called shallow verification since it checks the static semantic dependencies even though it does not check dynamic values.

For the most critical software, the highest level of analysis is appropriate. This involves generating verification conditions as well as performing flow analysis and requires proof annotations as will be explained later.

Information flow analysis should be considered the norm. However, for some programs or parts of programs, data flow analysis is sometimes all that is appropriate. It might be used for retrospective analysis performed after a program has been completely written (this is a far from ideal situation but sometimes happens). On the other hand, it should not be felt that data flow analysis is somehow inadequate; as we shall see in Chapter 10, many errors are detected by data flow analysis alone.

All three levels might be used in one program. Data flow analysis is often appropriate for the topmost level (including of course the main subprogram) where the derives annotations are often heavy and do not provide much added value. Proof might well be appropriate to some of the fine algorithmic detail with information flow analysis being appropriate for the bulk.

(In SPARK 83, the Examiner always carried out information flow analysis and data flow analysis alone was not an option. However, mode information was not supplied for global variables but was deduced from the derives annotation. The data flow analysis option of SPARK 95 (which does not require derives annotations) is only possible because mode information is explicitly given for global variables. Nevertheless, for backward compatibility, it is still possible to carry out information flow analysis (which does require derives annotations) without providing mode information for global variables although clearly if it is provided then additional consistency checks between the modes and derives annotation are possible.)

Whatever the level of analysis, the Examiner works, like an Ada compiler, on compilation units. In order to examine a compilation unit, the Examiner must have access to all other compilation units on which the unit depends. For instance, to analyse a compilation unit which inherits packages, the Examiner must have access to the specifications of those packages (the inherit clause was introduced in Section 2.9). Access to such other units is provided in various ways as explained in detail in Chapter 9.

The Examiner performs analysis in units of subprogram bodies and the initialization part of a package is treated rather like a parameterless subprogram for this purpose. In fact the SPARK language is such that there should be no executable code elsewhere at all; for example initial expressions in declarations are static and so do not give rise to executable code. (This is not quite true, there might be move instructions to load aggregates giving initial values to arrays and records, but there should be no expression evaluation.)

The interfaces presented by package and subprogram specifications are strictly adhered to for the purpose of analysis. Thus analysis of the body of a subprogram is performed assuming only the information in its specification (including annotations) and that this is correct. Equally, analysis of a call of a subprogram is performed assuming only the information in the specification and again that this is correct. The specification thus provides a rigid barrier between the internal and external views of a subprogram.

All errors are reported bearing in mind the fact that errors might impede further analysis. If the analysis is successful then a confirming message is given.

Examples of typical messages are illustrated by considering the procedure Exchange of Section 2.5.

```
procedure Exchange(X, Y: in out Float)
--# derives X from Y &
--#         Y from X;
is
  T: Float;
begin
  T := X;  X := Y;  Y := T;
end Exchange;
```

This is correct and at the end of analysis of this subprogram the Examiner outputs the message

```
+++        Flow analysis of subprogram Exchange performed:
           no errors found.
```

This is the normal confirmatory message obtained after information flow analysis. If we just ask for data flow analysis (in which case the derives annotations are not required and, if given, are ignored) then the final message becomes

```
Note: Information flow analysis not carried out.
```

Incidentally, if the reader wishes to try the Examiner on simple examples then this can be done as explained in Chapter 9. However, it should be remembered that a subprogram can only be a library unit if it is the main subprogram and so the Examiner will expect it to be preceded by the main program annotation. An alternative approach for such experiments is to wrap the subprogram in a package called perhaps Dummy. This has a number of practical advantages; several subprograms can be declared and so examined together and global variables can also be declared in the package body without more ado. All the significant examples in this book will be found on the CD as explained in Appendix 4; many are encapsulated in a package Dummy in this manner. Note that a pragma Elaborate_Body is required if the specification of Dummy is empty, see Section 7.1.

In order to illustrate some error messages suppose we make a foolish error in the procedure Exchange and inadvertently assign X to Y rather than T to Y as the last assignment so that it becomes

```
procedure Exchange(X, Y: in out Float)
--# derives X from Y &
--#         Y from X;
is
   T: Float;
begin
   T := X;  X := Y;  Y := X;
end Exchange;
```

Using information flow analysis, the Examiner reports a number of errors and also gives a final warning. The first error is marked explicitly against the statement T := X; thus

```
            T := X;  X := Y;  Y := X;
            ^1
!!! (  1)   Flow Error          : Ineffective statement.
```

This tells us that the assignment to T is useless because of course the value of T is never used. At the end of the subprogram the Examiner issues a number of messages

```
!!! (  2)   Flow Error          : Importation of the initial
            value of variable X is ineffective.

!!! (  3)   Flow Error          : The variable T is neither
            referenced nor exported.

!!! (  4)   Flow Error          : The imported value of X is
            not used in the derivation of Y.

??? (  5)   Warning             : The imported value of Y may
            be used in the derivation of Y.
```

These messages are all to be expected: (2) the initial value of X is not used at all whereas the derives annotation stated that it would be used in the determination of Y; (3) T is not used and so is indeed neither referenced nor exported; (4) this explicitly notes that the initial value of X was not used to determine Y contrary to the derives annotation. Item (5) is technically a warning as indicated by the **???** rather than the **!!!** used against formal errors; it warns that it seems that the final value of Y depends upon the initial value of Y (it gets copied into X and then back to Y) which is contrary to the derives annotation.

This last message is a warning because the flow analysis is conservative. In the general case where there are several execution paths, some paths might

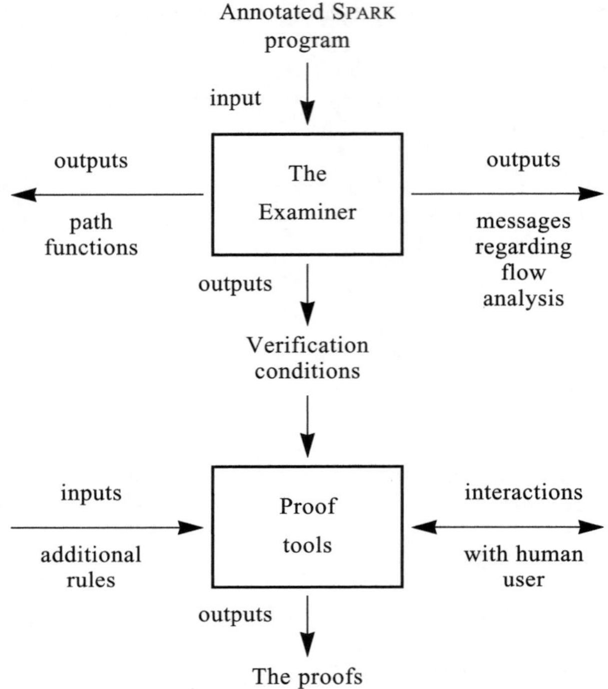


**Figure 3.1** The SPARK tools.

never be taken and so the potentially offending statements might not be executed. Nevertheless, all potential paths need to be inspected to determine whether the warning may be safely ignored. In this case there is only one path of course and so the warning has to be taken seriously.

The reader might feel that there are rather a lot of messages for such a simple error; but it really is a gross error. The origin of all the individual messages will be explained in detail when we look at some of the mathematics behind flow analysis in Chapter 10.

Incidentally, if we just request data flow analysis then we only get the first three messages. However, these are quite enough to identify this particular error!

The analysis of a compilation unit is performed in various phases and the messages are marked according to their origin and severity. Note that flow analysis is only performed if static and semantic analysis finds no errors.

Error messages from syntactic and semantic analysis are marked with `***`. Formal error messages from flow analysis are marked with `!!!` and warnings and notes are marked with `???`. In addition the Examiner produces messages marked with `---` which typically flag what is considered poor practice as well as messages marked with `+++` to confirm that all is well.

For the highest level of analysis, the Examiner is able to generate path functions and verification conditions which can then be analysed. We will first look at path functions because the ideas are very straightforward even though in practice they are not that useful. We will then consider the more important verification conditions and show how they can be proved to be true possibly with the aid of proof tools. The general relationship between the Examiner and the proof tools is illustrated in Figure 3.1. As this shows, path functions are typically read by the human reader whereas verification conditions are processed by the proof tools and may require additional information (rules) in order to complete a proof.

## 3.3 Path functions

The idea of a path function is that it reveals what happens when a particular path is traced through a subprogram. A subprogram without internal loops has a finite number of possible paths through it and for each of these there is a corresponding path function.

Each path function comprises two parts. First, a *traversal condition* which is a formula defining the conditions under which the path is traversed; this formula is written in terms of the initial values of the imported variables. And secondly, an *action part* which defines the final values of the modified variables (both exported and internal) in terms of the initial values of the imported variables.

As a very simple example consider the procedure Exchange once more

```
procedure Exchange(X, Y: in out Float)
--# derives X from Y &
--#         Y from X;
is
   T: Float;
begin
   T := X;  X := Y;  Y := T;
end Exchange;
```

This is so simple that there is only one possible path through it. It is in fact

```
    Path  1
      Traversal condition:
1:      true .
      Action:
        x' := y &
        y' := x &
        t' := x .
```

Since there is only one path that is always taken the traversal condition reduces to just the one condition which is true. The consequence of taking the path is shown by the action list to be that the final value of X is the initial value of Y (final values are denoted by the prime), the final value of Y is the initial value of X and the final value of T is the initial value of X. (Note that the Examiner outputs path functions using lower case letters; remember that in Ada there is no distinction between identifiers in upper or lower case and so no confusion can arise.)

Observe that the path function shows the state of all modified variables and not just the exported ones; this is sometimes helpful for spotting errors.

A more interesting example is

```
function Max(I, J: Integer) return Integer is
  Result: Integer;
begin
  if I > J then
    Result := I;
  else
    Result := J;
  end if;
  return Result;
end Max;
```

for which the path functions are

```
    Path  1
      Traversal condition:
1:     i > j .
      Action:
        max' := i &
        result' := i .
    Path  2
      Traversal condition:
1:     not (i > j) .
      Action:
        max' := j &
        result' := j .
```

In this case there are two possible paths and (not surprisingly) the condition for one is the negation of the condition for the other. In the actions the returned value is indicated by the name of the function.

Nested conditional statements give rise to multiple conditions. For example the following procedure is used to integrate faults and set a trip indicator appropriately

```
procedure Fault_Integrator(Fault_Found: in Boolean;
                           Trip: in out Boolean;
                           Counter: in out Integer)
--# derives Trip from Fault_Found, Trip, Counter &
--#         Counter from Fault_Found, Counter;
is
```

```
begin
  if Fault_Found then
    Counter := Counter + Up_Rate;
    if Counter >= Upper_Limit then
      Trip := True;  Counter := Upper_Limit;
    end if;
  else
    Counter := Counter - Down_Rate;
    if Counter <= Lower_Limit then
      Trip := False;  Counter := Lower_Limit;
    end if;
  end if;
end Fault_Integrator;
```

In this case there are four possible paths. (Incidentally Up_Rate, Down_Rate, Upper_Limit and Lower_Limit are constants declared outside the procedure. Constants are not included in the derives list.)

The path functions for this example are

```
   Path  1
     Traversal condition:
1:    fault_found .
2:    counter + up_rate >= upper_limit .
     Action:
       trip' := true &
       counter' := upper_limit .
   Path  2
     Traversal condition:
1:    fault_found .
2:    not (counter + up_rate >= upper_limit) .
     Action:
       counter' := counter + up_rate .
   Path  3
     Traversal condition:
1:    not fault_found .
2:    counter - down_rate <= lower_limit .
     Action:
       trip' := false &
       counter' := lower_limit .
   Path  4
     Traversal condition:
1:    not fault_found .
2:    not (counter - down_rate <= lower_limit) .
     Action:
       counter' := counter - down_rate .
```

In this example there are two conditions for each path and these must both apply. Note also that on paths 2 and 4, the variable Trip is not altered and so is not shown in the action list.

Path functions are sometimes useful for spotting inconsistencies, unused paths and unset variables. Path functions can be simplified using the SPADE Automatic Simplifier which searches for contradictions in the traversal conditions and simplifies both the conditions and action expressions.

In the above examples the Simplifier has little effect except that expressions such as not (i > j) are turned into i <= j. It also observes that in the function Exchange the one path is always traversed.

A contradiction would arise for example if we mistakenly wrote

```
if X > Y then
  ...
  if X < Y then
    ...
  end if;
end if;
```

so that the traversal condition for one of the paths becomes

```
     Path  2
       Traversal condition:
  1:     x > y .
  2:     x < y .
```

The Simplifier reports that the path could never be taken by reducing this to

```
     Path  2
               Path eliminated.  (Contradictory traversal condition)
```

and thereby draws our attention to a possible error.

(Incidentally, it has been estimated that around 10% of the paths in typical production programs can never be executed because the appropriate combination of conditions never arises. However, it is often easier to leave the code intact rather than make the conditions more elaborate.)

Path functions can become very laborious since the number of paths and the number of actions quickly become large for significant subprograms. There are also complexities regarding loops. As a consequence the task of checking all the paths is often much harder than developing a more formal proof using verification conditions. Nevertheless path functions are sometimes useful for retrospective analysis.

## 3.4 Verification conditions

The general idea is that we state certain hypotheses which we assert are always satisfied when a subprogram is called (the *preconditions*) and we also state the conditions which we want to be satisfied as a result of the call (the *postconditions*). These conditions are given as further annotations in the subprogram specification. We then have to show that the postconditions always follow from the preconditions.

The Examiner processes the text and generates one or more theorems which then have to be proved in order to show that the postconditions do indeed always follow from the preconditions. These theorems which are called *verification conditions* are often trivially obvious. If they are not then there are two tools which can help us in their proof. The first is the SPADE Automatic Simplifier which carries out routine simplification using a number of rules. The second is the SPADE Proof Checker which is an interactive assistant that enables the user to explore the problem and hopefully construct a valid proof.

In order for the proof tools to function correctly, they need to be aware of the various rules which can be used. For the predefined types these are built into the system but other rules can be provided and these then form additional inputs to the proof tools as was illustrated in Figure 3.1.

As a first example we will consider once more the procedure Exchange. In fact there is no precondition for this procedure since it is designed to work no matter what the values of the parameters happen to be. But there is of course a postcondition and so the procedure becomes

```
procedure Exchange(X, Y: in out Float)
--# derives X from Y &
--#         Y from X;
--# post X = Y~ and Y = X~ ;
is
   T: Float;
begin
   T := X;  X := Y;  Y := T;
end Exchange;
```

The conditions are written in a slightly extended form of SPARK which is described in Chapter 11. One immediate point of note is the use of the tilde character. An identifier which is both an import and an export of a procedure may be decorated with a tilde and the decorated form indicates the initial imported value of the identifier whereas the undecorated form indicates the final exported value. Thus

```
X = Y~
```

is the condition that the final value of X is the initial value of Y.

The verification condition generated by the Examiner for the procedure Exchange is simply

```
H1:   true .
      ->
C1:   y = y .
C2:   x = x .
```

The notation used here is that first we have a number of hypotheses (H1, H2, ...) and these are then followed by a number of conclusions (C1, C2, ...)

which have to be verified using the hypotheses. The whole verification condition is therefore

```
H1 and H2 and ...   ->   C1 and C2 and ...
```

where the arrow -> is the implies operator.

In this example there is no precondition and so effectively no hypotheses (this is represented as the single hypothesis H1 which is true). The two conclusions to be proved are that y = y and x = x which are reasonably self-evident and so it is pretty clear that the procedure Exchange is correct.

(The reader will see from the examples on the CD that there are often other hypotheses. They concern the type model and take the form n >= n_type__first, n <= n_type__last and so on. We will generally ignore these other hypotheses for the moment; they are described in detail in Section 11.9.)

Verification conditions often appear mysterious and not obviously related to the code; we will see how the Examiner arrives at them when we look at flow analysis in more detail in Chapter 10. Remember that the Examiner uses both the code and the annotations in arriving at the conditions.

Another point is that if there are several paths then several verification conditions are generated, one for each path.

If we were stubborn and wanted to be completely confident then we could submit the above verification condition to the Simplifier which would reduce it to simply

```
*** true .          /* all conclusions proved */
```

It is interesting to observe what would happen if we made a couple of silly errors. Suppose that we inadvertently added 1.0 to T so that the code was

```
procedure Exchange(X, Y: in out Float)
--# derives X from Y &
--#         Y from X;
--# post X = Y~ and Y = X~ ;
is
   T: Float;
begin
   T := X;  X := Y;  Y := T + 1.0;
end Exchange;
```

The Examiner would find no fault with flow analysis (the derives annotation is still consistent with the code) but the verification condition becomes

```
H1:   true .
      ->
C1:   y = y .
C2:   x + 1 = x .
```

Although such a set of conclusions cannot be proved nevertheless the Simplifier may be able to prove some and simplify others. Those that can be proved are removed. In this case the first one is removed and the second one is then renumbered so that the output of the Simplifier is

```
H1:   true .
      ->
C1:   false .
```

This shows that what was the second conclusion is not just unprovable but actually false. It follows that there are no circumstances at all under which the procedure meets its specification.

Note that verification conditions are written more as mathematics and not as program text. Thus the expression x + 1 in conclusion C2 does not express the literal as 1.0. In fact the conditions are written in a language known as FDL (Functional Description Language); this is described in some detail in Chapter 11. Floating point operations in SPARK are modelled as operations on rationals in FDL and so if the literal had been 1.5 then it would have become (3/2) in the verification condition.

We might also make actual flow errors in the code. For example consider

```
procedure Exchange(X, Y: in out Float)
--# derives X from Y &
--#         Y from X;
--# post X = Y~ and Y = X~ ;
is
   T: Float;
begin
   T := X;  X := Y;  Y := X;
end Exchange;
```

where, as in Section 3.2, we have inadvertently assigned X to Y rather than T to Y as the last assignment. We noted that the Examiner reports a number of difficulties with this such as that the assignment to T is ineffective, the initial value of X is not used, T is not used and so on. We are therefore likely to conclude that something is wrong but if we did persevere then the generated verification condition would show

```
H1:   true .
      ->
C1:   y = y .
C2:   y = x .
```

and the Simplifier would reduce this to

```
H1:   true .
      ->
C1:   y = x .
```

Incidentally this shows that the procedure is not always wrong since in fact the conclusions are satisfied if the values to be swapped happen to be the same!

The Examiner has a mode of operation enabling it to generate verification conditions corresponding to the run-time checks of Ada. The proof of these conditions shows that the checks would not be violated and therefore that the predefined exceptions as discussed in Section 3.1 will not be raised. It is important to note that no extra annotations are required for this and that these verification conditions can be generated whether data or information flow analysis is performed. Consider

```
type T is range -128 .. 128;

procedure Inc(X: in out T)
--# derives X from X;
is
begin
   X := X + 1;
end Inc;
```

The type T is an integer type whose values are constrained to lie in the range given. (In Chapter 6 we will see that strictly speaking the underlying type is unconstrained and that T denotes a subtype which is constrained. The mechanism is such that arithmetic is performed using the underlying machine hardware and it is only assignments to variables of the subtype T that are constrained.)

Calling the procedure Inc with the value 128 will cause Constraint_Error to be raised in full Ada on the attempt to assign 129 to X. We therefore have to ensure that this can never happen.

Applying the Examiner (with the run-time check option) results in two verification conditions. After simplification the conclusions of one become true and the other reduces to

```
H1:   x >= -128 .
H2:   x <= 128 .
      ->
C1:   x <= 127 .
```

Note that the Examiner knows about the type model and the meaning of the declaration of the type T; we do not have to explicitly give the preconditions that X >= -128 and X <= 128. However, the outcome is that we cannot prove the conclusion X <= 127 from the hypotheses. So there is a potential run-time error which will arise under conditions which are quite clear from the unproved conclusion.

There are a number of different approaches that can be used to prevent run-time errors. One approach is to insert preconditions to ensure that the parameters can never take values giving rise to run-time errors in the first place. Of course this simply shifts the problem to the calling code since we are then obliged to prove that at every call the relevant conditions are satisfied.

In the case of this example we can insert a precondition that X is never equal to T'Last thus

```
procedure Inc(X: in out T)
--# derives X from X;
--# pre X < T'Last;
is
begin
   X := X + 1;
end Inc;
```

The conclusions now reduce to true after simplification. However, we also have to show that X is indeed less than T'Last at every call of Inc.

Another approach is that of 'defensive programming' and to use a so-called saturated procedure thus

```
procedure Inc(X: in out T)
--# derives X from X;
is
begin
   if X < T'Last then
      X := X + 1;
   end if;
end Inc;
```

In this case the conclusions are again true and moreover there are no obligations on the calls of Inc. But of course it might be argued that the procedure does not really work any more. Nevertheless, this is an approach often used in practice where the program is modelling physical limits in the real world.

It is important to show that programs are free of exceptions at run time. Indeed it is usually easier to reason that a program is free of exceptions than to reason about the correct implementation of exception handlers that might be used in full Ada.

Moreover, certification often requires full test coverage and this is hard to achieve when the compiler inserts run-time checks and so it is much better to prove that the checks can never fail so that they can be omitted. This also results in smaller and faster code.

---

**EXERCISE 3.4**

1 Write the specification of a procedure Solve to solve the following pair of simultaneous linear equations

$$ax + by = p$$
$$cx + dy = q$$

Assume that the coefficients $a$, $b$, $c$ and $d$ are integers. Provide full annotations including an appropriate precondition and postcondition.

---

## 3.5 Iterative processes

Significant computations usually have loops and these cause complexity in proving correctness. The problems arise because the code of a loop is usually traversed a number of times with different conditions (otherwise it would never terminate). The conditions therefore have to take a rather more dynamic form.

The approach taken is to cut a loop so that the various parts can be treated separately. The cut is made by inserting an assert statement which gives conditions that are to be true at that point. The conditions can be thought of as postconditions for the sequence of code arriving at the cutpoint and as preconditions for the sequence going on from the cutpoint. The choice of an appropriate assertion is key to proving the correctness of the code.

A simple example is provided by the following integer division algorithm which might be used on a processor without a hardware divide instruction. It divides M by N to give remainder R and quotient Q.

```
procedure Divide(M, N: in Integer; Q, R: out Integer)
--# derives Q, R from M, N;
is
begin
   Q := 0;
   R := M;
   loop
      exit when R < N;
      Q := Q + 1;
      R := R - N;
   end loop;
end Divide;
```

(Those familiar with Ada 83 will note that this is not legal Ada 83 since the out parameters are being read. But it is allowed in Ada 95; permitting the reading of out parameters in Ada 95 may seem only a minor improvement but is of considerable practical and logical benefit.)

The idea of the algorithm is of course that we keep going around the loop adding one to the trial quotient and subtracting the divisor N from the corresponding trial remainder until the remainder first becomes less than the divisor. Clearly it only works if both M and N are not negative and also the divisor must not be 0. The precondition is therefore

```
--# pre (M >= 0) and (N > 0);
```

Note that the parentheses are not necessary but perhaps help to make the conditions easier to read.

The postcondition also has two parts. First the output parameters must have the appropriate mathematical relation implied by the division process and secondly the remainder must be less than the divisor and not negative, so we have

```
--# post (M = Q * N + R) and (R < N) and (R >= 0);
```

We now have to cut the loop at an appropriate point with a suitable assertion. A little thought and inspiration leads to the procedure finally becoming

```
procedure Divide(M, N: in Integer; Q, R: out Integer)
--# derives Q, R from M, N;
--# pre (M >= 0) and (N > 0);
--# post (M = Q * N + R) and (R < N) and (R >= 0);
is
begin
   Q := 0;
   R := M;
   loop
      --# assert (M = Q * N + R) and (R >= 0);
      exit when R < N;
      Q := Q + 1;
      R := R - N;
   end loop;
end Divide;
```

The choice of assertion is fairly obvious. As noted above, the final postcondition has two parts, the division relation and the upper and lower bounds on the remainder. All the loop does is keep the division relation true and reduce the remainder until it satisfies the upper bound (as well as keeping the lower bound satisfied). The assertion is simply that the division relation is true and that the remainder satisfies the lower bound; the exit statement is taken when the upper bound is satisfied as well. The initial statements before the loop are of course designed to ensure that the assertion is true when the loop is first entered.

There are therefore three sections of code to be verified, as illustrated in Figure 3.2. They are from the start to the beginning of the loop, around the loop, and from the loop to the end. The assert statement acts as the postcondition for the first section and as the precondition for the last section. It also acts as both precondition and postcondition for the loop itself; since it is unchanged by the loop it is also known as a loop invariant.

When the Examiner is applied to this subprogram, it produces verification conditions corresponding to the three sections. From the start to the loop invariant the verification condition is

```
H1:   m >= 0 .
H2:   n > 0 .
      ->
C1:   m = 0 * n + m .
C2:   m >= 0 .
```

Conclusion C2 is trivially obvious since it is just the hypothesis H1. Conclusion C1 is pretty obvious as well since it reduces to `m = m`. The Simplifier naturally reduces them both to true.

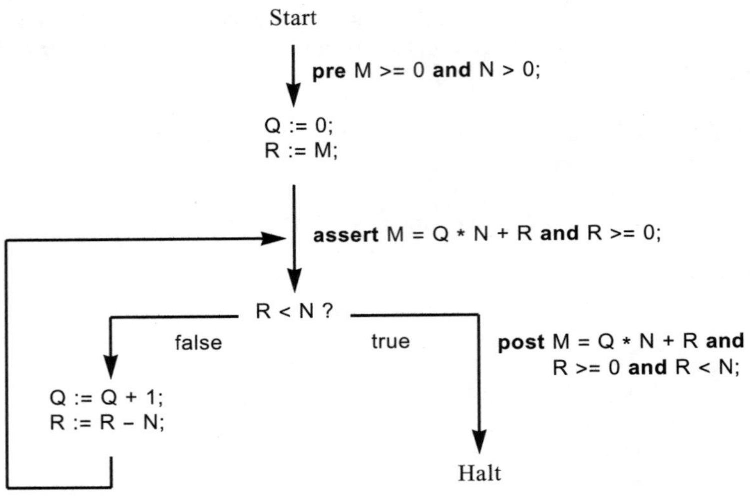

Start

pre M >= 0 and N > 0;

Q := 0;
R := M;

assert M = Q * N + R and R >= 0;

R < N ?

false

true

post M = Q * N + R and
R >= 0 and R < N;

Q := Q + 1;
R := R – N;

Halt

**Figure 3.2** Flowchart of integer division algorithm.

The verification condition for going around the loop from invariant to invariant is

```
H1:   m = q * n + r .
H2:   r >= 0 .
H3:   not (r < n) .
      ->
C1:   m = (q + 1) * n + (r – n) .
C2:   r – n >= 0 .
```

and that from the invariant to the final end is

```
H1:   m = q * n + r .
H2:   r >= 0 .
H3:   r < n .
      ->
C1:   m = q * n + r .
C2:   r < n .
C3:   r >= 0 .
```

In both cases the Simplifier reduces all the conclusions to true. It is also quite straightforward to show that they are true by hand – although perhaps a little tedious in the case of the loop itself which requires some manipulation. However, such trivial manipulation is prone to error if done by hand and the great advantage of the Simplifier is that it does not make careless mistakes.

Having shown that the verification conditions for the three separate sections of code are true it then follows that the procedure is correct. To be honest we have only proved that the program is partially correct; this means that it is correct provided that it terminates (and so does not loop forever). We have not formally shown that it terminates.

Termination of a loop is usually shown by considering some discrete expression whose value changes monotonically on each iteration and is such that exit from the loop occurs when its value passes some known target value. In the example here we know that R is reduced by N each time and that N is greater than zero. Consequently after a finite number of iterations R will become less than N so that the exit condition R < N is true (by coincidence N is the target value as well as the decrement). So this example does indeed terminate.

The Examiner does not offer any mechanical technique for proving termination but informal proofs are often obvious. Nevertheless, it is all too easy to forget to think about the problem of termination and to conclude that a subprogram is correct just because all the verification conditions are true.

It is hoped that this example has not seemed too tedious. In practice of course one does not bother to look at the unsimplified conditions and so the whole process is quite straightforward. However, it is important to realize just how much the Simplifier is doing. Without such tools, proving program correctness would not be a practical proposition.

## 3.6 Nested processes

Programming in the raw is about loops and subprogram calls. Fancy stuff regarding OOP and Abstract Data Types is all about visibility control; these are important but the ultimate power of the stored program machine is its ability to perform iterative and nested processes. The previous section addressed iterative processes and we now turn to nested processes or subprogram calls. But before doing so we consider check annotations which may be considered as a variation on assert annotations.

We have seen how iterative processes can be broken down through the use of assert annotations. An assert acts as a cutpoint and provides the postcondition for the end of one path and also the precondition for the start of a completely new path. Note that the hypotheses applicable to the first path do not carry over to the second; the hypotheses for the second path all have to be stated in the assert. (This is necessary because the prime purpose of the assert is to break a loop; if the conditions were propagated then the distinct cycles would be interlocked and this would cause difficulties.)

Sometimes it is convenient to ask for a condition to be checked but not for the existing hypotheses to be forgotten. This is done by a check annotation which takes the form

```
--# check X > 0 and X < 10;
```

This requests that verification conditions be generated corresponding to the check. The conclusions are then added to the existing hypotheses for the path

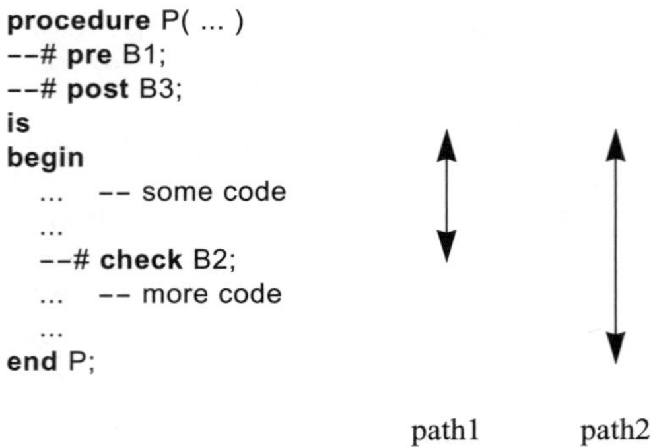

procedure P( ... )
--# pre B1;
--# post B3;
is
begin
... -- some code
...
--# check B2;
... -- more code
...
end P;
path1
path2


**Figure 3.3** Paths associated with a check.

thereafter. In effect the check causes a second path to be created but its starting point is that of the first path. This is illustrated in Figure 3.3 which shows the two paths associated with a precondition, a check and a postcondition.

The hypothesis for path1 is B1 and the conclusion to be proved is obtained from B2. The hypotheses for path2 are B1 plus the conclusion obtained from B2 (which is added by the check) and the conclusion to be proved is of course obtained from B3.

As a trivial example, suppose that a nervous programmer coding the procedure Exchange decides that it would be wise to check that the original value of Y has been safely assigned to X before overwriting Y by the final assignment. This could be done by

```
procedure Exchange(X, Y: in out Float)
--# derives X from Y &
--#         Y from X;
--# post X = Y~ and Y = X~ ;
is
  T: Float;
begin
  T := X;
  X := Y;
  --# check X = Y~ ;
  Y := T;
end Exchange;
```

The verification conditions for the two paths are

```
For path(s) from start to check:

H1:   true .
      ->
C1:   y = y .
```

For path(s) from start to finish:

```
H1:   true .
H2:   y = y .
      ->
C1:   y = y .
C2:   x = x .
```

As we can see, the first path generates a check for the correctness of Y and the second path then has this as an additional hypothesis.

Incidentally note that we can use Y~ to denote the original value of Y in a check and assert as well as in a postcondition. The undecorated form always represents the current value. Decoration with tilde is only permitted (and necessary) if a variable is both imported and exported (such as an **in out** parameter). If a variable is only imported then it behaves as a constant and so the undecorated form always refers to the initial value which is also the current value. If a variable is only exported then there is no initial value to refer to.

We can now turn to subprogram calls. If a subprogram has a precondition such as Divide then the precondition acts as a check on the actual parameters at the point of call. If a subprogram has a postcondition then this simply adds further hypotheses at that point.

Suppose we write a procedure to perform a cyclic rotation of three parameters A, B and C.

```
procedure CAB(A, B, C: in out Float)
--# derives A from C &
--#         B from A &
--#         C from B;
--# post A = C~ and B = A~ and C = B~;
is
begin
  Exchange(A, B);
  Exchange(A, C);
end CAB;
```

Each call of Exchange adds further hypotheses regarding the current state of the variables. In order to refer to the current state at different points the Examiner appends a double underline followed by a sequence number to the variables. Thus after the first call the value of A is denoted by a__1 and after the second it is denoted by a__2. The verification condition for CAB is

```
H1:   true .
H2:   a__1 = b .
H3:   b__1 = a .
H4:   a__2 = c .
H5:   c__2 = a__1 .
      ->
C1:   a__2 = c .
C2:   b__1 = a .
C3:   c__2 = b .
```

Two extra hypotheses are added at each call of Exchange corresponding to the two parts of the postcondition. The reader (with or without the aid of the Simplifier) will quickly verify that the conclusions are all true.

As a final example in this introductory chapter we will consider the algorithm to compute the greatest common divisor of two non-negative integers M and N. This is normally expressed recursively as

```
function GCD(M, N: Integer) return Integer is
begin
   if N = 0 then
      return M;
   else
      return GCD(N, M rem N);
   end if;
end GCD;
```

However, we cannot use recursion in SPARK (as explained in Section 1.2) and so we have to write it out as an iterative process. Note also that we would normally make the parameters and result of subtype Natural but since we want to defer a detailed discussion of run-time checks at this stage, it is simpler to avoid constraints for the moment.

In SPARK we might write it as a procedure thus

```
procedure GCD(M, N: in Integer; G: out Integer)
--# derives G from M, N;
is
   C, D: Integer;
   R: Integer;
begin
   C := M;  D := N;
   while D /= 0 loop
      R := C rem D;
      C := D;  D := R;
   end loop;
   G := C;
end GCD;
```

We have to copy the parameters into variables C and D because of course we cannot change M and N. We then divide one by the other, replacing the old dividend by the remainder and then swapping their roles for the next iteration until the remainder is zero. (The reason for writing this as a procedure rather than as a function is that it makes the complete proof slightly easier when we come to Chapter 11.)

If we assume that there is no hardware divide then we can use the Divide procedure of the previous section and we can also use a procedure Swap for additional illustration of the effect of nested subprogram calls. (Swap is like Exchange but has parameters of type Integer.) The procedure GCD then becomes

```
procedure GCD(M, N: in Integer; G: out Integer)
--# derives G from M, N;
is
   C, D: Integer;
   Q, R: Integer;
begin
   C := M;  D := N;
   while D /= 0 loop
      Divide(C, D, Q, R);
      C := R;
      Swap(C, D);
   end loop;
   G := C;
end GCD;
```

Note that we cannot write

```
Divide(C, D, Q, C);
```

because this creates aliasing between two of the parameters (this is discussed in depth in Section 6.7).

Furthermore the Examiner moans that Q is not used; we cannot do much about this, we have to put the quotient somewhere despite not being interested in it. (The pragmatic solution is to use some variable with an obvious name like Junk so that we can easily identify irrelevant messages relating to Junk.)

We are not yet in a position to give a satisfactory postcondition and so we cannot construct a proper proof for this procedure – this will be done in Chapter 11 when we discuss proof functions. However, we can add some minimal conditions which enable us to provide some degree of comfort.

In order to obtain verification conditions we have to cut the loop with an assert. At the very least we must ensure that C and D satisfy the preconditions for calling Divide. We also need conditions on M and N. So we might have

```
procedure GCD(M, N: in Integer; G: out Integer)
--# derives G from M, N;
--# pre M >= 0 and N > 0;
is
   C, D: Integer;
   Q, R: Integer;
begin
   C := M;  D := N;
   while D /= 0 loop
      --# assert C >= 0 and D > 0;
      Divide(C, D, Q, R);
      C := R;
      Swap(C, D);
   end loop;
   G := C;
end GCD;
```

There are in fact five paths and corresponding verification conditions

(1) from the start to the assertion,
(2) from the assertion around the loop back to the assertion,
(3) from the assertion to the check associated with the call of Divide,
(4) from the start to the finish,
(5) from the assertion to the finish.

The full details of the verification conditions are a bit boring but a number of points are worth noting. Incidentally, the Simplifier reduces all the conclusions to true – except for that for the second path which is indeed also true, but the Simplifier has a bit of a blind spot in some circumstances because of its fixed decision processes as explained in Section 11.7.

The procedure Divide implies a check and so as well as the path around the loop (2) there is also a path just from the assert to the call of Divide (3). The call of Swap produces no extra paths because it has no precondition. The two paths including the calls of Divide and Swap (2, 5) incorporate the additional hypotheses from the postconditions of the procedures.

The path from start to finish is interesting. It arises because we cut the loop *after* the exit condition which is implicit in the while condition. This is in contrast to the body of procedure Divide discussed in the previous section where the exit condition was explicit and the assert was placed *before* the exit condition. As a consequence there is a path through the procedure GCD which does not go around the loop at all. The verification condition for this path is

```
H1:   m >= 0 .
H2:   n > 0 .
H3:   not (n <> 0) .
      ->
C1:   true .
```

The conclusion is automatically true because we have given no postcondition (this also applies to path 5). But it is interesting to note that the hypotheses are contradictory. The third hypothesis (which uses the Pascal form <> for ≠ and thereby reveals the Pascal heritage of the tools) reduces to n = 0 which contradicts the second hypothesis. This contradiction arises because the loop is always executed at least once and so this path can never be taken anyway. In general, the Simplifier reports inconsistent hypotheses but in this particular case, since the conclusion is true anyway, it does not need to analyse them. An example of a report on inconsistent hypotheses will be found in Section 11.3.

Without a postcondition this example is a little futile although we have shown that the calls of Divide will always satisfy its precondition. The trouble with writing a suitable postcondition is making it complete. We can fairly easily express the condition that the answer G divides exactly into both M and N by writing

```
--# post G > 0 and (M rem G = 0) and (N rem G = 0)
```

But the difficulty is in stating that G is the largest such divisor. We will return to this example in Chapter 11.

We conclude this chapter with a very important observation. The verification conditions for the procedure GCD are generated without reference to the bodies of the procedures Divide and Swap. The only information about the called procedures that is required is given in their specifications including of course their pre- and postconditions. Thus the procedures might be compiled in a distinct library package P and then examination would only need access to the specification of P and not to its body. Of course the calls of Divide and Swap would then become P.Divide and P.Swap respectively.

The simple examples in this chapter have covered only a few aspects of the techniques available but should have given the reader some flavour of how we can prove that a program is correct. The topic will be covered in greater depth in later chapters. Meanwhile the next few chapters look in more detail at the SPARK core language as a subset of Ada plus the core annotations.

# Part 2

# The SPARK Language



This second part covers the SPARK core language and its relation to Ada. The core language consists of a kernel comprising a subset of Ada plus various annotations. The core annotations are

| | |
|---|---|
| --# **global** | permits access to global variables from within subprograms. |
| --# **derives** | defines interdependencies between imports and exports of subprograms. |
| --# **main_program** | indicates the main subprogram. |
| --# **own** | announces variables declared within packages which thus have state. |
| --# **initializes** | indicates that the given own variables are initialized before the main subprogram is entered. |
| --# **inherit** | permits access to entities in other packages. |
| --# **hide** | identifies text that is not to be examined. |

Chapter 4 acts as an introduction to the other chapters in this part. It deals with two aspects of SPARK, the overall structure and the fine lexical detail. The overall structure is very similar to Ada and includes hierarchical packages although there are a number of additional rules regarding visibility. The lexical details are given very briefly since they are almost identical to those of Ada.

Chapters 5, 6 and 7 then systematically describe the SPARK core language in detail. They show the full syntax as adapted from that of Ada and include notes on the major differences between SPARK and Ada. A number of examples are included. Chapter 5 deals with all aspects of the various types and their operations. Chapter 6 covers assignment, control structures and subprograms and hence covers the dynamic aspects of the language which govern the flow of data. Chapter 7 is concerned with visibility in general and includes packages, private types and the compilation process.

Chapter 8 is somewhat more informal and addresses the various ways in which SPARK interfaces to other parts of a system.

# SPARK Structure



The previous chapters will have given the reader a general idea of the approach used in SPARK. It is now time to consider SPARK in rather more detail and this is the first of several chapters covering the SPARK core language. Later chapters then consider how SPARK and its related tools are used in practice.

This chapter provides an opportunity to consider how SPARK is defined in relation to Ada and to describe both the small lexical details and the overall structure of the language.

## 4.1 The definition of SPARK

We present SPARK more or less in its own right but give the major variations from Ada on the grounds that most readers will be familiar with Ada. The full syntax of SPARK will be found in Appendix 1 but it is often convenient, especially when stressing the differences between Ada and SPARK, to give the syntax as part of the discussion.

The syntax is given in the familiar BNF form as used for Ada. Many productions (rules) are identical in Ada and SPARK; some productions are altered and these are prefixed with an asterisk (*) whereas some are additional and these are prefixed with a plus sign (+). Because SPARK omits several features of Ada, some productions have been coalesced if that simplifies the presentation; and of course many productions of Ada do not apply to SPARK at all.

The definition of SPARK falls into three major areas and these form the topics of the next three chapters

The type model: The type model of SPARK is considerably simpler than that of Ada. Two major differences are that all types and subtypes are named and all constraints are static. Other differences such as the absence of access (pointer) types ensure that there is no need for heap storage. These simplifications make it relatively easy to prove various properties of SPARK programs. The differences from Ada in this area are just these simplifications and no annotations are involved.

Control and data flow: The statements of SPARK and especially those concerning control flow are effectively those of Ada. Of course there is no tasking, gotos and labels are naturally omitted and there are also no exceptions. There are no block statements but this is really just a simplification to visibility. But the big difference is the core annotations describing the flow of data into and out of subprograms.

Packages and visibility: Packages and private types provide the main control of visibility in SPARK. Use package clauses are omitted so that names are more explicit and renaming is (largely) omitted on the grounds that it creates aliases. There are a number of restrictions on the nesting of subprograms and packages. Visibility is also controlled by core annotations which ensure that global variables are not unwittingly used. The separate compilation model is similar to that of Ada and includes child packages.

In the remainder of this chapter we briefly consider the overall structure of a SPARK program and the fine details of the lexical structure.

## 4.2 Program units

There are two forms of program units in SPARK, packages and subprograms, both of which we met in Chapter 2. The other program units of Ada (tasks, protected objects and generic units) do not exist in SPARK.

Both packages and subprograms can be given in two parts, a specification which defines the interface to the external client and the body which gives the implementation details.

The specification and body of a package are always textually distinct thus

```
package P is                -- specification
   ...      -- visible part
private
   ...      -- private part
end P;

package body P is           -- body
   ...
begin
   ...      -- initialization
end P;
```

Observe that according to the syntax the specification strictly excludes the final semicolon and the specification plus semicolon is called the package declaration. Informally however a package declaration is usually called its specification. The private part and initialization part are optional and certain packages do not have a body.

The specification and body of a subprogram may be given separately in certain circumstances (see Section 7.1) but the body always repeats the specification. Again specification plus semicolon is strictly termed a subprogram declaration.

Packages and subprograms can be nested within each other but there are a number of restrictions which are also discussed in Section 7.1. Top level packages and subprograms are termed library units and form the units of separate compilation. A SPARK program can only have one library subprogram and this is the main subprogram.

The specification and body of a library package may be compiled separately. However, the specification of the main subprogram cannot be compiled alone in SPARK but is always given complete with its body (a library subprogram specification can be compiled alone in Ada); subprogram specifications on their own only occur internal to packages in SPARK.

A library package can also have child packages and these are themselves library packages and can be compiled separately. The name of a child uses dotted notation in which the prefix is the name of its parent. So we might have

```
package P.Child is
   ...
end P.Child;
```

Such a child package is termed a public child. A public child is visible to an external client and a with clause is required as expected. Thus we might have

```
with P.Child;
package User is ...
```

The main differences between a child and an arbitrary package are that the private part and body of a child package can access the private part of its parent and that a child does not need a with clause for its parent. Moreover any with clause on the specification of its parent implicitly applies to the child as well (just as it applies to the body of the parent).

A child package can have with clauses for its siblings (provided they are already in the library of course). But unlike Ada, the body of the parent cannot have a with clause for one of its public children.

The other form of child package is the private child written as

```
private package P.Child is
   ...
end P.Child;
```

The key thing about a private child is that it is not visible to external users. It can only be used by the body of its parent and both specifications and bodies of private siblings (and their descendants). In each case a with clause is required. Unlike Ada, a private child is not visible to its public siblings.

Another difference between private and public children is that the whole of a private child (including the visible part) can see the private part of its parent. In essence, a public child can be seen as adding to the specification of a package whereas a private child is more like part of its body. Indeed a private child package behaves very much as a package embedded in the body of its parent.

Note carefully the two important differences between SPARK and Ada concerning child packages. One is that a package body cannot access its own public children; this is related to another SPARK rule, namely that a package cannot be embedded within a package specification but only within a body. The other difference is that a private child cannot access a public sibling or vice versa; thus the public and private siblings occupy two quite different regions of visibility (the reason for this rule is to avoid complexity with refinement).

A useful model for understanding the main visibility rules is that child packages are part of the declarative region of their parent. In Ada they effectively occur after the specification and before the body of the parent. But in SPARK we can think of a public child as occurring after the body of its parent whereas a private child occurs at the start of the body. This model explains why the parent body cannot have a with clause for a public child. The reasons for these differences concern inherit clauses and will become clear when we discuss the overall structure in more detail in Chapter 7.

The package structure is hierarchical. A child can have further children and so on. The basic rule is that a private child plus its children, if any, are not visible outside the hierarchy rooted at its parent. The visibility rules of SPARK then extend to the grandchildren in a natural manner. Thus a private child P.C.G of a private child P.C is only visible to the body of P.C and to other private children of P.C; it is not visible to the ancestor package P at all. On the other hand, a public child P.C.G of a private child P.C is visible to other public children of P.C, to private siblings of P.C and to the body of P. Questions of visibility between children of siblings and other remote relatives can be answered by considering the subtree concerned as a distinct structure.

A complete SPARK program comprises a number of library packages plus the one main subprogram which is especially annotated thus

```
--# main_program;
procedure My_Program ...
```

The program as a whole is started by calling the main subprogram from the environment and the subprogram then uses the resources of the various packages. Remember that SPARK does not permit separately compiled complete subprograms other than the main subprogram; thus SPARK does not permit child subprograms.

Note that just before entering the main subprogram, the initialization parts (if any) of all library packages are executed. However, the SPARK rules are such that the statements allowed in the initialization parts only involve statically known expressions and so could in principle be preelaborated (to use the Ada jargon).

It is also important to note that the order of the elaboration of packages cannot affect the meaning of a SPARK program although it can in full Ada. Suppose a package P has a locally declared variable B of the type Boolean and that two other packages Q and R assign the values True and False respectively to B in their initialization sequences, thus

```
package P is
   B: Boolean;
end P;

with P;
package Q is
   ...
end Q;

package body Q is
   ...
begin
   P.B := True;
end Q;

with P;
package R is
   ...
end R;

package body R is
   ...
begin
   P.B := False;
end R;
```

The value of B after the three packages have been elaborated will depend upon the order of the elaborations. But this is not defined in Ada and so the program is ambiguous. SPARK overcomes this by insisting that the initialization part of a package can only assign values to its own variables and not those of another package. There is an analogy here with the way in which the order of evaluation of an expression cannot affect the meaning of a SPARK program because functions cannot have side effects. In the case of the packages, the elaboration of one cannot have a side effect on another.

We conclude this section by observing that the predefined library of Ada comprises a notional package Standard and three library packages Ada, System and Interfaces. These in turn have a number of child packages such as Ada.Characters. This is discussed in a bit more detail in Section 8.4.

## 4.3 Lexical elements

As in Ada, the text of a compilation unit is a sequence of separate lexical elements. Each lexical element is either a delimiter, an identifier (which may be a reserved word), a literal, or a comment. The details of the lexical elements of SPARK differ little from Ada and so this summary concentrates on the differences.

A SPARK program is written using the same character set as Ada and so uses the full Latin-1 set. The characters are grouped into lexical elements such as identifiers, numbers and comments in the same way and the various separators and delimiters of SPARK are those of Ada. A notable variation is that comments which commence with a # symbol immediately after the double hyphen are treated specially as discussed below.

Individual lexical elements may not be split by spaces but otherwise spaces may be inserted freely. Care should be taken that the compound delimiters composed of adjacent characters do not contain spaces. They are

```
=>   ..   **   :=   /=   >=   <=   <>
```

This rule also applies to the combinations -> and <-> which occur in annotations.

## *Identifiers*

Identifiers in SPARK are exactly as in Ada and are formed of letters and digits with possibly embedded isolated underlines. The first character has to be a letter and the case of letters is irrelevant.

A difference from Ada is that identifiers predefined in the package Standard may not be redeclared. The package Standard of SPARK contains much less than Standard of full Ada and this rule applies to those identifiers in the Ada version.

The predefined identifiers in the SPARK version of Standard are those of the types Boolean, Integer, Float, Character and String, the subtypes Natural and Positive, the Boolean enumeration literals True and False and the package ASCII. Note however that ASCII is considered obsolescent in Ada 95 and is superseded by the package Ada.Characters.Latin_1.

The various reserved words may not be used as identifiers. The reserved words of SPARK are those of Ada 95 plus

| | | |
|---|---|---|
| **assert** | **hide** | **main_program** |
| **check** | **hold** | **own** |
| **derives** | **inherit** | **post** |
| **from** | **initializes** | **pre** |
| **global** | **invariant** | **some** |

These additional reserved words are associated with the annotations. (The words **hold**, **invariant** and **some** are reserved for historical reasons or possible future extensions.)

A number of other words should also be avoided if verification conditions or path functions are to be produced. These words are used in the Function Description Language (FDL) which is the underlying logic in which theorems about SPARK programs are expressed. These further words are listed in Appendix 2.

## *Numeric literals*

As in Ada, there are two classes of numeric literals: real literals and integer literals. A real literal is a numeric literal that includes a point; an integer literal is a numeric literal without a point.

Literals may be expressed in decimal form, that is in the conventional decimal notation, or in based form, with an explicit base. In the based form the base (which can be any numeral from 2 to 16) is followed by the digits surrounded by # characters. However, in SPARK only integer literals are expressible in based form.

A literal may conclude with an exponent comprising the letter E (either case) followed by a possibly signed numeral; the exponent gives the power of the base by which the simple literal is to be multiplied and must not be negative in the case of integer literals.

Embedded isolated underlines may also be inserted. Typical literals are

```
12            0          -- integer literals
12.0          0.0        -- real literals
1.34E-12      1.0E+6     -- real literals
2#1111_1111#  16#FF#     -- integer literals (value 255)
```

Finally, note that a literal is never itself negative. A form such as -7 consists of a literal preceded by the unary minus operator.

## *Characters and strings*

Character and string literals in SPARK take the same form as in Ada. Thus a character literal consists of a single Latin-1 character within a pair of single quotes whereas a string literal comprises a sequence of zero, one or more characters within double quotes.

Examples of character literals are

```
'A'    '*'    '''    ' '
```

Character literals in SPARK are always unambiguously of the type Character because it is not possible to declare other character types. However, unlikely expressions such as

```
'X' = 'L'              -- illegal
```

are not allowed in order to be compatible with Ada 95. This is because Ada 95 also has the type Wide_Character and so such an expression is ambiguous. There is no type Wide_Character in SPARK.

Characters that are not graphic characters may be referred to using the names of constants in the predefined package Ada.Characters.Latin_1. Thus we can refer to the various control characters as Ada.Characters.Latin_1.NUL and so on. As mentioned above, the package Ada.Characters.Latin_1 supersedes the package ASCII embedded within Standard which is considered obsolescent in Ada 95. Note furthermore that ASCII only gives the names of the 7-bit ASCII set whereas Ada.Characters.Latin_1 covers the full 8-bit Latin-1 set and so includes names for accented characters as well. See Appendix 2 for full details of the names and character values.

The syntax of string literals is as in Ada. Moreover they are always unambiguously of the type String. However, similarly to the type Character, expressions such as

```
"PIG" /= "pig"                -- illegal
```

are not allowed in order to be compatible with Ada 95. This is because Ada 95 also has the type Wide_String and so such an expression is ambiguous. There is no type Wide_String in SPARK.

A string literal must fit on one line. Long strings can be constructed by the use of the concatenation operator & as in Ada. Concatenation can also be used to embed control characters in strings. However, it should be noted that the rules of SPARK are such that the operands of & are always static and so all expressions involving & are statically evaluated. We can therefore look upon the use of & as creating extended literal values.

Examples of strings are

```
"Message of the day: "                              -- a string
" "        "A"        """"                          -- strings of one character

"String that includes the " &
Ada.Characters.Latin_1.ACK & " character" -- a single (static) string
```

Observe that, as in Ada, the double quote character in strings is represented by a pair of double quotes.

### *Comments and annotations*

A comment in SPARK, as in Ada, starts with two adjacent hyphens and extends up to the end of the line. Thus

```
-- this is an Ada and Spark comment
-- ## and so is this ##
```

However, if the two hyphens are immediately followed by a hash sign #, then although still a comment in Ada terms, it becomes an annotation in SPARK terms. For example

```
--# global in Input; out Current_Symbol;
--# derives Current_Symbol from Input;
```

Annotations are thus ignored by the Ada compiler but are processed by the SPARK Examiner. Annotations may extend over several lines but each line must start with --# (leading spaces and intervening blank lines are permitted). Annotations may include comments which are written starting with two hyphens in the usual way. So the meaningful text in an annotation is from the initial --# until any further pair of hyphens on the same line. For example we might have

```
--# global in X, Y;          -- This is a comment.
--# derives A from X,        -- This comment is embedded in
--#                 Y;       -- a derives annotation.
```

(Finally note that the SPARK Examiner can accept an alternative character to # should there be a clash with some other tool.)

---

**EXERCISE 4.3**

1 The following package is legal Ada but has a number of lexical errors in SPARK. What are they?

```
package Lexis is

   Start: constant Float := 0.0;
   Stop: constant Float := 16#0.FFFF#E+8;

   procedure Check(F: in Float; B: out Boolean);
   --# derives B
   --        note that B only depends upon F
   --        and not on Stop and Start
   --#             from F;

end Lexis;

package body Lexis is

   procedure Check(F: in Float; B: out Boolean) is
   begin
      B := F > Start and B < Stop;
   end Check;

end Lexis;
```

---

# 4.4 Pragmas

Pragmas in SPARK take the same form as in Ada. A typical Ada pragma is

```
pragma Inline(Exchange);
```

and this is a request to the compiler that all calls of the procedure Exchange be expanded in line.

Pragmas may only appear in certain places as in Ada. Thus they are generally allowed where a declaration or statement would be allowed, between a context clause and the following compilation unit, and where a compilation unit would be allowed.

Note that the Examiner does not check the legality of a pragma other than possibly restricting its position. The only pragmas explicitly recognized by the Examiner are Import (and the obsolete pragma Interface of Ada 83 which it replaces) and Elaborate_Body. The pragma Import enables a SPARK program to call a subprogram written in another language and is discussed in Section 8.1. The pragma Elaborate_Body concerns library packages and is discussed in Section 7.1.

## Summary

In the areas covered by this chapter, the main differences between SPARK and Ada are that in SPARK:

- A public child is not visible to the body of its parent.
- A public child is not visible to a private sibling and vice versa.
- Certain additional words are reserved.
- Real literals may not be expressed in the based form.
- The types Wide_Character and Wide_String do not exist.

# 5 The Type Model



As mentioned in the previous chapter, the type model of SPARK is considerably simpler than that of Ada. For example SPARK does not permit derived types or access types, there are no discriminants, and enumeration types may not contain character literals.

There is also a general principle that every type and subtype must have a name. As examples of this principle, SPARK does not allow anonymous array types and explicit constraints are not allowed in the declarations of objects.

In this chapter we look at all the types in SPARK and the operations associated with them. It is also convenient to explain the details of the syntax of expressions and names in this chapter.

## 5.1 Objects

An object is an entity that contains (has) a value of a given type. Objects are typically declared by object declarations but formal parameters of subprograms and loop parameters are also treated as objects; components of objects are also treated as objects as we have already mentioned.

Objects are either variables or constants. An object declaration gives the type of an object and if it is a constant also its initial value; this initial value must be a constant expression computed at compile time (constant expressions are described in Section 5.9). Variables can optionally be initialized in their declaration but again the initial value has to be constant. Thus we can write

```
Count, Sum: Integer;
Sorted: Boolean := False;
Limit: constant Integer := 10_000;
Level: constant Float := 3.5;
```

Note that several variables or constants can be declared together and that any initial value applies to them all. The syntax is

* object_declaration ::= defining_identifier_list :
    [**constant**] subtype_mark [:= *constant*_expression];

It is important to note that any initial value has to be a constant expression and so is known at compile time. In Ada, on the other hand, the initial value can be any expression of the relevant type and thus might not be known at compile time. The reason for insisting that initial values are constant is that it avoids requiring data flow analysis in a list of declarations.

The other important difference is that it is not possible to apply an explicit constraint when declaring objects as we can in Ada. This is revealed by the syntax which shows that the (sub)type of an object is always given by a subtype mark and not by a subtype indication (that is a subtype mark followed by an optional constraint).

So the following is not permitted in SPARK

```
I, J, K: Integer range 1 .. 10;   -- illegal Spark
```

and we have to spell it out in detail as for example

```
subtype Index is Integer range 1 .. 10;
I, J, K: Index;
```

We can summarize this rule by saying that all objects in SPARK have to have named subtypes (loop parameters are an exception, see Section 6.3). The reason for insisting that every subtype has a name is that it makes it much easier to reason about the correctness of a program.

Declarations of named numbers, which look rather like declarations of numeric constants but without a type name, are described in Section 5.9.

## 5.2 Types and subtypes

The *ARM* states 'A type is characterized by a set of values and a set of primitive operations ... ' [ISO, 1995]. The types in SPARK and Ada can be classified as shown in Figure 5.1. The categories of types shown in italics within parentheses do not exist in SPARK.

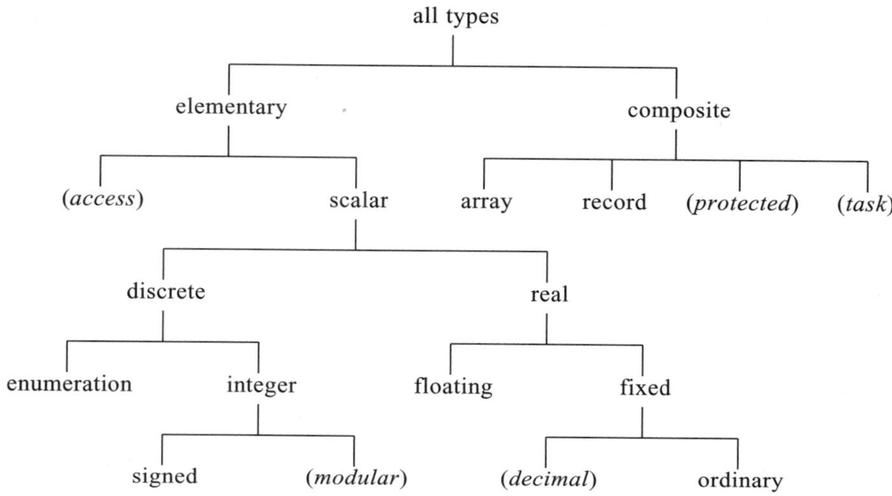


**Figure 5.1** SPARK and Ada type hierarchy.

We thus see that the composite types in SPARK are just the array and record types since there are no concurrent types. The categories of elementary types and scalar types are the same because there are no access types. The scalar types comprise the enumeration types, integer types and real types; the enumeration and integer types are collectively referred to as discrete types. The integer types are signed integer types in SPARK but there are no modular types as in Ada 95. The real types are subdivided into floating types and fixed types but there are no decimal types as in Ada 95.

The predefined types in SPARK are Integer, Float, Boolean, Character and String. The types Boolean and Character are enumeration types, Integer and Float are of course integer and floating types respectively and String is an array type. These predefined types are declared in the predefined package Standard.

Additional types can be defined as for example

```
type Colour is (White, Red, Yellow, Green, Blue, Brown);
type Column is range 1 .. 72;
type Table is array (Column) of Colour;
```

The first states that the enumeration type Colour has the six literal values given in the list. The type Column is an integer type with the range of values from 1 to 72. Finally the type Table is an array type composed out of the types Column and Colour. We could then declare a particular table by

```
The_Table: Table;
```

and then the object The_Table has 72 components denoted by The_Table(1) ... The_Table(72) each of which has a value of the enumeration type Colour.

It will be noted that a type declaration starts with the reserved word **type**, the identifier of the new type and then **is** followed by some means of describing the new type; this last bit is known as a type definition. The syntax of type declarations is as follows

```
* type_declaration ::= full_type_declaration | private_type_declaration
* full_type_declaration ::= type defining_identifier is type_definition;
* type_definition ::=
          enumeration_type_definition | integer_type_definition
        | real_type_definition         | array_type_definition
        | record_type_definition
```

Observe that this syntax confirms that access types, type extension, discriminants, and task and protected types are not permitted in SPARK. Private types are discussed in Chapter 7.

Subtypes are very important in SPARK because they enable us to express the important concept that a value can only lie within certain bounds. A subtype declaration enables us to give a name to a type together with a constraint. We saw an example in the previous section

```
subtype Index is Integer range 1 .. 10;
I, J, K: Index;
```

This declares Index to be a subtype of Integer with upper and lower bounds of 1 and 10 respectively; these bounds must be static and cannot be general expressions as they can in Ada.

The syntax for a subtype declaration is almost exactly as in Ada, namely

```
  subtype_declaration ::=
        subtype defining_identifier is subtype_indication;
  subtype_indication ::= subtype_mark [constraint]
  subtype_mark ::= subtype_name
  constraint ::= scalar_constraint | composite_constraint
* scalar_constraint ::= range_constraint
* composite_constraint ::= index_constraint
```

Note from the syntax that the constraint in a subtype_indication is optional as it is in Ada. Thus we can write

```
subtype Color is Colour;
```

thereby giving a full range subtype which effectively gives a different name to the type. This is often useful for eliminating package prefixes as we shall see when we discuss renaming in Section 7.7. However, this is only permitted for scalar types since it is strictly a shorthand for

```
subtype Color is Colour range Colour'First .. Colour'Last;
```

and in particular it is not possible to rename a private type in this way.

(The only differences from Ada revealed by the syntax are that there are no discriminant constraints in SPARK because there are no discriminants and no digits or delta constraints because there are no decimal types or reduced accuracy subtypes.)

Examples of subtypes of scalar types are

```
subtype Rainbow is Colour range Red .. Blue;
subtype Last10 is Column range Column'Last-9 .. Column'Last;
subtype Last5 is Last10 range Last10'Last-4 .. Last10'Last;
```

These examples illustrate the use of the attributes First and Last which apply to all scalar subtypes and give the first and last values of the range. The use of such attributes is important because they can eliminate repetition of related values.

Unlike Ada, all constraints in SPARK must be statically determined and so they cannot contain variables or function calls. Thus the syntax for a range constraint is

```
* range_constraint ::= range static_range

  range ::= range_attribute_reference
          | simple_expression .. simple_expression
```

Since constraints are always static in SPARK it follows that the attributes First and Last applied to scalar subtypes are themselves always static and can thus be used in a static expression.

A minor point is that a static range must not be null in SPARK, in other words the upper bound must be greater than or equal to the lower bound. (Null ranges are allowed in loops of course; see Section 6.3.)

It is important to note that a subtype declaration does not introduce a new type; thus if we write

```
R: Rainbow;
```

then the type of R is still Colour. We sometimes say that Colour is the base type of the subtype Rainbow although the *ARM* simply says type rather than base type (base type was the term used in Ada 83).

Having introduced the general ideas of types and subtypes, the remainder of this chapter deals with the various classes of types in SPARK together with their operations.

## 5.3 Enumeration types

We have already noted that the predefined types include the enumeration types Boolean and Character and have shown how to declare our own enumeration types such as Colour. The Boolean type is a predefined type with notional declaration

```
type Boolean is (False, True);
```

although the literals are not considered to be ordered in SPARK as discussed below. The type Character has a notional declaration

```
type Character is (nul, ... , '0', '1', '2', ... , 'A', 'B', 'C',
                                        ... , 'a', 'b', 'c', ... , 'ÿ');
```

which embraces the whole of the 8-bit Latin-1 set whose last character is lower case y diaeresis.

An important difference from Ada is that it is not possible to declare additional character types in SPARK. Thus all further enumeration literals must be identifiers and so the syntax becomes

```
* enumeration_type_definition ::=
        (defining_identifier {, defining_identifier})
```

Typical declarations of enumeration types and subtypes are

```
type Day is (Mon, Tue, Wed, Thur, Fri, Sat, Sun);
type Colour is (White, Red, Yellow, Green, Blue, Brown);
type Solo is (Alone);
subtype Rainbow is Colour range Red .. Blue;
subtype Weekday is Day range Mon .. Fri;
```

where we see that, as in Ada, an enumeration type can have just a single literal. We can also cascade scalar subtypes so we might have

```
subtype Mid_Week is Weekday range Tue .. Thu;
```

However, remember that a static range cannot be null in SPARK and so we cannot write

```
subtype Never is Day range Tue .. Mon;        -- illegal
```

The general SPARK philosophy of reducing the potential for ambiguity to a minimum means that enumeration literals may not be overloaded in the same scope with each other or with subprograms. Thus we cannot declare a type such as

```
type Traffic_Light is (Red, Amber, Green);
```

and the type Colour in the same list of declarations.

The usual attributes apply to enumeration types as in Ada. These are First, Last, Range (X'Range is a shorthand for X'First .. X'Last), Succ, Pred, Pos and Val and so we can write

```
X: Colour;
...
if X = Colour'Last then         -- rotate through colours
   X := Colour'First;
else
   X := Colour'Succ(X);
end if;
```

The attributes First, Last and Range apply to subtypes so that Rainbow'First is Red. However the functional attributes Succ, Pred, Pos and Val apply to the underlying type so that Rainbow'Succ(X) is the same value as Colour'Succ(X) even if X happens to be Blue.

The attributes Pos and Val convert between an enumeration value and its underlying integer position in the type definition considering the first element to have position zero. Thus Colour'Pos(Red) is 1 and Colour'Val(1) is Red.

Other operations which apply to enumeration types are = and /= and the relational operations <, <=, > and >=. The result of the relational operators is defined by the order in the type definition; thus Yellow is greater than Red for the type Colour. These operations of course return the value True or False of the type Boolean.

However, although the type Boolean is considered to be an enumeration type whose literals are True and False, there are a number of important special rules. The relational operators do not apply to the type Boolean although the equality operators do apply. The attributes Pred, Succ, Pos and Val do not apply but First and Last do apply and the type Boolean can be used as an array index type. However, explicit Boolean ranges are not allowed. As a consequence, SPARK Boolean expressions can never result in a run-time error.

It is possible to declare a full range subtype by writing

```
subtype Valve_Open is Boolean;
```

but we cannot write for example

```
subtype Valve_Open is Boolean range Boolean'First .. Boolean'Last;
```

Nor can we write something odd like

```
subtype Always is Boolean range True .. True;
```

because again explicit Boolean ranges are not permitted.

(One reason for these special rules is to avoid confusion arising from the fact that the binding of Boolean operations is different in Ada to that in Prolog and proof languages generally.)

The operations **and**, **or**, **xor** and **not** apply to the type Boolean and have their conventional meaning. Note that **xor** is the same as /=.

As mentioned above, the type Character is considered to be an enumeration type whose literals are the graphic characters. The relational operators and attributes apply to the type Character. But, unlike Ada, no other character types may be defined. In particular there is no type Wide_Character.

## 5.4 Numeric types

SPARK has integer, floating point and fixed point types as in Ada which are similarly considered to be descended from some hypothetical root types (see Section 5.9). This underlying mechanism is rather irrelevant from the point of view of the user since the effect is essentially the same as if they were just created individually as required as in SPARK 83. All the usual predefined operations apply.

The only predefined integer type is the type Integer. The user can define other integer types using an integer type definition which defines a signed integer type whose set of values includes those of a specified range. There are no modular types in SPARK. The syntax is simply

* integer_type_definition ::=
  **range** *static*_simple_expression .. *static*_simple_expression

Note that the bounds of the range must be static expressions of an integer type (such as Integer or a user-defined type). Thus we can write

```
Max_Line_Size: constant := 80;
type Page_Num is range 1 .. 2000;
type Line_Size is range 1 .. Max_Line_Size;
subtype Column_Ptr is Integer range 1 .. 10;
```

As in Ada, integer literals are literals of an anonymous predefined integer type known as universal_integer and these can be implicitly converted to any integer type. Other integer types do not therefore have their own literals. Note that Max_Line_Size is a named number as explained in Section 5.9.

The operations +, –, * and / apply to the integer types as expected with + and – allowed as both unary and binary operators; **abs** is a unary operator giving the absolute value. Division is with truncation towards zero; **rem** gives the corresponding remainder on division whereas **mod** is the modulus operation which we can look upon as giving the remainder corresponding to division with truncation towards minus infinity. There is also the exponentiation operator ** which takes a value of any integer type and raises it to a power given by a non-negative expression of the predefined type Integer. The comparison operators also apply to the integer types and return a value of the type Boolean. These operations are exactly as in Ada and elaborate expressions can similarly be formed using parentheses and paying due regard to the precedence rules. These are summarized at the end of this chapter.

It is useful to distinguish between the *range* and the *base range* of a type. Essentially the range is the range asked for in the type definition whereas the base range is that of the machine type actually used. For example, on a simple 16-bit machine the type Page_Num declared above would have range 1 .. 2000 whereas the base range would be –32768 .. +32767.

The various operators always work on the base range whereas assignment to variables is constrained to the range. The attribute Base provides access to the attributes of the base range. Thus Page_Num'Base'Last is +32767 whereas Page_Num'Last is 2000. In full Ada, the attribute Base can be used alone to enable objects of the underlying base type to be declared. This is not permitted in SPARK because the type would be anonymous.

The real types provide approximations to the real numbers, with relative bounds on errors for floating point types and absolute bounds on errors for fixed point types.

```
real_type_definition ::=
        floating_point_definition | fixed_point_definition
```

In a similar way to the integer literals, the real literals are literals of an anonymous predefined real type known as universal_real and these can be implicitly converted to any real type. Other real types do not therefore have their own literals.

The only predefined floating point type is the type Float. The user can declare other floating point types in terms of the error bound required; this is specified as relative precision by giving the required minimum number of significant decimal digits.

```
* floating_point_definition ::=
        digits static_simple_expression [real_range_specification]

  real_range_specification ::=
        range static_simple_expression .. static_simple_expression
```

The number of digits and the bounds of the range (if given) must be static as in Ada. For example

```
type Coefficient is digits 10 range -1.0 .. 1.0;
type Real is digits 8;
subtype Probability is Real range 0.0 .. 1.0;
```

On the other hand note that there are no reduced accuracy subtypes in SPARK and that they are considered obsolete in Ada 95; they did exist in Ada 83 but were little if at all used and were present in earlier versions of SPARK. Thus although a subtype can specify a reduced range, it cannot specify a reduced accuracy.

The numerical operations on floating point types are +, –, *, /, ** and **abs** with conventional meaning as in Ada. The exponentiation operator raises a floating point value to a positive or negative power given by a value of the type Integer.

The relational operators also apply to floating point types but the direct use of the equality operators is frowned upon on the grounds that we ought to think carefully about what we are doing. So rather than hopefully writing

```
if X = Last_X then
   Converged := True;
```

we are encouraged to more thoughtfully write something like

```
if abs (X - Last_X) < Epsilon then ...
```

which makes the criterion rather more explicit. So although using equality is not forbidden nevertheless the Examiner will give a warning.

The detailed behaviour of floating point operations naturally depends upon the hardware. However, the Numerics Annex of the *ARM* describes a set of numbers called model numbers associated with the implementation of each floating point type. Error bounds for the predefined operations are given in terms of these model numbers for implementations conforming to the Numerics Annex.

Fixed point types specify the error bound as an absolute value called the delta of the fixed point type. However, the decimal types of Ada 95 are not included in SPARK.

* fixed_point_definition ::= ordinary_fixed_point_definition

* ordinary_fixed_point_definition ::=
  **delta** *static*_simple_expression real_range_specification

An example is

```
type Volts is delta 0.125 range 0.0 .. 255.0;
```

Fixed point types are rather specialized and it is not appropriate to consider them in depth. However, it is worth mentioning one difference between SPARK and Ada.

Two values of any (possibly different) fixed point types can be multiplied or divided. A type conversion must be immediately applied to the result in order to define the type of the result. This follows the rules of Ada 83 which were more pedantic than the rules of Ada 95 which enable the result type to be determined from the context. However, SPARK never uses the context in this way and so the Ada 83 view still applies. Thus given

```
L, M, N: Fraction;
```

where Fraction is some fixed point type, we cannot write the following in SPARK

```
L := M * N;                  -- illegal in Spark
L := 0.5 * L;                -- illegal in Spark
```

Instead, we have to write

```
L := Fraction(M * N);
L := Fraction(0.5 * L);
```

although all are permitted in Ada 95. Note, however, that the last assignment had to be written as

```
L := Fraction(Fraction(0.5) * L);
```

in Ada 83 and earlier versions of SPARK.

## 5.5 Composite types

The only composite types in SPARK are arrays and records; moreover, records cannot have discriminants and cannot be tagged. Thus SPARK does not support type extension, inheritance and all the other dynamic aspects of OOP. Record types are therefore very simple and so we will consider them first.

A record type is a composite type consisting of named components. For example we might write

```
subtype Days is Integer range 1 .. 31;
type Months is (Jan, Feb, Mar, Apr, May, June,
                July, Aug, Sept, Oct, Nov, Dec);
subtype Years is Integer range 1 .. 4000;

type Date is
   record
      Day: Days;
      Month: Months;
      Year: Years;
   end record;

type Complex is
   record
      Re, Im: Real;
   end record;
```

Apart from there being no variants, the major changes are that a component cannot have a default initial value and the subtypes of the components must be given by an explicit subtype mark and not by a subtype indication.

The syntax of record types in SPARK is

```
* record_type_definition ::=
          record
             component_list
          end record;

* component_list ::= component_declaration {component_declaration}

* component_declaration ::=
          defining_identifier_list : component_definition;

* component_definition ::= subtype_mark
```

The various simplifications mean that the following which are legal in Ada are not allowed in SPARK

```
type Date is
   record
      Day: Integer range 1 .. 31;          -- illegal
      Month: Months;
      Year: Integer range 1 .. 4000;       -- illegal
   end record;
```

```
type Complex is
   record
      Re, Im: Real := 0.0;                  -- illegal
   end record;
```

The rationale for not permitting default initial values in records is that the values appear remote from where they are used; they can also give rise to partial initialization which is considered unwise.

The only operations applicable to record types as a whole are assignment, equality and inequality. Individual components are referred to by following the name of the record by a dot and the identifier of the component. Thus we can write

```
D, E: Date;
...
D := E;                    -- assign the whole record
D.Year := E.Year + 1;      -- assign to the Year component
```

Records in SPARK are thus very simple and have none of the structural complexities associated with discriminants in Ada. Arrays on the other hand are intrinsically much as in Ada although there are a number of restrictions designed to make a program more explicit and thereby simplify analysis.

An array type is a composite type consisting of components that have the same subtype as we saw in the example of the type Table whose components were of the type Colour.

Array types can be constrained (like Table) in which case the bounds are those of the index subtype following **array** as in the following

```
subtype Index is Integer range 1 .. 10;

type Brightness is array (Rainbow) of Natural;
type Row is array (Index) of Integer;

A_Row: Row;       -- bounds of A_Row are 1 and 10
```

Alternatively, array types can be unconstrained in which case the type definition contains the box symbol (<>) and the bounds then have to be given in a subtype declaration before an object can be declared

```
type Tuple is array (Integer range <>) of Real;
subtype Triple_Index is Integer range 1 .. 3;
subtype Triple is Tuple(Triple_Index);

type Daylight_Hours is array (Day range <>) of Natural;
subtype Weekday_Daylight is Daylight_Hours(Weekday);

Working_Hours: Weekday_Daylight;       -- bounds are Mon and Fri

type Matrix is array (Integer range <>, Integer range <>) of Real;

subtype Square is Matrix(Index, Index);

Box: Square;    -- a two-dimensional array with both bounds 1 and 10
```

An important difference from Ada is that the component subtype and the index subtype must both be given by a subtype mark and not by a subtype indication; this follows the general SPARK philosophy that all subtypes must have names. Moreover all array objects must be of named array types and cannot be of anonymous types.

The predefined type String is an example of an unconstrained one-dimensional array type. Its definition is the same as in Ada, thus

```
subtype Positive is Integer range 1 .. Integer'Last;
...
type String is array (Positive range <>) of Character;
...
subtype String_10 is String(Index);
Name: String_10 := "Cinderella";
```

All subtypes of the type String must have a lower bound of 1.

String literals in SPARK are always unambiguously of the type String. It is not possible to declare other character types and although it is possible to declare other array types with components of the type Character nevertheless the string literals do not apply to them in SPARK. (As a consequence such array types are rather inconvenient.)

The concatenation operator & only applies to the type String (and individual characters) and is always evaluated statically. (In Ada, the concatenation operator applies to all one-dimensional array types.)

The syntax of array types in SPARK is

```
array_type_definition ::=
        unconstrained_array_definition | constrained_array_definition

unconstrained_array_definition ::=
        array (index_subtype_definition
                {, index_subtype_definition}) of component_definition

index_subtype_definition ::= subtype_mark range <>

constrained_array_definition ::=
        array (discrete_subtype_definition
                {, discrete_subtype_definition}) of component_definition

* discrete_subtype_definition ::= discrete_subtype_mark

* index_constraint ::=
        (discrete_subtype_mark {, discrete_subtype_mark})
```

A very minor point is that, as in Ada, we cannot cascade array subtypes as we can with scalar types when we declared Mid_Week as a subtype of the subtype Weekday. In other words, we cannot impose narrower bounds on an already constrained array subtype.

We will now illustrate the various differences between SPARK and Ada regarding arrays. Note first that we cannot write

```
type Triple is array (1 .. 3) of Real;        -- illegal
```

but have to use a named index subtype such as Triple_Index. As a consequence, the Ada rule that such ranges are implicitly of type Integer is not required in SPARK.

A more elaborate example is provided by the following which is legal in Ada but not in SPARK

```
Upper_Case_Table: array (1 .. 10) of Character range 'A' .. 'Z';
```

Not only are anonymous array types not allowed in SPARK but we also have to explicitly give names to the index and component subtypes as already mentioned. So we have to write something like

```
subtype Index is Integer range 1 .. 10;
subtype Capital_Letter is Character range 'A' .. 'Z';
type Upper_Case_Array is array (Index) of Capital_Letter;
Upper_Case_Table: Upper_Case_Array;
```

Similarly, since an index constraint is expressed in terms of subtype marks and not more general ranges, we cannot write

```
Next_Line: String(1 .. 80);
```

but have to write

```
subtype Line_Index is Integer range 1 .. 80;
subtype Line is String(Line_Index);
Next_Line: Line;
```

It is important to realize that since all constraints have to be static it follows that all arrays have static bounds. Thus we cannot declare an array in SPARK whose bounds are not known until the program executes. This may be felt rather irksome but is necessary if the space occupied by the program is to be predictably bounded.

Components of arrays are referred to by following the name of the array by an index expression in parentheses. Naturally enough this expression can be dynamic. Thus

```
A_Row, B_Row: Row;
...
A_Row(I) := A_Row(J+K);          -- assign individual components
A_Row := B_Row;                  -- assign the whole array
```

Assignment, equality and inequality are allowed for all array types. But a major difference is that so-called sliding is never allowed in SPARK. This means that the bounds of both arrays must always be the same; the only exception to this rule is that equality and inequality are permitted between any values of type String. However, all subtypes of String have a lower bound of 1 anyway and if the upper bounds are different then the strings are of course not equal.

We shall see later that a parameter of a subprogram can be of an unconstrained array type such as Tuple or String in which case the formal parameter takes its bounds from the actual; because the bounds are not known until run time and sliding is never permitted, the operations permitted on such formal array parameters are somewhat limited. This is discussed in more detail in Sections 6.2 and 6.7.

The relational operators such as < and >= are defined for the type String but not for any other one-dimensional arrays. The logical operators are defined for one-dimensional arrays if the component type is Boolean.

The attributes First, Last, Length and Range apply to array objects and to constrained subtypes. Thus we have

```
Next_Line'First = 1
Line'Last = 80
```

and Range is short for First .. Last. The attribute Length gives the number of elements in the array and so we always have

```
T'Length = T'Pos(T'Last) - T'Pos(T'First) + 1
```

although it should be noted that this does not always apply in Ada because of the possibility of null ranges (there are no null ranges in SPARK).

Multidimensional arrays and arrays of arrays are both allowed. Suppose we wish to declare a type representing a chessboard. We can think of the board as a two-dimensional array or alternatively as a one-dimensional array of rows. So we can have

```
Board_Size: constant Integer := 8;
type Board_Index is range 1 .. Board_Size;
type Colours is (No_Colour, Black, White);
type Pieces is (No_Piece, Pawn, Knight, ... );
type Contents is
   record
      Colour: Colours;
      Piece: Pieces;
   end record;
```

and then either

```
type Boards2 is array (Board_Index, Board_Index) of Contents;
```

or

```
type Row is array (Board_Index) of Contents;
type Boards11 is array (Board_Index) of Row;
```

We can then declare the two kinds of boards

```
Square_Board: Boards2;
Rowed_Board: Boards11;
```

and the individual components can then be referred to as Square_Board(I, J) or Rowed_Board(I)(J) respectively.

It is generally easier to prove things about arrays of arrays (because the intermediate arrays have a named type) so they are generally to be preferred to multidimensional arrays. This especially applies to aggregates which are discussed in the next section.

Assignment, equality and inequality are permitted for multidimensional arrays; again sliding is not permitted so they must have the same number of dimensions and the same bounds in each dimension. As in Ada there are no other predefined operations on multidimensional arrays.

The attributes First, Last, Length and Range also apply to multidimensional arrays and the dimension number which has to be static is given in parentheses. So

```
Square_Board'Last(2) = 8
Rowed_Board(1)'First(1) = 1
```

The first dimension is assumed if the dimension is omitted.

Naturally enough, as in Ada, the subtype of a component of an array or a component of a record must not be an unconstrained array type such as String.

Another point which applies to both arrays and records is that flow analysis which is discussed in detail in Chapter 10 treats them as a whole and does not consider the inner components separately.

Array and record values can also be created by aggregates and these are discussed in the next section.

## 5.6 Aggregates

An aggregate is essentially an operation that combines component values into a composite value of a record or array type. There are a number of significant differences between SPARK and Ada aggregates both in their form and where they are allowed.

Aggregates are basically written as a list of values for the components in parentheses and separated by commas. The values for the individual components of an aggregate are either positional (in which case their order indicates the component they relate to) or named (by using an index value or component name preceding =>).

Thus an example of a positional aggregate for the type Date is

```
(4, July, 1776)              -- positional aggregate
```

and the values are given in the same order as in the type declaration. The following show the same aggregate in named notation

```
(Day => 4, Month => July, Year => 1776)
(Month => July, Day => 4, Year => 1776)
```

and of course the components can then be given in any order.

A major simplification for record aggregates is that an aggregate is either all named or all positional in SPARK whereas in Ada mixed forms are allowed with consequential complexity in the rules. Furthermore, the **others** form which is used to denote all components not explicitly mentioned is not allowed in record aggregates in SPARK and nor is the form with multiple choices.

The syntax is thus simplified to

* aggregate ::= record_aggregate | array_aggregate

* record_aggregate ::=
    positional_record_aggregate | named_record_aggregate

\+ positional_record_aggregate ::= (expression {, expression})

\+ named_record_aggregate ::=
    (record_component_association {, record_component_association})

* record_component_association ::=
    *component*_selector_name => expression

Aggregates must be complete in the sense that a value for every component must be specified once and only once.

An important difference regarding the use of aggregates in SPARK is that an aggregate is not an allowed form of primary in an expression as we shall see when we look at expressions in detail in Section 5.8. This means that all aggregates have to be used as part of a qualified expression. In other words, all aggregates have to be explicitly qualified with their subtype – this avoids the need for overload resolution. Thus whereas in Ada we might have written any of

```
Z: Complex := (0.0, 0.0);
Z: Complex := (Re | Im => 0.0);
Z: Complex := (others => 0.0);
```

in SPARK we have to write for example

```
Z: Complex := Complex'(0.0, 0.0);
Z: Complex := Complex'(Re => 0.0, Im => 0.0);
```

As mentioned in the previous section, a record type may not declare default values for the components. A useful alternative technique is to declare a constant of the type with the required initial value. This constant can then be used to provide the initial value for variables declared subsequently. The fact that the variables do have an initial value is then obvious.

A minor point is that the Ada rule that an aggregate with only one component must be given in named notation equally applies to SPARK. This is necessary so that the SPARK text can be compiled as Ada even though the potential ambiguity between a positional aggregate with one component and an expression in parentheses does not occur in SPARK because aggregates are always qualified. This rule applies to both record aggregates and array aggregates.

Array aggregates are much as in Ada. Both positional and named forms are allowed and an **others** clause may be used to cover components not explicitly mentioned. Any others clause naturally has to be last. Much of the complexity of use of array aggregates in Ada does not apply in SPARK because all aggregates have to be qualified and so the bounds are explicitly and statically known. Note that string literals do not have to be qualified; their lower bound is always 1 and the upper bound can be deduced from the length of the string.

Thus given

```
type Day is (Mon, Tue, Wed, Thur, Fri, Sat, Sun);
subtype Weekday is Day range Mon .. Fri;
type Busy is array (Day) of Boolean;
```

the following examples are equivalent (we qualify for emphasis).

```
Busy'(Tues | Thurs => True, Sat .. Sun => False, others => True)
Busy'(True, True, True, True, True, False, False)
Busy'(Weekday => True, others => False)
```

Observe that the named form can specify the choice of a group of components by using a range of index values, a subtype name or a series of such separated by vertical bars. Of course all choices and ranges have to be static because arrays in SPARK have static bounds. These various possibilities are shown by the syntax which is

```
  array_aggregate ::=
          positional_array_aggregate | named_array_aggregate

* positional_array_aggregate ::=
          (aggregate_item , aggregate_item {, aggregate_item})
        | (aggregate_item {, aggregate_item} , others => aggregate_item)

+ aggregate_item ::= aggregate | expression

* named_array_aggregate ::=
          (array_component_association {, array_component_association}
                                           [, others => aggregate_item])
        | (others => aggregate_item)

* array_component_association ::=
          discrete_choice_list => aggregate_item

  discrete_choice_list ::= discrete_choice { | discrete_choice}

* discrete_choice ::= static_simple_expression | discrete_range

* discrete_range ::= discrete_subtype_indication | static_range
```

Those familiar with the syntax of aggregates in Ada will note that the additional production aggregate_item has been introduced. This change to the syntax is necessary to permit aggregates for multidimensional arrays because, as mentioned above, an aggregate is not allowed as a primary in SPARK.

Naturally enough, each choice must specify values of the index type and each expression of each component association must be of the component type.

Other examples are

```
Triple'(1.0, 2.0, 3.0)
Line'(others => Ada.Characters.Latin_1.NUL)
```

where the last example shows that **others** is allowed on its own.

The nested structure in the case of aggregates within aggregates is interesting. Note especially the difference between the aggregate for an array of arrays as opposed to that for a multidimensional array. In the case of the array of arrays the inner aggregates have to be qualified. Thus pursuing the chessboard example, given

```
Empty: constant Contents := Contents'(No_Colour, No_Piece);
```

then in the case of an array of arrays we might write

```
Empty_Row: constant Row := Row'(Board_Index => Empty);

Initial_Board: constant Boards11 :=
   Boards11'(1 => Row'(Contents'(White, Rook),
                       Contents'(White, Knight),
                       Contents'(White, Bishop),
                       Contents'(White, Queen),
                       Contents'(White, King),
                       Contents'(White, Bishop),
                       Contents'(White, Knight),
                       Contents'(White, Rook)),
             2 => Row'(Board_Index => Contents'(White, Pawn)),
             3 .. 6 => Empty_Row,
             7 => Row'(Board_Index => Contents'(Black, Pawn)),
             8 => Row'(Contents'(Black, Rook),
                       Contents'(Black, Knight),
                       Contents'(Black, Bishop),
                       Contents'(Black, Queen),
                       Contents'(Black, King),
                       Contents'(Black, Bishop),
                       Contents'(Black, Knight),
                       Contents'(Black, Rook)));
```

This example illustrates a number of points. The inner aggregates are all qualified by Row but of course an inner element does not have to be an aggregate, it can be any appropriate expression of the type such as Empty_Row. Note also that the inner aggregates can be a mixture of positional and named aggregates although each individual inner aggregate must not be mixed.

The corresponding declaration in the case of the multidimensional array is

```
Initial_Board: constant Boards2 :=
   Boards2'(1 => (Contents'(White, Rook),
                  Contents'(White, Knight),
                  Contents'(White, Bishop),
                  Contents'(White, Queen),
                  Contents'(White, King),
                  Contents'(White, Bishop),
                  Contents'(White, Knight),
                  Contents'(White, Rook)),
            2 => (Board_Index => Contents'(White, Pawn)),
            3 .. 6 => (Board_Index => Empty),
            7 => (Board_Index => Contents'(Black, Pawn)),
            8 => (Contents'(Black, Rook),
                  Contents'(Black, Knight),
                  Contents'(Black, Bishop),
                  Contents'(Black, Queen),
                  Contents'(Black, King),
                  Contents'(Black, Bishop),
                  Contents'(Black, Knight),
                  Contents'(Black, Rook)));
```

Note that the inner aggregates do not have to be qualified and indeed they cannot be because they are not objects of a named type in their own right.

---

**EXERCISE 5.6**

1 Declare a constant of the type Complex with value zero. Then declare a variable Z with initial value equal to this constant.

2 Write an aggregate of the type Stack of Section 2.5 with all components set to 0.

---

## 5.7 Names

The remainder of this chapter covers the evaluation of expressions in SPARK. We start by considering the details of names and then survey all the various operators.

Names denote declared entities and their components.

* name ::= direct_name | indexed_component | selected_component
    | attribute_reference | function_call

* direct_name ::= identifier

* prefix ::= name

Many of the forms of names permitted in Ada are not relevant to SPARK. Dereferencing does not apply because there are no access types. SPARK does not have array slices and type conversions are never treated as names. The direct name for an entity is the identifier associated with that entity in its declaration. Note that new operators cannot be declared in SPARK and operators are always called with infixed notation; as a consequence a direct name never takes the form of an operator symbol.

Indexed and selected components include a prefix that is a name. If this name is a function call then it denotes a component of the result of that function call.

Indexed components are used to denote components of arrays.

indexed_component ::= prefix (expression {, expression})

The prefix must be of an array type – either the name of an array or a function call returning an array value. The expressions specify the index values for the component; there must be one expression for each index position of the array type. Each expression must be of the type of the corresponding index.

Examples are

```
Schedule(Sat)
Square_Board(M, I+J)
Rowed_Board(3)(7)
```

Remember that distinct notations are used for components of multidimensional arrays such as Square_Board and components of arrays of arrays such as Rowed_Board.

Selected components are used to denote record components and also to denote entities declared in the visible part of a package.

selected_component ::= prefix . selector_name

* selector_name ::= identifier

In the case of a record, the prefix must denote an object of a record type either directly or indirectly as the result of a function call. The selector must be the identifier of a component of that record type such as

```
Today.Month
```

The selected component notation may also be used to select an entity in a package in which case the prefix denotes the package, thus

```
Stacks.Push(S, 1)
```

denotes a call of the subprogram Push in the package Stacks. The notation can of course be used recursively to any depth and so

```
Table_Manager.Get_Entry(Key).Field(N)
```

might denote component N of the array Field of some record returned by calling the function Get_Entry in the package Table_Manager with the parameter Key.

As we shall see later when we discuss visibility in Chapter 7, we cannot redundantly use the selected notation to refer to an entity in a package from immediately within that package as we can in Ada.

The final form of name is an attribute. An attribute denotes a basic operation on a type or object given as a prefix.

attribute_reference ::= prefix ' attribute_designator

* attribute_designator ::= identifier [(*static*_expression)] | Delta | Digits

The allowed attributes of SPARK are given in Appendix 2 and further details will be found in Annex K of the *ARM* [ISO, 1995].

Examples of attributes using previous examples are

```
Colour'First            -- White
Rainbow'First           -- Red
Rainbow'Base'First      -- White
Date'Size
Colour'Succ(Red)        -- Yellow
```

Remember that the attribute Base which gives the underlying base type cannot be used alone in SPARK but only as the prefix of a further attribute.

## 5.8 Expressions

An expression is a formula that defines the computation of a value. Expressions are much as in Ada except that there are no allocators (because there are no access types) and, as mentioned in Section 5.6, aggregates are treated differently and always have to be qualified. The syntax is

```
expression ::=
      relation {and relation}  | relation {and then relation}
    | relation {or relation}   | relation {or else relation}
    | relation {xor relation}

relation ::=
      simple_expression [relational_operator simple_expression]
    | simple_expression [not] in range
    | simple_expression [not] in subtype_mark

simple_expression ::=
    [unary_adding_operator] term {binary_adding_operator term}

term ::= factor {multiplying_operator factor}

factor ::= primary [** primary] | abs primary | not primary
```

* primary ::= numeric_literal | character_literal | string_literal
| name | type_conversion | qualified_expression | (expression)

It should also be noted that type conversions and character literals are not considered to be names in SPARK and so have to be included as possible forms of primaries.

Since SPARK has no overloading (apart from the predefined overloading of operators such as + for numeric types), there is no need for overload resolution and so the type of every expression is determined by the types of its constituents and its operators and does not depend upon its context.

The operators fall into six precedence levels just as in Ada. In increasing order of precedence they are

logical_operator ::= **and** | **or** | **xor**

relational_operator ::= = | /= | < | <= | > | >=

binary_adding_operator ::= + | – | &

unary_adding_operator ::= + | –

multiplying_operator ::= * | / | **mod** | **rem**

highest_precedence_operator ::= ** | **abs** | **not**

There are also the short circuit forms **and then** and **or else** as in Ada and they both have the same precedence as the logical operators. Similarly, the membership tests **in** and **not in** have the same precedence as the relational operators.

Operators of higher precedence are associated with their operands before operators of lower precedence in the usual way. For a sequence of operators of the same precedence the operators are associated from left to right.

The association of operators and operands is important for type checking and selection of the correct operator implementation. The actual order of evaluation is undefined but the association of operators can be imposed by the use of parentheses. Thus considering

```
X := A * B * C * D;
Y := (A * B) * (C * D);
```

the order of the multiplications in the assignment to X is not defined at all. However, in the case of Y we are assured that the final multiplication is that of (A * B) by (C * D). But it is not possible to impose an order on the evaluation of A * B with respect to that of C * D; however, this does not matter since functions in SPARK cannot have side effects.

We will now briefly survey the various operators.

### *Logical operators*

The logical operators are defined for the type Boolean and any one-dimensional array type whose components are of type Boolean. They have their conventional meaning for Boolean types. For arrays whose components are of the type Boolean, the operations are performed on a component by component basis. The arrays must have the same bounds and so sliding cannot occur.

The short circuit forms **and then** and **or else** are defined for the type Boolean. The left operand of a short circuit form is always evaluated first. Depending on the value of the left operand the right operand may or may not be evaluated.

Examples of logical and short circuit forms are

```
Busy(Sat) and Busy(Sun)
Col_Ptr in Line'Range and then Current_Line(Col_Ptr) /= CR
```

### *Relational operators*

The equality operators = and /= are predefined for any type that is not limited (see Section 7.6 for limited types).

The ordering operators <, <=, >, >= are defined for any scalar type, other than Boolean, and for the predefined type String. The differences from Ada therefore are that they are not defined for the type Boolean nor for one-dimensional arrays of discrete types other than String.

The relational operators have their conventional meaning and return a result of type Boolean. Two objects of composite types, that is arrays or records, are equal if their corresponding components are equal.

Remember from Section 5.5 that sliding is never permitted for arrays. So if we have

```
type Vector is array (Integer range <>) of Integer;
subtype Range_03 is Integer range 0 .. 3;
subtype Range_14 is Integer range 1 .. 4;
subtype Vector_03 is Vector(Range_03);
subtype Vector_14 is Vector(Range_14);
X03: Vector_03 := Vector_03'(1, 2, 3, 4);
X14: Vector_14 := Vector_14'(1, 2, 3, 4);
```

then not only is X03 not equal to X14 but we cannot even compare them. Thus

```
if X03 = X14 then            -- illegal Spark
```

is illegal in SPARK whereas of course it is perfectly legal in Ada and the result is True. It is vital that it is illegal in SPARK rather than return False otherwise SPARK would not be a subset of Ada. So the lower bounds of operands of = and /= must always be the same; the upper bounds must also be the same except in the case of the type String.

The membership tests **in** and **not in** are predefined for all types as in Ada; they enable a value to be tested to see whether it lies within a given range or subtype. The evaluation of the membership test **in** yields the result True if the value of the expression is within the given range or if this value belongs to the subtype denoted by the given subtype mark. The test **not in** gives the complementary result.

Examples of relational operators and membership tests are

```
X /= Y
5 > 6
N in 1 .. 10
N >= 1 and N <= 10
Today in Weekday
```

### *Binary adding operators*

The binary adding operators + and – are defined for any numeric type and have their conventional meaning. The two operands must be of the same base type. The result will also be of that type.

So we might have

```
A: Integer;
Z: Float;
M, N: Fraction;
...
A + 1                    -- result of type Integer
Z + 1.0                  -- result of type Float
M + N                    -- result of type Fraction
```

As mentioned before the operator & is always evaluated statically in SPARK.

### *Unary adding operators*

The unary adding operators + and – are defined for any numeric type and have their conventional meaning. The operand and the result have the same type.

### *Multiplying operators*

The multiplying operators * and / are defined for any integer or floating point type and have their conventional meaning. The two operands must be of the same (base) type. The result will also be of that type.

The special rules for fixed point were given earlier in this chapter. Other examples using multiplying operators in SPARK are

```
A, B: Integer;
X: Float;
L, M, N: Fraction;
...
A * B                    -- result of type Integer
X * 2.0                  -- result of type Float
L * 2                    -- result of type Fraction
M / N                    -- conversion required
Fraction(M / N)          -- result of type Fraction
```

In addition, for integer types, the operators **rem** and **mod** are defined as explained in Section 5.4. The right operand may not be zero. For positive operands **mod** and **rem** return the same result.

### *Highest precedence operators*

The unary operator **abs** is defined for any numeric type in the usual way. The unary operator **not** is defined for the type Boolean and any one-dimensional array with Boolean components.

The left operand of the exponentiation operator ** can be of any integer or floating point type. The right operand is always of the predefined type Integer. The right operand cannot be negative if the left operand is of integer type.

Examples are

```
A, B: Integer;
X: Float;
...
A ** B                    -- result of type Integer
X ** A                    -- result of type Float
X ** 2                    -- result of type Float
```

### *Type conversions*

The evaluation of a type conversion evaluates the expression given as the operand and converts the resulting value to the specified target subtype. Type conversions are only allowed between closely related types (or the same type).

The syntax is

* type_conversion ::= subtype_mark (expression)

The conversion is allowed if the target type and the operand type are both numeric. The conversion of a real value to an integer type rounds to the nearest integer with a value midway between two integers rounding away from zero. Thus

```
A, B: Integer;
X: Float;
...
Integer(1.6)              -- result type Integer, value 2
Integer(-1.5)             -- result type Integer, value -2
Float(A) * X              -- result type Float
A * Integer(X)            -- result type Integer
```

Conversion is also allowed if the operand type and the target type are array types of the same dimensions, and with the same (or convertible) index types and statically matching component subtypes. Sliding is never allowed so the bounds also have to be the same; one consequence is that conversion is not possible on formal array parameters of an unconstrained type. (Convertible means that the index types could be different integer types. Statically matching subtypes are those with the same type and same static bounds.)

An important difference between Ada and SPARK is that SPARK does not permit so-called view conversions. Most view conversions concern tagged types or access types neither of which exist in SPARK and so are not relevant. However, another consequence is that it is not possible to use a type conversion as an actual parameter corresponding to a formal parameter of mode **in out** or **out**.

### *Qualified expressions*

A qualified expression is used to state explicitly the subtype of an expression or aggregate.

```
qualified_expression ::=
        subtype_mark ' (expression) | subtype_mark ' aggregate
```

Qualified expressions are chiefly used in SPARK with aggregates as we have already noted in a number of previous examples. Thus

```
D := Date'(25, Dec, 1990);
```

Qualified expressions can be used in other contexts but are not needed to resolve ambiguities in SPARK as they often are in Ada because SPARK has no overloading. The subtype mark must not be that of an unconstrained array type.

## 5.9 Constant and static expressions

A big difference between SPARK and Ada is that objects declared as constants have to be initialized with values known at compile time in SPARK. Constant in Ada means read-only whereas in SPARK it also implies statically known. Thus in Ada a constant can be initialized with the value of a variable whereas this is not permitted in SPARK. (Variables can also be initialized when declared in SPARK and the initial values follow the same rules as for constants.)

It is thus tempting to say that a constant in SPARK has to be initialized with a static expression. However, this is not really acceptable because a static expression in Ada cannot be of a general composite type (static expressions in Ada are scalar or strings). Moreover, there are even some scalar expressions which are acceptable as initial values since they can be evaluated statically even though they are not static expressions in the technical sense.

It is easier to state what is not permitted by defining a constant expression as any expression not containing

- the name of a variable (including a parameter of any mode),
- a function call other than a call of a predefined operator or attribute,
- an indexed component,
- a selected component whose prefix denotes a record.

The initial value in an object declaration then has to be given by a constant expression. Note that such an expression can contain aggregates and the names of other constants.

Parameters of mode **in** are not considered to be constant in this discussion since, although their value cannot be changed, the actual parameter can of course be any expression of the appropriate type and is usually not known until the program is executed.

Examples of constant expressions are

```
25
Float(4 * 12)
Date'(25, Dec, 1990)
"1234567890"
```

As we have just noted, static expressions are more restrictive than constant expressions. Static expressions are expressions of a scalar type or the type String whose constituents are limited to the following

- an enumeration literal (including character literals),
- a numeric literal or named number (see below),
- a string literal,
- a constant object (but not an **in** parameter),
- a static attribute or a functional attribute with static parameters (including most attributes of arrays),
- a qualified static expression,
- a membership test or short circuit form,
- a type conversion of a static expression.

Static expressions are required in a number of contexts such as in the definition of types and in choices occurring in aggregates and case statements.

Static expressions are very similar to those of Ada 95. Thus short circuit forms, membership tests and type conversions are all permitted. A subtle point is that all type conversions of a static expression are themselves static in SPARK because all named subtypes are static in SPARK. (The only unnamed subtypes occur in loop statements, see Section 6.3.)

We conclude by discussing the types of numeric literals and static expressions. SPARK uses a similar model to Ada 95 by introducing the notions of universal and root types. The general goal is to permit literals and static expressions to be used in any appropriate numeric context without having to introduce tedious explicit conversions.

As mentioned in Section 5.4, the integer literals are of a fictitious type known as universal_integer and the real literals (those with a point) are of the type universal_real. These universal types can be implicitly converted to any other integer or real type and this explains why the literals can be used in any appropriate context without qualification or conversion.

We can give a name to a numeric literal by using a number declaration. The syntax is

```
number_declaration ::=
        defining_identifier_list : constant := static_expression;
```

Thus we might give names to commonly used literals such as

```
Max_Line_Size: constant := 80;
Pi: constant := 3.14159_26536;
```

The value of an integer named number can be given by a static expression of any integer type. Similarly the value of a real named number can be given by a static expression of any real type.

Static numeric expressions are evaluated using arithmetic of the expected type. Thus if we write

```
C: constant Integer := 2 + 2;
```

then the addition is notionally done using that of the type Integer. However, in some circumstances, the expected type is not explicit in which case two other notional types, root_integer and root_real, are used. This would arise for example if we wrote

```
type Tiny_Integer is range 0 .. 2 + 2;
```

in which case the addition is performed using the type root integer.

All the normal operations applicable to all integer and floating types apply to the root types. We can think of root integer as having the biggest range of the integer types and root real as similarly being the most accurate of the real types. But of course all the operations are actually performed at compile time because the expressions are static. For convenience it is also possible to multiply or divide a value of type root real by a value of type root integer to give a result of type root real.

Although static expressions are required in a number of situations such as giving the initial values for constants and the bounds of constraints, nevertheless it is important to note that an expression is static if it looks static and not just because it occurs in a context demanding a static expression. Thus 2 + 2 is always evaluated statically to give 4 and not just in static contexts.

Some examples of static expressions are

```
25                    -- universal integer
Max_Line_Size         -- universal integer
2 + 2                 -- root integer
30 / 5                -- root integer
5 * 2.0               -- root real
2.0**5                -- root real
Integer'First         -- integer
```

A minor point is that the attribute Pos delivers a result of the type universal integer; this result may not be statically known and is the only situation where a dynamic universal value can occur. But of course it will immediately be converted to another integer type anyway.

## Summary

In the areas covered by this chapter, the main differences between SPARK and Ada are that in SPARK:

- All types and subtypes must be given names. In particular, anonymous array subtypes are not allowed. (But loop parameters are an exception and may be of an anonymous and dynamic subtype.)
- Dynamic expressions may not be used in declarations. All initial values and constraints must be determinable prior to program execution.
- The only unconstrained types are unconstrained arrays. Records with discriminants or variant parts are not allowed. Tagged record types are also not allowed.
- Access types are not allowed.
- Derived types are not allowed.
- Modular and decimal types are not allowed.
- Overloading of enumeration literals is not permitted. One consequence is that no user-defined character types are allowed.
- Slices are not allowed. This would lead to the introduction of anonymous subtypes.
- All subtypes of the type String must have a lower bound of 1.
- Operators cannot be called using prefix notation. That is they cannot be used as functions.
- Aggregates may only be used within qualified expressions. Named and positional associations cannot be mixed.
- The ordering relations are not defined for Boolean or arrays other than the type String.
- A type conversion cannot be an actual parameter where the formal parameter is of mode **in out** or **out**.

# Control and Data Flow



This chapter covers the various statements which govern the flow of control though a program. There are two main topics, the compound control statements such as the if, case and loop statement and then subprograms and their calls. Subprograms provide the conventional mechanism for abstraction through parameterization and take two forms, procedures and functions. Procedures are called as distinct statements whereas functions are called as part of an expression. It is also convenient to discuss assignment statements in this chapter.

The sequential control statements of SPARK are much as in Ada with only relatively minor differences to make analysis more straightforward. A big difference however is that subprograms have annotations describing the flow of data through parameters and global variables.

Minor aspects of control flow such as the initialization of packages are dealt with in the next chapter. A detailed discussion of the analysis of data and information flow is in Chapter 10.

## 6.1 Statements

The executable statements of SPARK are divided into two categories, the compound control statements which contain other statements nested within and the simple statements which cannot be decomposed.

The most important simple statements are the assignment statement and the procedure call. There is also the exit statement for leaving loops and the return statement for defining the result of a function. Finally the null statement does nothing but is useful for places where a statement is required by the syntax but no action is to be performed.

The syntax relating to statements is as follows

sequence_of_statements ::= statement {statement}

* statement ::= simple_statement | compound_statement

* simple_statement ::= null_statement
| assignment_statement | procedure_call_statement
| exit_statement | return_statement

* compound_statement ::= if_statement | case_statement | loop_statement

null_statement ::= **null**;

Many of the forms of statement in Ada do not apply in SPARK. Thus there are no goto statements, block statements or raise statements or the various statements involved in tasking. Naturally enough there are no labels either.

The omission of most of these is as expected. One would not expect a language of the rigour of SPARK to have labels and gotos. And of course, SPARK does not support exceptions. Perhaps of more surprise is the omission of block statements. However, block statements complicate the visibility model and are considered unnecessary especially since most of their uses in Ada do not apply to SPARK; for example there are no exception handlers in SPARK and moreover all subtypes are static and so inner blocks are not needed for dynamic array declarations. In any event a block can always be replaced by an inlined procedure.

There are also rather different rules regarding the position of exit and return statements as we shall see in a moment.

In addition to the above, SPARK also allows the use of *proof statements*; these enable the Examiner to generate verification conditions and other theorems relating to the correctness of a SPARK text as outlined in Chapter 3.

Proof statements are given in the form of annotations. They are not mandatory, and like comments, their presence or absence has no influence on the legality or the effect of a SPARK program; they are accordingly not shown in the syntax in this part of the book which is devoted to the core aspects of SPARK.

## 6.2 Assignment statements

An assignment statement replaces the current value of a variable with a new value specified by an expression.

assignment_statement ::= *variable*_name := expression;

The named variable and the right-hand side expression must be of the same type and of course this must not be a limited type. Before the variable is updated, a check is made that the value of the expression belongs to the subtype of the variable, that is the value must satisfy any constraints on the variable. If this check fails then the program terminates.

The following illustrates the possibility of checks

```
subtype Index is Integer range 1 .. 10;
I, J: Index;
K: Integer;
...
J := 6;
I := J;                    -- identical ranges
...
K := J;                    -- compatible ranges
J := K;                    -- illegal if K > 10 or K < 1
```

The assignment of J to I requires no check because I and J have the same subtype. The assignment of J to K also requires no check because the range of possible values of J is a subset of the range for I. However, the assignment of K to J requires a check since some possible values of K are outside the permitted values for J. If the check fails, the assignment is not performed and the program terminates.

SPARK does not have exceptions so the program shudders to a grinding halt when something goes wrong. The general philosophy is that for critical programs it is not acceptable for anything to go wrong and so the world might as well end if it does! Indeed, as we saw in Chapter 3, the SPARK philosophy is that we should be able to prove that the program cannot raise an exception and so the checks can be omitted by using the pragma Suppress with parameter All_Checks.

Actually one of the problems with checks is that it is difficult to verify the code associated with them if they never fail! In practice of course a SPARK program is an Ada program and so if it does have checks and one fails then an exception will be raised and so since SPARK has no exception handlers then the program will terminate. However, it is often convenient to place a **when others** exception handler at the end of the main subprogram which will then catch any exception; such a handler would have to be in code covered by a hide directive and so hidden from the Examiner. See Section 8.2.

Array assignments need careful consideration. Remember that sliding never occurs in SPARK and so not only must both the destination variable and the expression be of the same array type but the bounds must also be identical. So using the example of the previous chapter, if we have

```
type Vector is array (Integer range <>) of Integer;
subtype Range_03 is Integer range 0 .. 3;
subtype Range_14 is Integer range 1 .. 4;
subtype Vector_03 is Vector(Range_03);
subtype Vector_14 is Vector(Range_14);
```

```
X03: Vector_03;
X14: Vector_14;
```

then it is not possible to assign X03 to X14 directly in SPARK

```
X14 := X03;                    -- illegal in Spark
```

even though both sides are of type Vector. The effect can of course be obtained by writing a loop statement.

## 6.3 Compound control statements

The compound control statements are the if statement, case statement and loop statement. They are called compound statements because they contain internal sequences of statements. They all take a bracketed form with a closing **end if**, **end case** or **end loop** as appropriate.

It should also be noted that statements in Ada and SPARK are terminated by semicolons rather than separated by semicolons and so the last statement of a sequence also has a semicolon (this is unlike Pascal).

### *If statements*

If statements are exactly as in Ada. Simple examples are

```
if X > Max_X then
   Max_X := X;
end if;

if X > Y then
   Max := X;
else
   Max := Y;
end if;
```

The condition after **if** is an expression of the type Boolean and the **else** part is optional. It is also possible to have one or more **elsif** parts as revealed by the syntax

```
if_statement ::=
        if condition then
           sequence_of_statements
       {elsif condition then
           sequence_of_statements}
       [else
           sequence_of_statements]
        end if;

condition ::= boolean_expression
```

In the case of an if statement containing elsif parts, the associated conditions are evaluated in order until one (if any) is found to be true and then the corresponding sequence of statements is executed. Of course if none of the conditions is true and there is no else part then no statements are executed.

### *Case statements*

Case statements are also as in Ada and allow one or more alternative sequences to be chosen according to the value of an expression. Thus we might do different actions according to the day of the week

```
case Today is
   when Mon .. Thurs => Work;
   when Fri => Work; Party;
   when Sat | Sun => null;
end case;
```

This reflects that we go to work on Monday to Thursday. We also work on Friday and then go to a party. At the weekend we do nothing and this shows the use of an explicit null statement. The statements Work; and Party; are calls of appropriate procedures that happen to have no parameters.

The rules are similar to those for array aggregates and an others clause is permitted as the last choice. So the weekend activity in the above example could be rewritten as

```
when others => null;
```

The syntax in SPARK is somewhat rewritten in order to show the others choice explicitly

```
* case_statement ::=
        case expression is
           case_statement_alternative
          {case_statement_alternative}
          [when others => sequence_of_statements]
        end case;

  case_statement_alternative ::=
        when discrete_choice_list => sequence_of_statements
```

Apart from the rewritten syntax, case statements are exactly as in Ada. In particular, every possibility must be covered exactly once. The range of possibilities is usually known at compile time because named types and subtypes are static in SPARK. But loop parameters may have a dynamic range and so if such a loop parameter is used in a case expression then an others clause will usually be required.

### *Loop statements*

Loop statements are much as in Ada but there are a number of important differences. The simplest form of loop is one that essentially goes on for ever and can only be broken by an exit statement that takes control to just after the end of the loop

```
loop
   Get(Current_Character);
   exit when Current_Character = '*';
end loop;
```

The other two forms of loop statement commence with **while** and **for** respectively. A while statement continues as long as the Boolean expression after **while** remains true whereas a for statement repeats with the loop parameter taking a sequence of values. For example

```
while Bid(N).Price < Cut_Off.Price loop
   Record_Bid(Bid(N).Price);
   N := N + 1;
end loop;

for I in Index_Range loop
   Sum := Sum + A(I);
end loop;
```

In the case of the for statement, the loop parameter I has the subtype given by the range after **in** and the loop repeats with I taking each value of the range in turn (normally in ascending order but inserting **reverse** after **in** gives descending order).

The full syntax of loop statements in SPARK is

loop_statement ::= [*loop_*statement_identifier :]
        [iteration_scheme] **loop**
            sequence_of_statements
        **end loop** [*loop_*identifier];

iteration_scheme ::=
        **while** condition | **for** loop_parameter_specification

* loop_parameter_specification ::=
    defining_identifier **in** [**reverse**] *discrete_*subtype_mark [**range** range]

One important simplification compared with Ada is that a for statement cannot have a range without a subtype mark. Thus the shorthand form

```
for I in 1 ..10 loop
```

which is permitted in Ada, is not allowed in SPARK so that we always have to give the type explicitly thus

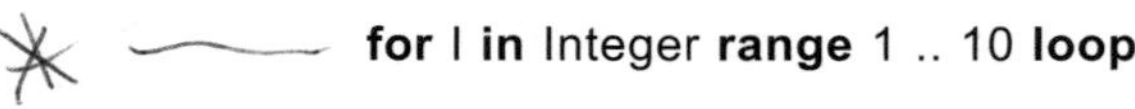

```
for I in Integer range 1 .. 10 loop
```

However, note that the subtype of I is effectively anonymous. This is the one case in SPARK where a subtype is anonymous and moreover need not be static in the sense that the limits of the range may be dynamic; thus a loop can be null.

A small difference is that although a SPARK loop can be named nevertheless the name cannot be used in an exit statement. The name is however used for the construction of a unique identifier for a control parameter occurring in verification conditions; see the answer to Exercise 11.3(**1**).

The syntax of the exit statement therefore simplifies to

* exit_statement ::= **exit** [**when** condition];

This means that an exit statement always transfers control out of the innermost loop. Exit statements are allowed in while and for statements as well as in simple loop statements.

Incidentally, if we need to write a program that runs for ever then it is best to write

```
while True loop
   ...
end loop;
```

rather then

```
loop
   ...
end loop;
```

The reason is that in the first case the Examiner only produces a single message to the effect that the condition is stable whereas in the second case the Examiner complains that every statement in the loop is ineffective if the loop has no exit statements. See Section 10.8 for a discussion on loop stability.

We will now discuss the rules regarding the position of exit statements which are necessary to ensure that data and information flow analysis can be carried out as discussed in Chapter 10.

If an exit statement contains a when clause then its closest containing compound statement must be a loop statement. Thus we cannot use such an exit statement to jump out of a nested construction. So the following is illegal in SPARK

```
loop
   ...
   if some_condition then
      ...
      exit when some_other_condition;        -- illegal Spark
   end if;
   ...
end loop;
```

On the other hand, if an exit statement does not contain a when clause then it must be immediately within an if statement which has no else or elsif parts

and the exit statement must be the last statement of the if statement. Moreover, the if statement must itself be immediately within the loop. So the following is permitted

```
loop
   ...
   if some_condition then
      ...   -- last wishes
      exit;
   end if;
   ...
end loop;
```

Note that these rules do not prevent multiple exit statements within a loop since we can still write

```
loop
   ...
   exit when this_condition;
   ...
   exit when that_condition;
   ...
end loop;
```

The consequence of these rules is that every execution path through the body of a loop traverses all its conditional exit statements and all its conditional statements that contain unconditional exit statements. In other words, the rules ensure that all exit statements are effectively at the outermost layer of the loop and not buried inside nested statements.

These rules also accord with sensible guidelines on good programming practice such as those recommended in *Ada 95 Quality and Style* [SPC, 1995].

---

**EXERCISE 6.3**

1 Rewrite the following legal Ada in SPARK

```
My_Loop:
for I in 1 .. 100 loop
   A(I) := A(I) + 1;
   if A(I) = 10 then
      exit My_Loop;
   else
      A(I+1) := 0;
   end if;
end loop My_Loop;
```

---

## 6.4 Return statements

Return statements are used in subprograms in Ada in order to transfer control back to the point of call. However, in SPARK a return statement cannot be used in procedures at all but only in functions. Thus a return statement must always have a return expression

* return_statement ::= **return** expression;

Moreover a function has to have precisely one return statement and this has to be the last statement of the function.

These rules simplify the process of analysis by ensuring that there is only one exit path from a procedure or function. It is also clearer for the reader since internal return statements cannot be buried in the middle of the code.

## 6.5 Subprograms

A subprogram is a program unit whose execution is invoked by a subprogram call. As in Ada, subprograms come in two forms: procedures and functions. A simple example of a procedure from Chapter 2 is

```
procedure Exchange(X, Y: in out Float) is
   T: Float;
begin
   T := X;  X := Y;  Y := T;
end Exchange;
```

A procedure starts with its specification which includes the formal parameter list if any. Local variables can be declared between **is** and **begin** and the statements occur between **begin** and the final **end**. Functions take a similar form but commence with the word **function** and give the result (sub)type after the parameter list. For example

```
function Max(I, J: Integer) return Integer is
   Result: Integer;
begin
   if I > J then
      Result := I;
   else
      Result := J;
   end if;
   return Result;
end Max;
```

Remember that a SPARK function must have a single return statement and that must be its last statement. So this example cannot be written with a return in each branch.

As in Ada, subprograms may have distinct specifications and bodies although this is only allowed in certain circumstances in SPARK as discussed in the next chapter. In the remainder of this section we will just consider the detail of subprogram specifications; bodies will be described in Section 6.7.

There are a number of differences regarding subprogram specifications in SPARK. One difference is that default expressions are not allowed for the formal parameters as they are in Ada; this fits in with the general principle that values should not appear remote from where they are used. Another difference is that the designator of a function may not be an operator; this is simply because all operators in SPARK are predefined.

Moreover, SPARK also requires subprograms to have global and derives annotations as we saw in Chapter 2.

The syntax is

```
* subprogram_declaration ::=
          procedure_specification ; procedure_annotation
        | function_specification ; function_annotation

+ procedure_specification ::=
        procedure defining_identifier parameter_profile

+ function_specification ::=
        function defining_designator parameter_and_result_profile

  parameter_profile ::= [formal_part]

  parameter_and_result_profile ::= [formal_part] return subtype_mark

  formal_part ::= (parameter_specification {; parameter_specification})

* parameter_specification ::=
        defining_identifier_list : mode subtype_mark

  mode ::= [in] | in out | out
```

This rather long-winded syntax follows that of Ada 95 except that procedure and function specifications are treated distinctly in order to aid the discussion on annotations below.

Other points to note about the syntax are that the name of a subprogram is always just an identifier because there are no child subprograms in SPARK and moreover there are no access parameters because SPARK does not have access types. The parameter modes are otherwise the same as in Ada as discussed in Chapter 2.

In accordance with the general philosophy of uniqueness of names, a user-defined subprogram is not allowed to overload any other subprogram (predefined or user-defined).

Finally, the result subtype of a function cannot be an unconstrained array type such as String. The subtype must be constrained such as String_10. The reason for this rule is to avoid problems with allocating temporary storage for a result whose size is not known at compile time. But of course there is no similar rule regarding **out** parameters of a procedure which can be of an unconstrained array type since storage allocation problems do not arise with parameters.

## 6.6 Procedure and function annotations

Procedures may be annotated with a global definition giving information about the use of global variables and they may also be annotated with a dependency relation giving information about the relationships between imported and exported parameters and globals. The global annotation may give mode information similar to parameters indicating whether a global is read, updated or both. If there are no globals then the global annotation is omitted.

If information flow analysis is required then the dependency relation is necessary although the global annotation need not supply modes. On the other hand, if only data flow analysis is required, then the dependency relation may be omitted but the global annotation must supply modes. It is recommended that the modes of globals always be supplied, the option to omit them being necessary for backward compatibility with SPARK 83.

The syntax is

```
+ procedure_annotation ::=
          [global_definition | moded_global_definition]
          [dependency_relation]
```

If a procedure has distinct specification and body then the annotation follows the distinct specification otherwise it follows the specification in the body; the annotation is never repeated unless refined, see Section 7.3. The following example from Chapter 2 shows an annotation after a specification

```
procedure Random(X: out Float);
--# global in out Seed;
--# derives X, Seed from Seed;
```

The parameter list plus global annotation states that Random reads the global variable Seed and updates X and Seed. The derives annotation more explicitly states that the updated value of X only depends upon the prior value of Seed and the updated value of Seed only depends upon the prior value of Seed.

Note that the global definition (if there is one) has to precede any dependency relation because the latter will inevitably use the global variables.

The following shows an annotation in a body

```
procedure Exchange(X, Y: in out Float)
--# derives X from Y &
--#         Y from X;
is
   T: Float;
begin
   T := X;  X := Y;  Y := T;
end Exchange;
```

In this case there is no global definition and the dependency relation states that the new value of X depends only upon the old value of Y and vice versa.

As noted in Section 2.5 the whole purpose of a procedure is to update some external variables. Usually a procedure has both imports and exports. Sometimes a procedure has exports but no imports such as the procedure Clear of Section 2.6

```
procedure Clear(S: out Stack);
--# derives S from ;
```

As a special case it is possible for a procedure to have no imports or exports; it would then do nothing but a null procedure is often useful thus

```
procedure Nothing;
--# derives ;
```

But the final case of a procedure with imports but no exports is forbidden. So we cannot have

```
procedure Strange(X: in T);
--# derives   from X;      -- illegal
```

Note that if a derives annotation is supplied then this last situation is prevented by the syntax which is given below. However, if no derives annotation is supplied (because information flow analysis is not required) then any global annotation must have modes and there is also a check that at least one parameter or global variable has mode **out** or **in out**. See also the discussion on external sequences in Section 8.3.

A function may also have an annotation although this is often not necessary since functions can never have dependency relations (because their parameters can only be of mode **in** and SPARK functions never have side effects and so can never update global variables). Note that since all globals are necessarily of mode **in**, the form of annotation without modes is always used with functions. So the syntax reduces to

```
+ function_annotation ::=
        [global_definition]
```

The detailed rules for the formation of global definitions and dependency relations are as follows

```
+ global_definition ::= --# global entire_variable_list;

+ entire_variable_list ::= entire_variable {, entire_variable}

+ entire_variable ::= [package_name .] direct_name

+ moded_global_definition ::=
        --# global global_mode entire_variable_list;
                                {global_mode entire_variable_list;}

+ global_mode ::= in | in out | out
```

+ dependency_relation ::=
  **--# derives** [dependency_clause {& dependency_clause}];

+ dependency_clause ::=
  entire_variable_list **from** imported_variable_list

+ imported_variable_list ::= [*] | [* ,] entire_variable_list

Note that the mode **in** may not be omitted in a global annotation giving modes as it can in a parameter list. The modes all have to be supplied in a particular annotation or not at all.

The syntax permits several variables on the left hand side of a dependency relation. Thus

```
--# derives X, Seed from Seed;
```

is short for

```
--# derives X from Seed &
--#         Seed from Seed;
```

Another abbreviation is permitted in the common case of a variable depending upon itself which can then be represented by the use of * which if present must be the first item on the right. Thus

```
--# derives A, B, C from *, X, Y;
```

is equivalent to

```
--# derives A from A, X, Y &
--#         B from B, X, Y &
--#         C from C, X, Y;
```

The * notation is permitted even if the variable is already explicitly in the list on the right. Thus

```
--# derives A, B from * , A;
```

is equivalent to

```
--# derives A from A &
--#         B from A, B;
```

Note carefully that all variables mentioned in these annotations must be entire variables; this means they must not be components of composite variables. Thus if a procedure accessed just the component Day of some record variable Today of the type Date, then we could not write

```
--# global in Today.Day;        -- illegal
```

but must give the entire variable name

```
--# global in Today;
```

The need to provide annotations in terms of entire variables can give rise to warning messages in the case of exported variables. Consider for example the procedure Clear in Section 2.6 (the Ada comment echoes the annotation which cannot strictly be repeated since it was given in the specification)

```
procedure Clear(S: out Stack)
-- derives S from ;
is
begin
   S.Stack_Pointer := 0;
end Clear;
```

Although the logic of the program is such that it is not necessary to give an initial value to the component S.Stack_Vector, nevertheless since annotations are in terms of entire variables, the Examiner warns that the undefined initial value of S.Stack_Vector may be used to derive the final value of S.

Also note that the items in the annotations must be variables (including parameters); there is never any need to mention a constant in a global or derives annotation and indeed to do so would be illegal.

There are a number of rules of completeness and consistency concerning the variables appearing in these annotations. Most of these are quite obvious.

First, the derives annotation, if given, must be consistent with the parameter list and any global annotation. Every parameter and every global variable must appear as either an imported variable or as an exported variable in the dependency relation as appropriate. It could appear as both as does Seed which illustrates the very common situation of a variable depending upon itself. An **in out** parameter or global must be both imported and exported.

Moreover the various lists may not contain redundancies; a variable cannot appear in both a global definition and in a parameter list, and a variable cannot be repeated in a global definition or as an exported variable in a dependency relation. It could of course appear several times as an imported variable in a dependency as for example Seed in the procedure Random, but again cannot be repeated in the same imported variable list (except that the use of * does not constitute repetition).

A rather different rule regarding global definitions is that a name in the global definition of a procedure cannot be redeclared immediately (or as a loop parameter) within the procedure. Thus an internal name cannot hide an imported global one. This is illustrated by the nested procedures Outer and Inner of Section 2.4. The annotated version of Inner is

```
procedure Inner(K: in Integer)
--# global in out I;
--# derives I from I, K;
is
   J: Integer;
begin
   J := K + I;
   I := J + 2;
end Inner;
```

An attempt to redeclare I locally would be detected (whereas in normal Ada without annotations it would simply result in the local I being used instead of the global one).

But of course this does not prevent another declaration of I inside a subprogram or package which is itself internal to Inner because it would not then be immediately redeclared within Inner.

The subprogram body must be consistent with the annotations given with the subprogram specification. Every imported variable (one read by the subprogram) must either be an **in** or **in out** parameter or be in a global definition (with mode **in** or **in out** if supplied). Similarly every exported variable (one updated by the subprogram) must be an **out** or **in out** parameter or be in a global definition (with mode **out** or **in out** if supplied). Reading and updating may be direct or indirect via calls of other subprograms.

Finally, the dependency relation, if given, must be consistent with the information flow relations of the subprogram body. However, every path though a procedure need not update all the exported variables. Some may simply pass through unchanged. Thus we might write

```
procedure Quadratic(A, B, C: in Float;
                    Root_1, Root_2: in out Float; Real_Roots: out Boolean);
--# derives Root_1, Root_2, from *, A, B, C &
--#         Real_Roots from A, B, C;
```

where Root_1 and Root_2 are not updated if the quadratic equation does not have real roots. The resulting possible dependency of Root_1 and Root_2 on their initial values is shown in the derives annotation and illustrates the use of the * abbreviation.

However, if Root_1 and Root_2 are **out** parameters thus

```
procedure Quadratic(A, B, C: in Float;
                    Root_1, Root_2: out Float; Real_Roots: out Boolean);
--# derives Root_1, Root_2, Real_Roots from A, B, C;
```

then it is necessary that Root_1 and Root_2 be updated on every path even if Real_Roots is false (since otherwise Constraint_Error might be raised by a junk value). Parameters can only 'pass through' if they have mode **in out** and so will at least have some benign value.

Finally it is worth emphasizing that the global annotation should be looked upon as simply an extension of the parameter list with the purpose of making it quite clear which variables are used by the subprogram. Globals can indeed be looked upon as parameters for which the actual parameters are always the same.

---

## EXERCISE 6.6

**1** Rewrite the procedure Clear so that the entire variable S is correctly given a value.

**2** Consider the derives annotation of the procedure Multiply of Section 1.5. Is it really consistent with the body?

It is sometimes felt that derives annotations add little to the information in the parameter and global annotations especially if the latter give the modes. The following somewhat bizarre exercises show that this is almost inevitably not so.

**3** The following specifications are typical of those used for external communication as we shall see in Section 8.3.

```
procedure Write(X: in T);
--# global in out S;

procedure Read(X: out T);
--# global in out S;
```

What derives annotations would be consistent with these specifications?

**4** How many different derives annotations would be consistent with

```
procedure Change(X, Y: in out Float);
```

---

## 6.7 Subprogram bodies and calls

Subprogram bodies comprise their specification followed by an implementation part. The implementation part is much as in Ada but cannot have an exception handler.

```
* subprogram_body ::=
        procedure_specification [procedure_annotation] is
           subprogram_implementation
      | function_specification [function_annotation] is
           subprogram_implementation

+ subprogram_implementation ::=
           declarative_part
        begin
           sequence_of_statements
        end designator;
```

Remember that an annotation must not be included if a subprogram has been declared in a package specification since the annotation will already have been given with the subprogram specification. (This does not apply in the case of refinement to abstract variables which was briefly introduced in Chapter 2 and is discussed in detail in the next chapter.)

If a procedure specification is given separately then the specification given as part of the body must be the same. The technical term used in Ada is that they must have full conformance. Some slight variation is allowed provided they have the same meaning. Thus an explicit mode **in** could be omitted in one and not the other and parameters of the same subtype could be given in a list or distinctly. Thus the following conform

```
function Max(I, J: Integer) return Integer
function Max(I: in Integer; J: in Integer) return Integer
```

A minor difference from Ada is that the designator after the final **end** is mandatory in SPARK whereas it is optional in Ada.

We now turn to subprogram calls. A procedure call is a statement standing alone whereas a function call returns a value as part of an expression. Actual parameters are provided of the appropriate type corresponding to the formal parameters. Such calls may use positional or named notation as for aggregates. So we might write

```
Exchange(U, V);
Exchange(X => U, Y => V);
P := Max(Q, R);
```

The syntax is much the same as in Ada except that positional and named notation must not be mixed (remember that the same applies to record aggregates – this is a general rule in SPARK) and there are no default parameters in SPARK.

* procedure_call_statement ::= *procedure*_name [actual_parameter_part];

* function_call ::= *function*_name [actual_parameter_part]

* actual_parameter_part ::= (parameter_association_list)

\+ parameter_association_list ::= named_parameter_association_list
   | positional_parameter_association_list

\+ named_parameter_association_list ::=
   *formal_parameter*_selector_name => explicit_actual_parameter
   {, *formal_parameter*_selector_name => explicit_actual_parameter}

\+ positional_parameter_association_list ::=
   explicit_actual_parameter {, explicit_actual_parameter}

explicit_actual_parameter ::= expression | *variable*_name

Each actual parameter is associated with a corresponding formal parameter. For a named association the correspondence between a formal parameter and an actual parameter is made explicitly. For a positional association the actual parameter corresponds to the formal parameter with the same position in the formal part. A subprogram call must specify exactly one corresponding actual parameter for each formal parameter. As mentioned above, unlike Ada, named and positional parameters cannot be mixed in a given subprogram call.

The actual parameter corresponding to an **in** parameter must be an expression of the appropriate type; the expression gives the value of the **in** parameter which behaves as a constant in the body. The actual parameter corresponding to an **in out** or **out** parameter must be a variable of the appropriate type.

An actual parameter whose corresponding formal parameter is an exported variable (has mode **in out** or **out**) has to be an entire variable if it is an array. So we cannot write A_Row(K) or indeed A_Row(7) as the actual parameter in a call of

```
procedure Increment(I: in out Integer);
--# derives I from I;
```

However, records are treated more flexibly and it is possible to pass a component such as Some_Date.Year to a call of Increment. Note that the restriction on arrays only applies to exported variables; an actual parameter which is just imported can of course be a component of an array.

In the case of array parameters, if the formal is constrained then the actual must have the same bounds (sliding is not allowed whereas it is in Ada). If the formal is of an unconstrained type then the actual can be of any subtype and the bounds of the formal array are taken from the actual parameter. In the case of a function returning an array the expression in the return statement must have the same bounds as the required result (sliding is again not allowed); remember that the result of a function cannot be of an unconstrained array type.

The type

```
type Vector is array (Integer range <>) of Integer;
```

is a typical example of an unconstrained array type. A procedure with a parameter of this type such as

```
procedure Scan(V: in Vector);
```

can be called with a parameter of any subtype of Vector. So we can write

```
subtype Five_To_Ten is Integer range 5 .. 10;
subtype Vector_5_10 is Vector(Five_To_Ten);
A_Vector: Vector_5_10 := Vector_5_10'(others => 0);
...
Scan(A_Vector);
```

and then in this case within Scan we will find that V'First is 5 and V'Last is 10. However these attributes are not static when applied to such a parameter because their value depends upon the bounds of the array passed as actual parameter.

A consequence of the absence of array sliding in SPARK is that it is not possible to perform whole array operations such as assignment and comparison for equality on the formal parameter V. The operations permitted on an unconstrained formal array parameter V are to pass it on to another call, take attributes of it such as First and Last, and index into it. It is not possible to perform type conversions on unconstrained array types.

An important difference between SPARK and Ada is that recursion is forbidden in SPARK. The reason for this is of course so that space requirements are bounded and can be computed statically. Recursion is not prohibited explicitly but as a consequence of various rules many of whose prime purpose is to ensure that analysis can be performed linearly.

One rule is that every call of a subprogram in the compilation unit containing the declaration of the subprogram body (or stub, see Section 7.9) has to follow the declaration of the body (or stub); this forbids direct recursion and mutual recursion within a compilation unit. Mutual recursion between a parent unit and its children is similarly prevented by the conceptual order of their declaration; mutual recursion between unrelated compilation units or between siblings is prevented by the rules regarding inherit clauses (see Section 7.2) and the fact that private and public siblings are not visible to each other.

There are also a number of rules to prevent aliasing of variables in the execution of procedures. Aliasing means the same variable being known through two different names. An important potential example of aliasing is where parameters might overlap and the rules of SPARK therefore prevent parameters overlapping where this might cause problems.

A variable V given in a global definition and exported from a procedure cannot be an actual parameter of a call of that procedure; if the exported variable is composite then the same restriction applies to its components. So we cannot have

```
procedure P(X: in T; ... );
--# global out V;
--# derives V from ... ;     -- exports V
...
P(V, ... );                  -- illegal call with V
```

A variable V given in the global definition of a procedure cannot occur as an actual parameter of that procedure if the corresponding formal parameter is an exported variable. So we cannot have

```
procedure P(X: in out T; ... );
--# global V;
--# derives X from ... ;     -- exports X
...
P(V, ... );                  -- illegal call with V
```

These last two rules are essentially two sides of the same coin. The intent is to prevent an assignment to X or V also causing an update to the other.

If a variable V occurs as an actual parameter and the corresponding formal parameter is exported, then neither V nor any of its subcomponents can occur as another actual parameter in the same call. So we cannot have

```
procedure P(X: in T; Y: out T);
--# derives Y from X;        -- exports Y
...
P(V, V);                     -- illegal call repeats V
```

This prevents an assignment to Y also updating X.

The above rules are designed to prevent aliasing; a very important consequence of the absence of aliasing is that it does not matter whether a parameter is passed by copy or by reference.

These three rules may seem a bit hard to remember but they are really all the same rule. This can be seen by considering all globals as simply parameters where the actual parameter is always the same. With this transformation the rules concerning globals reduce to the last rule, namely that an actual parameter cannot be repeated if any of the corresponding formal parameters are exported.

It is important to note that although we can pass a component of a record as an out parameter, nevertheless the aliasing rules always apply to entire variables and individual components are not distinguished for this purpose. Thus (assuming T is Integer) both of the following

```
P(Some_Date.Day, Some_Date.Year);        -- illegal call
P(A_Row(J), A_Row(K));                   -- illegal call
```

are not permitted. (Remember that there is a general principle that all interfaces are defined in terms of entire variables because to do otherwise would generally hinder abstraction but internal flow analysis treats record components as individual entities.)

Note finally that there are no restrictions on a variable just being imported. So we can write

```
procedure P(X, Y: in T; Z: out T);
--# derives Z from X, Y;
...
P(V, V, W);                     -- OK
```

Such multiple reading can do no harm; it is potential multiple update paths that cause the problems of aliasing.

We conclude this chapter with some examples of aliasing which illustrate the application of the above rules. First consider the following procedure which monitors how many times it is called through the global variable Call_Count

```
Call_Count: Integer := 0;
...
procedure Inc(X: in out Integer)
--# global in out Call_Count;
--# derives X, Call_Count from *;
is
begin
   X := X + 1;
   Call_Count := Call_Count + 1;
end Inc;
...
Y: Integer;
...
Inc(Y);
```

However, an attempt to apply Inc to Call_Count itself thus

```
Inc(Call_Count);              -- illegal Spark
```

is illegal since it violates the rule that a global cannot also be an actual parameter corresponding to an exported formal parameter. Of course scalar parameters are always passed by copy and so even if permitted the result is that Call_Count would always just increase by 1. However, this might be considered surprising since quite clearly two additions take place.

A more severe example is provided by the following nasty procedure

```
subtype Index is Integer range 1 .. 10;
type Vector is array (Index) of Float;

A: Vector;                    -- bounds of A are 1 and 10
...
procedure Sly(V: in Vector)
--# global in out A;
--# derives A from A, V;
is
begin
   A(1) := V(1) + V(1);
   A(1) := A(1) + V(1);
end Sly;
...
A(1) := 1.0;
Sly(A);
```

This very artificial example illustrates how the behaviour may depend upon the parameter mechanism. Array parameters in Ada may be passed by copy or by reference. If the parameter A is passed by copy the final value of A(1) is 3.0 whereas if it is passed by reference the final value of A(1) is 4.0. This possible variation arises because of the aliasing since within Sly both A and V refer to the same array. However, using SPARK, this uncertainty is detected because of the aliasing rules and the program is thus rejected.

Another example is provided by the procedure Multiply of Section 1.5.

## Summary

In the areas covered by this chapter, the main differences between SPARK and Ada are that in SPARK:

- There are no labels or goto statements.
- There are no blocks.
- There are no exceptions.
- Arrays never slide on assignment, parameter passing or conversion.

- There are restrictions on return and exit statements.
- Subprograms may require annotations.
- There must be a designator after the closing end of a subprogram body.
- Formal parameters cannot have default expressions associated with them.
- Named and positional associations may not be mixed.
- Subprograms cannot be called recursively.
- A user-defined subprogram may not overload any other subprogram.

# Packages and Visibility



This chapter discusses various aspects of the control of visibility which is of major importance in defining abstractions.

Subprograms control visibility to some extent through the introduction of local variables hidden from the outside user. However, the most important means of controlling visibility is through packages and private types which as we saw in Chapter 2 provide the means of implementing abstract data types.

It is also convenient to discuss separate compilation in this chapter because the rules of dependency are also related to visibility.

This chapter completes the general discussion of the SPARK core language. The predefined library and similar implementation-dependent issues are discussed in Chapter 8.

## 7.1 Packages

Packages allow the specification of groups of logically related entities, including subprograms, in such a way that they can be used from outside the package, whilst their inner workings remain hidden and protected from the user.

A package is generally provided in two parts: a package specification and a package body. Every package has a package specification, but not all packages have a package body. The usual reason for requiring a package body is in order to provide a body for a subprogram whose specification has been given in the package specification. Thus a typical structure is

```
package P is

   procedure Q( ... );
   --# derives ...

end P;

package body P is

   procedure Q( ... ) is
   begin
      ...
   end Q;

end P;
```

In Ada, a library package is only permitted to have a body if one is required by some language rule. Many of the Ada rules requiring a body do not apply to SPARK. The main one that does apply is that a package body is required if a subprogram body has to be provided to correspond to a subprogram specification in the package specification. The only other reason is if pragma Elaborate_Body is specified; this can be useful so that we can provide a body to initialize own variables of the package even if the package has no subprograms. Thus we might write

```
package P
--# own V;
--# initializes V;
is
   pragma Elaborate_Body(P);
   V: T;
end P;

package body P is
begin
   V := initial_value;
end P;
```

In full Ada the main purpose of this pragma is to ensure that the package body is elaborated immediately after the package specification. However, such order of elaboration is immaterial in SPARK as we saw in Section 4.2.

Before embarking on the details of packages in SPARK, it would seem appropriate to outline the rules regarding what can be declared and where.

In Ada the rules are such that bodies cannot be declared inside package specifications. This is expressed by classifying declarative items (declarations) as basic declarative items or bodies. And then only basic declarative items are allowed inside specifications whereas any declarative items are allowed inside bodies (and blocks but there are no blocks in SPARK anyway).

Thus in Ada the nesting of declarations is permitted quite freely with the single proviso that bodies are only allowed in bodies (and blocks). Moreover subprograms can always have distinct specifications and bodies in Ada.

The rules in SPARK are stricter. A distinct subprogram specification is not allowed inside a package body unless it is immediately followed by the pragma Import and thus denotes an external subprogram (see Section 8.1). Moreover, as mentioned in Section 4.2, a subprogram specification cannot be compiled alone in SPARK. There are similar rules regarding packages; thus a package specification is not permitted inside another package specification. The rules are best phrased in terms of where specifications are allowed and are

- A (distinct) subprogram specification is only allowed immediately within a package specification (including the private part), or immediately within a package body provided it is followed by a pragma Import.
- A package specification is only allowed as a library unit or immediately within a subprogram body or package body.

Given that recursion is not permitted, allowing a distinct subprogram specification inside a package body would be somewhat superfluous. The rule regarding package specifications simplifies the visibility model by preventing visibly nested structures but explicitly permits the use of embedded packages to represent abstract state machines for refinement.

The rules are enforced through the syntax for SPARK by excluding package and subprogram declarations (the proper term for a specification plus semicolon) from the category of basic_declaration and then treating them separately. In fact the syntax rules are

```
* basic_declaration ::= object_declaration | number_declaration
          | type_declaration | subtype_declaration

* declarative_part ::=
          {renaming_declaration}
          {declarative_item | embedded_package_declaration
                                   | external_subprogram_declaration}

* basic_declarative_item ::= basic_declaration | representation_clause

  declarative_item ::= basic_declarative_item | body

  body ::= proper_body | body_stub

* proper_body ::= subprogram_body | package_body

+ embedded_package_declaration ::=
          package_declaration {renaming_declaration}

+ external_subprogram_declaration ::=
          subprogram_declaration
          pragma Import(pragma_argument_association,
                        pragma_argument_association,
                        {pragma_argument_association});
```

Package declarations and external subprogram declarations are thus explicitly permitted embedded in a more general declarative part. The rules regarding both the form and position of renaming declarations are discussed in detail in Section 7.7.

Turning now to the syntax for packages, we have

```
   package_declaration ::= package_specification;

*  package_specification ::=
           [inherit_clause]
           package defining_program_unit_name
              package_annotation
           is
             {renaming_declaration}
             {package_declarative_item}
           [private
             {renaming_declaration}
             {package_declarative_item}]
           end [parent_unit_name .] identifier;

+  package_declarative_item ::= basic_declarative_item
           | subprogram_declaration | external_subprogram_declaration

*  package_body ::=
           package body defining_program_unit_name
           [refinement_definition]
           is
              declarative_part
           [begin
              sequence_of_statements]
           end [parent_unit_name .] identifier;

   defining_program_unit_name ::=
           [parent_unit_name .] defining_identifier

   parent_unit_name ::= name
```

There are a number of differences from the syntax of Ada. Note in particular how a subprogram declaration (with or without a pragma Import) is explicitly allowed in both the visible part and private part of a package specification; as mentioned above, these are the only places where a subprogram specification can be declared on its own (without a body or pragma Import).

Package bodies are much as in Ada except that the optional initialization part is simply a sequence of statements and cannot have an exception handler. Entities declared in a body are not visible outside the body except that an own variable declared in a package body may appear in an annotation occurring in the specification (in the package annotation itself or in a subprogram annotation in the package).

Child packages are permitted as discussed in Section 4.2. A child package can have further children and so the parent unit name can itself be the name of a child package. The full name must be repeated at the end of the specification and body. The rules regarding visibility are enforced by with and inherit clauses. 

The annotations applicable to packages are described in the following sections.

## 7.2 Inherit clauses

A package specification (or a main subprogram) may begin with an inherit clause. Inherit clauses control access to global entities outside packages in much the same way as global clauses of subprograms control access to variables outside subprograms.

One reason for introducing inherit clauses is to give better control of visibility from within a package. We have good control of visibility from outside a package because entities in the package have to be referred to using the dotted notation. Thus a variable V declared in the visible part of a package P has to be referred to as P.V from outside (remember that use package clauses are forbidden). However, if the package P is embedded in a package Q then any variable declared in Q can (in Ada) be simply referred to as V from within P and it is not at all clear that it is actually declared in Q. Thus

```
package body Q is
   V: Integer;

   package P is
      -- V can be referred to here simply as V in Ada
      ...
   end P;

   package body P is
      ...
   end P;

end Q;
```

In order to give greater clarity SPARK insists that such variables use dotted notation and so we have to write Q.V in SPARK. Furthermore, in order to indicate that the package P refers to entities in Q we have to add an inherit clause to P that mentions Q thus

```
package body Q is
   V: Integer;

   --# inherit Q;
   package P is
      -- V has to be referred to here as Q.V in Spark
      ...
   end P;
```

```
   package body P is
      ...
   end P;
end Q;
```

Incidentally we cannot pedantically refer to V as Q.V from immediately within Q but must just write V.

In a way inherit clauses serve two purposes; they make entities visible to the code in the Ada sense and they also make entities visible within the SPARK annotations. As we saw in Section 2.9, there are important circumstances where an entity such as The_Stack.State does not need to be mentioned specifically in the code itself but nevertheless does have to be mentioned in an annotation.

The syntax of an inherit clause is

\+ inherit_clause ::= **--# inherit** *package*_name {, *package*_name};

We say that a package P inherits a package Q if the inherit clause of P mentions the package Q. This is only allowed if

- the declaration of P is within the scope of Q (note that Q could be a library unit), and
- every package (or main subprogram) whose body contains the declaration of P, but not that of Q, inherits Q.

An appropriate interpretation is required for private child packages which are considered to be declared at the start of the body of their parent as was explained in Section 4.2.

The first of these rules is obvious from the normal Ada scope rules and the nested case is illustrated above; an inherit clause is also required if the packages are declared at the same level (even if not library units).

```
package Q is
   ...
end Q;

--# inherit Q;
package P is
   ...
end P;
```

The second rule is more subtle and essentially says that in the case of multiple nesting then the inherit mechanism has to be done step by step. For example

```
--# inherit Q;
package R is
   ...
end R;
```

```
package body R is
   --# inherit Q;
   package P is
      ...
   end P;

   package body P is
      ...
   end P;
end R;
```

This illustrates that the package P nested in R can only inherit Q if R inherits Q first. Remember that packages can only be nested in bodies. Of course if P wishes to refer to a variable declared in R then it will also have to inherit R.

```
--# inherit Q, R;
package P
```

In the case of library units a package P that inherits a package Q will have a with clause for Q as well. However, the with clause might only be on the body whereas the inherit clause always goes on the specification. So we might have

```
with Q;
--# inherit Q;
package P is
   ...
end P;

package body P is
   ...
end P;
```

or, if only the body of P depends upon Q in the Ada sense, we would write

```
--# inherit Q;
package P is
   ...
end P;

with Q;
package body P is
   ...
end P;
```

In a sense SPARK always causes the specification to be dependent although this dependency might not exist in Ada. A similar phenomenon occurs with importing own variables as we saw in the example of the variable Seed in Section 2.5. However, the use of abstract own variables and refinement can be used to prevent such dependencies being a problem as illustrated by The_Stack in Section 2.8.

Child packages follow similar rules. A child package (public or private) always requires an inherit clause in order to access its parent even though no with clause is required. From within a child, entities of the parent must be referred to without using the parent name as a prefix (whereas it could optionally be provided in Ada). So we might have

```
package P is
   type T is ... ;
   ...
end P;

--# inherit P;
package P.Child is
   -- T has to be referred to here as just T and not P.T in Spark
   ...
end P.Child;

package body P.Child is
   ...
end P.Child;
```

On the other hand a parent can never have an inherit clause for its child. In the case of a public child, the parent body is not allowed a with clause for the child anyway and in the case of a private child although a with clause is allowed on the parent body, nevertheless an inherit clause is not required. Thus the following is permitted

```
package P is
   ...
end P;

private package P.Child is
   type T is ... ;
   ...
end P.Child;

with P.Child;
package body P is
   -- T has to be referred to here as Child.T and not P.Child.T
   ...
end P;
```

Note that within the body, an entity of the child is referred to without the common prefix. This is an example of a general rule that when referring from one package to another any common ancestor name is omitted. But the full hierarchical name is always used in with and inherit clauses and in refinement.

Private child packages are treated very like embedded packages in SPARK. Thus an embedded package P requires an inherit clause in order to refer to an outer package Q but not vice versa. In the same way, a private child requires an inherit clause in order to refer to its parent but not vice versa. Moreover, transitive inheritance has to be explicitly stated as for embedded packages. Thus a private child can only have inherit clauses for its parent, other private siblings and any packages inherited by its parent. In contrast, however, a public child is considered to be outside its parent and can inherit any package at all and not just those inherited by its parent.

The similarity between private child packages and embedded packages with regard to names is important. Thus an entity T within P.Child has to be referred to as Child.T from within the body of P in the same way that an entity within an embedded package C has to be referred to as C.T from within the rest of the body of P. As a consequence it is quite easy to restructure a program using embedded packages into one using private child packages.

There is a general rule within a package that a subprogram cannot be called until after its body has been declared (see Section 6.7). This similarly applies to private children which, we recall from Section 4.2, are conceptually declared at the start of the body of their parent. As a consequence a package can call a subprogram in a private child but not vice versa; however the reverse holds for public children – a public child can call a subprogram in its parent but not vice versa. One consequence of these rules is that mutual recursion is forbidden.

The rules regarding two public siblings or two private siblings are as for two unrelated library packages and the rules for a public child of one package and an unrelated package are also as for unrelated packages. Thus one package can inherit the other provided its specification is already in the library and the inherit clause always goes on the specification. However a public child cannot see a private sibling and vice versa.

A minor rule is that an inherit clause for a child implies one for its parent. Thus the following are both permitted and equivalent

```
--# inherit P, P.Child;
--# inherit P.Child;
```

Apart from this case, the gratuitous repetition of a package name in an inherit clause is not permitted.

Inherit clauses are sometimes vital in order to enable annotations to be written; this applies when a chain of packages is used transitively. We discussed this in some detail in Section 2.9 where we showed a main subprogram calling the procedure Use_Stack declared in an intermediate package. Even though the main subprogram does not use The_Stack directly but only indirectly, it does need an inherit clause for The_Stack so that the global annotations can be written correctly. Thus

```
package The_Stack
--# own State;
--# initializes State;
is
   procedure Push(X: in Integer);
   --# global in out State;
   --# derives State from State, X;

   procedure Pop(X: out Integer);
   --# global in out State;
   --# derives State, X from State;
end The_Stack;
```

```
--# inherit The_Stack;
package Go_Between is

   procedure Use_Stack;
   --# global in out The_Stack.State;
   --# derives The_Stack.State from The_Stack.State;

end Go_Between;

with The_Stack;
package body Go_Between is

   procedure Use_Stack is
   begin
      ...
      The_Stack.Push( ... );
      ...
      The_Stack.Pop( ... );
      ...
   end Use_Stack;

end Go_Between;

with Go_Between;
--# inherit The_Stack, Go_Between;
--# main_program;
procedure Main
--# global in out The_Stack.State;
--# derives The_Stack.State from The_Stack.State;
is
begin
   ...
   Go_Between.Use_Stack;
   ...
end Main;
```

The global annotation on the main subprogram reveals that it changes the state of The_Stack even though the details of that state are hidden by the indirection of the code. The inherit clause for The_Stack is necessary so that the annotation can be written; however, there is no need for a with clause for The_Stack because it is not explicitly used by the Ada text.

## 7.3 Own variables

Package annotations concern own variables and their initialization. We discuss own variables in this section and their initialization in the next section. Note that package annotations always go in package specifications whereas any related refinement definitions go in the corresponding package bodies.

The general idea is that an own variable of a package is a variable declared within that package; it could be in the specification or in the body such as Random_Numbers.Seed. It naturally preserves its value between successive calls of subprograms of the package. This basic idea is extended by the concept of refinement outlined in Section 2.8 where we saw how the abstract own variable The_Stack.State was defined in terms of concrete variables S and Pointer declared in the body.

(The geriatric reader will recall that the term own was used in Algol 60 to denote a variable local in scope to a procedure but whose value was nevertheless preserved between successive calls. However, Algol 60 had no concept of packages and also provided no easy way to initialize own variables so the feature was somewhat half-baked.)

An own variable in SPARK is defined as a variable in a package annotation such as

```
--# own Seed;              -- see Section 2.5
--# own State;             -- see Section 2.8
```

Note that the syntax is the same whether the variable is concrete (Seed) or abstract (State); this is as expected since the user of the package does not need to know whether the variable is refined or not. (As we shall see in Section 11.2, it is also possible to give the type of an own variable; this is mandatory for concrete own variables if verification conditions are to be generated.)

The abstract own variable State was then the subject of a refinement definition in the package body thus

```
--# own State is S, Pointer;                -- refinement
```

Note carefully that we do not refer to S and Pointer as own variables at all even though they are declared in the package. It is only the variables in package annotations that are referred to as own variables.

The syntax of a package annotation is

+ package_annotation ::=
  [own_variable_clause [initialization_specification]]

+ own_variable_clause ::= **--# own** own_variable_list;

+ own_variable_list ::= own_variable {, own_variable}

+ own_variable ::= direct_name

The general idea is that own variables should only be updated from outside the package containing them by calling a procedure in the package as for example calling Random updates Seed. However an own variable can be declared in the visible part and can then be updated directly by assignment from outside the package. Nevertheless this is considered bad practice and the Examiner issues a warning. The initialization of own variables is discussed in detail in the next section.

We now consider abstract own variables and the process of refinement in more detail. The stack example from Chapter 2 in outline was

```
package The_Stack
--# own State;
--# initializes State;
is
   procedure Push(X: in Integer);
   --# global in out State;
   --# derives State from State, X;
   ...
end The_Stack;

package body The_Stack
--# own State is S, Pointer;                -- refinement
is
   ...
   S: Vector;
   Pointer: Pointer_Range;

   procedure Push(X: in Integer)
   --# global in out S, Pointer;
   --# derives S       from S, Pointer, X &
   --#         Pointer from Pointer;
   is
   begin
      Pointer := Pointer + 1;
      S(Pointer) := X;
   end Push;
   ...
begin                          -- initialization
   Pointer := 0;
   S := Vector'(Index_Range => 0);
end The_Stack;
```

The abstract own variable thus appears in two distinct package annotations, first to indicate that it is an own variable in the package specification and then in the refinement definition in the body.

The refinement definition has a similar syntax to a dependency relation

+ refinement_definition ::=
    --# **own** refinement_clause {& refinement_clause};
+ refinement_clause ::= subject **is** constituent_list
+ subject ::= direct_name
+ constituent_list ::= constituent {, constituent}
+ constituent ::= [*package*_name .] direct_name

Thus a single refinement definition can give the refinements for several abstract own variables and is typically written over several lines

```
--# own This is A, B, C &
--#     That is P, Q, R;
```

The various constituents must either be variables declared immediately within the package body (such as S and Pointer) or they could be own variables of private child packages or embedded packages declared immediately within the body. These various cases are illustrated by

```
package P
--# own State;
is
   ...
end P;

private package P.C
--# own Z;
is
   ...
end P.C;

with P.C;
package body P
--# own State is X, Q.Y, P.C.Z;
is
   X: Integer;

   package Q
   --# own Y;
   is
      ...
   end Q;
   ...
end P;
```

It is likely although not necessarily the case that the package body will have a with clause for the private child as shown; there will inevitably be one or more procedures in P that manipulate P.C.Z but they might do it indirectly by calling a procedure in a sibling child P.D in which case P would have a with clause for P.D but not necessarily for P.C.

Note that the full hierarchical name is always used in a refinement. Thus we write P.C.Z and not C.Z despite being inside the body of P.

The process of refinement can clearly be repeated since an own variable in the constituent list such as Q.Y might itself be an abstract own variable of the internal package Q. It is important that the constituents are all local to the package (or to a private child or embedded package) so that they truly belong uniquely to the package which is the essence of ownness.

There are various obvious rules of completeness concerning own variables and refinement. Every variable declared immediately within a package must either appear in a package annotation as an own variable or must appear as a constituent in a refinement. Every own variable of an embedded package such as Q.Y or of a private child package such as P.C.Z must also appear in a refinement in the embracing or parent package. And of course a variable cannot be a constituent of more than one refinement. (Incidentally, any own variables of a *public* child are completely independent of the parent.)

Finally, we note that if the specification of a subprogram such as Push has a global annotation mentioning an abstract own variable such as State then the subprogram body has to have refined global and derives annotations written in terms of the concrete variables. (Remember that a subprogram body does not normally have annotations if there is a separate specification.)

There are various consistency rules regarding the original and refined annotations which ensure that the original annotations reflect the correct abstract view of the refined versions. The basic idea is that the original version mentions only those abstract variables whose constituents appear in the refined version.

The refined version must of course be written in terms of how it is implemented and may not need to mention all the variables appearing in the refinement.

Thus suppose the package The_Stack had a function indicating whether the stack was empty. The specification would be

```
function Empty return Boolean;
--# global State;
```

and the body would be

```
function Empty return Boolean
--# global Pointer;
is
begin
   return Pointer = 0;
end Empty;
```

and we note that the global annotation of the refined version does not and indeed must not mention the array S since the code does not use S.

## 7.4 Package initialization

If the own variables of a package are initialized either in their declaration or in the initialization part of the package then the package annotation must contain an initialization specification giving the names of those own variables. For example

```
package Random_Numbers
--# own Seed;
--# initializes Seed;
```

The initialization specification always immediately follows an own variable clause. The syntax is

+ initialization_specification ::= **--# initializes** own_variable_list;

The purpose of an initialization specification is to enable data flow analysis of the clients of the package to be carried out without looking at the details of the package body. Indeed, initialization is always performed during package elaboration and thus before the main subprogram is entered. We are therefore assured that all variables will have been given their initial values before any other code is executed.

Remember that an own variable can also be given a first value by calling a procedure specifically for that purpose. This is not formally considered to be initialization since it will occur after the main subprogram has been called; an initializes specification is therefore not required in this case. The use of undefined values in this dynamic situation is prevented by data flow analysis using the annotations on the procedure in the usual way.

If we mention a variable in an initialization specification then it must either be updated by the package initialization or be initialized in its declaration. Thus the initialization part of the package Random_Numbers can and must update Seed since it is not initialized in its declaration.

In the case of an abstract own variable such as State which is mentioned in an initialization specification then all variables in the refinement must themselves be initialized (but the refinement itself does not have a further initialization specification). Thus the variable State is refined into S and Pointer and so both S and Pointer must be initialized even though we know (from dynamic considerations) that the initialization of S is really unnecessary. We shall return to this problem of partial initialization in Section 12.5 when we consider various categories of state.

There are rules regarding the statements permitted in a package initialization which ensure that elaboration order problems such as shown in Section 4.2 cannot arise. Thus user-defined subprograms cannot be called and variables inherited from other packages cannot be read or updated. The only variables of the package that may be read or updated are the own variables or those appearing in a refinement; moreover the variables must be those which are required to be initialized and no others. (But it is possible to write a for statement and the loop parameter can then be read; an example will be found in Section 9.2.)

For example if we have two own variables of type Integer

```
--# own J, JJ;
```

then the initialization part might be

```
begin
   J := 3;
   JJ := J * J;
end P;
```

In a nested situation where an abstract own variable is refined and one of the constituents of the refinement is an own variable of a private child or an embedded package, then the initialization specifications must be consistent. Thus if this variable in the refinement is required to be initialized (directly or indirectly) then it must be mentioned in an initialization specification in its defining package as in the following

```
package P
--# own State;
--# initializes State;
is
   ...
end P;

package body P
--# own State is X, Q.Y;
is
   X: Integer;

   package Q
   --# own Y;
   --# initializes Y;
      ...
   end Q;
   ...
end P;
```

The reverse is also true. If an own variable of a private child or embedded package is initialized then the outer variable must also be given in an initialization specification.

## 7.5 Global definitions and visibility

We now turn to a further consideration of global definitions of subprograms which were discussed in some detail in the previous chapter.

There are a number of structural visibility rules whose underlying principle is simply that access to global variables should be visibly performed a step at a time. We can access a global variable several layers out but each intervening layer must import the variable using an appropriate mechanism (global or inherit). The rules are best illustrated with examples.

A variable V can only appear in the global definition of a subprogram P (including a main subprogram) if one of the following patterns holds.

(1) P and V are both local to an immediately enclosing declarative region.

```
package Q is
   V: T;

   procedure P ...
   --# global V;

end Q;
```

The enclosing declaration could also be a subprogram. The rule says declarative region so V could be in the specification and P in the body of Q, or both could be in the specification or both in the body.

(2) P is immediately enclosed by a subprogram having V in its global list or as a parameter (that is V must be an imported or exported variable of the subprogram).

```
procedure Q(V: T ... )
--# global W, ...
--# derives ... V ...
is
   procedure P ...
   --# global V, W;
   is ...

begin
   ...
end Q;
```

This shows both possibilities, V is a parameter of Q and W is global to Q; note that V must appear somewhere in a derives list of Q. (Strictly speaking the case of the parameter V is covered by pattern 1.)

(3) V is an own variable of a package Q, and P and Q are both in the same declarative region.

```
procedure M is

   package Q
   --# own V;
      ...
   end Q;

   procedure P ...
   --# global Q.V;
   is ...

begin
   ...
end M;
```

In this case the dotted notation is required to refer to V in the global list (use package clauses are not allowed in SPARK). The embracing declarative region (shown here as the procedure M) could also be a package as in pattern 1.

(4) V is an own variable of an immediately enclosing package. In this case P could be in the package specification or just in the body.

```
package Q
--# own V;
is
   procedure P1 ... ;
   --# global V;

end Q;
```

```
package body Q is

   procedure P1 ... is
   begin
      ...
   end P1;

   procedure P2 ...
   --# global V;
   is
   begin
      ...
   end P2;

end Q;
```

In this case the variable V could be in the specification or in the body of Q. This example shows P1 in the specification of Q and P2 just local to the body. Remember that if a subprogram has both specification and body then the annotations are not repeated in the body. (This is really another case of pattern 1 unless V is abstract.)

(5) V is an own variable of a package inherited by a package immediately enclosing P.

```
--# inherit Q;
package R is

   procedure P ... ;
   --# global Q.V;

end R;
```

This again shows the use of the dotted notation for referring to V.

(6) The final case is where P is the main subprogram and V is inherited by P.

```
--# inherit Q;
--# main_program;
procedure P ...
--# global Q.V;
   ...
end P;
```

Note that we do not necessarily also need a with clause for Q. This was illustrated by the example in Section 7.2 where the main subprogram referred to The_Stack in the global definition but nevertheless did not need a with clause for The_Stack.

All these various cases may seem rather tiresome but remember that the underlying principle is that access to global variables has to be done a step at a time. Note that in the above templates any packages at library level could be child packages.

Finally it should be observed that all variables imported by the main subprogram must be initialized somehow. Such imported variables will be own variables of packages (nothing else could be visible) and these own variables must therefore be initialized. Again this is illustrated by the example in Section 7.2 where State is initialized.

## 7.6 Private types

The declaration of a type as a private type in the visible part of a package makes the type available to other packages whilst hiding the details of its definition. The general idea was illustrated by the type Stack in Section 2.6. Thus the visible part of the package contained

```
type Stack is private;
```

and then in the private part we gave the full declaration

```
private
   Stack_Size: constant := 100;
   type Pointer_Range is range 0 .. Stack_Size;
   subtype Index_Range is Pointer_Range range 1 .. Stack_Size;
   type Vector is array (Index_Range) of Integer;

   type Stack is
      record
         Stack_Vector: Vector;
         Stack_Pointer: Pointer_Range;
      end record;
```

where we also declared a number of auxiliary items.

The syntax of a private type declaration is simply

```
* private_type_declaration ::=
        type defining_identifier is [limited] private;
```

It is also possible to declare a constant of a private type in the visible part even though an initial value cannot be given because the full type is not yet known. Thus we might have

```
Empty_Stack: constant Stack;
```

in the visible part and then in the private part we have to give a further declaration for the constant including its initial value

```
Empty_Stack: constant Stack := Stack'(Vector'(others => 0), 0);
```

Such a constant is termed a deferred constant. A deferred constant need not necessarily be of a private type; for example the type might be a record type one of whose components is itself private.

If a private type (or deferred constant) declaration is given in the visible part of a package then a corresponding declaration of the type (or constant) must appear in the private part of that package.

Between the private declaration and the full type declaration, the type name can only be used in certain contexts. An important restriction is that it cannot be used to declare variables. But it can be used as the type of formal parameters of subprograms and in other type declarations. These rules are all as in Ada. However, many of the minor complexities of Ada do not occur in SPARK because all subtypes in SPARK have to have names.

A private type declaration that includes the reserved word **limited** declares a limited type. A limited type is a type for which neither assignment nor the predefined comparison for equality and inequality is allowed. The full type will generally not be limited and so within the private part and body both assignment and predefined equality and inequality are available. Note that a type is also limited if it has one or more limited components.

A private part can also contain the declarations of renamings and subprogram specifications as well as objects and types not related to the private types mentioned in the visible part. Such declarations are particularly useful with private children since they are visible to child packages but not to client packages in general. Note, however, that subprograms declared here cannot be called by a private child as mentioned in Section 7.2.

## 7.7 Visibility and renaming

The visibility rules are essentially the same as those of Ada except that they are simplified largely as a consequence of the general principle that there should be only one way to refer to a given entity.

The most dramatic difference is that the use package clause is forbidden. This is a fairly common restriction in many user environments on the grounds that use package clauses obscure the origin of variables and consequently make programs hard to read and understand. It is therefore to be expected that SPARK should forbid use package clauses. However, as we shall see in a moment, the use *type* clause is permitted although only within a context clause at the start of a compilation unit. (Use type clauses were added in Ada 95.)

A good illustration of the principle that there should be only one way to refer to an entity is that we cannot gratuitously supply a prefix. Thus within the package The_Stack of Section 2.7 we cannot refer to Pointer as The_Stack. Pointer. So we cannot use the dotted notation when we do not have to.

A subtle aspect of this is that although a loop may be named thus

```
Outer:
for I in Integer range 1 .. 100 loop
   ...
end loop Outer;
```

we cannot refer to the loop variable as Outer.I within the loop (which we can in Ada although it is not very useful).

A number of other rules are essentially consequences of the annotations and have already been mentioned. Thus

- within subprograms and their calls, the uses of parameters and global variables have to be consistent with the dependency clause and global definitions (Section 6.6);
- within a package (or main subprogram), access to entities outside the package has to be consistent with inherit clauses (Section 7.2);
- in a package initialization, the only variables that can be read or updated are those declared immediately within the package (Section 7.4).

There are a number of rules regarding redeclarations some of which we have already mentioned. Overload resolution is not used in SPARK. Every identifier has a unique meaning in a given context and users may not redefine identifiers declared in Standard or overload subprograms in any way. This also implies that enumeration literals may not be overloaded.

There is a general principle regarding redeclarations in nested scopes. The purpose is to ensure that something is not accidentally redeclared with the result that a reference to an existing entity changes accidentally into a reference to the newly declared entity thereby silently changing the meaning of the program. This is sometimes known as preventing an accidental 'hole in the scope'.

The principle is that an identifier that is directly visible (that is by writing X rather than P.X and taking into account the SPARK rules regarding global and inherit annotations) can never be redeclared.

In fact, the identifier of an existing declaration can only be used for a new declaration in the following cases

- The new declaration is in a subprogram and the existing declaration is a variable or parameter that occurs outside the subprogram and is not mentioned in a global annotation of the subprogram.
- The new declaration is in a package and the existing declaration is outside that package and not directly visible in SPARK.
- The new declaration is that of a component of a record type.

One consequence of the first rule is that an imported global variable may not be redeclared immediately inside a subprogram. However, a variable declared external to a subprogram and not mentioned in a global annotation can be redeclared inside the subprogram.

Another consequence is that an identifier used to denote a constant or type may not be redeclared in an inner scope.

The main consequence of the second rule is that the name of a package P inherited by a package Q cannot be used inside Q to declare some other entity. This applies even if the package Q does not have a with clause for P so that P can only be used in annotations anyway. It also applies to nested packages as well as to library packages.

The third rule confirms that we are quite free to use whatever names we like for components of records – subject of course to other rules such as that preventing the reuse of identifiers in Standard.

The absence of use package clauses is a potential problem with operators because the SPARK syntax forbids the notation P."+" for calling an operator and so, without some other technique, operators on user-defined types could not be used at all. Remember that although we cannot explicitly declare our own operators nevertheless the relevant predefined operators are implicitly declared in a package whenever we declare a type in that package.

So if we write

```
package Real_Numbers is
   type Real is digits 9;
   type Long_Real is digits 15;
end Real_Numbers;
```

then we implicitly declare all the operators +, –, * and so on for the types Real and Long_Real in the package Real_Numbers. Outside the package we cannot write

```
X := Real_Numbers."+"(Y, Z);
```

because the prefix notation is not allowed in SPARK. Nor can we write a use package clause for Real_Numbers.

However, as in Ada, we can provide a use type clause within the context clause at the start of a compilation unit. The use type clause must follow a with clause for the package containing the declaration of the types concerned. The syntax is

use_type_clause ::= **use type** subtype_mark {, subtype_mark};

We can now write

```
with Real_Numbers; use type Real_Numbers.Real;
--# inherit Real_Numbers;
--# main_program;
procedure Main
--# derives ... ;
is
   X, Y, Z: Real_Numbers.Real;
begin
   ...
   X := Y + Z;
   ...
end Main;
```

which shows the normal infixed notation within that unit. Note that Ada also permits a use type clause within any declaration list; this is not permitted in SPARK.

It should be noted that use type clauses do not suffer from the evils of use package clauses because we cannot declare new operators nor (in SPARK) give new meanings to existing operators.

The effect of a use type clause also extends to any internal packages although such internal packages would almost inevitably need further inherit clauses for the package containing the type as discussed in Section 7.2. (But of course an internal package never has a with clause.)

Even with use type clauses, the absence of use package clauses can be cumbersome and so renaming is permitted in strictly controlled circumstances. At the beginning of this chapter we noted that renaming declarations were treated specially in the syntax. Renaming is only permitted for subprograms (including operators) and only in certain places. Renaming of a subprogram is only allowed for a subprogram declared in a package P and then

- renamings are allowed immediately after the declaration of the specification of a package P if it is an embedded package;
- renamings are allowed at the start of the body of a package (or main subprogram) which inherits P or is the parent of P (remember that a package does not need an inherit clause for a private child);
- renamings of operators are allowed at the start of the visible part or private part of a package which inherits P.

Another vital point is that the new name must be the same as the old name without the package prefix and moreover all formal parameters have to have the same name and the same named subtype as well. So renaming just enables us to omit the prefix and otherwise we cannot change the name. But of course the important point is that, unlike use clauses, the full name is still visible in the unit using the abbreviation because the renaming shows exactly what is going on.

If we do provide a renaming then we must use the abbreviated form and the old dotted name is no longer allowed. This accords with the general principle stated at the beginning of this section that there should be only one way to refer to an entity.

The syntax is

* renaming_declaration ::=
  **function** defining_operator_symbol formal_part **return** subtype_mark
      **renames** *package*_name . operator_symbol;
  | function_specification
      **renames** *package*_name . *function*_direct_name;
  | procedure_specification
      **renames** *package*_name . *procedure*_direct_name;

The various possibilities can be illustrated by the package The_Stack. If this package were embedded then we could rename Push and Pop immediately after its specification as shown below. But note that renaming can only be applied to subprograms and so we still have to refer to the own variable as The_Stack.State.

```
package body Q is

   package The_Stack
   --# own State;
      ...
   end The_Stack;            -- end of specification

   procedure Push(X: in Integer) renames The_Stack.Push;
   procedure Pop(X: out Integer) renames The_Stack.Pop;
   ...
   procedure Use_Stack
   --# global in out The_Stack.State;
   --# derives The_Stack.State from The_Stack.State;
   is
   begin
      ...
      Push( ... );            -- rather than The_Stack.Push
      ...
      Pop( ... );
      ...
   end Use_Stack;

end Q;
```

On the other hand suppose that The_Stack were declared outside and then inherited as in the chained example with the package Go_Between in Section 7.2. We could then rename Push and Pop immediately within the body of Go_Between thus

```
--# inherit The_Stack;
package Go_Between is

   procedure Use_Stack;
   --# global in out The_Stack.State;
   --# derives The_Stack.State from The_Stack.State;

end Go_Between;

with The_Stack;
package body Go_Between is

   procedure Push(X: in Integer) renames The_Stack.Push;
   procedure Pop(X: out Integer) renames The_Stack.Pop;

   procedure Use_Stack is
   begin
      ...
      Push( ... );
      ...
      Pop( ... );
      ...
   end Use_Stack;

end Go_Between;
```

Renaming for operators was vital before the introduction of use type clauses because, as mentioned above, the prefix notation is not permitted. It should now be considered somewhat obsolescent although it is retained for compatibility. We can use renaming either immediately after the package (note that a use type clause is not permitted at this position) or at the start of a body which inherits the package. So the earlier example could be rewritten as

```
with Real_Numbers;
--# inherit Real_Numbers;
--# main_program;
procedure Main
--# derives ... ;
is
   function "+" (Left, Right: Real_Numbers.Real)
                return Real_Numbers.Real renames Real_Numbers."+";
   X, Y, Z: Real_Numbers.Real;
begin
   ...
   X := Y + Z;
   ...
end Main;
```

It is clear that the use type clause is more compact particularly since it embraces all the operators of the type whereas a renaming has to be supplied for each one.

Incidentally we could also write

```
subtype Real is Real_Numbers.Real;
```

in order to avoid the tedium of the full type name. This is a bit of a trick and cannot be used for composite types.

Without use type clauses, renaming of operators in a package specification was vital for writing initial values such as negative constants. So

```
with Real_Numbers;
--# inherit Real_Numbers;
package Limits is
   function "-" (Right: Real_Numbers.Real)
                return Real_Numbers.Real renames Real_Numbers."-";
   Lower_Limit: constant Real_Numbers.Real := -5.5;
   Upper_Limit: constant Real_Numbers.Real := 6.5;
   ...
end Limits;
```

Observe that in the case of operators the formal parameters are always Left and Right (or just Right if only one) which are the curious names of the formal parameters of the predefined operators. Actually these names never get used in SPARK other than in renaming declarations.

Operator renaming, like use type clauses, is effective within inner packages and does not have to be repeated.

## 7.8 Compilation units

The full details of how the various parts of a program are compiled and linked to form a complete program are somewhat outside the domain of the Ada language itself and depend upon the implementation.

However, the general idea is that the program is written as a number of library units and these can be compiled separately. The source and object of these units are typically held in a program library and one important aspect of the library system is to ensure that the various units are consistent. The means by which this is done is not prescribed but we are assured that it is impossible to link a program out of inconsistent units.

The various library items (specifications, bodies or subunits) may be compiled separately or can be grouped together into one or more compilations. Thus each compilation is a succession of compilation units.

```
  compilation ::= {compilation_unit}

  compilation_unit ::=
          context_clause library_item | context_clause subunit

* library_item ::=
        [private] package_declaration | package_body | main_subprogram

+ main_subprogram ::=
          [inherit_clause]
          main_subprogram_annotation
          subprogram_body

+ main_subprogram_annotation ::= --# main_program;
```

As in Ada, within a program library the names of all library units must be distinct. The main differences from Ada are that renaming is not allowed at the library level and that separate subprogram specifications are not allowed. There are also no child subprograms.

Note that the main subprogram in SPARK has an annotation indicating that it is the main subprogram (for historic reasons it is **main_program**). The main subprogram also has an optional inherit clause as discussed in Section 7.2. In fact the only subprogram allowed at the library level is the main subprogram and there can only be one such subprogram in a library. The main subprogram can have parameters as in Ada.

Context clauses specify the interdependence of library units. Observe that since a subprogram is only allowed at the library level if it is a main subprogram, it follows that a context clause cannot refer to subprograms but only to packages.

```
  context_clause ::= {context_item}

* context_item ::= with_clause | use_type_clause

* with_clause ::=
          with library_package_name {, library_package_name};
```

A context clause may have several with clauses and use type clauses. A use type clause must follow the with clauses mentioning the packages concerned. The following lines are equivalent

```
with A, B, C; use type A.S, B.T;
with A; with B; use type A.S, B.T; with C;
with A; use type A.S; with B; use type B.T; with C;
```

Note that a package name or type name cannot gratuitously appear more than once in the same context clause except that a with clause for a child package implies one for its parent which could also be given explicitly (a similar rule applies to inherit clauses as mentioned in Section 7.2). But a context clause might repeat items already visible through other context clauses. Thus the body of package P could have a with clause for another package Q even though it was already given on the specification of P – this might be useful for placing a use type clause for a type Q.T just on the body of P.

An important rule in Ada which equally applies to SPARK is that the context clause on a package specification also applies implicitly to the specifications of all its child packages. But this is not true of inherit clauses which must always be given explicitly in this situation.

## 7.9 Subunits

Subunits just as in Ada are used for the separate compilation of the body of a program unit declared within another compilation unit. Both subprograms and packages can be subunits. The general idea is that the body is removed from its parent unit and replaced by a stub and then the body can be compiled separately.

Thus taking the first version of The_Stack in Section 2.7, the package body would become

```
package body The_Stack is
   Stack_Size: constant Integer := 100;
   subtype Index_Range is Integer range 1 .. Stack_Size;
   type Vector is array (Index_Range) of Integer;
   S: Vector;
   subtype Pointer_Range is Integer range 0 .. Stack_Size;
   Pointer: Pointer_Range;

   procedure Push(X: in Integer) is separate;

   procedure Pop(X: out Integer) is separate;
begin                          -- initialization
   Pointer := 0;
end The_Stack;
```

and the subunit for Push would become

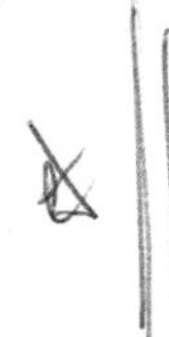

```
separate(The_Stack)
procedure Push(X : in Integer) is
begin
   Pointer := Pointer + 1;
   S(Pointer) := X;
end Push;
```

and similarly for Pop. Note the separate clause which indicates the name of the body from which the unit has been taken. The syntax is

* body_stub ::= subprogram_body_stub | package_body_stub

* subprogram_body_stub ::=
        procedure_specification [procedure_annotation] **is separate**;
      | function_specification [function_annotation] **is separate**;

package_body_stub ::= **package body** defining_identifier **is separate**;

subunit ::= **separate** (parent_unit_name) proper_body

A body stub may only occur immediately within the declarative part of a compilation unit. The process can be repeated to any level, thus a subunit can have its own subunits. It is important to note that the visibility within the subunit is exactly that at the stub and so the procedure Push can still refer to the global variables S and Pointer.

There is never any annotation on the subunit itself although there might be on the stub. Thus if we take the refined version of The_Stack from Section 2.8, then the procedure body Push has a refined global and derives annotation and this is applied to the stub which therefore becomes

```
procedure Push(X : in Integer)
--# global in out S, Pointer;
--# derives S       from S, Pointer, X &
--#         Pointer from Pointer;
is separate;
```

and the subunit itself remains as before.

Subunits are very useful for subprograms. But in the case of packages, private child packages offer advantages because both specification and body are then compiled separately. This means that a change to the specification of one private child need not cause recompilation of all its siblings; on the other hand, using subunits, a change to the specification of one causes the whole of the package body including all other subunits to be recompiled.

## 7.10 Compilation order

The rules for order of compilation follow those of Ada and are designed to ensure that the units in a total program are consistent. The details of the library system depend upon the implementation, but the general principle is that a unit cannot be compiled until after all those units it depends upon are entered into the library. Some implementations may follow the austere Ada 83 rules and insist that a dependent unit must not only be entered into the library but also be compiled as well before units dependent on it can themselves be compiled.

Remember that a unit is dependent upon the specifications of all those mentioned in with clauses and that a body is also dependent upon the corresponding specification. A child unit is dependent upon the specification of its parent and a subunit is dependent upon its parent unit (which will be a library unit body or another subunit).

The rules for the order of compilation are thus

- A compilation unit can only be compiled after the specifications of all packages named by its with clause are entered into the library.
- A package body can only be compiled after its specification has been entered into the library.
- A child unit can only be compiled after the specification of its parent has been entered into the library.
- Any subunit of a compilation unit can only be compiled after the compilation unit in which its body stub occurs is entered into the library.

Another consequence of the need for consistency is that if a compilation unit is changed then all compilation units dependent upon it must be recompiled.

The SPARK system has similar rules for the order of examination by the SPARK Examiner. However, the dependencies are indicated by the inherit clauses rather than the with clauses. Moreover, it should be remembered that inherit clauses (unlike with clauses) always go on a specification and never on a body as discussed in Section 7.2. As a consequence this may impose stricter orders of examination and need for reexamination.

Thus suppose we have three packages User, Servant and Slave where the body of the package Servant directly accessed by the User is in turn implemented using the package Slave. Moreover suppose that the specification of Servant does not depend upon Slave in the Ada sense; in other words the User does not need to be aware of the Slave at all. The Ada structure is

```
package Servant is
   ...
end;

with Slave;
package body Servant is
   ...
end Servant;

with Servant;
package User is ...
```

The structure is such that the package User does not depend upon the Slave and so any changes to the Slave will not require recompilation of the User.

However, if we now add the SPARK annotations the structure becomes

```
--# inherit Slave;
package Servant is
   ...
end;

with Slave;
package body Servant is
   ...
end Servant;

with Servant;
--# inherit Servant, Slave;
package User is ...
```

The SPARK dependency is tighter and if the Slave is changed then the Servant will need to be reexamined and so will the User even though the User will not need to be recompiled.

Note that the User might not need an inherit clause for the Slave. It only needs one if the Slave directly changes some internal state. It would not need an inherit clause if the Slave just computed some function or if the Slave only changed the state of the Servant. But of course the User will need reexamining anyway because of the inherit clause for the Servant.

Another difference between inherit and with clauses is that with clauses only apply to library units whereas inherit clauses apply also to the internal structure. However the Examiner always works in terms of library units and so internal inherit clauses are irrelevant to the order of examination.

## Summary

In the areas covered by this chapter, the main differences between SPARK and Ada are that in SPARK:

- A package may not be declared within an enclosing package specification.
- Subprograms may only be declared separately from their bodies (or body stubs) in package specifications.
- Inherit clauses are required.
- Own variables must be named in a package specification.
- A package initialization can only be used to initialize own variables of that package.
- Private types cannot have discriminants. (In fact no type can have a discriminant.)
- Use package clauses are not allowed.

- Use type clauses are only allowed in context clauses.
- A public child is not visible to the body of its parent.
- A public child is not visible to a private sibling and vice versa.
- There are no child subprograms.
- The only subprogram that can be separately compiled is the main subprogram.

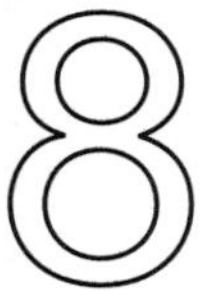

# Interfacing



We have now covered essentially all aspects of the SPARK core language. We have seen that SPARK is a rich language by some standards (for example it has packages and private types unlike Pascal and C) but, on the other hand, is necessarily simpler than full Ada in order to enable programs to be proved. As a consequence it may not be possible to write the whole of a system in SPARK. We may need to use full Ada for certain parts or we may need to interface to possibly preexisting code written in some other language such as assembler or C. An important example is interfacing to Commercial Off The Shelf (COTS) software.

In this chapter we discuss how such interfacing is achieved and also illustrate the techniques by discussing the predefined library and other peripheral matters.

## 8.1 Interfacing pragmas

The normal way in which an Ada program interfaces to programs in other languages is through the use of various pragmas. A SPARK program can use the same technique and indeed a SPARK program can interface to a program written in full Ada in this way.

We can call a subprogram written in another language by using the pragma Import. Thus to call a procedure P written in the C language we would declare just a specification for P followed by the pragma Import as follows

```
procedure P( ... );
--# derives This from That;
pragma Import(C, P);
```

The pragma tells the compiler and the Examiner not to expect a body for P. It also indicates that the calling convention is that of C. Note that the Examiner requires the normal annotations on the specification.

A SPARK program could call a procedure Action written in full Ada by giving the language convention as Ada thus

```
procedure Action( ... );                    -- the Spark code
--# derives This from That;
pragma Import(Ada, Action);
```

In its turn the full Ada program has to export the name of the procedure so that it can be called from outside (since the Ada program does not know that the procedure is being called by a SPARK program of course). This is done by placing a pragma Export after the specification of the procedure in the full Ada code.

```
procedure Action( ... );                    -- the full Ada code
pragma Export(Ada, Action);
```

A consequence of this technique is that the checking of parameters between the call in the SPARK program and the code in the Ada program is lost. The pragmas Import and Export may have other parameters giving the name of the subprogram in the foreign language and the link name if these are different.

The Examiner generally ignores pragmas other than checking their syntax. But it does recognize Import since it has to know not to expect a body. Note that Import was known as Interface in Ada 83.

## 8.2 Hidden text

Using the pragmas Import and Export to interface to another language suffers from the disadvantage that it only works in terms of complete subprograms. An alternative is to use hidden text which is a piece of the program which will be ignored by the Examiner. It may be of any form, including full Ada.

The parts of a program which may be hidden are

- a subprogram body,
- the private part of a package,

- a package body (including a possible initialization part),
- the initialization part of a package.

The hidden text is indicated by the hide directive which takes the form of an annotation consisting of the reserved word **hide** followed by the name of the subprogram or package concerned. For example a subprogram implementation can be hidden from the Examiner thus

```
procedure Secret
--# global out This; in That;
--# derives This from That;
is
   --# hide Secret
   ...   -- hidden text
end Secret;
```

The hide directive has to follow the **is** of the body; its effect is to tell the SPARK Examiner not to analyse the hidden text but just to skip looking for the **end** and the name of the subprogram. (It is perhaps neater to follow the directive with a semicolon although this is naturally hidden and thus ignored!)

In the case of a package, the hide directive is allowed immediately after **private**, after the **is** of the body and after **begin** of the body. The Examiner then skips the private part, the whole of the body or the initialization part respectively until it finds the final **end** and package name.

The form of the hidden text is not specified in SPARK although typically it will just be Ada code which for some reason we do not want to be analysed. This is often helpful to support program development by successive refinement whereby we want the Examiner to ignore parts of a program which are not complete or not yet written at all.

Indeed, as mentioned in Section 2.5 where the private part of the package Stacks was hidden, the hide directive enables parts of a program to be examined even though the program cannot be compiled. Thus we had

```
package Stacks is

   type Stack is private;

   function Is_Empty(S: Stack) return Boolean;
   function Is_Full(S: Stack) return Boolean;

   procedure Clear(S: in out Stack);
   --# derives S from ;

   procedure Push(S: in out Stack; X: in Integer);
   --# derives S from S, X;

   procedure Pop(S: in out Stack; X: out Integer);
   --# derives S, X from S;

private
   --# hide Stacks;
end Stacks;
```

The specification of the package Stacks can be examined and other packages using it can also be examined even though the package specification cannot be compiled because the private part is incomplete.

Hidden text may thus be used either to ignore incomplete parts of a program during examination or to hide parts of a program where one needs to use full Ada or even another language. This often happens when it is necessary to employ a predefined package, or a package provided by a compiler vendor, where the specification does not obey the rules of SPARK. Good examples are provided by input–output as we shall see in a moment.

Strictly speaking the hide directive is considered to be a tool directive and not part of the SPARK language itself. This explains why the syntax of SPARK does not include hidden text and indeed it is difficult to express in syntactic terms the concept of skipping to the appropriate **end**. A more important philosophical thought is that any program unit including a hide directive is really not a SPARK program unit at all because anything could be included. Interfacing using pragma Import does not suffer from this difficulty because a proper interface is provided by the SPARK specification of the imported subprogram whereas no interface is prescribed when using the hide directive.

## 8.3 External sequences

In Section 2.8 we saw how abstract own variables could be refined to correspond to concrete variables declared in a package body. Another use for abstract own variables occurs where the variable in the annotation does not actually correspond to explicit variables in the Ada program at all but only exists in the SPARK annotations for the purpose of reasoning about part of the program from the point of view of the calling code.

Consider the problem of reading some external gadget such as the clock. Successive reads will deliver a new value and this means that the clock cannot be read by a function since functions in SPARK always return the same value unless some other procedure call updates the state. This was illustrated by the random number generator where we decomposed the original procedure Random into a procedure Update and a function Random. In the case of the clock there is no other procedure to intervene and so we have to read the clock with a procedure rather than a function. We might consider

```
procedure Read_Clock(T: out Time);
--# derives T from ;
```

and then

```
procedure Read_Clock(T: out Time) is
   --# hide Read_Clock;
   ... -- this part is not analysed by the Spark Examiner
   ... -- and so can use full Ada or code and so on
end Read_Clock;
```

However, this is not acceptable because it implies that the time never changes. Although there would be no problem in writing the body (which is hidden so that we can use full Ada and thus perhaps call Ada.Calendar.Clock) nevertheless there are likely to be problems when examining the calling code. The Examiner is likely to complain that certain calls of Read_Clock are ineffective since they seem to produce the same value; this might result in so-called stable loops (loops which seem to do nothing) and as a consequence the program would be rejected.

The proper approach is to recognize the existence of some time state which changes independently of the program. We can consider this as represented by an external sequence of values and that each time we read the clock we consume an item of the sequence. This sequence can then be modelled as an abstract variable of a time package such as

```
package Timing
--# own Time_Sequence;
--# initializes Time_Sequence;
is
   procedure Read_Clock(T: out Time);
   --# global in out Time_Sequence;
   --# derives T, Time_Sequence from Time_Sequence;

end Timing;
```

The package body can then be hidden thus

```
package body Timing is
   --# hide Timing;
   -- package body is not analysed by the Spark Examiner

   procedure Read_Clock(T: out Time) is
   begin
      ...
   end Read_Clock;

end Timing;
```

and there is no refinement for Time_Sequence nor is it declared in any other way.

Another example which illustrates the same sort of problem might be a procedure which simply causes the process to wait for a certain time. Just writing

```
procedure Wait(T: in Time);
--# derives ;
```

is not permissible since a procedure with an import must also have at least one export as explained in Section 6.6. Moreover, if a derives list is given then T must appear in it anyway.

The solution is again to use an external sequence thus

```
procedure Wait(T: in Time);
--# global in out Time_Sequence;
--# derives Time_Sequence from Time_Sequence, T;
```

The technique of external sequences can be used for input and output generally. Thus packages for reading from and writing to input and output ports might have specifications as follows

```
package Input_Port
--# own Input_Sequence;
--# initializes Input_Sequence;
is
   procedure Read_From_Port(Input_Value: out Integer);
   --# global in out Input_Sequence;
   --# derives Input_Sequence, Input_Value from Input_Sequence;

   function End_Of_Input_Sequence return Boolean;
   --# global Input_Sequence;

end Input_Port;

package Output_Port
--# own Output_Sequence;
--# initializes Output_Sequence;
is
   procedure Write_To_Port(Output_Value: in Integer);
   --# global in out Output_Sequence;
   --# derives Output_Sequence from Output_Sequence, Output_Value;

end Output_Port;
```

Again the state is represented by sequences which are abstract own variables. The sequence of all items which may be read successively from the input port is represented by the own variable Input_Sequence and similarly for Output_Sequence.

---

## EXERCISE 8.3

1 Write a main subprogram to read a sequence of unsigned integers from an input port and then write the sequence to an output port in reverse order. Both sequences are terminated with the value zero. Assume the existence of the packages Input_Port and Output_Port of this section and the package The_Stack of Section 2.8.

2 Rewrite the previous exercise using the abstract type Stack of Section 2.6. Also assume that the end of the sequence is detected by the function End_Of_Input_Sequence so that the sequence can contain any values and thus is not restricted to being terminated by a zero.

---

## 8.4 The predefined library

The Ada predefined library comprises three packages Ada, System and Interfaces. Each of these contains a number of child packages. The package System is concerned with intrinsic aspects of the implementation such as heap storage and is almost entirely outside the scope of SPARK. The package Interfaces is concerned with interfacing to other languages such as Fortran, COBOL and C. The package Ada contains traditional predefined material such as mathematical functions and input–output facilities.

Much of the predefined library of Ada cannot be directly accessed by a SPARK program simply because the predefined library uses facilities not supported by SPARK (such as exceptions and generics). The library therefore has to be used indirectly using hiding introduced above; this is illustrated in the next section when we consider the package Spark_IO which provides text input–output and may be used instead of the package Ada.Text_IO of full Ada.

The only package that has an interface that conforms to the rules of SPARK and so can be accessed directly is Ada.Characters.Latin_1.

The reader will recall that the predefined packages of Ada 83 are structured as child packages such as Ada.Text_IO of the package Ada in Ada 95. However, Ada 95 provides library renamings such as

```
with Ada.Text_IO;
package Text_IO renames Ada.Text_IO;
```

so that compatibility with the Ada 83 view is preserved. (Such renamings are not permitted in SPARK.) Note moreover that the package Spark_IO is not a child of Ada.

The package Standard is a vital part of the Ada predefined library and indeed all library units are considered as children of Standard in Ada 95. However, the package Standard does not necessarily really exist; it is simply that the compiler behaves much as if it does. When compiling a SPARK program we are of course using a normal Ada compiler and so the full package Standard automatically applies. However, when examining a SPARK program the Examiner will reject the program if it uses certain features of full Ada which are normally represented as being declared in Standard. Thus we can think of SPARK as having a somewhat simpler package Standard which is used by the Examiner.

The main differences are

- the functions "<", "<=", ">", ">=" are not defined for Boolean,
- the functions "*" and "/" for universal fixed are treated differently,
- there are no types Wide_Character and Wide_String,
- there is no type Duration,
- there are no predefined exceptions.

In addition, remember that the embedded package ASCII is obsolescent and superseded by the child package Ada.Characters.Latin_1.

## 8.5 Spark_IO

Because the standard Ada input–output packages contain features not supported by SPARK, a special package called Spark_IO is provided for the manipulation of text.

Of course, Spark_IO does not have to be used; it is simply an example of a possible means of interfacing to the predefined package Ada.Text_IO and is provided as a convenience. Nevertheless we will consider it in some detail because it provides a good illustration of the use of hiding and external sequences.

Spark_IO contains facilities for file manipulation and input–output of the predefined types Character, String, Integer and Float. Facilities for the input and output of user-defined integer and floating point types, fixed point types and enumeration types must be provided by the user if required. (These can be based on procedures in Spark_IO, whose specification and body are provided in full on the CD that accompanies this book.)

Spark_IO is implemented in terms of Text_IO and so follows its general principles. Thus values input from the external environment of the program, or output to the environment, are considered to occupy external files. An external file can be anything external to the program that can produce a value or receive a value to be written.

As in Text_IO, an external file is identified by a string giving the name of the file. A second string – the form – gives further system-dependent characteristics that may be associated with the file. Input and output operations are expressed as operations taking a parameter of the internal type Spark_IO.File_Type, rather than directly in terms of the external files. Procedures enable the external file and the internal file object to be associated.

The package Spark_IO has an abstract own variable File_Sys, which can be considered to represent the set of external files used by a program. File_Sys is a global variable of all the predefined input–output procedures and is updated by many of them. The abstract variable File_Sys is not refined because the body of Spark_IO is hidden and thus behaves much like the abstract variable Time_Sequence discussed in Section 8.3.

The set of external files represented by File_Sys always contains the standard input file, identified by the constant Spark_IO.Standard_Input, and the standard output file, identified by the constant Spark_IO.Standard_Output.

If something goes wrong with Text_IO in full Ada then one of various exceptions is raised. However, SPARK does not support exceptions and so this approach is not possible in Spark_IO. Instead a status type is defined

```
type File_Status is (OK, Status_Error, Mode_Error, Name_Error, ... );
```

whose literals correspond to the exceptions of Ada.IO_Exceptions in full Ada plus the literal OK. The various subprograms then have a parameter of the type File_Status which indicates whether an error condition has arisen. If a status parameter indicates that an error has occurred then any other returned values are undefined and the onus is on the programmer to perform appropriate recovery actions.

The text of the specification of Spark_IO is shown below and illustrates the use of various SPARK annotations. For convenience it is interspersed with a few brief notes of explanation emphasizing the differences from the corresponding facilities of Text_IO.

```
with Ada.Text_IO;
package Spark_IO
   --# own File_Sys;
   --# initializes File_Sys;
is
   type File_Type is limited private;
   type File_Mode is (In_File, Out_File, Append_File);

   type File_Status is (OK, Status_Error, Mode_Error, Name_Error,
         Use_Error, Device_Error, End_Error, Data_Error, Layout_Error);

   subtype Number_Base is Integer range 2 .. 16;

   Standard_Input: constant File_Type;
   Standard_Output: constant File_Type;

-- File Management

   procedure Create(File: in out File_Type;
                    Name_Of_File: in String;
                    Form_Of_File: in String;
                    Status: out File_Status);
   --# global in out File_Sys;
   --# derives File_Sys, File, Status from File_Sys, File,
   --#                                  Name_Of_File, Form_Of_File;

   procedure Open(File: in out File_Type;
                  Mode_Of_File: in File_Mode;
                  Name_Of_File: in String;
                  Form_Of_File: in String;
                  Status: out File_Status);
   --# global in out File_Sys;
   --# derives File_Sys, File, Status from File_Sys, File,
   --#                    Mode_Of_File, Name_Of_File, Form_Of_File;

   procedure Close(File: in out File_Type;
                   Status: out File_Status);
   --# global in out File_Sys;
   --# derives File_Sys, Status from File_Sys, File &
   --#         File from File;

   procedure Delete(File: in out File_Type;
                    Status: out File_Status);
   --# global in out File_Sys;
   --# derives File_Sys, Status from File_Sys, File &
   --#         File from File;
```

```
procedure Reset(File: in out File_Type;
                Mode_Of_File: in File_Mode;
                Status: out File_Status);
--# global in out File_Sys;
--# derives File_Sys, Status from File_Sys, File, Mode_Of_File &
--#         File from File, Mode_Of_File;
```

The procedures Create, Open, Close, Delete and Reset are much as expected. However, there are no default parameters in SPARK and so actual parameters for Name_Of_File and Form_Of_File always have to be supplied. Another point is that Create does not have a parameter Mode and so any new file is automatically of mode Out_File; this seems sensible and Out_File is the default value in Text_IO anyway. Note also the mode Append_File which is additional in SPARK 95 and corresponds to the similar change to Text_IO in Ada 95. All these procedures have a final parameter Status which, as mentioned above, returns a status value indicating whether the call was successful or not.

```
function Valid_File(File: in File_Type) return Boolean;
--# global File_Sys;

function Mode(File: in File_Type) return File_Mode;
--# global File_Sys;

procedure Name(File: in File_Type;
               Name_Of_File: out String;
               Stop: out Natural);
--# global in File_Sys;
--# derives Name_Of_File, Stop from File, File_Sys;

procedure Form(File: in File_Type;
               Form_Of_File: out String;
               Stop: out Natural);
--# global in File_Sys;
--# derives Form_Of_File, Stop from File, File_Sys;

function Is_Open(File: in File_Type) return Boolean;
--# global File_Sys;
```

Procedures Name and Form replace the corresponding functions of Text_IO because functions in SPARK are not permitted to return an unconstrained type such as String. The result is instead returned through the out parameter Name_Of_File or Form_Of_File with the parameter Stop indexing the last character copied; if the out parameter is not long enough then the result is truncated and Stop set equal to one more than the length of the parameter.

Incidentally note that the names of the parameters are Name_Of_File, Mode_Of_File and Form_Of_File rather than the briefer Name, Mode and Form as in Text_IO. This is because of the rule in SPARK that an identifier cannot be redeclared in a local scope and therefore a formal parameter of a subprogram cannot have the same identifier as the subprogram itself.

The functions Mode and Is_Open directly correspond. The function Valid_File is additional and checks that the parameter is valid.

There is no concept of default files in SPARK largely because the spirit of the language requires things to be stated explicitly. There are therefore no subprograms such as Set_Output for manipulating default files. The standard files are explicitly represented by the constants Standard_Input and Standard_Output.

The files always have unbounded line and page length and so there are no subprograms such as Set_Line_Length. Otherwise column manipulation within a line is much as in Text_IO although line manipulation on a page is not fully supported.

```
-- Column, Line and Page Control

  procedure New_Line(File: in File_Type;
                     Spacing: in Positive);
  --# global in out File_Sys;
  --# derives File_Sys from File_Sys, File, Spacing;

  procedure Skip_Line(File: in File_Type;
                      Spacing: in Positive);
  --# global in out File_Sys;
  --# derives File_Sys from File_Sys, File, Spacing;

  procedure New_Page(File: in File_Type);
  --# global in out File_Sys;
  --# derives File_Sys from File_Sys, File;

  function End_Of_Line(File: in File_Type) return Boolean;
  --# global File_Sys;

  function End_Of_File(File: in File_Type) return Boolean;
  --# global File_Sys;

  procedure Set_Col(File: in File_Type;
                    Posn: in Positive);
  --# global in out File_Sys;
  --# derives File_Sys from File_Sys, File, Posn;

  function Col(File: in File_Type) return Positive;
  --# global File_Sys;

  function Line(File: in File_Type) return Positive;
  --# global File_Sys;
```

The procedures New_Line (for output) and Skip_Line (for input) always have to give both the file and the number of lines because there are no default parameters. The number of lines is sensibly of the subtype Positive rather than the peculiar subtype Positive_Count of Text_IO. The subprograms Set_Col and Col set and read the current column position within a line (the first being 1). There is also the function End_Of_Line. The corresponding facilities for pages are limited. There is a procedure New_Page but no procedure Skip_Page. The function Line gives the current line on the page but there is no corresponding procedure Set_Line or function End_Of_Page or Page. Finally there is the function End_Of_File.

```
-- Character Input-Output

  procedure Get_Char(File: in File_Type;
                     Item: out Character);
  --# global in out File_Sys;
  --# derives File_Sys, Item from File_Sys, File;

  procedure Put_Char(File: in File_Type;
                     Item: in Character);
  --# global in out File_Sys;
  --# derives File_Sys from File_Sys, File, Item;

-- String Input-Output

  procedure Get_String(File: in File_Type;
                       Item: out String;
                       Stop: out Natural);
  --# global in out File_Sys;
  --# derives File_Sys, Item, Stop from File_Sys, File;

  procedure Put_String(File: in File_Type;
                       Item: in String;
                       Stop: in Natural);
  --# global in out File_Sys;
  --# derives File_Sys from File_Sys, File, Item, Stop;

  procedure Get_Line(File: in File_Type;
                     Item: out String;
                     Stop: out Natural);
  --# global in out File_Sys;
  --# derives File_Sys, Item, Stop from File_Sys, File;

  procedure Put_Line(File: in File_Type;
                     Item: in String;
                     Stop: in Natural);
  --# global in out File_Sys;
  --# derives File_Sys from File_Sys, File, Item, Stop;

-- Integer Input-Output

-- Spark_IO only supports input-output of
-- the predefined integer type Integer

  procedure Get_Integer(File: in File_Type;
                        Item: out Integer;
                        Width: in Natural;
                        Read: out Boolean);
  --# global in out File_Sys;
  --# derives File_Sys, Item, Read from File_Sys, File, Width;

  procedure Put_Integer(File: in File_Type;
                        Item: in Integer;
```

```
                          Width: in Natural;
                          Base: in Number_Base);
   --# global in out File_Sys;
   --# derives File_Sys from File_Sys, File, Item, Width, Base;

   procedure Get_Int_From_String(Source: in String;
                                 Item: out Integer;
                                 Start_Pos: in Positive;
                                 Stop: out Natural);
   --# derives Item, Stop from Source, Start_Pos;

   procedure Put_Int_To_String(Dest: in out String;
                               Item: in Integer;
                               Start_Pos: in Positive;
                               Base: in Number_Base);
   --# derives Dest from Dest, Item, Start_Pos, Base;

-- Floating point Input-Output

-- Spark_IO only supports input-output of
-- the predefined real type Float

   procedure Get_Float(File: in File_Type;
                       Item: out Float;
                       Width: in Natural;
                       Read: out Boolean);
   --# global in out File_Sys;
   --# derives File_Sys, Item, Read from File_Sys, File, Width;

   procedure Put_Float(File: in File_Type;
                       Item: in Float;
                       Fore: in Natural;
                       Aft: in Natural;
                       Exp: in Natural);
   --# global in out File_Sys;
   --# derives File_Sys from File_Sys, File, Item, Fore, Aft, Exp;

   procedure Get_Float_From_String(Source: in String;
                                   Item: out Float;
                                   Start_Pos: in Positive;
                                   Stop: out Natural);
   --# derives Item, Stop from Source, Start_Pos;

   procedure Put_Float_To_String(Dest: in out String;
                                 Item: in Float;
                                 Start_Pos: in Positive;
                                 Aft: in Natural;
                                 Exp: in Natural);
   --# derives Dest from Dest, Item, Start_Pos, Aft, Exp;

-- Spark_IO does not support input-output of fixed point types

   pragma Inline(Valid_File, End_Of_Line, End_Of_File, Get_Char);
```

```
private
   --# hide Spark_IO;
   ...
end Spark_IO;
```

Since SPARK does not support overloading, the various procedures Put and Get of Text_IO are replaced with procedures with explicit names giving the type of value being transferred. Thus we have Put_Char, Get_Char, Put_String, Get_String, Put_Integer, Get_Integer, Put_Float and Get_Float.

Note that Put_String and Get_String have an additional parameter Stop indicating the index of the last character in the string transferred. (If Stop is zero for Put_String then the whole string is output.)

Since there are no defaults, the procedures Put_Integer and Put_Float always have to pass full formatting information; otherwise their behaviour is as for the corresponding procedures Put of Text_IO. The procedures Get_Integer and Get_Float have an additional Boolean parameter Read which indicates whether the operation is successful (rather than raising Data_Error as would happen in Text_IO).

The procedures Put_Line and Get_Line are again similar to the corresponding procedures of Text_IO but have a further parameter Stop like Put_String and Get_String.

Finally there are procedures such as Get_Int_From_String which enable Integer and Float values to be transferred to and from a string rather than a file. Incidentally it should be noticed that the parameter indicating the starting position in the string is Start_Pos rather than Start; this is because Start is an FDL reserved word and although it is unlikely that proof would be required of programs using Spark_IO nevertheless it is felt good practice to avoid such words in general utilities.

## 8.6 Implementation of Spark_IO

It is instructive to consider how Spark_IO is implemented in terms of Text_IO. The private part is

```
private
   --# hide Spark_IO;

   type IO_Type is (Stdin, Stdout, Namedfile);
   type File_Ptr is access Ada.Text_IO.File_Type;
   type File_Type is
      record
         File: File_Ptr := null;
         IO_Sort: IO_Type := Namedfile;
      end record;

   Standard_Input: constant File_Type := File_Type'(null, Stdin);
   Standard_Output: constant File_Type := File_Type'(null, Stdout);
end Spark_IO;
```

The first point to note is the hide directive. This is necessary because the type File_Type is implemented as a record having a component of the type File_Ptr which is an access type referring to the type File_Type of Text_IO.

Incidentally this reference to Text_IO means that the specification of Spark_IO requires a with clause for Text_IO. However, it does not need an inherit clause since there is no reference to Text_IO within the code to be examined because of the hide directive.

The body of Spark_IO is also hidden since it needs to use many facilities of full Ada such as exceptions. Moreover, it has calls of the subprograms in Text_IO and these calls cannot be processed by the Examiner because the corresponding specifications (in Text_IO) are not annotated and so the Examiner can know nothing about them.

We will not show the whole of the body of Spark_IO but just a fragment illustrating typical techniques

```
package body Spark_IO is
--# hide Spark_IO;
   ...

   procedure Create(File: in out File_Type;
                    Name_Of_File: in String;
                    Form_Of_File: in String;
                    Status: out File_Status) is
   begin
      Status := OK;
      if File.File = null then
         File.File := new Ada.Text_IO.File_Type;
      end if;
      Ada.Text_IO.Create(File.File.all, Ada.Text_IO.Out_File,
                                  Name_Of_File, Form_Of_File);
   exception
      when Ada.Text_IO.Status_Error => Status := Status_Error;
      when Ada.Text_IO.Name_Error => Status := Name_Error;
      when Ada.Text_IO.Use_Error => Status := Use_Error;
      when Ada.Text_IO.Device_Error => Status := Device_Error;
   end Create;

   ...

   function Is_In(File: in File_Type) return Boolean is
   begin
      return Is_Open(File) and then Mode(File) = In_File;
   end Is_In;

   ...

   package Integer_IO is new Ada.Text_IO.Integer_IO(Integer);

   procedure Get_Integer(File: in File_Type;
                         Item: out Integer;
                         Width: in Natural;
                         Read: out Boolean) is
```

```
   begin
      if Is_In(File) then
         Integer_IO.Get(File_Ref(File), Item, Width);
         Read := True;
      else
         Read := False;
      end if;
   exception
      when others => Read := False;
   end Get_Integer;

   ...

end Spark_IO;
```

The procedure Create shows the cascaded call of Create in Text_IO followed by an exception handler to turn any exception into a status value. Note also how a new object of type Text_IO.File_Type is created if necessary.

The procedure Get_Integer is implemented in terms of an instantiation of Text_IO.Integer_IO with the type Integer. The slave function Is_In is declared for convenience. Again an exception handler is necessary to set the status value.

The user can define input–output for any type in the same way as Spark_IO. A package specification can be given which obeys the rules of SPARK and this package can then be implemented using a hidden package body.

## 8.7 Example of Spark_IO

The use of Spark_IO is illustrated by the following complete program which also happens to use all the core annotations of SPARK. The body of the package Inventory is not shown.

```
package Inventory
   --# own Content;
   --# initializes Content;
is
   Max_Size: constant := 100;

   type Inventories is limited private;
   type Part_Numbers is range 1000 .. 9999;

   procedure Add(Part: in Part_Numbers;
                 Number: in Positive;
                 Full: out Boolean);
   --# global in out Content;
   --# derives Content from Part, Number, Content &
   --#         Full from Part, Content;
```

```
   procedure Look_Up(Part: in Part_Numbers;
                     Number: out Natural);
   --# global in Content;
   --# derives Number from Part, Content;

private
   type Sizes is range 0 .. Max_Size;
   subtype Indices is Sizes range 1 .. Sizes'Last;
   type Items is
      record
         Part_Number: Part_Numbers;
         Amount: Positive;
         Empty: Boolean;
      end record;
   type Inventories is array (Indices) of Items;
end Inventory;

with Spark_IO, Inventory;
--# inherit Spark_IO, Inventory;
--# main_program
procedure Dialogue
   --# global in out Spark_IO.File_Sys, Inventory.Content;
   --# derives Inventory.Content from * &
   --#         Spark_IO.File_Sys from *, Inventory.Content;
is
   Number: Inventory.Part_Numbers;
   Amount: Natural;
   Found: Boolean;

   procedure Set_Up_Inventory
   --# global Inventory.Content;
   --# derives Inventory.Content from *;
   is separate;

   procedure Enter_Part(Number: out Inventory.Part_Numbers)
   --# global in out Spark_IO.File_Sys;
   --# derives Spark_IO.File_Sys from * &
   --#         Number from Spark_IO.File_Sys;
   is
      Number_Read: Integer;
      OK: Boolean;
   begin
      loop
         Spark_IO.Put_String(Spark_IO.Standard_Output,
                                                "Part number? ", 0);
         Spark_IO.Get_Integer(Spark_IO.Standard_Input,
                                              Number_Read, 0, OK);
         exit when OK and then
            (Number_Read >= Integer(Inventory.Part_Numbers'First) and
             Number_Read <= Integer(Inventory.Part_Numbers'Last));
```

```
            Spark_IO.Put_Line(Spark_IO.Standard_Output,
                                "Invalid part number, try again", 0);
            Spark_IO.New_Line(Spark_IO.Standard_Output, 1);
         end loop;
         Number := Inventory.Part_Numbers(Number_Read);
      end Enter_Part;

   begin   -- Dialogue
      Set_Up_Inventory;

      while True loop
         Enter_Part(Number);
         Inventory.Look_Up(Number, Amount);

         Spark_IO.Set_Col(Spark_IO.Standard_Output, 5);
         Spark_IO.Put_String(Spark_IO.Standard_Output,
                                          "part number: ", 0);
         Spark_IO.Put_Integer(Spark_IO.Standard_Output,
                                      Integer(Number), 0, 10);
         Spark_IO.Put_String(Spark_IO.Standard_Output,
                                      " - Items available:", 0);
         Spark_IO.Set_Col(Spark_IO.Standard_Output, 50);

         if Amount = 0 then
            Spark_IO.Put_Line(Spark_IO.Standard_Output, "NONE", 0);
            Spark_IO.New_Line(Spark_IO.Standard_Output, 1);
         else
            Spark_IO.Put_Integer(Spark_IO.Standard_Output,
                                              Amount, 5, 10);
            Spark_IO.New_Line(Spark_IO.Standard_Output, 2);
         end if;
      end loop;

   end Dialogue;
```

A typical interaction might then be

```
Part number? 450
Invalid part number, try again
Part number? 3456
    Part Number: 3456 - Items available:        NONE
Part number? 9214
    Part Number: 9214 - Items available:          10

...
```

where those characters typed by the user are shown in italics.

It should be noted that this program goes on for ever. The main loop is a while statement with condition True as recommended in Section 6.3. The report resulting from examining this program is given in Section 9.5 and shows the corresponding message from the Examiner concerning the stable loop.

## 8.8 Shadows

We now illustrate a technique (trick) for interfacing often referred to as using a shadow.

In Section 8.2 we introduced the use of the hide directive to indicate text which was to be hidden from the Examiner and thus not analysed. We saw how this could be used where the private part or body of a package needed to use some aspect of full Ada and therefore could not be examined. The technique was illustrated by showing how Spark_IO (which presents a legal SPARK interface to the user) was implemented in terms of Ada.Text_IO (which is not legal SPARK).

A more severe situation arises where the interface itself cannot be written in SPARK and thus cannot be presented to the Examiner. The problem is not that we might want to examine such an interface but that we want to examine calls to the interface from other parts of the program and so the Examiner has to be aware of the interface. The general idea is that we introduce a semantically equivalent piece of legal SPARK (the shadow) that stands in for the interface for the purposes of examination but then we use the proper text for compilation.

In other words, a 'shadow' specification is written in SPARK, to represent the original specification. The original specification is used for compilation, but its shadow is used for examination.

(The technique is typically organized by using a variant index file which refers to the shadow text rather than the real text; see Section 9.4.)

For example the real package which is compiled might be

```
package Bits is
   type Byte is range 0 .. 255;
   function "and" (Left, Right: Byte) return Byte;
end Bits;
```

whereas the shadow version which is processed by the Examiner might be

```
package Bits is              -- shadow
   type Byte is range 0 .. 255;
end Bits;
```

which omits the declaration of the operator which is forbidden in SPARK.

Of course it is not possible to access the new operator "and" from SPARK. This can be overcome by providing additional packages with specifications written in SPARK but bodies written in full Ada which can therefore access the features of the original package which were not written in SPARK.

So we might have

```
with Bits;
--# inherit Bits;
package Local_Bits is
   function Byte_And(Left, Right: Bits.Byte) return Bits.Byte;
   pragma Inline(Byte_And);
end Local_Bits;
```

```
package body Local_Bits is
   function Byte_And(Left, Right: Bits.Byte) return Bits.Byte is
   --# hide Byte_And;
   begin
      return Bits."and"(Left, Right);
   end Byte_And;
end Local_Bits;
```

If code optimization is not performed during compilation, the introduction of a function body will add a function call overhead. If this is unacceptable it can be eliminated using renaming by writing

```
with Bits;
package Local_Bits is
   function Byte_And(Left, Right: Bits.Byte) return Bits.Byte
         renames Bits."and";
end Local_Bits;
```

Of course the Examiner doesn't know about Bits."and" and so this has to have a shadow package as well.

Care is needed to ensure that shadow and real versions are kept consistent.

## 8.9 Representation clauses

Those familiar with Ada will recall that representation clauses are used to control the fine detail of how a type is represented and where objects are located in the address space. They are especially important for mapping variables onto locations used for direct memory access by external devices (but of course this technique should not be used for attempting to create aliases). We will not give the details here because they do depend somewhat upon the implementation.

However, the important point to note is that representation clauses are permitted in SPARK although the Examiner merely checks their syntax and warns of their existence. A warning is appropriate because in extreme cases they can affect the semantics of a program and hence compromise the validity of the SPARK analysis.

The syntax of representation clauses is given in Appendix 1.

# Part 3

# The SPARK Tools



This third part covers those aspects of SPARK which relate to the proof process and the use of the SPARK tools in general. The annotations used for proof are as follows

| | |
|---|---|
| **--# pre** | defines preconditions for a procedure or function. |
| **--# post** | defines the postcondition for a procedure. |
| **--# return** | defines (explicitly or implicitly) the result of a function. |
| **--# assert** | defines a predicate that is required to be true at that point and which forms the sole hypothesis for the following code. |
| **--# check** | like assert but adds its conclusions to the existing hypotheses. |
| **--# function** | declares a proof function whose meaning is given by distinct rules. |

Chapter 9 introduces the Examiner which is the main tool and its invocation through the Windows Interface. It then discusses the various options controlling identification of files, levels of analysis and reporting.

Chapter 10 is rather mathematical. It discusses the theory behind flow analysis. This chapter can be skipped since a deep understanding is not necessary in order to use the tools. Nevertheless it does give greater insight into the workings of the tools. Moreover, it justifies many of the rules in SPARK as opposed to Ada by showing how they are necessary for analysis.

Chapter 11 expands on the process of verification outlined in Chapter 3 and covers the other main tools, the SPADE Automatic Simplifier and the Proof Checker. It includes a general discussion of the main principles of the proof process and the Functional Description Language (FDL) used for verification conditions and associated proof rules. Unfortunately space precludes a detailed discussion of the interactive use of the Proof Checker.

Chapter 12 addresses a number of design issues. Program design is more of an art than a science but nevertheless it is hoped that the notes given here will be of help to the SPARK user.

The final Chapter 13 looks at a number of case studies and thereby shows some rather larger examples than have been introduced earlier. The first example is a lift controller which illustrates outline design and decomposition using subunits. The second example concerns an autopilot and illustrates the use of refinement and private child packages. The final example is a simple sorting algorithm with full proof annotations and outlines the complete proof.

There are then four appendices. Appendix 1 gives the full syntax of SPARK and relates it to that of Ada; Appendix 2 lists the reserved words and attributes and also gives the names of all the Latin-1 characters; Appendix 3 summarizes the differences between SPARK 95 (the language described here) and SPARK 83 (based on Ada 83); and Appendix 4 is an introduction to the CD which accompanies this book.

The book concludes with answers to the various exercises, bibliography and index.

# 9 The SPARK Examiner



The previous chapters were mostly concerned with the SPARK core language (including the core annotations) and its relation to Ada. We now turn to a more detailed consideration of the tools associated with SPARK which were briefly introduced in Chapter 3.

The most important tool is of course the Examiner and the simple use of the Examiner forms the topic of this chapter. More advanced uses of the Examiner and the other tools (the Simplifier and Proof Checker) and some of the mathematics behind them are then discussed in subsequent chapters.

## 9.1 Examination order

The SPARK Examiner is a stand-alone tool which analyses source files in order to check their conformance to the rules of SPARK. Each source file may contain many SPARK compilation units and these may be fully implemented or partially hidden using the hide directive discussed in Section 8.2.

As mentioned in Section 7.10, in order to analyse a compilation unit, the Examiner needs access to certain other units in much the same way that the compiler needs access to certain information about other units in order to compile a given unit. The rules are slightly different for the Examiner because they are based on inherit clauses as well as with clauses.

The rules are as follows

- to analyse a package body, the Examiner needs access to its specification and to the specifications of its private children;
- to analyse a package specification or main subprogram that inherits other packages, the Examiner needs access to the specifications of those other packages (and those that they inherit and so on);
- to analyse a child unit, the Examiner needs access to the specification of its parent;
- to analyse a subunit, the Examiner needs access to the unit containing its stub.

In trivial cases all the units to be examined can be in one file – this follows the syntax for a compilation given in Section 7.8. More generally, an ordered list of several files is specified in some way. The Examiner then analyses all the units in the files, in the order in which the files are mentioned.

Access to any other files that are required according to the rules given above can be provided by the use of index files (see Section 9.4). Otherwise the order of the files and the units within the files must be such that the Examiner only requires access to units which it has already analysed.

It should be observed that this all works in terms of source text files and is therefore very simple to understand. There is no concept of a program library as used by typical Ada compilers. Those familiar with the transition from Ada 83 to Ada 95 will recall that in Ada 83 a unit could only be compiled after all those it depends upon have been compiled, whereas Ada 95 is less demanding and simply insists that these units are present in some form in the library (it could be simply as program text). Thus we can think of the examination model as being more akin to the compilation source text model permitted by Ada 95 rather than to the object code model required by Ada 83.

For each source file examined, the Examiner produces a listing file which includes error and warning messages plus a report file summarizing the analysis. This summary also includes the error and warning messages. The level of warnings can be controlled by a warning control file.

In the examples in this book we assume that the Examiner supplied on the associated CD is being used and therefore is being run on a PC under Microsoft Windows 95 or later compatible systems. We also assume that installation has been carried out according to the instructions given in Appendix 4 and that the system has been installed in the directory **c:\winspark**.

The very simplest situation is where the whole program is in one file called perhaps **myprog.ada** within some directory such as **c:\winspark\examples\chap9\9_1**. This is in accordance with the structure of the files containing the text of the examples as described in Appendix 4.

From within Windows, the SPARK Interface is entered by double-clicking on the icon labelled SPARK for Windows within the SPARK program group. This opens the main SPARK window which contains the usual drop-down menus plus a small toolbar. Click on File and then Open (or click on the first icon in the toolbar or type Ctrl-O). This opens a dialogue box entitled Open File showing the directory structure. Select the appropriate directory and then click on Open.

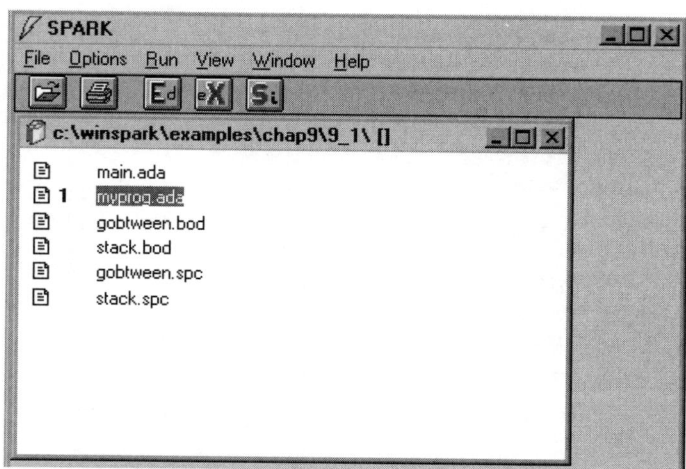


**Figure 9.1** The SPARK and directory windows.

This should open a window containing the names of all the files in the directory and hopefully includes **myprog.ada**. Click on this and the number 1 will appear against it. The situation should now be as illustrated in Figure 9.1 which shows the names of all the files associated with the examples in this section.

The Examiner can be invoked with the current default options by just clicking on Run and then Examiner (or by clicking on the red X icon in the toolbar or typing Ctrl-E).

A report is by default sent to the file **spark.rep** and a listing with embedded messages is sent to the file **myprog.lst** in the current directory. (The various defaults can be overridden and changed as discussed in Section 9.3.) The names of these files should then appear in the directory window. Clicking on a file name with the *right* mouse button will call an associated editor and open the file. Messages can then be inspected and any changes can be made to the source file by a similar use of the editor.

In the general case a program will be spread across several files. As a concrete example consider the program at the end of Section 2.9 which comprises the package The_Stack, the package Go_Between and the main subprogram Main. We will assume that Use_Stack in Go_Between is rather more explicit such as

```
procedure Use_Stack is
   A: Integer;
begin
   The_Stack.Push(55);
   The_Stack.Pop(A);
end Use_Stack;
```

although of course this is pretty useless (but most small examples are anyway).

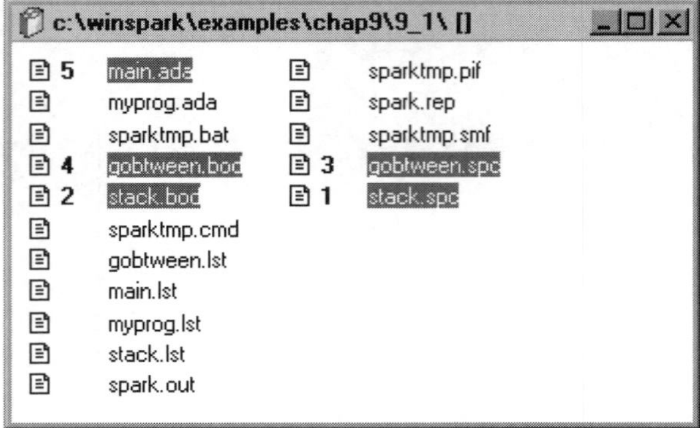


**Figure 9.2** Directory window after the stack example.

We will also assume that the units are in the five files **stack.spc**, **stack.bod**, **gobtween.spc**, **gobtween.bod** and **main.ada** where an obvious convention for file extensions is used.

(Many conventions are possible; one is to use extensions **ads** and **adb** for specification and body respectively. Another is to make the file extension always the same (such as **ada**) and then to distinguish specification and body by appending a trailing underscore to the file name in the case of the specification.)

We can then click on the file names in turn in the following order

```
stack.spc, stack.bod, gobtween.spc, gobtween.bod, main.ada
```

and numbers 1 to 5 will appear against the file names. Invoking the Examiner will now cause the whole program to be examined.

A report is sent to **spark.rep** and three listing files **main.lst**, **stack.lst** and **gobtween.lst** are generated. The directory window should now be as in Figure 9.2. Note that in the case of Stack and Go_Between the listing relates to the analysis of the body which actually overwrites that of the analysis of the specification since by default they both go to the same file. More specific listing files can be requested as explained in Sections 9.3 and 9.4. (The window also shows a number of other files such as **sparktmp.bat**; these are temporary files created by the Windows Interface for calling the Examiner as explained in Section 9.7.)

Note that a file can be unselected by clicking on its name once more (in which case the list of numbers is shuffled up) and that two files can be interchanged within the list by dragging the name of one file to that of the other.

The SPARK rules permit other orders of examination although there is less flexibility than for compilation because the inherit clause means that **gobtween.spc** has to be examined after **stack.spc**. The SPARK dependencies and the Ada dependencies for this example are illustrated in Figures 9.3 and 9.4. Only the direct dependencies are shown. The differences are quite striking.

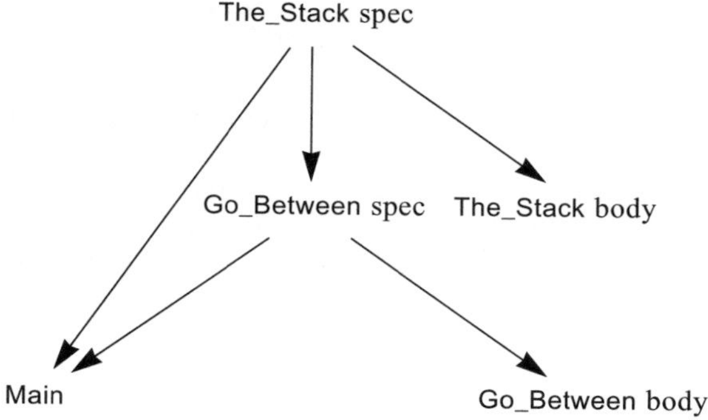


**Figure 9.3** SPARK dependencies.

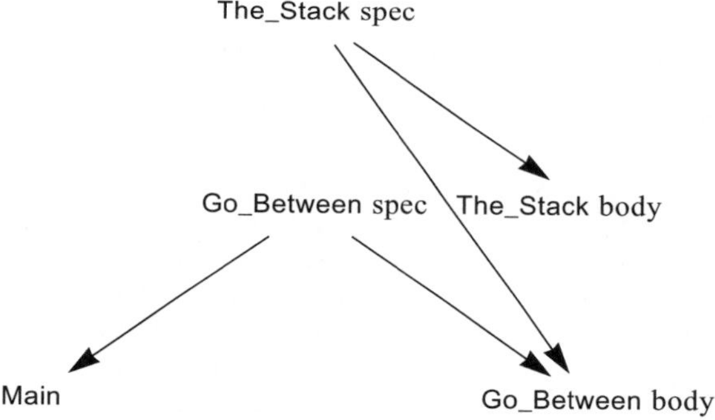


**Figure 9.4** Ada dependencies.

Thus if we change the specification of The_Stack then only the bodies of The_Stack and Go_Between will also need to be recompiled. On the other hand the whole program will need to be reexamined.

Since the result of examination is not retained between distinct invocations of the Examiner, it is often the case that much of the program needs reexamination anyway. For example, if we change the body of Go_Between, then the specifications of The_Stack and Go_Between will also have to be reexamined as part of the process of reexamining the body of Go_Between. To do this we select in order

```
stack.spc, gobtween.spc, gobtween.bod
```

Other sensible combinations might be just the package The_Stack or the two package specifications plus the main subprogram thus

```
stack.spc, stack.bod
stack.spc, gobtween.spc, main.ada
```

It is clearly somewhat of a burden having to individually select all the files each time and this can be alleviated by the use of metafiles and index files as described in Section 9.4.

It is important to realize that the Windows Interface merely establishes various command line parameters and then invokes the Examiner as a batch job. The mechanism used is discussed briefly in Section 9.7. Note that the Command Line Interface is common to all implementations of the Examiner such as those on the DEC VAX and the Sun as well as on the PC. However, the Graphical User Interface naturally varies between implementations.

## 9.2 Messages

The Examiner analyses a unit in several passes. The first pass carries out lexical and syntax analysis; this also identifies the other units required in order to analyse the unit in question. These will already have been read if the files were selected directly in the directory window but if index files are used as described in Section 9.4 then the Examiner may have to find some source files using the information in the index files. When all these other units have been read, the Examiner then carries out static semantic analysis and, if this is successful, data or information flow analysis as requested.

The result of analysis may be a number of error and warning messages typical of those produced by compilers. The user has to be aware that the point of view of the Examiner may not always be quite that expected by the programmer and so appropriate sympathy is sometimes necessary.

For example it must be remembered that aggregates are always qualified in SPARK. Omitting the qualification will lead the Examiner to expect an expression after the opening parenthesis and the resulting message might at first sight thus seem surprising.

The messages produced during the earlier passes include those relating to inconsistencies between annotations and the code. The rules of Section 6.7 concerning derives and global annotations, which are designed to prevent aliasing, are typical of those checked during semantic analysis. For example, the aliasing in the call of Sly results in

```
            Sly(A);
                ^1
*** (  1)  Semantic Error    : This parameter is overlapped
           by an exported global variable.
```

More interesting messages are produced by flow analysis some of which we have already encountered in Section 3.2. In analysing such messages it is important to be aware that flow analysis is done in terms of individual components for records but treats arrays as entire variables.

For example, the analysis of the sample program of the last section results in several messages. The analysis is carried out in units of subprograms and the initialization part of a package is treated rather like a parameterless subprogram. Recall that the body of The_Stack is

```
package body The_Stack
--# own State is S, Pointer;                  -- refinement
is
   Stack_Size: constant := 100;
   type Pointer_Range is range 0 .. Stack_Size;
   subtype Index_Range is Pointer_Range range 1 .. Stack_Size;
   type Vector is array (Index_Range) of Integer;
   S: Vector;
   Pointer: Pointer_Range;

   procedure Push(X: in Integer)
   --# global in out S, Pointer;
   --# derives S       from S, Pointer, X &
   --#         Pointer from Pointer;
   is
   begin
      Pointer := Pointer + 1;
      S(Pointer) := X;
   end Push;

   procedure Pop(X: out Integer)
   --# global in S; in out Pointer;
   --# derives Pointer from Pointer &
   --#         X       from S, Pointer;
   is
   begin
      X := S(Pointer);
      Pointer := Pointer - 1;
   end Pop;
begin                                -- initialization
   Pointer := 0;
   S := Vector'(Index_Range => 0);
end The_Stack;
```

The Examiner confirms that both Push and Pop are satisfactory by messages of the form

```
+++        Flow analysis of subprogram Push performed: no
           errors found.
```

At the end of the initialization part of the package The_Stack, it reports

```
+++        Flow analysis of package initialization
           performed: no errors found.
```

However, in the procedure Use_Stack inside Go_Between (as shown in the previous section) it reports

```
!!! (  1)  Flow Error          : Assignment to A is
           ineffective.
```

```
!!! (  2)  Flow Error        : The variable A is neither
           referenced nor exported.
```

These are to be expected – they arise because we have written a silly program as an example which ultimately does nothing. The variable A which was declared simply as a destination for Pop is never used and so the assignment to A resulting from the call of Pop is itself ineffective.

It is interesting to consider the effect of omitting the initialization for S which we know from dynamic considerations is not necessary. This would result in the following messages at the end of the initialization part of the package

```
!!! (  1)  Flow Error        : The variable S is neither
           imported nor defined.

!!! (  2)  Flow Error        : The variable S is exported
           but not (internally) defined.
```

Of course, the Examiner is not aware of the deeper relationship between the usage of the individual components of S and the value of the variable Pointer and the protocol of use of the procedures Push and Pop. Indeed, looked at as a whole, S is not defined and a call of Pop (without a previous call of Push) might on the face of it access the undefined S.

Note that an attempt to initialize the array S with a loop such as

```
begin                        -- initialization
   Pointer := 0;
   for I in Index_Range loop
      S(I) := 0;
   end loop;
end The_Stack;
```

results in the messages

```
!!! (  1)  Flow Error        : Statement contains
           reference(s) to undefined variable S.

??? (  2)  Warning           : The undefined initial value
           of S may be used in the derivation of S.
```

The problem is that we must look at the array S as a whole. The assignment to S(I) is seen as an assignment to only part of the entire variable S and the Examiner considers that S as a whole is not defined. In other words the undefined value of S is used in the assignment to derive a new value for S.

A discussion of the techniques used by the Examiner in the detection of information flow errors will be found in Chapter 10. We will return to the problem of giving more information about the values of individual components of entire variables in Chapter 11.

A full description of all the messages that the Examiner can produce and their causes will be found in the detailed documentation on the CD.

## 9.3 Option control

We will now look at the various options and their defaults. Selecting Options produces a menu of four items, options for the Examiner, options for the Simplifier, more General options and finally, the ability to Save the currently established options as the default for future use. We will look at the Examiner options first and then the General options; those for the Simplifier are discussed in Section 11.6.

Selecting Examiner now brings up the dialogue box shown in Figure 9.5. This allows control of three areas, Analysis, Reporting and Files.

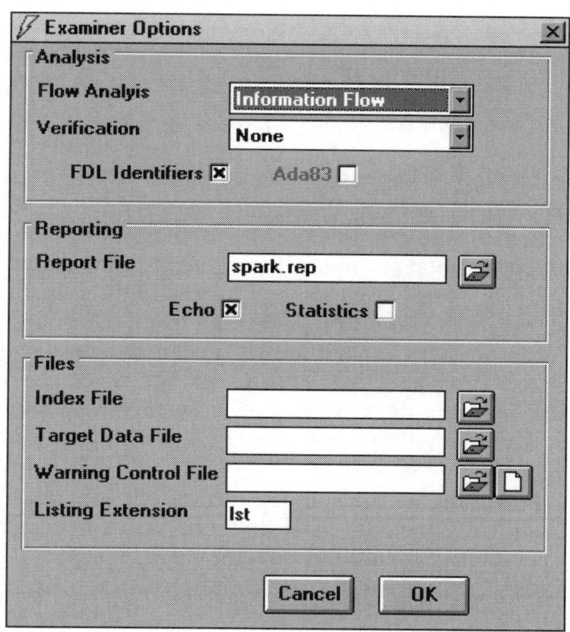


**Figure 9.5** The Examiner Options dialogue box.

Under Analysis, the Flow Analysis menu offers three possibilities. Data Flow and Information Flow carry out flow analysis according to whether data flow or the more comprehensive information flow analysis is required (remember that information flow analysis requires derives annotations). Information flow analysis is the initial default. The other possibility is Syntax Check Only whose purpose is self-evident.

The Verification menu should be left as None unless path functions or verification conditions are to be generated; these options are discussed in Section 9.6. The box marked FDL Identifiers controls whether the additional words in FDL are to be reserved or permitted as identifiers; the initial default is that the box is checked which means that the identifiers are reserved. There is also a box marked Ada 83; this is inactive using the demonstration release but normally enables the Examiner to carry out analysis according to the rules of SPARK 83.

Under Reporting, the box marked Report File gives the name of the file to which the overall report is to be sent; this is normally **`spark.rep`**. If no file is specified then no report is produced. The button to the right of the box enables the name of an existing file to be selected (this applies generally to boxes which require file names). The box marked Echo controls whether summary messages should be sent to the 'screen'; the box is normally checked and the messages then appear in a standard output file. The box marked Statistics enables the generation of statistics. It is normally not checked.

(As mentioned earlier, the Examiner is itself written in SPARK and therefore cannot use dynamic storage. Accordingly, it has a number of fixed size tables. Invoking the statistics option produces a report on usage of these tables. Note that the Examiner comes in different sizes and so this information may be used to decide that a larger version should be installed. The demonstration version supplied on the CD is relatively small.)

Under Files, the first three boxes give the names of any index file, target data file or warning control file. The initial default is that there are none; index files are described in Section 9.4, target data files are associated with proof and are described in Section 9.6, warning control files are described below. Again, the button to the right enables the name of an existing file to be selected. The last box gives the default extension for listing files, this is normally **lst**.

For each file analysed, a listing is sent to a file whose identifier consists of that of the source file with extension changed to that given as the listing extension. The listing includes any error or other messages embedded at appropriate places. If two files have the same file name (but of course different extensions) such as **stack.spc** and **stack.bod** then the listing for the latter overrides that for the former as mentioned earlier.

This can be overcome by specifying a **?** in the listing extension in which case the corresponding characters of the source extension are not changed. Thus writing **ls?** as the extension would result in listing files with names **stack.lsc** and **stack.lsd**. An alternative approach is to use a metafile as explained in the next section; this allows any listing file to be specified. Note that if the listing extension is set to nothing then the normal default extension of **lst** applies.

The report file summarizes the activity and findings of the Examiner. For simple exercises, it is hardly necessary since the listing file contains all that is needed. But for serious development the report file is a useful management tool since it includes a list of all options used, files analysed and listings produced as well as repeating the error messages also given in the listings. An example of a report file is given in Section 9.5.

The optional warning control file provides the user with control over how warnings are reported. The Examiner provides a number of warnings of various kinds and these are normally reported in full using the same format as for full errors. Although warnings are generally of interest, nevertheless too many trivial warnings can result in genuinely interesting warnings being ignored. It is possible to suppress warnings of certain categories and they are then only reported in a summary form (in both listing and report) giving the total number of warnings in each category. The warning control file describes the warnings to be suppressed; it is a text file and it is conventional to give it the extension **wrn**. The syntax of the text of the file is

warning_file ::= {warning_entry}

warning_entry ::= language_feature | pragma_selection

language_feature ::=
**representation_clauses** | **hidden_parts**
| **direct_updates** | **with_clauses**
| **static_expressions** | **type_conversions**
| **unused_variables** | **constant_variables**
| **notes**

pragma_selection ::= **pragma all** | **pragma** pragma_identifier

Comments in the Ada style can also be inserted. An example of a warning control file is

```
-- a warning control file
direct_updates
pragma List
pragma Page
```

and this has the effect of providing only summary information regarding the use of pragmas Page and List (warnings of other pragmas are given in full) and direct updates. Direct updating refers to the updating of own variables of other packages and, as mentioned in Section 7.3, is considered bad practice. Another example of a warning control file will be found in Section 9.5. Further details regarding warnings will be found in the documentation on the CD.

For convenience it is possible to build a warning control file using the Interface. This is done by clicking on the second button to the side of the Warning Control File box. This brings up a dialogue box which has entries for the various language features as shown in Figure 9.6. The features can then be selected as required. In the case of pragmas, a list of permitted pragmas can be created, extended or reduced by entering pragma names in the appropriate box and then clicking on + or – alongside the box. Alternatively the box marked All Pragmas can be checked. Finally, the created warning control file can be saved by inserting its name and then selecting OK in the usual manner.

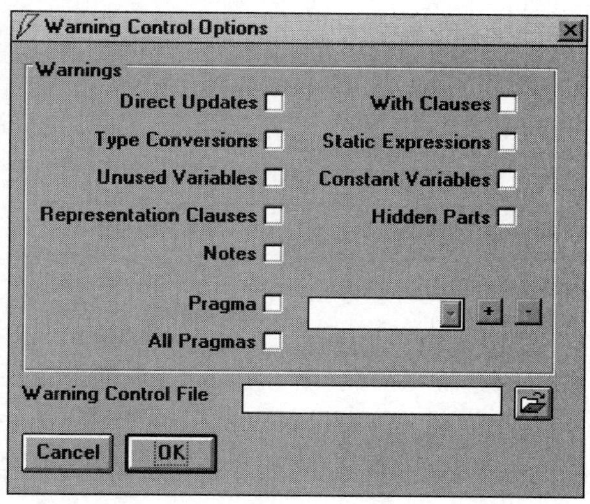


**Figure 9.6** The Warning Control File dialogue box.

The General Options dialogue box shown in Figure 9.7 enables a number of attributes to be set concerning the Windows Interface itself.

The first group controls the display in the directory windows. The box Filer Filter lists the extensions of the files to be displayed; for example setting **ada, lst** will ensure that files with other extensions are not shown; if the box is empty then all files are shown. The box Filer Order enables the files to be displayed in alphabetical order of the whole file name (by Name) or grouped in alphabetical order of extension (by Type). These options can also be selected on an individual directory window basis by selecting Window from the main menu. It is possible to have two windows open for the same directory; one could be used to show the source files while the other shows listing files.

The next group gives the exact location of the various tools to be used. The Examiner will typically be **c:\winspark\examiner\dosspark.exe**; other entries are the Simplifier (usually **c:\winspark\simplify\simp.exe**), the Proof Checker (which is not available on the demonstration version), and the Editor which is to be invoked when the right mouse button is clicked (perhaps **c:\windows\notepad.exe**).

The final group mainly concerns the temporary files to be used behind the scenes in executing the Examiner as a batch job. However, the first box gives the directory which is to be used for all output if the input directory is read-only; this might be **c:\temp**. This would arise, for instance, if the examples are examined directly from the CD. Since the resulting files such as listing files and report cannot be written to the CD they have to be put somewhere else. The other boxes give the names within the output directory (which is the input directory except in the case just discussed) of the Batch File, Meta File, and Output File respectively; see Section 9.7 for more details. The final check box controls whether 'screen' output is also copied to the output file.

Once options have been established they are used for all invocations of the Examiner within the session until changed. However, the Save Options item in the Options menu must be selected if the options are to be remembered between different invocations of the overall SPARK for Windows system. This applies to both the specific options for the Examiner as well as to the more general options we have just been discussing.

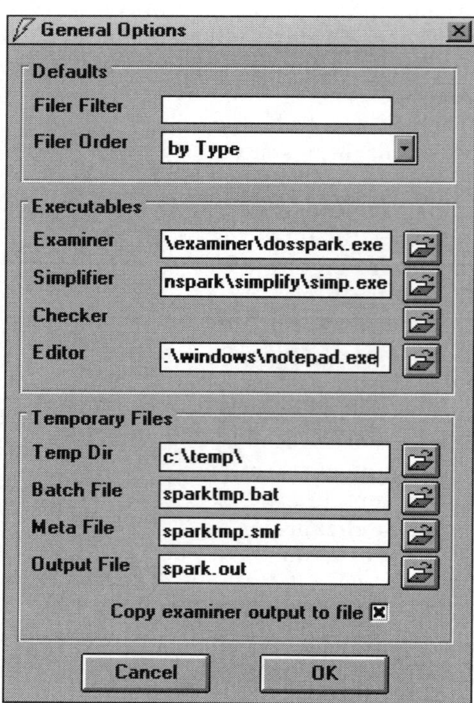


**Figure 9.7** The General Options dialogue box.

## 9.4 Metafiles and index files

For anything other than the most trivial exercises it is a nuisance having to select all the files individually each time the Examiner is invoked. This problem is overcome by the introduction of metafiles and index files which may be used to indirectly provide the required information. Metafiles are the simplest and will be discussed first.

A metafile is simply a text file containing the names of the files to be analysed one to a line; the extension is conventionally **smf**. For example rather than selecting the five files of the stack example each time we could create a metafile **main.smf** consisting of

```
-- metafile for stack example
stack.spc
stack.bod
gobtween.spc
gobtween.bod
main.ada
```

The whole program can then be analysed by just selecting this one file before invoking the Examiner. A metafile can contain the names of other metafiles (they have to be prefixed by **@**) and so a hierarchy can be created. One possibility is to create metafiles for pairs of specifications and bodies. Thus we might have a metafile called **stack.smf** just containing

```
stack.spc
stack.bod
```

and similarly for **gobtween.smf**. The overall metafile **main.smf** could then be

```
-- example of nested metafiles
@stack.smf
@gobtween.smf
main.ada
```

Incidentally, an explicit listing file can be given for a source file named in a metafile by following it by **/l=** and the name of the listing file; any explicit extension would then override the default listing extension given in the Examiner options dialogue box. So the metafile **stack.smf** might be

```
stack.spc /l= stackspc.lst
stack.bod /l= stackbod.lst
```

Metafiles are thus a convenient way of grouping files together. However, all files mentioned are completely analysed and a listing is generated for each one. The other situation which often arises is that the Examiner needs access to other files in order to analyse a particular file but a full analysis and listing of such other files is not required. This is where index files are useful.

An index file is a text file (the conventional extension is **idx**) which associates compilation units with the files that contain them.

As a first example, our illustrative program comprising The_Stack, Go_Between and Main might be examined through the use of an index file consisting of the following text

```
The_Stack  specification  is in  stack.spc
The_Stack  body           is in  stack.bod
Go_Between  specification is in  gobtween.spc
Go_Between  body          is in  gobtween.bod
Main  main_program        is in  main.ada
```

Assuming that this file is called **example.idx** and is in the current directory then the main program can be examined by typing the name of the index file in the Index File box in the Examiner options dialogue box, selecting just the one file **main.ada** and then invoking the Examiner.

On examining the subprogram Main, the Examiner discovers that it needs access to the specification of The_Stack and the specification of Go_Between as can be seen from the dependency diagram in Figure 9.3. However, these were not selected explicitly and so the Examiner searches the index file in order to discover where they are located. The index file contains the required information and so the examination can proceed.

In effect the Examiner has to fully analyse the specifications of both The_Stack and Go_Between in order to analyse Main. However, the only listing file produced is that for Main (it will be **main.lst**) and so any errors found in the specifications will only be reported in the overall report file **spark.rep**. Of course the expectation is that the specifications have already been examined and found to be correct and we are only having to reexamine them on the fly as a prerequisite to examining Main.

Similarly if we wish to examine just the body of Go_Between then we only need to select **gobtween.bod** assuming that the index file is still set in the options box.

In this case the Examiner searches for the specification of Go_Between using the index file since the body is dependent on the specification. It also then recursively searches for the specification of The_Stack because the specification of Go_Between depends upon it in turn. (It is interesting to note from Figures 9.3 and 9.4 that the Ada dependency of the body of Go_Between on the specification of The_Stack is direct whereas the SPARK dependency is indirect.) Again we only get a listing file for the body of Go_Between.

Index files can be arranged into a hierarchy using a superindex and child units and subunits can be factored out using an auxiliary index as will be explained in a moment.

The syntax rules for an index file are

index_file ::= [super_index] {index_entry}

super_index ::= superindex **is in** file_spec

index_entry ::= unit_name entry_type **is in** file_spec

entry_type ::= **auxindex** | **main_program**
| **specification** | **body** | **subunit**

unit_name ::= Ada_unit_name

The usual Ada lexical rules apply. Spaces and newlines may be inserted freely but are not allowed in individual lexical items such as the words **is**, **in** and **specification**. It is also possible to insert comments in the Ada style.

The first entry in an index file can be the designation of a so-called superindex. If the search of an index file fails then any superindex is searched in a similar manner. This process can be repeated and thus a number of indexes can be linked in a hierarchical manner.

If we have a number of standard files common to various projects (such as Spark_IO) then these can be described in a file called perhaps **library.idx** thus

```
Spark_IO  specification  is in  sparkio.spc
Spark_IO  body           is in  sparkio.bod
Spark_Elementary_Functions  specification is in  sparkef.spc
...
```

and so on.

The index file for a specific project can then start with

```
superindex                is in  library.idx
My_Package specification is in  ...
```

and there is no need to repeat the information regarding the standard library.

Auxiliary index files are useful with subunits and private child units. Suppose that the bodies of procedures Push and Pop of the package The_Stack have been made into subunits as illustrated in Section 7.9; assume that the body of The_Stack is now in the file **stacksep.bod** and that the subunits are in **push.sub** and **pop.sub**. The index file could then be written as

```
The_Stack  specification  is in  stack.spc
The_Stack  body           is in  stacksep.bod
The_Stack.Push  subunit   is in  push.sub
The_Stack.Pop  subunit    is in  pop.sub
Go_Between  specification is in  gobtween.spc
Go_Between  body          is in  gobtween.bod
Main  main_program        is in  main.ada
```

An alternative approach however is to recognize that the body of The_Stack should be treated as the root of a hierarchy in its own right. We can place the information regarding the body in its own index file (**stackaux.idx** say) and then refer to this from the main index file. The main file (now called **main.idx** say) then becomes

```
The_Stack  specification  is in  stack.spc
The_Stack  auxindex       is in  stackaux.idx
Go_Between  specification is in  gobtween.spc
Go_Between  body          is in  gobtween.bod
Main  main_program        is in  main.ada
```

and the auxiliary file (**stackaux.idx**) is

```
The_Stack  body            is in  stacksep.bod
The_Stack.Push  subunit    is in  push.sub
The_Stack.Pop  subunit     is in  pop.sub
```

Assuming that the Index File option has been set to **main.idx**, then we can examine the body of Push by just selecting the one file **push.sub** and invoking the Examiner.

When the Examiner attempts to analyse the subunit Push, it first discovers that it needs the body of The_Stack because the subunit depends upon it. The Examiner then searches the index file and although it does not find an entry for The_Stack body nevertheless it finds an auxiliary file with the same unit name. It then searches the auxiliary file and finds the body successfully. The Examiner then of course discovers that it needs to examine the specification of The_Stack as well and so has to search the main index file again and of course finds it successfully.

An alternative approach might be to reverse the roles and make **main.idx** a superindex file so that the index file given in the option box (now called **stackbod.idx** perhaps) becomes

```
superindex                 is in  main.idx
The_Stack  body            is in  stacksep.bod
The_Stack.Push  subunit    is in  push.sub
The_Stack.Pop  subunit     is in  pop.sub
```

We can then select **push.sub** and invoke the Examiner as before. In this case the Examiner finds the body of The_Stack immediately in the given index file. However, when it comes to search for the specification of The_Stack it does not find it; but the index file does mention a superindex and so the Examiner searches that and is then of course successful.

Note that an auxiliary file used as such must not contain an entry for a superindex since there is a risk of a search then looping.

Incidentally we could have also placed the specification of The_Stack in the auxiliary file. The only requirement is that all units in an auxiliary file must have the same ultimate ancestor unit name.

The reader will note that this example is too trivial, there is never any point in an index file mentioning units which are not required for the analysis of some other unit – or, in other words, units that are the leaves of the dependency tree. In this example the leaf units are Main.Ada, the body of Go_Between and the two subunits Push and Pop. The reason is obvious, if the subunit Pop is to be examined then it must be directly selected anyway and no other unit ever requires it.

However, it is often convenient for documentation purposes to complete the index file as a record of the structure. But of course index files can usefully contain subunits if they in turn have other subunits.

The auxiliary index file structure can be used in a similar way with a hierarchy of child units and is especially useful with private children.

## 9.5 Example of report file

As a further example we reconsider the program discussed in Section 8.7 regarding the control of an inventory. The program consists of a main subprogram which carries out the dialogue with the user and a package which maintains the inventory. It also uses Spark_IO to communicate with the user.

We might choose to have three index files. The main one is **dialog.idx** and its content is

```
superindex          is in  common.idx
Inventory auxindex  is in  invent.idx
```

The file **common.idx** is essentially a subset of the hypothetical library discussed in the previous section. In this case all we need is

```
spark_io specification is in spark_io.spc
```

The third file **invent.idx** refers to the package Inventory and is

```
Inventory specification is in invent.spc
Inventory body          is in invent.bod
```

Note that the main index file contains no direct entries but just references to the superindex and the auxiliary index. In principle we could include an entry for the main subprogram Dialogue but in practice there is no need since the main subprogram is always referred to explicitly in the command line and of course is never needed for the analysis of any other part of the program – this applies to any main subprogram and indeed to any unit which is a leaf of the dependency tree as mentioned in the previous section.

We can now set the Index File box to **dialog.idx**, select the one source file **dialog.ada**, and then invoke the Examiner.

The report file that might be produced is as follows.

```
     *******************************************************
                     Report of SPARK Examination
   SPARK95 Examiner with VC and RTC Generator Release 5.01 / 08.00
                        Demonstration Version
     *******************************************************

                    DATE : 16-AUG-2000 10:41:09.30

     Options:
         index_file=C:\WINSPARK\EXAMPLES\CHAP9\9_5\DIALOG.IDX
         nowarning_file
         notarget_compiler_data
         source_extension=ADA
         listing_extension=LST
         nodictionary
         report_file=SP0905A.REP
         no_html
```

```
    nostatistics
    fdl_identifiers
    flow_analysis=information
    ada95
    annotation_character=#

Selected files:
   @SPARKTMP.SMF

Index Filename(s) used were:
   C:\WINSPARK\EXAMPLES\CHAP9\9_5\DIALOG.IDX
   C:\WINSPARK\EXAMPLES\CHAP9\9_5\INVENT.IDX
   C:\WINSPARK\EXAMPLES\CHAP9\9_5\COMMON.IDX

Meta File(s) used were:
   SPARKTMP.SMF
      C:\WINSPARK\EXAMPLES\CHAP9\9_5\DIALOG.ADA

Full warning reporting selected

Source Filename(s) used were:
   C:\WINSPARK\EXAMPLES\CHAP9\9_5\DIALOG.ADA
   C:\WINSPARK\EXAMPLES\CHAP9\9_5\INVENT.SPC
   C:\WINSPARK\EXAMPLES\CHAP9\9_5\SPARKIO.SPC

Source Filename:  C:\WINSPARK\EXAMPLES\CHAP9\9_5\INVENT.SPC
No Listing File

   Unit name:  Inventory
   Unit type:  package specification
   Unit has been analysed, any errors are listed below.

No errors found

Source Filename:  C:\WINSPARK\EXAMPLES\CHAP9\9_5\SPARKIO.SPC
No Listing File

   Unit name:  Spark_IO
   Unit type:  package specification
   Unit has been analysed, any errors are listed below.

3 error(s) or warning(s)

Line
  22  with Ada.Text_IO;
           ^1
--- (  1)  Warning       :  1: The identifier Ada is
           either undeclared or not visible at this point.

 269    pragma Inline(Valid_File, End_Of_Line, End_Of_File,
               ^2
--- (  2)  Warning       :  3: Pragma - ignored by the
           SPARK Examiner.
```

```
 284  end Spark_IO;

--- (  3)  Warning       : 10: The private part of package
           Spark_IO is hidden - hidden text is ignored by
           the SPARK Examiner.

Source Filename:  C:\WINSPARK\EXAMPLES\CHAP9\9_5\DIALOG.ADA
Listing Filename:  C:\WINSPARK\EXAMPLES\CHAP9\9_5\DIALOG.LST

   Unit name:  Dialogue
   Unit type:  main program
   Unit has been analysed, any errors are listed below.

2 error(s) or warning(s)

Line
  49     while True loop
               ^1
!!! (  1)  Flow Error    : 40: Exit condition is stable, of
           index 0.

  69  end Dialogue;

--- (  2)  Warning       :400: Variable Found is declared
           but not used.

--End of file--------------------------------------------
```

As can be seen, the report file describes the various options and files that were used and also summarizes any errors or warnings.

There are three warnings regarding the specification of Spark_IO which are reasonable. The first reflects that there is a with clause for Ada.Text_IO but of course we did not make the specification of Ada.Text_IO available to the Examiner because the reference to Ada.Text_IO is in the hidden private part. There are also warnings about the pragma and the fact that the private part was hidden. These warnings are common and it is convenient to suppress them. We can provide a warning control file called perhaps **dialog.wrn** as follows

```
hidden_parts
with_clauses
pragma Inline
```

If we now set the Warning option to **dialog.wrn** then the difference in the report is that the description of the options selected includes the fact that the warning control file is used and the three warnings regarding Spark_IO are suppressed and replaced by the following summary

```
3 summarised warning(s), comprising:
     1 pragma(s)*
     1 hidden part(s)*
     1 with clause(s) lacking a supporting inherit
(*Note: the above warnings may affect the validity of the
 analysis.)
```

There are two remaining messages regarding the main subprogram Dialogue. One is a warning that the variable Found has not been used; this is true and maybe the writer of the procedure had some future use for it in mind.

Finally there is an actual error message regarding the loop to the effect that the exit condition is stable of index 0. This reflects the fact that the loop never ends and so the poor user is involved in the dialogue until eternity or some extraneous event stops the program. We will return to the topic of loop stability in more detail in Chapter 10.

## 9.6 Proof options

The Examiner generates path functions or verification conditions if one of the following items in the Verification menu is selected

Path Functions
Verification Conditions
Run Time Checks
RTC plus Overflow

As well as performing flow analysis and generating the normal listing and report files, the Examiner creates additional files containing the path functions or verification conditions. We will briefly consider verification conditions first.

The options Verification Conditions, Run Time Checks and RTC plus Overflow generate verification conditions at different levels. The option Verification Conditions produces the usual conditions and the others in addition generate conditions concerning run-time checks as discussed in Section 11.9. The conditions themselves are output in a file with extension **vcg**. Two other kinds of files are also generated, one has extension **fdl** and the other has extension **rls**. The use of these two files will be described in Chapter 11 when we come to a more detailed look at proving correctness.

The various files form a tree structure corresponding to the structure of the unit analysed. Thus if the unit comprises the package The_Stack containing subprograms Push and Pop, then a directory called **the_stac** is created (note truncation to eight characters) and this will contain files **push.vcg**, **push.fdl**, **push.rls**, **pop.vcg**, **pop.fdl** and **pop.rls**.

Under Files in the Examiner Options dialogue box, the Target Data File option is useful if verification conditions are being generated especially in the case of conditions for run-time checks. The file can be used to supply values for various attributes, the file extension is usually **dat** and an example is

```
Integer'First = -32768
Integer'Last = 32767
```

This gives the values of the attributes Integer'First and Integer'Last for the target machine which might not be the same as those for the host machine running the Examiner, compiler and other tools. The values can also be expressed in based notation. The use of this information is discussed in Section 11.9; further details of the format of target data files will be found in the documentation on the CD.

The option Path Functions generates path functions. A similar file structure is used. The path functions themselves are in a file with extension **pfs** and another file with extension **dec** is also generated. Note that information flow analysis is required if path functions are requested.

## 9.7 DOS interface

This final section contains a very brief explanation of the background working of the Windows Interface. The main point is that the Interface creates a DOS command line and then invokes the Examiner as a batch job.

The names of the files selected are placed in a metafile (normally **sparktmp.smf**) and it is this metafile which is processed by the Examiner. The parameters controlling the various options including the name of this metafile are placed in a command file (normally **sparktmp.cmd**). Finally, a batch file (normally **sparktmp.bat**) contains the executable commands which actually invoke the Examiner and pass it the names of the command file and the output file, if any (usually **spark.out**).

The names of the metafile, the batch file and the output file can be changed in the General options dialogue box. The name of the command file is taken from that of the batch file as is a mysterious **pif** file which ensures that the Examiner behaves nicely under Windows. Further details of the syntax of the commands will be found in the documentation on the CD.

# Flow Analysis



This chapter looks at some of the mathematics behind the workings of the Examiner. It is of course not really necessary for the reader to understand how the Examiner works in order to use it and so this chapter can perhaps be considered optional reading. However, a little understanding will help in interpreting some of the messages.

Moreover, it is comforting to know that there is some mathematics behind it all. And to know that there are genuine reasons for the restrictions on control flow and that it is not simply a dictatorial whim that, for example, exit and return statements cannot be used quite freely.

## 10.1 Production of verification conditions

In Section 3.4 we remarked that verification conditions often appear to be mysterious and not particularly related to the code under examination. This section will hopefully reveal some of the mysteries.

We have seen that verification conditions apply to paths between two assertions, one at the beginning of a path and one at the end. Assertions are given by annotations which can take the form of preconditions and postconditions as well as assert statements. Some simple subprograms such as

Exchange (Section 3.4) just have one path whereas the subprogram Divide (Section 3.5) has three paths corresponding to how the loop is cut by the assert statement.

The general idea is that we take the final condition and then consider what must hold in order for the final condition to be true as we go backwards through the code step by step.

For example consider an assignment statement

```
X := Y + Z;
```

and suppose that we want to show that the postcondition

```
--# post X > 3
```

holds immediately *after* the assignment has been performed. The condition that must hold *before* the assignment is clearly that Y + Z > 3. We obtain this condition by simply replacing all instances of X (the left hand side of the assignment) by all instances of Y + Z (the right hand side) in the desired condition. The resulting condition is then known as the *weakest precondition*. If we can prove this weakest precondition then the desired postcondition automatically follows. This process of moving a postcondition backwards through some operation is known as *hoisting*.

The conclusion of the verification condition for a path is thus the weakest precondition obtained by hoisting its postcondition to the beginning of the path. The hypothesis for the path is of course the given precondition for it. So proving the verification condition amounts to showing that the weakest precondition is implied by the given precondition.

For example consider the procedure Exchange once more

```
procedure Exchange(X, Y: in out Float)
--# derives X from Y &
--#           Y from X;
--# post X = Y~ and Y = X~ ;
is
   T : Float;
begin
   T := X;  X := Y;  Y := T;
end Exchange;
```

If we hoist the desired postcondition back through the assignment Y := T we get

```
X = Y~ and T = X~          -- replacing Y by T
```

and then back through X := Y

```
Y = Y~ and T = X~          -- replacing X by Y
```

and finally back through T := X

```
Y = Y~ and X = X~          -- replacing T by X
```

In doing these transformations we have to remember that X~ means the initial value of X and so is not changed by the transformations – the initial value is just the initial value whereas X means the current value at a particular point.

So we end up with the condition that at the beginning the current value of X must equal the initial value of X and similarly for Y. Of course at the beginning the current value *is* the initial value and so the tildes can be dropped resulting in the final condition

```
Y = Y and X = X
```

Turning back to Section 3.4 we find that this corresponds exactly to the output of the Examiner

```
H1:   true .
      ->
C1:   y = y .
C2:   x = x .
```

where the hypothesis H1 is just true because there is no precondition in this case. Note that the Examiner always separates out individual subconditions as separate conclusions in order to simplify the presentation. This analysis incidentally reveals why the Examiner gives the y conclusion first (a human being would surely give them in alphabetical order!).

The other important statement with regard to hoisting is the if statement. (Other control flow statements can be broken down into if statements.) Consider

```
if X > Y then
   --# assert Z = 3;
```

At the point of the assert statement we know that X > Y is true and we need to ensure that, as a consequence of having taken that branch of the if statement, it follows that Z = 3 is true also. This is often expressed in the form

```
X > Y -> Z = 3
```

which is read as 'X > Y implies Z = 3'. This is therefore the weakest precondition for the truth of the assertion.

So in the case of an if statement the precondition is the implication that the condition for taking the branch gives rise to the desired postcondition. Of course we also have to consider the condition for taking the other branch and this will impose other preconditions on the state before the if statement.

We are now in a position to consider the procedure Divide which is rather more interesting and has an explicit precondition as well as a postcondition.

```
procedure Divide(M, N: in Integer; Q, R: out Integer)
--# derives Q, R from M, N;
--# pre (M >= 0) and (N > 0);
--# post (M = Q * N + R) and (R < N) and (R >= 0);
is
```

```
begin
   Q := 0;
   R := M;
   loop
      --# assert (M = Q * N + R) and (R >= 0);
      exit when R < N;
      Q := Q + 1;
      R := R - N;
   end loop;
end Divide;
```

Remember that there are three paths, from the start to the assert statement, around the loop, and from the assert to the end as was illustrated in Figure 3.2. We will consider these in turn.

The postcondition for the first path is that of the assert statement

```
(M = Q * N + R) and (R >= 0)
```

and hoisting this up to the beginning through the two assignment statements gives successively

```
(M = Q * N + M) and (M >= 0)          -- replacing R by M
(M = 0 * N + M) and (M >= 0)          -- replacing Q by 0
```

This last expression is the required conclusion for the first path and the hypothesis is the precondition for the procedure as a whole. This corresponds exactly to the verification condition produced by the Examiner which as we saw in Section 3.5 is

```
H1:   m >= 0 .
H2:   n > 0 .
      ->
C1:   m = 0 * n + m .
C2:   m >= 0 .
```

The path corresponding to the loop is processed by hoisting the assert condition backwards around the loop and taking account of the condition for not leaving the loop. First we go back through the two assignment statements in the loop; we start from the desired assert condition

```
(M = Q * N + R) and (R >= 0)
```

and hoist this twice giving

```
(M = Q * N + R - N) and (R - N >= 0)          -- replacing R by R - N
(M = (Q + 1) * N + R - N) and (R - N >= 0)    -- replacing Q by Q + 1
```

We now hoist this through the exit statement – which adds the condition **not** (R < N) – and finally obtain

```
(not R < N) -> (M = (Q + 1) * N + R - N) and (R - N >= 0)
```

So this is the weakest precondition for going around the loop and the condition in the assert statement is the given precondition. It follows that the verification condition to be proved is that the given precondition implies this weakest precondition.

We can generally write that some condition implies some other condition as

```
A -> Z
```

If the conclusion Z itself takes the form of an implication B -> C then the overall condition becomes

```
A -> (B -> C)
```

and this can alternatively be written as

```
(A and B) -> C
```

The Examiner always makes this transformation as shown by its output for this path which is

```
H1:   m = q * n + r .
H2:   r >= 0 .
H3:   not (r < n) .
      ->
C1:   m = (q + 1) * n + (r - n) .
C2:   r - n >= 0 .
```

The hypotheses H1 and H2 come directly from the given precondition (the assert statement) whereas H3 comes from the part of the weakest precondition before the -> (which is the condition for traversing the path). The conclusions C1 and C2 come from the part of the weakest precondition after the ->.

The final path is processed similarly with the assert statement again providing the given precondition. The final postcondition in this case is that for the procedure as a whole. Hoisting it through the exit statement gives

```
(R < N) -> (M = Q * N + R) and (R < N) and (R >= 0)
```

which is the required weakest precondition. Again the Examiner moves the first part into the hypotheses to give the result

```
H1:   m = q * n + r .
H2:   r >= 0 .
H3:   r < n .
      ->
C1:   m = q * n + r .
C2:   r < n .
C3:   r >= 0 .
```

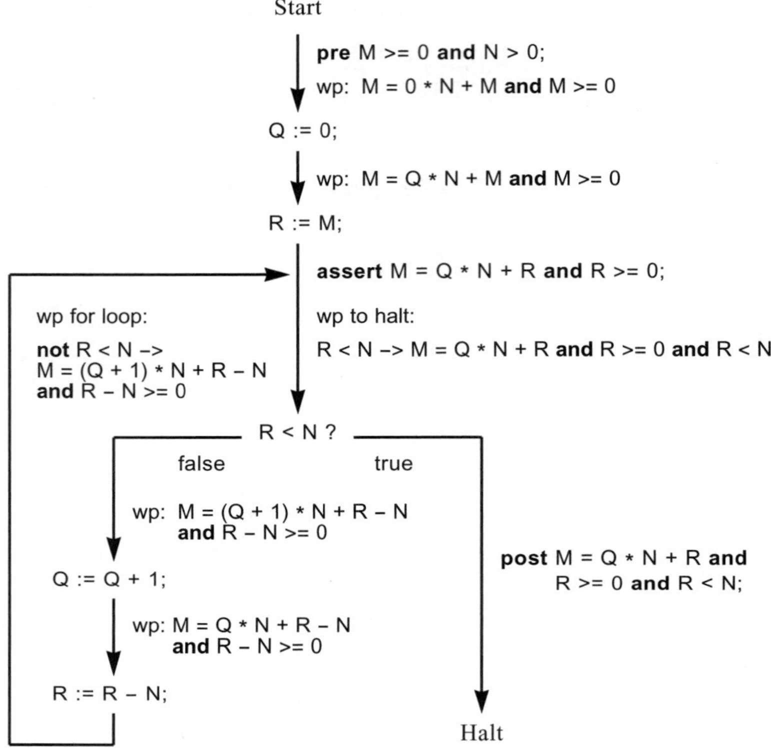


**Figure 10.1** Hoisting the conditions.

The various hoisted conditions and the resulting weakest preconditions for the three paths are shown in Figure 10.1.

Other control statements such as case statements and other forms of loops are treated similarly by breaking them down into one or more conditional statements.

The hoisting process also works with hypotheses as can be seen by considering the overall verification condition for the version of Exchange with the check in Section 3.6. The hypothesis

```
X = Y~
```

is introduced by the check and this is hoisted through the assignments to the beginning of the procedure resulting in the additional hypothesis

```
H2:    y = y
```

A similar process applies to the other examples in Section 3.6. For example the calls of the procedures Swap and Divide in the procedure GCD add many hypotheses and in fact the main loop has ten hypotheses in total (two from the assert, one from the while condition, five from the call of Divide and two from the call of Swap). It is worth emphasizing that the normal user need not be bothered by the apparent complexity introduced by all these hypotheses since the Simplifier reduces these verification conditions to true anyway.

Incidentally, it is important to appreciate that hoisting only works because of the absence of aliasing and side effects. The rules of SPARK forbidding such things are not to make life hard for the programmer but to make the proof process feasible.

---

**EXERCISE 10.1**

1 Show step by step the effect of hoisting the postcondition back through the assignments in the case of the two incorrect versions of procedure Exchange in Section 3.4.

---

## 10.2 Control flow composition

We recall from Chapter 6 that there are a number of restrictions on the flow of control in SPARK as compared to Ada. These are

- Goto statements are forbidden.
- Exit statements cannot give a loop name and so always refer to the innermost loop.
- Exit statements with a when clause must be at the outermost level of a loop.
- Exit statements without a when clause must be immediately within an if statement which is itself at the outermost level of a loop. The if statement must have no else or elsif part and the exit statement must be the last statement of the if statement.
- Return statements are not permitted in procedures.
- A function must have precisely one return statement which must be its last statement.

Without restrictions it would be impossible to carry out program analysis in the general case. Indeed, it has been known for a long time [Böhm and Jacopini, 1966] that sequential composition, conditional statements and while loops (plus assignment of course) are all that is necessary to program any computation. For example, a program with gotos can always be transformed to eliminate them although additional variables may be required. The control flow graphs for the permitted structures are shown in Figure 10.2.

However, being restricted to just these structures is inconvenient and it is often helpful to permit multiple exits from loops in order to avoid introducing

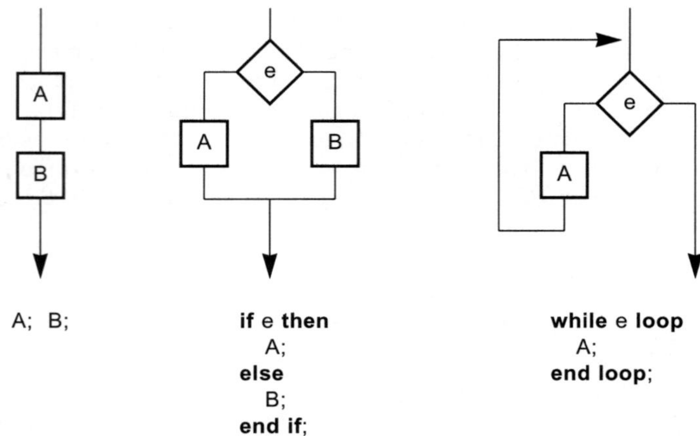


**Figure 10.2** Flow graphs of Böhm and Jacopini units.

additional variables. Accordingly SPARK permits multiple exits and in fact the flow graph of a SPARK subprogram obeys the rules of a Semi-Structured Flow Graph (SSFG) grammar [Farrow, Kennedy and Zucconi, 1975]. The SSFG rules ensure that the control flow graph of a subprogram is composed out of simple units in a unique manner and moreover that information flow analysis is straightforward.

The atomic unit is of course the assignment statement. The primitive compound statements are conditional statements and simple loop statements. All other allowed forms such as case statements and multi-exit loops can be composed out of these by various transformations. The most important transformations are composition by nesting (making one unit the controlled part of another unit such as a conditional statement) and composition by sequencing (putting two units in sequence). Subprogram calls are considered as a series of assignments to and from their parameters plus sequential composition.

Recursive transformations are often useful for deriving algorithms as we shall see later. For example the while statement

```
while e loop
   A;
end loop;
```

can be expressed as

```
if e then
   A;
   while e loop
      A;
   end loop;
end if;
```

In practice the various restrictions are not a burden. The absence of the goto statement is not a hindrance since there are other appropriate control structures that can be used. Moreover, the restrictions on return and exit statements are often imposed on the grounds that it is bad practice to bury them inside other control structures because this impedes program readability.

## 10.3 Information flow relations

In the remainder of this chapter we look in some detail at the mathematics of information flow analysis. As well as giving some insight into how the Examiner works this also reveals the origins of many of the error messages that it can produce. Understanding the underlying cause of an error message is often helpful in determining what is really wrong with a program. The techniques are based on a seminal paper to which the reader is referred for further details [Bergeretti and Carré, 1985].

Before setting out, it is worth emphasizing that information flow analysis takes no heed of the specific values of any of the variables involved. It is purely concerned with their dependency on one another and thus corresponds to the information in the derives annotation. But it is more than data flow analysis which simply relates to which variables are imports and exports of a subprogram and is not concerned with their interdependence. However, data flow analysis alone is quite effective and discovers many important anomalies such as the use of undefined variables and ineffective statements.

Information flow analysis is based on a number of relationships between variables and expressions. A statement group S (which might be a single statement, a sequence of statements, or a complete subprogram) has a set of variables $V$ and a set of expressions $E$. For example the sequence

```
X := Y + Z;  W := 2 * X;
```

has four variables (X, Y, Z, W) and two expressions ($e_1 \equiv$ Y + Z and $e_2 \equiv$ 2 * X).

The expressions depend on the variables and the variables depend on the expressions. As a consequence the final values of the variables depend upon the initial values of the variables through the intermediary of the expressions. The idea therefore is to develop formulae for the two relationships between the expressions and the variables and then to compute the overall relationship between the variables using these intermediate formulae.

We define

$D$ the set of variables that the statement group *may* Define.

$P$ the set of variables that the statement group *may* Preserve.

Note carefully the use of the word *may*. This relates to the fact that if a statement group has conditional statements or loops then the path taken may not traverse all assignments. What we are interested in is the possibility that a variable may be defined or preserved taking into account all possible paths. The actual values of variables are of course ignored in this analysis.

In the case of the above sequence we have

$$D = \{\mathsf{X}, \mathsf{W}\}, \qquad P = \{\mathsf{Y}, \mathsf{Z}\}$$

Note that the two sets do not overlap. But the sets can overlap if conditions are involved. For example in the case of

```
if W > 0 then X := Y + Z; else Z := 2; end if;
```

then we have four variables and three expressions ($e_1 \equiv \mathsf{W} > 0$, $e_2 \equiv \mathsf{Y} + \mathsf{Z}$, $e_3 \equiv 2$) and

$$D = \{\mathsf{X}, \mathsf{Z}\}, \qquad P = \{\mathsf{W}, \mathsf{X}, \mathsf{Y}, \mathsf{Z}\}$$

In this case the two sets overlap and in fact the set $P$ comprises all the variables involved.

We define three Boolean relationships between the variables $V$ and the expressions $E$.

$L(u, e)$ true if the initial value of variable $u$ *may* be used in computing the expression $e$.

$M(e, v)$ true if the expression $e$ *may* be used in computing the final value of variable $v$.

$R(u, v)$ true if the initial value of variable $u$ *may* be used in computing the final value of variable $v$.

Note once more the use of the word *may* in these definitions.

In the case of the sequence of two assignment statements

```
X := Y + Z; W := 2 * X;
```

the relations are true for the following pairs of arguments

$$L_{true} = \{(y, e_1), (z, e_1), (y, e_2), (z, e_2)\}$$

$$M_{true} = \{(e_1, w), (e_1, x), (e_2, w)\}$$

$$R_{true} = \{(y, w), (z, w), (y, x), (z, x), (y, y), (z, z)\}$$

Note that $L(x, e_2)$ is not true since although X does appear in the second expression, the initial value of X is overwritten by the first assignment. On the other hand, $L(y, e_2)$ and $L(z, e_2)$ are both true since although Y and Z are not explicitly mentioned in the second expression, they affect it indirectly through the assignment to X. The overall process is illustrated by Figure 10.3.

For the purpose of manipulation it is convenient to represent the relations by binary matrices so that for example

$$L_{ij} = 1, \text{ if } L(v_i, e_j) \text{ is true, and 0 otherwise}$$

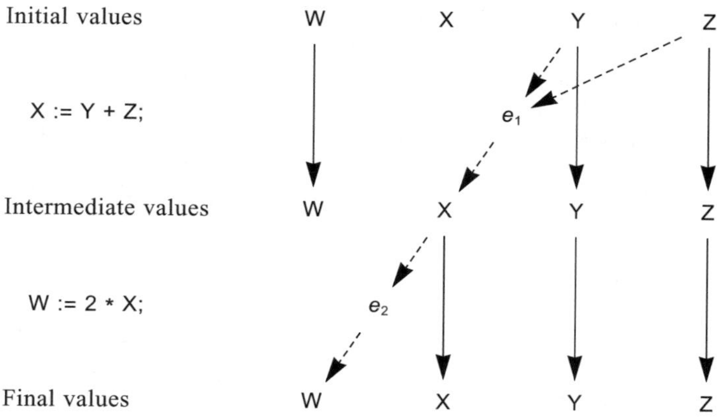


**Figure 10.3** Flow of information in two assignments.

So identifying W, X, Y, Z as $v_1$, $v_2$, $v_3$, $v_4$, the three matrices are

$$L = \begin{pmatrix} 0 & 0 \\ 0 & 0 \\ 1 & 1 \\ 1 & 1 \end{pmatrix} \qquad M = \begin{pmatrix} 1 & 1 & 0 & 0 \\ 1 & 0 & 0 & 0 \end{pmatrix} \qquad R = \begin{pmatrix} 0 & 0 & 0 & 0 \\ 0 & 0 & 0 & 0 \\ 1 & 1 & 1 & 0 \\ 1 & 1 & 0 & 1 \end{pmatrix}$$

It is also convenient to introduce the diagonal matrices $D$ and $P$ which have a 1 only in those entries corresponding to a variable that may be defined or preserved respectively. Thus for the pair of assignment statements we have

$$D = \begin{pmatrix} 1 & 0 & 0 & 0 \\ 0 & 1 & 0 & 0 \\ 0 & 0 & 0 & 0 \\ 0 & 0 & 0 & 0 \end{pmatrix} \qquad P = \begin{pmatrix} 0 & 0 & 0 & 0 \\ 0 & 0 & 0 & 0 \\ 0 & 0 & 1 & 0 \\ 0 & 0 & 0 & 1 \end{pmatrix}$$

In this particular case (in which the defined and preserved sets do not overlap) we have

$$D \textbf{ xor } P = I$$

where $I$ is the unit matrix.

When performing operations on binary matrices remember that the components 0 or 1 really represent truth values false and true respectively. In the above expression the operation **xor** is performed component by component.

The product of two binary matrices can be defined in the expected way with component addition replaced by **or** and multiplication by **and**. In other words the product $N$ of two matrices $L$ and $M$ with components $L_{ij}$ and $M_{jk}$ is the matrix with components

$$N_{ik} = (L_{i1} \textbf{ and } M_{1k}) \textbf{ or } (L_{i2} \textbf{ and } M_{2k}) \textbf{ or } \ldots \textbf{ or } (L_{in} \textbf{ and } M_{nk})$$

where $L$ has $n$ columns and $M$ has $n$ rows.

There is an important relation between $L$, $M$, $R$ and $P$ that holds for any statement group. A variable $u$ may be used in computing the value of a variable $v$ by two routes. First, it may be that $u$ is used in some expression that in turn is used to compute $v$. Secondly, in the case where $u$ and $v$ are the same variable, it may be that the variable is a member of the set of preserved variables $P$ and so it may affect itself by virtue of not being altered at all. This can be expressed symbolically as

$$R = LM \textbf{ or } P$$

When writing and manipulating matrices remember that the set of expressions and variables are in some overall context such as that of a particular subprogram body. Another general point is that initialized variable declarations can be treated as assignments just after the **begin** of a subprogram; since the initial values are always constant it follows that no flow analysis is required within declarations.

In the next sections we will show how the relations for various forms of statement group may be computed from those for the individual statements.

---

**EXERCISE 10.3**

1 Calculate the matrices $L$, $M$ and $R$ for the following individual statements within the context of them both (so that there are two expressions and four variables)

$S_1 \equiv$ X := Y + Z; $S_2 \equiv$ W := 2 * X;

Then compute $R_1R_2$ and show that this is the same as the matrix $R$ for the statement group comprising the sequence of the two statements.

2 Confirm that $R = LM$ **or** $P$ for the sequence of the previous exercise.

3 What are the various matrices for the null statement? Assume a context containing $V_n$ variables and $E_n$ expressions.

---

## 10.4 Sequences of statements

We now consider sequences of statements and show how the relations for a complete sequence may be computed from those of the individual statements.

Suppose we have two statement groups $S_1$ and $S_2$ and the various relations $L_1$, $L_2$ and so on. We are not assuming that $S_1$ and $S_2$ are assignment statements – they can be any groups of one or more statements. Consider the group $S$ comprising $S_1$ followed by $S_2$.

The first things to note are that the sets of defined and preserved variables are simply given by

$D = D_1$ **or** $D_2$
$P = P_1$ **and** $P_2$

And we note incidentally that $P_1$ **and** $P_2$ is the same as $P_1P_2$ because they are diagonal matrices.

In order to compute $L$ note that an expression $e$ of $S$ can be affected by a variable $v$ in two ways according to whether $e$ occurs in $S_1$ or in $S_2$. If it is an expression of $S_1$ then, as an expression of $S$, it is affected by $v$ if it is affected as an expression of $S_1$ in the usual way. On the other hand, if it is an expression of $S_2$ then it is affected by $v$ if there is some variable $u$ that affects it and $u$ is in turn affected by $v$ as a consequence of $S_1$. This can be expressed as

$L = L_1$ **or** $R_1L_2$

A similar argument regarding which expressions affect the final values of the variables shows that

$M = M_1R_2$ **or** $M_2$

In order to compute $R$ we use the general theorem of the last section

$R = LM$ **or** $P$

to give

$R = (L_1$ **or** $R_1L_2)(M_1R_2$ **or** $M_2)$ **or** $(P_1$ **and** $P_2)$

Now $L_1M_2 = 0$ (the matrix of all zeros) since no expression $e$ can be in both $S_1$ and $S_2$. Similarly $L_2M_1 = 0$. And as observed above $P_1$ **and** $P_2 = P_1P_2$. This gives

$R = L_1M_1R_2$ **or** $R_1L_2M_2$ **or** $P_1P_2$

If we now replace $R_1$ by $L_1M_1$ **or** $P_1$ and $R_2$ similarly by $L_2M_2$ **or** $P_2$ we get

$R = L_1M_1(L_2M_2$ **or** $P_2)$ **or** $(L_1M_1$ **or** $P_1)L_2M_2$ **or** $P_1P_2$
$= (L_1M_1$ **or** $P_1)(L_2M_2$ **or** $P_2)$
$= R_1R_2$

which is a neat result.

Sequences of several groups can be computed by repeated application of the formulae. The binary operations are all associative and so it follows that the order of application does not matter.

As an example we will consider the procedure Exchange yet again.

```
procedure Exchange(X, Y: in out Float)
--# derives X from Y &
--#         Y from X;
is
   T: Float;
```

```
begin
  T := X;  X := Y;  Y := T;
end Exchange;
```

There are three variables X, Y and T and three expressions. The matrices for the individual statements are trivial such as

$$L_1 = \begin{array}{c} \\ x \\ y \\ t \end{array}\!\!\begin{array}{c} \begin{array}{ccc} 1 & 2 & 3 \end{array} \\ \begin{pmatrix} 1 & 0 & 0 \\ 0 & 0 & 0 \\ 0 & 0 & 0 \end{pmatrix} \end{array} \qquad M_1 = \begin{array}{c} \\ 1 \\ 2 \\ 3 \end{array}\!\!\begin{array}{c} \begin{array}{ccc} x & y & t \end{array} \\ \begin{pmatrix} 0 & 0 & 1 \\ 0 & 0 & 0 \\ 0 & 0 & 0 \end{pmatrix} \end{array} \qquad R_1 = \begin{array}{c} \\ x \\ y \\ t \end{array}\!\!\begin{array}{c} \begin{array}{ccc} x & y & t \end{array} \\ \begin{pmatrix} 1 & 0 & 1 \\ 0 & 1 & 0 \\ 0 & 0 & 0 \end{pmatrix} \end{array}$$

and the matrices for the whole procedure are easily shown to be

$$L = \begin{array}{c} \\ x \\ y \\ t \end{array}\!\!\begin{array}{c} \begin{array}{ccc} 1 & 2 & 3 \end{array} \\ \begin{pmatrix} 1 & 0 & 1 \\ 0 & 1 & 0 \\ 0 & 0 & 0 \end{pmatrix} \end{array} \qquad M = \begin{array}{c} \\ 1 \\ 2 \\ 3 \end{array}\!\!\begin{array}{c} \begin{array}{ccc} x & y & t \end{array} \\ \begin{pmatrix} 0 & 1 & 1 \\ 1 & 0 & 0 \\ 0 & 1 & 0 \end{pmatrix} \end{array} \qquad R = \begin{array}{c} \\ x \\ y \\ t \end{array}\!\!\begin{array}{c} \begin{array}{ccc} x & y & t \end{array} \\ \begin{pmatrix} 0 & 1 & 1 \\ 1 & 0 & 0 \\ 0 & 0 & 0 \end{pmatrix} \end{array}$$

The Examiner computes these matrices and then checks them for various errors and anomalies. There is nothing untoward in this case. Note in particular from the matrix $R$ that the initial value of T is not used to compute the final value of X or Y; this is as it should be.

Now suppose that the last statement is replaced by Y := X; as in Section 3.2 so that the statement part is

```
T := X;  X := Y;  Y := X;
```

As we saw this gave rise to a number of error and warning messages. The matrices now become

$$L = \begin{array}{c} \\ x \\ y \\ t \end{array}\!\!\begin{array}{c} \begin{array}{ccc} 1 & 2 & 3 \end{array} \\ \begin{pmatrix} 1 & 0 & 0 \\ 0 & 1 & 1 \\ 0 & 0 & 0 \end{pmatrix} \end{array} \qquad M = \begin{array}{c} \\ 1 \\ 2 \\ 3 \end{array}\!\!\begin{array}{c} \begin{array}{ccc} x & y & t \end{array} \\ \begin{pmatrix} 0 & 0 & 1 \\ 1 & 1 & 0 \\ 0 & 1 & 0 \end{pmatrix} \end{array} \qquad R = \begin{array}{c} \\ x \\ y \\ t \end{array}\!\!\begin{array}{c} \begin{array}{ccc} x & y & t \end{array} \\ \begin{pmatrix} 0 & 0 & 1 \\ 1 & 1 & 0 \\ 0 & 0 & 0 \end{pmatrix} \end{array}$$

In examining the matrices we pay particular attention to those entries corresponding to the imported and exported variables of the procedure. In this case X and Y are expected to be both imported and exported according to the derives list.

The first anomaly is that $M$ contains a row (the first row) for which all entries corresponding to the exported variables are 0. This means that the statement containing this expression can have no effect on the exported values and so is *ineffective*. This is the origin of the message

```
!!! (  1)  Flow Error          : Ineffective statement.
```

Another test is to look at the matrix $R$ and to ensure that every imported variable has a 1 against some exported variable. In this case the row for variable X has 0 against all the exported variables. Hence we get

```
!!! (  2)  Flow Error          : Importation of the initial
           value of variable X is ineffective.
```

There are also checks of a general nature not related to the matrices. One such check is to scan the text to ensure that all variables are used somewhere. This gives rise to

```
!!! (  3)  Flow Error          : The variable T is neither
           referenced nor exported.
```

More specific checks ensure that the relationships stated in the derives annotation are correctly described by the matrix *R*. The derives annotation is in fact a precise description of the submatrix of *R* corresponding to the imported and exported variables. In this case the derives annotation states that Y is derived from X (and nothing else) and so we would expect a 1 in the Y column against X. However, there is a 0 and this results in

```
!!! (  4)  Flow Error          : The imported value of X is
           not used in the derivation of Y.
```

And finally there should of course not be a 1 against any other imported variable in the column for Y but in fact there is a 1 against the entry for Y itself. This produces the warning

```
??? (  5)  Warning             : The imported value of Y may
           be used in the derivation of Y.
```

Note that this is a warning. This is because the analysis is generally based on the syntactic possibility that a variable may impact on others. Remember that the relationships *L*, *M* and *R* all have *may* in their definition. For example a body might comprise

```
X := Y - Y;  Y := X;
```

in which case the operations are such that the initial value of Y does not influence the final value of Y. Nevertheless information flow analysis as summarized by the matrix *R* predicts that Y depends on Y. The other reason for writing *may* is that there might be several paths and allowance has to be made for this fact in the relationships.

The above discussion has been based on the assumption that we have requested information flow analysis. If on the other hand, we only ask for data flow analysis, then the derives annotation is not required and if given is ignored. The analysis is then based on a synthetic derives annotation constructed from the mode information in the parameter list and global annotation which assumes that all exports depend upon all imports. Naturally enough, the analysis between the derives annotation and the matrix *R* is then not performed; as a consequence the last two messages are not produced. Throughout this chapter we will assume that information flow analysis is being performed.

## 10.5 Undefined variables

The previous section showed how the $M$ and $R$ matrices are used to detect certain errors. The $L$ matrix could be used to detect expressions that depend upon undefined variables. However, experience shows that extensive use of the $L$ matrix for this results in an unhelpful number of messages; this is because one expression depending upon an uninitialized variable will in turn typically cause many other expressions to depend upon that uninitialized variable.

In fact the Examiner only uses the $L$ matrix to report on the use of uninitialized variables in expressions in conditions such as

```
if X > Y then
```

In other contexts it is enough to detect only those expressions which *directly* depend upon undefined variables. In order to do this we introduce two other relations similar to the $L$ relation.

$T(u, e)$ true if the initial value of variable $u$ *may be used directly* in computing the expression $e$.

$T'(u, e)$ true if the initial value of variable $u$ *is always used directly* in computing the expression $e$.

The difference between $T$ and $L$ is that $T$ requires the use of $u$ to be direct, that is $u$ appears explicitly in the text of the expression $e$. The $T$ relation has the normal *may* caveat which means that $T$ is true only if there is *some* path from the start to $e$ that does not change $u$; this path need never be taken and so $T$ like $L$ can only give rise to warnings. The $T'$ relation is stronger and is true if *all* paths from the start to $e$ do not change $u$. This means that if $T'(u, e)$ is true and $u$ is not an imported variable then there is definitely an error.

The matrices $T$ and $T'$ are both the same as $L$ for a single assignment statement. For a sequence of two statement groups $S_1$ and $S_2$ they are

$$T = T_1 \textbf{ or } T_2P_1$$
$$T' = T'_1 \textbf{ or } T'_2P'_1$$

where $P'$ is the strong version of $P$. In other words $P'$ gives the variables that *are* preserved whereas $P$ gives the variables that *may* be preserved. Note that $P' = D \textbf{ xor } I$ where $I$ is the unit matrix.

As an example suppose that we make an error in the first statement of procedure Exchange so that the sequence becomes

```
Y := X;  X := Y;  Y := T;
```

The various matrices now become

$$L = \begin{array}{c} \\ x \\ y \\ t \end{array}\begin{array}{c} 1\ 2\ 3 \\ \begin{pmatrix} 1 & 1 & 0 \\ 0 & 0 & 0 \\ 0 & 0 & 1 \end{pmatrix}\end{array} \qquad M = \begin{array}{c} \\ 1 \\ 2 \\ 3 \end{array}\begin{array}{c} x\ y\ t \\ \begin{pmatrix} 1 & 0 & 0 \\ 1 & 0 & 0 \\ 0 & 1 & 0 \end{pmatrix}\end{array} \qquad R = \begin{array}{c} \\ x \\ y \\ t \end{array}\begin{array}{c} x\ y\ t \\ \begin{pmatrix} 1 & 0 & 0 \\ 0 & 0 & 0 \\ 0 & 1 & 1 \end{pmatrix}\end{array}$$

$$T = \begin{array}{c} \\ x \\ y \\ t \end{array} \overset{\begin{array}{ccc} 1 & 2 & 3 \end{array}}{\begin{pmatrix} 1 & 0 & 0 \\ 0 & 0 & 0 \\ 0 & 0 & 1 \end{pmatrix}} \qquad T' = \begin{array}{c} \\ x \\ y \\ t \end{array} \overset{\begin{array}{ccc} 1 & 2 & 3 \end{array}}{\begin{pmatrix} 1 & 0 & 0 \\ 0 & 0 & 0 \\ 0 & 0 & 1 \end{pmatrix}}$$

The matrix $T$ is different from $L$ since the initial value of X affects expression $e_2$ only indirectly and so $L(x, e_2)$ is true whereas $T(x, e_2)$ is false. Of course $T$ and $T'$ are the same in this example because there is only one path.

The matrix $T$ (strictly $T'$) reveals that the initial value of the variable T is used in $e_3$ (the row for the variable T has a 1 in the third column). However, the variable T is not imported and so its initial value is undefined. The Examiner reports

```
Y := X;  X := Y;  Y := T;
                       ^1

!!! (  1)  Flow Error          : Expression contains
           reference(s) to undefined variable T.
```

In the previous section we saw that there is a general check that all variables are used somewhere (either by occurring in an expression or by being exported) and that this gave rise to message (3) in the incorrect example of that section. There is a corresponding general check relating to the setting of variables. This checks that all variables are set somewhere, by being the destination of an assignment or an export from some called procedure or by being imported in the first place. This check fails for the example considered here and this gives rise to

```
!!! (  3)  Flow Error          : The variable T is neither
           imported nor defined.
```

A related message concerning the undefined nature of T is deduced from the matrix $R$ when checking the derives annotation for Y. This is a warning because the definition of $R$ is based on which variables *may* affect other variables. The message is

```
??? (  7)  Warning             : The undefined initial value
           of T may be used in the derivation of Y.
```

Other messages are similar to those produced by the incorrect example of the previous section.

---

**EXERCISE 10.5**

1 Predict the four other messages produced by the Examiner for the last example of this section by considering the $R$ matrix.

---

## 10.6 Subprogram calls

Subprogram calls are modelled as assignments to their exported variables where the expressions involve the relevant imported variables. Only the information in the derives annotation is needed in order to do this. The details of the body are not required. This is a very important point; not only is it important for logical development but it also ensures that the time taken for the Examiner to perform its analysis does not increase exponentially with the size of the program.

Consider a call of the procedure Exchange such as in the procedure CAB of Section 3.6

```
procedure CAB(A, B, C: in out Float)
--# derives A from C &
--#         B from A &
--#         C from B;
is
begin
  Exchange(X => A, Y => B);
  Exchange(X => A, Y => C);
end CAB;
```

where we have used named notation for clarity. The derives annotation of Exchange is

```
--# derives X from Y &
--#         Y from X;
```

and so the first call is modelled as the two statements

```
A := f(B);  B := g(A);
```

where f and g are some expressions of their arguments. Note that these statements are considered to be performed simultaneously. So the A in g(A) is always the initial value of A.

It is always the case that the number of expressions in the model of the procedure call equals the number of exported variables whereas the number of variables involved is that of the context. The $L$, $M$ and $R$ matrices are easily computed from the derives annotation.

For the procedure CAB as a whole there are three variables and four expressions (two for each call of Exchange). The $R$ matrices for the two calls are

$$R_1 = \begin{array}{c} \\ a \\ b \\ c \end{array} \begin{array}{c} \begin{array}{ccc} a & b & c \end{array} \\ \begin{pmatrix} 0 & 1 & 0 \\ 1 & 0 & 0 \\ 0 & 0 & 1 \end{pmatrix} \end{array} \qquad R_2 = \begin{array}{c} \\ a \\ b \\ c \end{array} \begin{array}{c} \begin{array}{ccc} a & b & c \end{array} \\ \begin{pmatrix} 0 & 0 & 1 \\ 0 & 1 & 0 \\ 1 & 0 & 0 \end{pmatrix} \end{array}$$

Note that C is unchanged by the first call and B is unchanged by the second call. The matrix for the procedure as a whole is then $R_1R_2$ which is

$$R = \begin{array}{c|ccc} & a & b & c \\ \hline a & 0 & 1 & 0 \\ b & 0 & 0 & 1 \\ c & 1 & 0 & 0 \end{array}$$

and this correctly matches the derives annotation of the procedure CAB.

Functions are treated in a very simple manner. Remember that functions in SPARK cannot have side effects and have no exported variables. All the variables in the actual parameters of a call are simply treated as variables of the expression containing the call.

---

**EXERCISE 10.6**

1 Suppose that the second call of Exchange in CAB is accidentally written as Exchange(B, C). Compute the $R$ matrix and consider what messages you might expect from the Examiner.

2 Suppose that the second call of Exchange in CAB simply repeats the first one. Compute the various matrices and predict the messages from the Examiner.

---

## 10.7 Conditional statements

Conditional statements introduce the possibility of several paths. Since we are only considering the syntactic form this means that we cannot know which path will be taken and so the *may* in the various relations becomes important.

Consider the general conditional statement

```
if e then S1; else S2; end if;
```

where $S_1$ and $S_2$ are arbitrary statement groups.

The sets of defined and preserved variables are obviously given by

$$D = D_1 \textbf{ or } D_2$$
$$P = P_1 \textbf{ or } P_2$$

In order to compute the other matrices it is convenient to define $L$ and $M$ matrices for the expression $e$ that defines the condition. We define $L_e$ as the matrix where the only 1s are in the column corresponding to the expression $e$ and in the rows corresponding to the variables appearing in $e$. We define the matrix $M_e$ as that with a 1 in every entry of the row corresponding to $e$; this is an appropriate definition for an expression standing alone since it reflects the fact that (without knowing its context) the expression may affect any variable at all.

It is then straightforward to see that

$$L = L_e \textbf{ or } L_1 \textbf{ or } L_2$$
$$M = M_eD \textbf{ or } M_1 \textbf{ or } M_2$$

And then

$$R = LM \textbf{ or } P$$
$$= (L_e \textbf{ or } L_1 \textbf{ or } L_2)(M_eD \textbf{ or } M_1 \textbf{ or } M_2) \textbf{ or } (P_1 \textbf{ or } P_2)$$

Now remember that $L_xM_y$ is null for distinct statement groups $S_x$ and $S_y$ since no expression can be in two different places at the same time. And so most terms vanish when the above is expanded giving

$$R = L_eM_eD \textbf{ or } L_1M_1 \textbf{ or } L_2M_2 \textbf{ or } P_1 \textbf{ or } P_2$$
$$= L_eM_eD \textbf{ or } R_1 \textbf{ or } R_2$$

The matrix $L_eM_eD$ has a 1 in the rows corresponding to the variables of $e$ and the columns corresponding to the variables of $D$.

It is also easily seen that

$$T = L_e \textbf{ or } T_1 \textbf{ or } T_2$$
$$T' = L_e \textbf{ or } T'_1 \textbf{ or } T'_2$$

The rules for the case where there is no else part are obtained by treating $S_2$ as a null statement (see Exercise 10.3(**3**)). So for

```
if e then S1; end if;
```

we have

$$D = D_1$$
$$P = I$$
$$L = L_e \textbf{ or } L_1$$
$$M = M_eD \textbf{ or } M_1$$
$$R = L_eM_eD \textbf{ or } R_1 \textbf{ or } I$$
$$T = L_e \textbf{ or } T_1$$
$$T' = L_e \textbf{ or } T'_1$$

Note in particular that $P$ is $I$. This is because all variables are preserved if $e$ is false.

Conditional statements with elsif parts and case statements can be treated as sequences of simple if statements.

---

## EXERCISE 10.7

**1** Calculate the matrices $L$, $M$ and $R$ for the conditional statement discussed in Section 10.3 which was

```
if W > 0 then X := Y + Z; else Z := 2; end if;
```

---

## 10.8 Loop statements and stability

Loop statements have interesting properties concerning information flow. They provide opportunities for the Examiner to issue messages warning of possible errors associated with the concept of loop stability.

The simplest form of loop (other than the infinite loop without an exit) is the classic while statement.

```
while e loop
   A;
end loop;
```

The sets of defined and preserved variables for the while statement are clearly exactly the same as for the simple conditional statement, namely

$$D = D_A$$
$$P = I$$

In order to obtain the other formulae we first note that the loop can be expressed recursively (unrolled) as

```
if e then
   A;
   while e loop
      A;
   end loop;
end if;
```

We can then use the formulae for the simple if statement where the statement group $S_1$ is the statement A followed by the while statement itself. So we can express $L$ for the loop as

$$\begin{aligned} L &= L_e \textbf{ or } L_1 \\ &= L_e \textbf{ or } L_A \textbf{ or } R_A L \end{aligned}$$

and then by repeatedly substituting for $L$ on the right we have

$$\begin{aligned} L &= (I \textbf{ or } R_A \textbf{ or } R_A{}^2 \textbf{ or } R_A{}^3 \textbf{ or } \ldots)(L_e \textbf{ or } L_A) \\ &= R_A{}^*(L_e \textbf{ or } L_A) \end{aligned}$$

where $X^*$ denotes the transitive closure of $X$ which is the infinite union of all powers of $X$. In a similar manner we can show that

$$R = R_A{}^*(L_e M_e D_A \textbf{ or } I)$$
$$M = M_e D_A \textbf{ or } M_A R$$

The transitive closure of $R_A$ thus plays an important role in determining the relations for the while statement. There are a number of well-known algorithms for computing transitive closures such as that based on Warshall's theorem [Warshall, 1962]. Thus, given a matrix $A$, the transitive closure may be computed (in SPARK) by

```
for K in Integer range 1 .. N loop
   for I in Integer range 1 .. N loop
      for J in Integer range 1 .. N loop
         A(I, J) := A(I, J) or (A(I, K) and A(K, J));
      end loop;
   end loop;
end loop;
```

This computation is fast since it is only of the order of $N^3$ which is perhaps surprising since the infinite union of all powers suggests a potentially unbounded computation.

As an example consider the procedure GCD of Section 3.6 in the form

```
procedure GCD(M, N: in Integer; G: out Integer)
--# derives G from M, N;
is
   C, D: Integer;
   R: Integer;
begin
   C := M;  D := N;          -- 1, 2
   while D /= 0 loop         -- 3
      R := C rem D;          -- 4
      C := D;  D := R;       -- 5, 6
   end loop;
   G := C;                   -- 7
end GCD;
```

Comments have been added in order to simplify identification of the seven expressions. There are six variables M, N, G, C, D and R. However, the essence of the calculation concerns only the three variables C, D and R and the four expressions of the loop and so we will ignore the others for the moment.

The matrices for the body of the loop are

$$L_A = \begin{array}{c} \\ c \\ d \\ r \end{array} \begin{array}{c} 3\ 4\ 5\ 6 \\ \begin{pmatrix} 0 & 1 & 0 & 1 \\ 0 & 1 & 1 & 1 \\ 0 & 0 & 0 & 0 \end{pmatrix} \end{array} \qquad M_A = \begin{array}{c} \\ 3 \\ 4 \\ 5 \\ 6 \end{array} \begin{array}{c} c\ d\ r \\ \begin{pmatrix} 0 & 0 & 0 \\ 0 & 1 & 1 \\ 1 & 0 & 0 \\ 0 & 1 & 0 \end{pmatrix} \end{array} \qquad R_A = \begin{array}{c} \\ c \\ d \\ r \end{array} \begin{array}{c} c\ d\ r \\ \begin{pmatrix} 0 & 1 & 1 \\ 1 & 1 & 1 \\ 0 & 0 & 0 \end{pmatrix} \end{array}$$

We now have to compute the transitive closure of $R_A$. It is easy to see that $R_A{}^2$ and all higher powers are the same and so

$$R_A{}^2 = \begin{array}{c} \\ c \\ d \\ r \end{array} \begin{array}{c} c\ d\ r \\ \begin{pmatrix} 1 & 1 & 1 \\ 1 & 1 & 1 \\ 0 & 0 & 0 \end{pmatrix} \end{array} \qquad R_A{}^* = I \textbf{ or } R_A \text{ or } R_A{}^2 = \begin{array}{c} \\ c \\ d \\ r \end{array} \begin{array}{c} c\ d\ r \\ \begin{pmatrix} 1 & 1 & 1 \\ 1 & 1 & 1 \\ 0 & 0 & 1 \end{pmatrix} \end{array}$$

(Incidentally, the powers might oscillate and never reach a stable point but the union always becomes stable. Note that we cannot say converge because we are not talking about continuous functions.)

We are now in a position to compute the matrix $R$ for the loop as a whole (we will refer to this matrix as $R_{loop}$ in order to distinguish it from the variable R). First note that the matrix $L_eM_eD_A$ has a 1 in the rows corresponding to the variables in the expression of the condition and in the columns corresponding to all the variables that may be defined by the body. Since only the variable D occurs in the expression but all three variables are defined by the body, it follows that

$$L_eM_eD_A = \begin{array}{c} \\ c \\ d \\ r \end{array} \begin{array}{c} c\ d\ r \\ \begin{pmatrix} 0 & 0 & 0 \\ 1 & 1 & 1 \\ 0 & 0 & 0 \end{pmatrix} \end{array} \qquad L_eM_eD_A \textbf{ or } I = \begin{array}{c} \\ c \\ d \\ r \end{array} \begin{array}{c} c\ d\ r \\ \begin{pmatrix} 1 & 0 & 0 \\ 1 & 1 & 1 \\ 0 & 0 & 1 \end{pmatrix} \end{array}$$

And then finally

$$R_{loop} = R_A{}^*(L_eM_eD_A \textbf{ or } I) = \begin{array}{c} \\ c \\ d \\ r \end{array} \begin{array}{c} c\ d\ r \\ \begin{pmatrix} 1 & 1 & 1 \\ 1 & 1 & 1 \\ 0 & 0 & 1 \end{pmatrix} \end{array}$$

Note the two differences between the matrices $R_{loop}$ and $R_A$. First, the initial value of the variable R for the loop can affect its final value because the loop may not be executed at all in which case it keeps its initial value; on the other hand the initial value of R for the body does not impact on the final value because it always gets overwritten. Secondly, the initial value of C can affect the final value of C for the loop whereas it does not for the body; this is because the loop may be executed more than once in which case the value of C affects D the first time and this in turn affects C the second time. It is easy to see intuitively how the possible different number of executions of the loop (including none) are taken into account by the transitive closure of $R_A$.

Another point in this example is that the matrix $R_{loop}$ is actually the same as $R_A{}^*$. This is because the only variables in the expression controlling the loop are changed by the body of the loop. But of course if the expression contained variables not manipulated by the body then the matrices would be different because the variables in the expression would affect those in the loop (by affecting how many times the loop is executed). This would happen if the loop were perhaps

```
while D /= M loop
   R := C rem D;
   C := D;  D := R;
end loop;
```

This code is wrong in the sense that it does not solve the problem but there are no information flow errors as such and the Examiner reports that none are found.

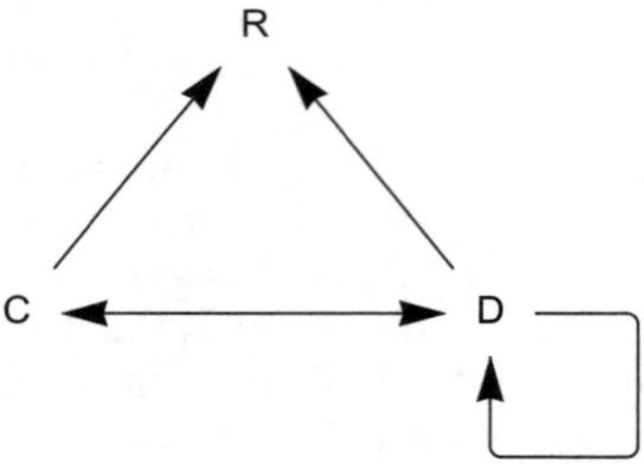


**Figure 10.4** Flow graph of body of loop.

If none of the variables affected by the body occur in the expression then the loop will execute for ever (or not at all). This would happen if we had accidentally written

```
while M /= 0 loop
   R := C rem D;
   C := D;  D := R;
end loop;
```

The Examiner notices this anomaly and reports

```
          while M /= 0 loop
                 ^1
!!! (  1)  Flow Error          : Exit condition is stable, of
           index 0.
```

This message means that the loop condition is unchanged by the loop body and therefore stable. We will now look at the meaning of the index value mentioned in the message.

The matrix $R_A$ can be represented as a flow graph as shown in Figure 10.4. The nodes are the variables of $D_A$, that is those that may be affected by the body of the loop; other variables are omitted. The arcs represent elements whose values are 1 and so correspond to a dependency between the variables at the nodes.

We see that the graph exhibits cycles. There is a cycle of length 2 between the variables C and D and also a cycle of length 1 just involving D.

A variable is said to be *stable* if it is not on a cycle and moreover there are no paths to it from a cycle. In this example the only variable not on a cycle is R but in any event there are paths to R from both C and D. So none of the variables are stable. (Remember that we are only discussing variables that may be defined by the loop body.)

The examples in Figure 10.5 show graphs of loop bodies with stable variables. In the first graph there is a cycle but the variables P and Q do not have paths from the cycle. In the second graph there are no cycles at all. The variables P, Q, A, B and C are therefore stable.

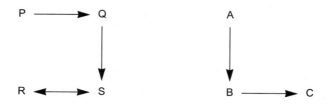


**Figure 10.5** Flow graphs exhibiting stable variables.

The stability index of a variable is defined as the maximum length of path that leads to the variable. Thus A and P have index 0, B and Q have index 1 and C has index 2. It is easy to see that stable variables do not change after the loop has been executed once more than the number of times given by their index. Thus A is changed only by the first iteration and does not change thereafter; B is changed by the first and second and not thereafter and so on.

Stability is defined for expressions as well as for variables. An expression in a loop is said to be stable if every variable in it is either not changed by the loop at all or is stable. The stability index for an expression is zero if none of its variables are changed by the loop and otherwise is one more than the maximum index values of its stable variables. This definition applies not only to expressions in the body of the loop but also to the expression which is the loop exit condition as well.

The Examiner checks loop exit conditions and issues an error message if they are stable as in the example above. An index of zero means that the loop will never be executed or will execute for ever – the program is presumably in error (but it might be the outermost loop of a continuous process). If the index is one then the program may be in error or alternatively the loop can be replaced by an if statement. Higher values are just suspicious.

As another example suppose we accidentally write the loop as

```
while D /= 0 loop
   R := M rem N;
   C := D;  D := R;
end loop;
```

where the assignment to R mistakenly uses the initial parameters rather than C and D. It is easily seen that both C and D are then stable; D has index 0 and C has index 1. The loop condition involves D and so has index one more than that of D namely 1. The Examiner reports this accordingly.

The Examiner also issues messages regarding stable expressions within a loop that influence the path taken through the loop – that is expressions occurring in the conditions of if and case statements within the loop. Experience has shown that issuing messages regarding other stable expressions is unhelpful.

The above discussion has been in terms of the simple while statement. The more general loop statement with multiple exits of the form

```
loop
   exit when e1;
   S1;
   exit when e2;
   S2;
   ...
   exit when en;
   Sn;
end loop;
```

can be treated in a similar manner. It can be shown for example that

$$R = X_n^*((Q_1 \text{ or } I) \text{ or } X_1(Q_2 \text{ or } I) \text{ or } X_2(Q_3 \text{ or } I) \ldots \text{ or } X_{n-1}(Q_n \text{ or } I))$$

where

$$X_i = R_1 R_2 R_3 \ldots R_i, \quad Q_i = L_{e_i} M_{e_i} D, \quad D = D_1 \text{ or } D_2 \text{ or } D_3 \ldots \text{ or } D_n$$

Further examples and discussion will be found in the paper [Bergeretti and Carré, 1985]. This paper also discusses the concepts of partial statements associated with a variable and how they can be used as an aid to program analysis, debugging and maintenance.

---

## EXERCISE 10.8

1 Draw the flow graph for the loop

```
while D /= 0 loop
   R := C rem D;
   C := D;  D := 1;
end loop;
```

where the final assignment has been changed. Predict any message from the Examiner concerning loop stability.

2 Prove the formula for the matrix $R$ for the while statement and then for the multi-exit loop statement.

# 11 Verification



This chapter looks in more detail at the topic of verification which was introduced in Chapter 3 when we looked at some simple path functions and verification conditions.

This chapter also introduces the general concepts of the FDL language in which verification conditions and proofs are written and shows how information is presented to the Simplifier and Proof Checker. However, a complete description of FDL and the interactive use of the Proof Checker is outside the scope of this book.

We start with some philosophical remarks concerning the difference between testing and verification.

## 11.1 Testing and verification

It is important to understand the difference between testing and verification. Testing is rather like carrying out a scientific experiment whereas verification is akin to a mathematical proof.

All that testing typically does is possibly show the presence of a bug. If a test passes, then we know that the program behaves as hoped given one particular set of inputs, but that says nothing about correctness as a whole. Similarly, a typical scientific experiment (e.g. is light deflected by the planet Mercury as predicted by Einstein?) might show that a given hypothesis is not invalid for one set of conditions. Thus if light is not deflected by Mercury then Einstein was wrong but if it is deflected then it only shows that Einstein is right in that one case. It doesn't prove the theory but just adds supporting evidence for it. Scientific experiments also suffer from the problems of measurement errors and so have confidence bounds as well; was the light bent the correct amount and how accurate are our instruments? Quantum mechanics adds yet another dimension which we need not contemplate!

At least in program testing, we normally get a clear answer since we are usually dealing with discrete values. Similarly, the more tests that pass, the more confidence we have in the program. In a very simple case it may be possible to test all combinations of inputs and then we have a full proof but this is unlikely. Experience in testing shows that it is a good idea to test extreme values since these are the cases that are likely to have bugs. But generally speaking, testing is a very hit and miss affair. Lots of tests may give general confidence but it is hard to quantify the confidence in a mathematical way such as required for Hazard Analysis.

Mathematical proof is quite different to scientific experiment. Given certain axioms, a proof covers all cases and there are no exceptions; thus we show indisputably that all isosceles triangles do have equal base angles and we don't have to go around measuring lots of them. Of course a proof may have a flaw (in which case it wasn't a proof anyway) but that is another matter. Sometimes we may not be able to prove a potential theorem one way or the other from a set of axioms as shown by Gödel. Thus Pappus' theorem cannot be proved from the propositions of incidence even though it is stated entirely in terms of incidence.

Program verification is like mathematical proof. If we can prove that a program is correct (given certain conditions defined as part of its specification) then we have absolute confidence that it will work for all circumstances covered by the conditions. Sometimes we might not be able to find a proof; that might not mean that the program is incorrect but simply that we have not got the right approach to proving it. Moreover, the proof of a program has to be complete and correct. Whereas in mathematics, the theorem might be true even if the proof is incomplete, what ultimately matters in a program is the code and not the specification since it is the code that is executed.

The above remarks should not be taken to mean that testing is a waste of time. In a large program a full mathematical proof may be impossible for all but the most critical parts and testing is then vital for the rest of it. Moreover, the specification might be incorrect, the compiler might generate the wrong code, the hardware might not work and so on; for all these more general reasons, testing is *always* required.

An interesting point that is easily overlooked is that we cannot prove that a program is correct if it is not correct. And so failure to find a proof may simply mean that the program is actually wrong. We must therefore remove all the bugs before a program can be proved to be correct. The very process of attempting a proof is likely to reveal bugs but testing is also a pretty useful way of finding bugs.

## 11.2 Proof contexts

Assert and check annotations and pre- and postconditions were introduced in Chapter 3. These annotations all relate to the proof process and are collectively referred to as proof contexts. Note that these proof annotations are not considered to be part of the core SPARK language and so were not covered by the syntax in Part 2 of this book.

Pre- and postconditions form part of the specification of a subprogram and follow global and derives annotations. If a subprogram has separate specification and body then they only appear in the specification and not in the body. In our examples, however, it is generally convenient to assume that there is no separate specification.

It is important that pre- and postconditions are part of the specification because, of course, they are part of the interface. Preconditions impose a requirement at the point of call and postconditions provide a further hypothesis which can be assumed on the return from the call as we saw in Section 3.6.

It is also possible to provide preconditions for functions in a similar manner to procedures. However, rather than a postcondition, the value of the result is given by a return annotation. The simplest form of return annotation is shown by the following trivial example

```
function Inc(X: Integer) return Integer
--# return X + 1;
is
begin
   return X + 1;
end Inc;
```

This may seem a bit repetitive but the return annotation forms part of the specification and so the formula for the result is made known to the calling code (via a proof function as described below) where it provides a hypothesis for the purposes of proof whereas in the Ada code it is just known to the body. The conclusion of the verification condition produced by the Examiner is simply `x + 1 = x + 1` which is obviously true.

A very important point is that we are not simply repeating the expression of the return statement in the annotation. That is completely the wrong point of view. One should consider the annotation as specifying the function and thus coming first and then the development of the code of the body coming second. Thus the specification alone says

```
function Inc(X: Integer) return Integer;
--# return X + 1;
```

It is then just a matter of good fortune that in very simple cases the return statement enables the result to be implemented in the body in an identical manner to the expression in the annotation.

In more elaborate situations another form of return annotation can be used as illustrated by

```
function Max(X, Y: Integer) return Integer
--# return M => (X > Y -> M = X) and
--#             (Y > X -> M = Y);
is
   Result: Integer;
begin
   if X > Y then
      Result := X;
   else
      Result := Y;
   end if;
   return Result;
end Max;
```

The return annotation introduces M to stand for the result and this is then followed by an extended expression which provides values for M according to various conditions.

There are two verification conditions because there are two paths.

```
For path(s) from start to finish:

function_max_1.
H1:    true .
H2:    x > y .
       ->
C1:    (x > y) -> (x = x) .
C2:    (y > x) -> (x = y) .

function_max_2.
H1:    true .
H2:    not (x > y) .
       ->
C1:    (x > y) -> (y = x) .
C2:    (y > x) -> (y = y) .
```

The conclusions C1 and C2 for both these paths themselves take the form of implications which means that the condition after the arrow has to be proved true only if the condition before the arrow is true.

For the first path, the first condition in C1 is true by H2 and so we have to show that (x = x) is true which it is. In the case of C2, however, (y > x) is always false by H2 and so C2 as a whole is true irrespective of the fact that (x = y) may or may not be true (this is often loosely stated as false implies anything). The second path is similarly correct.

However, it is important to note that the return annotation does not specify the value for M when X = Y. Any value such as 210 would satisfy the specification. So we could write the conditional statement as

```
if X > Y then
   Result := X;
elsif Y > X then
```

```
        Result := Y;
    else
        Result := 210;
    end if;
```

and we would then get a third path with verification condition

```
function_max_3.
H1:    true .
H2:    not (x > y) .
H3:    not (y > x) .
       ->
C1:    (x > y) -> (210 = x) .
C2:    (y > x) -> (210 = y) .
```

All the verification conditions can still be proved to be true; in the case of the third path the conditions before the arrow in both conclusions are always false and so the conditions involving 210 are irrelevant.

Care is clearly needed to avoid incomplete specifications. One approach is to use the form

```
--# return M => (A -> M = X) and
--#             (B -> M = Y) and
--#             (C -> M = Z) and
--#             (A or B or C);
```

where A, B and C are conditions such as X > Y. The final condition (A **or** B **or** C) then ensures that all cases are covered.

Another possibility is that the return annotation might have overlapping ranges thus

```
function Max(X, Y: Integer) return Integer
--# return M => (X >= Y -> M = X) and
--#             (Y >= X -> M = Y);
is
   Result: Integer;
begin
   if X > Y then
      Result := X;
   else
      Result := Y;
   end if;
   return Result;
end Max;
```

In this case the ranges overlap but they indicate the same result anyway and so the verification conditions can still all be proved. However, unlike the earlier examples in this section, the Simplifier does not quite manage to reduce all the conclusions to true. For the second path we are left with

```
function_max_2.
H1:    x <= y .
       ->
C1:    x >= y -> y = x .
```

That this is true can be seen by considering the first part of the conclusion C1 as two distinct cases corresponding to x = y and x > y respectively. In other words the one conclusion can be split into two thus

```
C1:    x = y -> y = x .
C2:    x > y -> y = x .
```

In the case of x = y, the conclusion immediately follows; in the case x > y, there is a contradiction with the hypothesis H1 and so this case need not be considered further. The net result is that the overall original conclusion is true. This technique is not one of those built into the Simplifier but is typical of the strategies used with the Proof Checker.

The syntax of most proof contexts (such as assert and check annotations and pre- and postconditions) consists of the appropriate reserved word followed by a predicate (Boolean expression). The syntax of a return annotation consists of **return** followed by an expression of the appropriate type.

The expressions in proof contexts are written in SPARK with a few extensions some of which we have already met.

- The expression in a return annotation can take the form of some identifier followed by => and an extended expression as illustrated above.
- The operators -> (implies) and <-> (is equivalent to) are available. Their precedence is the same as **and**, **or** and **xor**. They similarly cannot be mixed in an expression without the use of parentheses.
- Predicates can be quantified using **for all** and **for some**. Thus we can write **for all** M **in** Index => (A(M) = 0) as will be illustrated later.
- There are forms representing composite objects with some components changed. Thus A[I => A(J); J => A(I)] denotes the array A with components I and J interchanged. Similarly D[Year => 1994] denotes the record D of type Date with the Year component changed. Such array and record updates are treated as names and so can be further indexed or selected all within the one expression. Their use will also be illustrated later.
- The initial value of an **in out** parameter X can be represented by X~. The same applies to a global variable that is both imported and exported.

The position of the tilde character needs care. For an array parameter A the initial value of the component with index I where I is a local variable is referred to as A~(I). But of course if I is itself both imported and exported and we wish to refer to the initial value of the component using the initial value of I then we write A~(I~). Similarly the initial value of the component C of some record R is referred to as R~.C. However, if a global variable V is in an inherited package P so that it is normally referred to as P.V then its initial value is P.V~ and not P~.V.

It is also possible to declare proof functions such as

```
--# function F(I: Integer) return Integer;
```

As we shall see in the next section, such functions do not form part of the Ada program but may be used in proof contexts. Moreover, a proof function is implicitly declared whenever verification conditions are generated for code calling a SPARK function. For example, if we have a function with the following specification

```
function Fn(A, B: Integer) return Boolean;
--# global G;
```

where the global variable G is of type T, then a proof function with signature

```
--# function Fn(A, B: Integer; G: T) return Boolean;
```

is implicitly declared. Note that any global imports are made into formal parameters so that the proof function is a pure function. Verification conditions for code calling Fn will contain calls of the corresponding proof function.

The reader might wonder why the verification condition for the calling sequence is always written in terms of a call of an implicit proof function rather than directly incorporating the expression of the return annotation. Thus a call of the trivial function Inc as in

```
procedure Bump(Y: in out Integer)
--# derives Y from Y;
--# post Y = Y~ + 1;
is
begin
   Y := Inc(Y);
end Bump;
```

results in the verification condition

```
H1:    true .
       ->
C1:    inc(y) = y + 1 .
```

There are two main reasons. One is that the called function might not have a return annotation anyway and so there would be a hole in the expression; the corresponding problem does not arise with procedures since the effect is simply that no further hypotheses are added at the point of the procedure call. The other reason is that a combinatorial explosion might occur since a return annotation might contain calls of other functions thereby resulting in deeply nested expressions which would be hard to disentangle. It is considered better practice to break each level down through the implicit proof functions. Again there is no corresponding problem with procedure calls since each postcondition is self-contained.

There are two other extensions to the normal SPARK syntax regarding proof contexts. One is the ability to give the type of an own variable. For concrete variables this is mandatory if verification conditions are to be generated. The

**Table 11.1** Mapping of while and for statements.

| *Original form* | *Treated as* |
|---|---|
| **while** E **loop**<br>  S;<br>**end loop**; | **loop**<br>  **exit when not** E;<br>  S;<br>**end loop**; |
| **for** I **in** T **range** L .. U **loop**<br>  S;<br>**end loop**; | **if** L <= U **then**<br>  I := L;<br>  **loop**<br>    S;<br>    **exit when** I = U;<br>    I := T'Succ(I);<br>  **end loop**;<br>**end if**; |
| **for** I **in** T **loop**<br>  S;<br>**end loop**; | I := T'First;<br>**loop**<br>  S;<br>  **exit when** I = T'Last;<br>  I := T'Succ(I);<br>**end loop**; |

Ada type declaration may even occur later in the same package in which case its early appearance is called a type announcement. For example

```
--# own X: Integer;          -- using a predefined type
--# own B: Buffer;           -- announcement of type Buffer
```

The identifier Buffer can only be used before its Ada declaration in other annotations. An abstract own variable can optionally be given a proof type thus

```
--# own State: Stack_Type;
--# type Stack_Type is abstract;
```

The use of such proof types for refinement will be illustrated in Section 11.8.

The other minor extension is that an assert annotation can be placed just before the word **loop** in a for statement or while statement thus

```
while Some_Condition
--# assert ...
loop ...

for I in Some_Type range Some_Range
--# assert ...
loop ...
```

This is particularly useful with while statements since the assertion is considered to be immediately before the implied test as if it had been written

```
loop
   --# assert ...
   exit when not Some_Condition;
   ...
```

This avoids a path bypassing the assertion which occurs with while statements if we place the assert statement inside the loop as we saw when dealing with GCD in Section 3.6.

The notional code corresponding to loop statements and thus the effective location of assert statements is intuitively obvious in most cases. For completeness the mappings are shown in Table 11.1. For statements containing **reverse** are similar with the initial value assigned to the loop parameter I being U or T'Last, the test of I in the exit statement being against L or T'First, and the attribute Succ being replaced by Pred.

The full syntax of proof contexts will be found in Appendix 1.

---

**EXERCISE 11.2**

1 Rewrite the function Max containing the foolish path returning 210 with the extra condition in the return annotation of the form (A **or** B **or** C). Explain why the verification conditions can no longer be proved.

2 Consider the validity of

```
function Dec(X: Integer) return Integer
--# return X + 1;
is
begin
   return X + 1;
end Dec;
```

---

## 11.3 Proof functions

The conditions in proof contexts that we have seen so far have been written in terms of the variables of the SPARK program plus the usual predefined operations. As mentioned in the last section we can also declare proof functions and these are only available in proof contexts.

Consider once more the procedure for computing the Greatest Common Divisor introduced in Section 3.6. We observed at the time that we were unable to prove correctness because we were unable to express the postcondition in a suitable form.

In order to simplify the discussion we will assume that hardware division is available so that we can avoid the confusion of the procedures Divide and Swap. The procedure is therefore

```
procedure G_C_D(M, N: in Natural; G: out Natural)
--# derives G from M, N;
is
   C, D: Integer;
   R: Integer;
begin
   C := M;  D := N;
   while D /= 0 loop
      R := C rem D;
      C := D;  D := R;
   end loop;
   G := C;
end G_C_D;
```

The approach we take is to introduce a mathematical function gcd which we can use in the annotations even though it is not defined in the Ada program text. Interestingly enough, although we cannot define our procedure G_C_D in a recursive manner because of the dynamic space required to implement recursion, nevertheless we can introduce recursive definitions in our proofs because the proofs are performed independently of program execution.

So we introduce a proof function as follows

```
--# function Gcd(A, B: Natural) return Natural;
```

This declaration is another form of proof context and is typically declared in the same package as the procedure G_C_D. The syntax is just as for a normal Ada function declaration and it follows the usual visibility rules (so its identifier has to be different to that of the procedure). The proof function Gcd can then be referred to in the annotations within G_C_D thus

```
procedure G_C_D(M, N: in Natural; G: out Natural)
--# derives G from M, N;
--# pre M >= 0 and N > 0;
--# post G = Gcd(M, N);
is
   C, D: Integer;
   R: Integer;
begin
   C := M;  D := N;
   while D /= 0 loop
      --# assert C >= 0 and D > 0 and Gcd(C, D) = Gcd(M, N);
      R := C rem D;
      C := D;  D := R;
   end loop;
   G := C;
end G_C_D;
```

The key to proving correctness is the assertion in the loop. The whole point about the algorithm is that the variables C and D are reduced by each iteration in a way that ensures that their gcd remains unchanged. Eventually D becomes zero and C is then the answer.

The Examiner is now able to produce verification conditions; note that the Examiner does not need to know what the proof function Gcd actually means because the process of producing conditions simply involves formal substitution through the hoisting process described in Section 10.1.

There are in fact four paths including one from start to finish which bypasses the loop as in the example in Section 3.6 and similarly can never be taken because the loop is always executed at least once. We will look at the others in detail.

The verification condition for the first path is

```
For path(s) from start to assertion:

H1:   m >= 0 .
H2:   n > 0 .
H3:   n <> 0 .
      ->
C1:   m >= 0 .
C2:   n > 0 .
C3:   gcd(m, n) = gcd(m, n) .
```

This is clearly correct. C1 is H1, C2 is H2 and C3 is a tautology irrespective of the meaning of gcd.

The verification condition for going around the loop is

```
For path(s) from assertion to assertion:

H1:   c >= 0 .
H2:   d > 0 .
H3:   gcd(c, d) = gcd(m, n) .
H4:   c - c div d * d <> 0 .
      ->
C1:   d >= 0 .
C2:   c - c div d * d > 0 .
C3:   gcd(d, c - c div d * d) = gcd(m, n) .
```

C1 follows from H2 since if d is greater than zero then, *a fortiori*, d is also greater than or equal to zero.

C2 is simply an expansion of c rem d > 0. Now c rem d is greater than or equal to zero since both c and d are not negative from H1 and H2. But by H4, c rem d is not equal to zero and therefore it must be greater than zero. So C2 is proved.

C3 requires more thought. We need the following mathematical theorems about the gcd function

*T1*: $\text{gcd}(a, b) = \text{gcd}(b, a)$
*T2*: $\text{gcd}(a \bmod b, b) = \text{gcd}(a, b) \qquad b \neq 0$

C3 can then be successively transformed as follows

```
gcd(d, c – c div d * d) = gcd(m, n)
gcd(d, c mod d) = gcd(m, n)          -- definition of mod
gcd(c mod d, d) = gcd(m, n)          -- T1
gcd(c, d) = gcd(m, n)                -- T2 and H2
gcd(m, n) = gcd(m, n)                -- H3
true
```

and so the result is proved. (Remember that **mod** and **rem** are the same for positive operands.)

And finally, the verification condition from the loop to the end of the procedure is

```
For path(s) from assertion to finish:

H1:   c >= 0 .
H2:   d > 0 .
H3:   gcd(c, d) = gcd(m, n) .
H4:   not (c – c div d * d <> 0) .
      ->
C1:   d = gcd(m, n) .
```

In order to prove this we need another theorem about the function gcd

$$T3: \quad \mathrm{gcd}(a, 0) = a \qquad\qquad a \neq 0$$

We can then transform C1 as follows

```
d = gcd(m, n)
d = gcd(c, d)                        -- H3
d = gcd(c mod d, d)                  -- T2 and H2
d = gcd(0, d)                        -- c mod d = 0 by H4
d = gcd(d, 0)                        -- T1
d = d                                -- T3
true
```

and so this condition is true as well.

We have now shown that all the verification conditions are true and so the procedure is also shown to be correct (strictly, partially correct). Of course we did all the proof by hand. Indeed we have not told the Examiner anything about the meaning of gcd and so it could not help. However, as we shall see in the next section, we can tell the Proof Checker about the various theorems to be used and the proofs can then be mechanized.

It is interesting to apply the Simplifier to the verification conditions. It reduces the first one to true but it cannot do much with those for going around the loop and from the loop to the end because it does not know anything about gcd. However, it notices that the path from the start to the finish cannot be taken. Before simplification this verification condition is

```
For path(s) from start to finish:

H1:   m >= 0 .
```

```
H2:    n > 0 .
H3:    not (n <> 0) .
       ->
C1:    m = gcd(m, n) .
```

and the Simplifier reduces this to

```
*** true .   /* contradiction within hypotheses. */
```

Note that it does this without knowing about the meaning of gcd.

This spurious fourth path can be avoided by placing the assertion immediately before the word **loop** as explained at the end of the previous section. The assertion has to be changed to take account of the fact that D will be zero the last time the assertion is encountered. The loop then becomes

```
while D /= 0
   --# assert C >= 0 and D >= 0 and Gcd(C, D) = Gcd(M, N);
loop
   R := C rem D;
   C := D;  D := R;
end loop;
```

The resulting verification conditions are similar to before and can be proved in the same way.

Incidentally, the declaration of the proof function

```
--# function Gcd(A, B: Natural) return Natural;
```

can be placed anywhere that a declaration is allowed.

If a function such as Gcd is to be used in various proofs then it may be convenient to declare it perhaps with other similar declarations in a distinct package

```
package Proof_Stuff is
   --# function Gcd(A, B: Natural) return Natural;
   ...
end Proof_Stuff;
```

In order to use the proof function Gcd within our procedure G_C_D, the package containing G_C_D must have an inherit clause for Proof_Stuff and the full extended name is then required in all references to Gcd. So we might write

```
--# inherit Proof_Stuff;
package P is
   procedure G_C_D(M, N: in Integer; G: out Integer)
   --# derives G from M, N;
   --# pre M >= 0 and N > 0;
   --# post G = Proof_Stuff.Gcd(M, N);
   ...
end P;
```

```
package body P is
   procedure G_C_D(M, N: in Integer; G: out Integer) is
      ...
   begin
      ...
   end G_C_D;
end P;
```

It is important to note that there is no need for a with clause for Proof_Stuff because it is only used in annotations and not in the actual Ada code.

A final point about proof functions is that they provide a way to introduce proof constants since we can always define a proof function which returns a known constant value.

---

**EXERCISE 11.3**

1 Write a package P containing a function Factorial with specification

```
function Factorial(N: Natural) return Natural;
--# pre N >= 0;
--# return Fact(N);
```

where Fact is a suitable proof function which should also be declared in P. Generate the verification conditions and show that they are true by assuming relevant theorems regarding the proof function.

---

## 11.4 Proof declarations and rules

In order that the Simplifier or Proof Checker can manipulate verification conditions it is necessary that they understand the meaning of all variables and functions used in the conditions. As mentioned in Section 3.4, these conditions are written in FDL. The mapping of SPARK expressions into FDL which is performed by the Examiner is generally obvious. In addition the tools need to be aware of various rules regarding how conditions may be manipulated in order to show that they are true.

In this section we look at the general way in which the rules and conditions are written and supplied to the tools. The next section looks at FDL in more detail and a further discussion on the rules will be found when we consider the general properties of the Proof Checker in Section 11.7.

FDL has predefined types integer and real and predefined arithmetic operations such as + and * operating upon values of these types. An important principle is that FDL deals with mathematics and so the FDL type real includes the type integer because the field of real numbers includes the integral domain of integers. FDL also has enumeration types such as boolean. (Note that FDL identifiers are in lower case in order to distinguish them from SPARK identifiers.) Various rules concerning the properties of these types are built into the proof tools.

All other information has to be passed to the tools along with the conditions to be proved. Some information is automatically produced by the Examiner in rule files with extensions **fdl** and **rls**.

The FDL declarations of all the variables used in the verification conditions will be found in the **fdl** file. As a specific example, the **fdl** file for the procedure G_C_D contains

```
function round__(real) : integer;
var d : integer;
var c : integer;
var n : integer;
var m : integer;
function gcd(integer, integer) : integer;
```

The variables d, c, m and n are declared to be of the FDL type integer using a Pascal-like syntax. There is also a profile of the function gcd which we declared as a proof function. Again note that the FDL identifiers are all in lower case.

Another important point which emphasizes that FDL concerns the mathematics of the program is that the numerical types in the declarations of variables and proof functions are the underlying mathematical types. Thus the subtype Natural used in the declaration of the proof function Gcd in the SPARK text becomes the type integer in the FDL text.

The file also always includes the declaration of a general round function from real to integer; note that its identifier has two trailing underlines and so cannot clash with any Ada identifier. There is no need for a corresponding reverse conversion because, as mentioned above, the type real covers the type integer anyway.

Other items that might appear in an **fdl** file are the declarations of constants corresponding to attributes used in conditions. For example if we declare a subtype

```
subtype Index is Integer range 1 .. 10;
```

then the **fdl** file will contain

```
const index__last : integer := pending;
const index__first : integer := pending;
```

and the actual values (promised by pending) are then supplied in the **rls** file as explained in a moment. Note again how the attributes use a double underline in the FDL identifier to avoid a clash with any SPARK identifier.

In order for the tools to be able to manipulate the conditions for the procedure G_C_D successfully, it is necessary to supply the theorems concerning the proof function Gcd which we used when doing the proof by hand. These are written in a special rules language which has affinity to both FDL and Prolog. This rules language has the specific types of FDL and also more general types which are used for declaring the parameters of operations. These are

| | |
|---|---|
| i | integer |
| ir | integer or real |
| e | enumeration |
| ire | integer, real or enumeration |
| any | all types |

Note again that there is no need for a distinct type 'r' because we are dealing with mathematical concepts and the set of real numbers includes the integers.

Rules are grouped into families. There are many predefined rules available to the tools covering the usual theorems of mathematics and logic. An **rls** file is automatically produced by the Examiner for each subprogram processed and additional rules can be supplied in **rul** files.

In the case of G_C_D the **rls** file just contains

```
rule_family g_c_d_rules:

    X       requires [X:any] &
    X <= Y requires [X:ire, Y:ire] &
    X >= Y requires [X:ire, Y:ire].
```

which are dummy declarations in this instance.

The additional rules that we need for our proof can be placed in a **rul** file and would be written as a rule family as follows

```
rule_family gcd:

    gcd(X, Y) requires [X: i, Y: i] .

gcd(1): gcd(A, B) may_be_replaced_by gcd(B, A) .
gcd(2): gcd(A, 0) may_be_replaced_by A if [A <> 0] .
gcd(3): gcd(A mod B, B) may_be_replaced_by gcd(A, B) if [B <> 0] .
```

This starts with the name of the rule family and then gives the parameter types for the function gcd and then the various rules themselves (these are often referred to as rewrite rules). The rules use upper case identifiers to represent patterns to be matched whereas lower case is used for FDL identifiers such as gcd.

The **rls** file produced by the Examiner will also contain rules relating to attributes which are used in verification conditions. Thus corresponding to the declarations of constants index__first and index__last in the **fdl** file we would find the following rules in the **rls** file

```
p_rules(5): index__first may_be_replaced_by 1.
p_rules(6): index__last may_be_replaced_by 10.
```

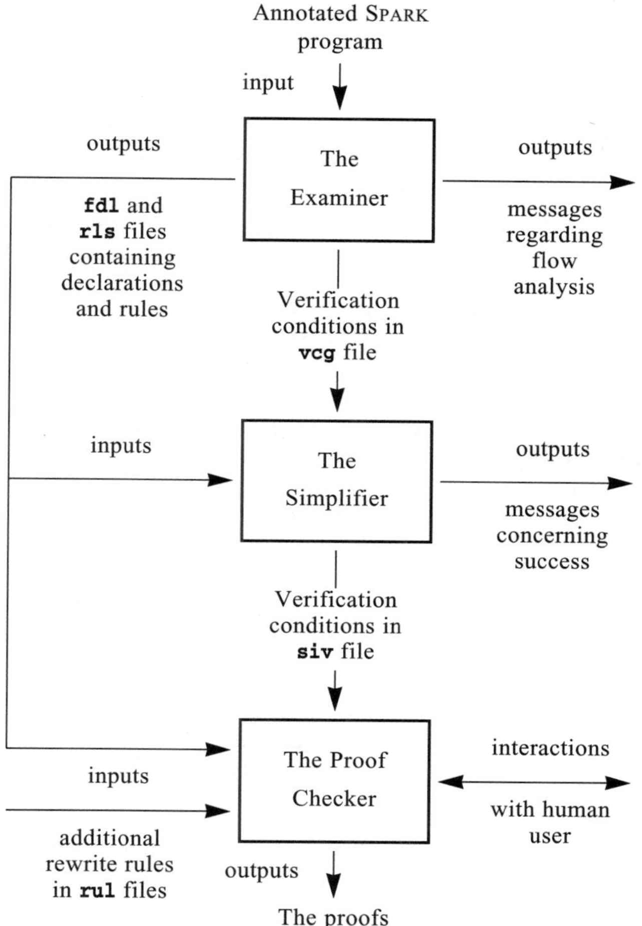


**Figure 11.1** Overall proof process.

where P is the name of the procedure being analysed.

There is no technical difference between an **rls** and **rul** file. The Examiner always produces an **rls** file and it is conventional for additional rules to be placed in an **rul** file. But in principle the **rls** file could be edited with additional rules.

For reasons explained in Section 11.7, the Simplifier is not able to use general additional rewrite rules such as those for gcd but only the simple ones generated by the Examiner such as those giving values for the constants index__first and index__last. Indeed the Simplifier accepts just one **rls** file whereas the Proof Checker also accepts **rul** files. This is illustrated in Figure 11.1 which shows the various files involved and their relationship to the

Simplifier and the Proof Checker.

If the Simplifier is unable to reduce a verification condition to true then that may be for a number of reasons.

- The verification condition may not be true. This could be because the program is wrong or alternatively because some proof statement such as a precondition or assertion is wrong.
- The Simplifier is unable to process any necessary additional rules.
- The Simplifier may not be clever enough.

In the second and third cases the condition may be proved by hand or (preferably) by using the Proof Checker. Thus the general strategy is to use the Simplifier to simplify conditions as much as possible and then to pass them (together with any additional rules) to the Proof Checker.

We conclude with an obvious warning. If we write our own rules and then deduce (by hand, or by using the Proof Checker) that a condition is true then we are very much relying upon our rules being correct. If the rules are not correct then a proof might be invalid and the whole edifice of proof thus destroyed.

And always remember that the verification conditions only ensure partial correctness. The subprogram might still be incorrect because it does not terminate.

---

**EXERCISE 11.4**

**1** Write an appropriate rule family for the proof function Fact of Exercise 11.3(**1**).

**2** The following function is a possible declaration of Factorial. Its verification conditions are all true but yet it is not satisfactory. Why?

```
function Factorial(N: Natural) return Natural
--# pre N >= 0;
--# return Fact(N);
is
   Result: Natural := 1;
   Term: Natural := 1;
begin
   loop
      Result := Result * Term;
      --# assert Term > 0 and Result = Fact(Term);
      exit when Term = N;
      Term := Term + 1;
   end loop;
   return Result;
end Factorial;
```

---

## 11.5 The FDL language

We have introduced a number of aspects of FDL through examples and although it is not possible in the space available to give a complete description of FDL, nevertheless this short summary should clarify the general principles and cover those features required in SPARK verification conditions. Further examples will also be seen in later sections.

The notation of FDL has some resemblance to Pascal because of its origins in the development of the original SPADE tools which, as mentioned in Section 1.1, were based on proving programs in a subset of Pascal. FDL uses a number of reserved words in addition to those of SPARK and these are listed in Appendix 2; we saw the use of const, pending, var and may_be_replaced_by in the previous section.

### *Simple types*

These comprise the type integer, the type real and enumeration types including the predefined type boolean.

The types integer and real should be thought of as the true mathematical types. Thus the type integer of FDL is not the type Integer of Ada with its range from Integer'First to Integer'Last but rather the integer type of mathematics embracing all the integer values. We can perhaps think of the FDL types integer and real as corresponding to the Ada types universal_integer and universal_real. A difference however is that in FDL the type real covers the type integer whereas the Ada universal types are disjoint. Operations on the types integer and real are performed with infinite range and precision. As we saw in Section 3.4, numeric literals that are not whole numbers are replaced by rational pairs of integers in verification conditions.

Enumeration types are defined by the usual set of literal values such as

```
type day = (mon, tue, wed, thu, fri, sat, sun);
```

and the type boolean has the literals true and false although they are not ordered.

It is also possible to declare subranges of integer and enumeration types in the Pascal style thus

```
type zone = 1 .. 48;
type weekday = mon .. fri;
```

Finally note that it is possible to define one type as being the same as another such as

```
type index = integer;
```

This is essentially just a renaming and can be used with both simple and composite types. (It does not introduce a new type as would a derived type definition in full Ada.)

Such a declaration might appear in the **fdl** file if we declare

```
type Index is range 1 .. 10;
```

in the SPARK text.

As a language, FDL ignores the constraints and also the strong typing distinction between Index and Integer in the SPARK. This does not lead to a loss of integrity because the strong typing has already done its job by ensuring static consistency at the SPARK level and the constraints can be checked using the run-time check option of the Examiner. The purpose of FDL is to provide a framework for proving dynamic correctness. Moreover, it should not usually be necessary to declare types since the Examiner declares them for us.

### *Object declarations*

Variables are declared using var as seen from the **fdl** files. Constants can similarly be declared using const. Constants must be given an initial value although this can be declared as pending (rather like a deferred constant in Ada). In the case of integer constants the initial value can be a signed integer literal. More generally an initial value is written as a literal in a string delimited by single quotes. This quoted form can also be used for large integer constants. The following examples illustrate various possibilities

```
var x, y : integer;
const answer : integer = 42;
const pi : real = '3.1415926536';
const order : integer = pending;
```

It will not usually be necessary to declare variables and constants because they are automatically declared for us by the Examiner. Moreover the Examiner always declares constants as pending in the **fdl** file and then gives the values as rules in the **rls** file.

### *Structured types*

FDL has array and record types. Array types may have several dimensions and each of the index types may be an enumeration or subrange type. An array index type can also be integer in which case objects of the array type might appear to have an infinite number of components, but of course the FDL simply models the SPARK program in which the actual array is constrained. Record types have fields (components) named in the usual way. There are no restrictions on the types of the components of arrays or records. Some examples are

```
type row = 1 .. 10;
type column = 1 .. 5;
type vector = array [column] of real;
type matrix = array [row, column] of real;
```

```
type daynumber = 1 .. 31;
type monthname = (jan, feb, mar, apr, may, jun,
                  jul, aug, sep, oct, nov, dec);
type yearnumber = 1 .. 2100;
type date = record
              day : daynumber;
              month : monthname;
              year : yearnumber
            end;
```

Note that FDL uses semicolons as in Pascal; that is as separators rather than terminators and so there is no semicolon after the field year in the definition of the type date.

FDL also has set and sequence types. For example

```
type hue = set of colour;
type message = sequence of integer;
```

### *Functions*

Functions in FDL are pure mathematical functions. They do not have side effects and all parameters must be passed explicitly. Thus, unlike SPARK functions, an FDL function cannot read global data.

The syntax of a function declaration takes a straightforward form as illustrated by the declaration of gcd in the **fdl** file for G_C_D.

```
function gcd(integer, integer) : integer;
```

Observe that the parameters are not named. A function need have no parameters in which case it will always return the same value. There are no procedures in FDL.

There are a number of predefined functions such as

```
abs(x)    -- absolute value, x is real or integer
sqr(x)    -- square, x is real or integer
pred(x)   -- predecessor, x is integer or enumeration type
succ(x)   -- successor, x is integer or enumeration type
odd(x)    -- true if x is odd, false otherwise, x is integer
```

There are also functions for manipulating arrays and records and for creating structured values. These are necessary because FDL takes an entire variable approach with regard to accessing components of structured objects.

The element of an array a with index i may be read by using the general function element thus

```
element(a, [i])
```

whereas it may be updated by using the general function update. Thus

```
update(a, [i], x)
```

represents the value of the array a with the value of the element with index i replaced by x. But note that this does not actually change the array. To do that we have to make an entire assignment thus

```
a := update(a, [i], x);
```

and this corresponds to the assignment A(I) := X; in Ada. Multidimensional arrays use a sequence of index expressions such as [i, j, k].

A similar approach is taken with records. Functions fld_fn and upf_fn are defined for manipulating a field fn of a record type t. Thus for the type date we might write

```
d := upf_month(d, feb);
```

It is important to note that the words Element, Update and words commencing Fld_ and Upf_ should be avoided as identifiers in programs for which verification conditions are to be analysed.

Note also that this is not the same notation as that used for modifying arrays and records in SPARK proof contexts. The relationship between the two notations will become clear when we introduce quantification in Section 11.8.

Structured values may be defined using the function mk__t for an array or record type t. Note that this has a double underline and so cannot conflict with Ada identifiers. The form is similar to an Ada aggregate using named notation although the syntax is rather different. For example

```
mk__date(day := 25, month := dec, year := 1999)
mk__vector([1 .. 3] := 0, [4] := 1, [5] := 2)
mk__vector(0, [4] := 1, [5] := 2)
```

The last illustrates a default value appearing first and has the same value as the previous example.

### *Operators*

The various operators are much as in Ada. There are, however, some important differences which should be noted.

- +, –, * Addition, subtraction, multiplication. The operands can be integer or real and the result is type real unless both arguments are type integer in which case it is type integer. So mixed operands are allowed. There is also unary minus.
- / Real division. The operands are integer or real; result is real.
- div Integer division. The operands and result are integer.
- mod Modulus. The operands and result are integer.
- ** Exponentiate. The first operand can be integer or real; the second operand must be a non-negative integer.

Integer division truncates towards zero as in Ada. So div in FDL corresponds to / for integer operands in Ada. There is no rem in FDL and so the Examiner expands **rem** in Ada text into an expression using div and * in verification conditions.

The user should be aware that **mod** in Ada is just transformed into mod in FDL. However there are no built-in rules given for mod and so they have to be supplied by the user. The reason for this is that the tools are also used with other languages such as Pascal in which mod has a different meaning. So although **mod** may be technically the correct thing to use, there are practical advantages in using **rem** which is the same for positive operands anyway.

The Boolean operators and, or, not are as in Ada. There is no xor but there are operators for implication and equivalence.

-> Implication. The expression true -> false is false; other combinations are true.

<-> Equivalence. The result is true if both operands have the same truth value. The same as equality.

The equality and relational operators are much as in Ada. An important notational difference is that <> is used for inequality. The equality operators apply to all types; the relational operators only to simple types.

Although <-> and = have the same meaning for the type boolean, it is preferable to use <-> in conditions because the built-in rules for <-> are more extensive. The use of <-> is also the more natural mathematical style.

Finally, there are membership operators in and not_in for use with set types.

### *Expressions*

Be aware that the precedence order is slightly different to that in Ada (moreover it is not the same as in Pascal). In increasing order, the levels in FDL are

```
->   <->
or
and
not
=   <>   <   <=   >   >=   in   not_in
+   – (binary)
*   /   div   mod
– (unary)
**
```

The precedence can always be overruled by parentheses. The redundant use of parentheses is especially advised when there might be the risk of confusion with Ada. (The Examiner generates redundant parentheses for this reason.)

Most of the differences in precedence between FDL and Ada do not matter because the operators are different anyway. The most significant difference is that of unary minus in relation to the multiplication operators. But even this does not show up very much because $-(x \times y)$ and $(-x) \times y$ are the same. But care is needed with modulus when providing our own rules.

## 11.6 The Simplifier

The Simplifier is written in Prolog which as the reader will be aware is especially designed for logical manipulation.

The main purpose of the Simplifier is to simplify verification conditions prior to developing a proof. In many cases the Simplifier is able to reduce all the conclusions to true anyway. The Simplifier can also be used to simplify path functions.

A version of the Simplifier is provided on the CD accompanying this book. The Simplifier, like the Examiner, is invoked through the Windows Interface described in Chapter 9.

The Simplifier is extremely easy to run since there are no complex options as with the Examiner. In fact the Simplifier options dialogue box which is obtained by selecting Options and then Simplifier is rather boring. It has only one entry, namely for the heap size but in the demonstration version this is fixed anyway.

Assuming that we have some verification conditions in a **vcg** file and that corresponding **fdl** and **rls** files are in the same directory, then we just select the **vcg** file so that a 1 appears against it and then invoke the Simplifier by clicking on Run and then Simplifier (or by clicking on the S icon in the toolbar or by typing Ctrl-S). The Simplifier automatically looks for the **fdl** and **rls** files and there is no need to mention them.

The simplified verification conditions are produced in an **siv** file which can be inspected using the editor in the usual manner. A log of activity is also produced in an **slg** file.

A similar process is used to simplify path functions. We just select the **pfs** file (the Simplifier finds the **dec** file automatically) and invoke the Simplifier. The simplified path functions are produced in an **sip** file and a log of activity is produced in an **slg** file.

## 11.7 The Proof Checker

The Proof Checker is a sophisticated program and not easily described other than by interactive demonstration. It is a very powerful program although considerable experience is required in order to make best use of its facilities. It is not provided on the CD with this book and a thorough discussion is thus really outside our scope. However, in view of the importance of the Proof Checker in performing that last step in verifying the correctness of many programs, an outline description of its abilities seems appropriate.

The Proof Checker, like the Simplifier, is written in Prolog; many of its commands thus have a Prolog flavour. It is important to realize that the Proof Checker is not completely automatic. A fully automatic proof checker embracing the range of conditions that we wish to deal with using reasonable time and other resources is beyond our capabilities. Despite advances in inference engine technology, it remains a fact that the human mind is capable of inspired leaps of the imagination that as yet defy automation. On the other hand the human mind is also capable of lapses of accuracy which mean that manual proofs are extremely unreliable.

The Proof Checker provides the best of both worlds. It couples human abilities to judge fruitful avenues of exploration with the accuracy of the machine. The Proof Checker is thus an interactive program; this enables the user to direct the Checker to explore the use of various strategies and rules on the condition to be proved. Subgoals can be established and proved and retained for further use.

An important aspect of the Proof Checker is its ability to keep a log of the progress of a proof. Such a log is vital for audit and certification. The log also shows which hypotheses and rules have been used in the proof so that in the event of changes to the rules and hypotheses, it can be immediately seen whether a particular proof remains true or needs to be reworked. The log itself is produced in a **plg** file and a file of the commands actually typed is produced in a **cmd** file. This latter file is useful for replaying a proof session.

The Proof Checker proceeds by applying various strategies and rules. We have already met the idea of rules when discussing the function gcd. There are many families of built-in rules available to us. A random selection will give some idea of their scope. First there are simple arithmetic rules such as

```
arith(3): X + 0 may_be_replaced_by X .
assoc(4): A * (B * C) may_be_replaced_by (A * B) * C .
distrib(1): A*(B+C) & A*B + A*C are_interchangeable .
```

Whether a rule is written as may_be_replaced_by (which implies one way replacement only) or as are_interchangeable (which implies replacement both ways) is largely pragmatic. Clearly it does not make sense to go around adding +0 everywhere because that is not likely to lead to simplification. Moreover, interchangeability implies twice as many possibilities and can slow the proving process. It is also often redundant, because for example

```
commut(1): A + B may_be_replaced_by B + A .
```

is the same rule when written in reverse anyway and the one way rule covers both directions.

Some rules have one or more conditions. For example

```
arith(12): (X / Y) * Y may_be_replaced_by X if [ Y <> 0 ] .
```

The above rules are examples of substitution rules enabling one expression to be replaced by another. There are also inference rules which enable new facts to be deduced from existing facts. Examples are

```
transitivity(1): I <= K may_be_deduced_from [ I <= J, J <= K ] .
odd(5): odd(X) may_be_deduced_from [ odd(-X) ] .
abs(3): abs(X) >= 0 may_be_deduced .
```

Note that in the last case we write may_be_deduced rather than may_be_deduced_from since there is no list of previous conditions because the formula is always true.

There are also special rules regarding logical manipulation such as

```
inference(2): X may_be_deduced_from [ Y -> X, Y ] .
```

Rules are grouped into families such as the predefined families arith, assoc, distrib and so on. In addition we can declare our own families such as gcd. For each family of rules we have to give a family declaration thus

```
rule_family arith:

   X * Y requires [ X : ir, Y : ir]
   X + Y requires [ X : ir, Y : ir]
   X - Y requires [ X : ir, Y : ir]
   X div Y requires [ X : i, Y : i]
   X / Y requires [ X : ir, Y : ir]
```

Note that the result type is not given. Indeed the parameter types are not really necessary either because they are known from the properties of the FDL operators and functions but are an expediency to eliminate unnecessary searching for matching rules. In any case the Proof Checker always checks that the result type is unchanged by a transformation.

Several families of rules may be given in the same file. The family declaration giving the parameters must precede the rules of the family but otherwise the items may be given in an arbitrary order. Each family declaration must be self-contained and mention all the operations required by the rules of the family.

It is important to distinguish between the use of upper case and lower case identifiers in rules. An upper case identifier such as X stands for any pattern of appropriate type. A lower case identifier represents an FDL entity such as the type integer. In writing our own rules we may refer to constants such as index__last declared in the FDL, in which case these represent bound values such as 10 and not arbitrary patterns.

Care is indeed needed when writing our own rules to ensure that they are correct. Otherwise we might conclude that a particular program is correct when it is not. Taking gcd as an example we actually supplied rules for gcd rather than giving a definition of gcd. However, we can indeed give a definition and then use the Proof Checker to prove our rules. The technique is to write the definition in the rules file, write the potential rules as verification conditions (by hand) and then use the Proof Checker to prove them in the normal way. The proved rules can then be added to the rule base.

We conclude this section with a few remarks about proof strategies. We mentioned earlier that the Proof Checker proceeds by applying various strategies and rules. The rules are the hard facts available to the Checker whereas strategies are the dynamic approaches available. The interactive user directs the proof process by telling the Checker which strategies to apply. Typically the rules remain unchanged throughout a proof although rules might be added in the course of developing a proof.

Strategies available include

- simple inference by pattern matching against the rules,

- deduction using truth tables,
- proof by cases; thus cases for $x = 0$ and $x \geq 1$ might need different approaches,
- proof by contradiction; a frequent technique in mathematics,
- proof by induction; again familiar from mathematics (but rare in practice).

An important aspect of the workings of the Proof Checker is the ability to break down a proof into a number of subgoals (called proof frames). Thus if the direction of a proof is not obvious we can establish a subgoal and attempt to prove that; if successful this is added as a further hypothesis and then the main proof returned to. We met a trivial example of this in Section 11.2 when we saw how the final conclusion for the last example of the function Max could be proved by considering the cases of x = y and x > y separately.

The Simplifier has many components in common with the Proof Checker but is automatic and not driven interactively. Because it is automatic it has to use fixed decision processes and these are chosen so that it makes positive progress and never gets into a loop or stuck in a blind alley. One consequence of using fixed processes is that the Simplifier sometimes fails to prove something which looks obvious to the human reader. It is largely because of the risk of error in user-supplied rules which might cause chaos that the Simplifier does not accept them. An important strategy used by the Simplifier is to look for contradictions.

## 11.8 Quantification and refinement

We have now covered the main scope of the workings of the various tools and showed how they can be used to prove procedures such as G_C_D. But we have really only covered the proof of a very simple class of algorithms. Indeed all our examples have been about the manipulation of simple variables and the use of subprograms. However, a major aspect of programming is the ability to manipulate composite types such as arrays and to index through them.

(Programming in some mathematical sense is about subprograms and arrays. Features such as records and OO generally are management gloss giving control of visibility – important but not of the essence. Another way of looking at this is that visibility control is important in helping the frail human in developing and proving programs by hand. But visibility control is of less significance when proofs are developed mechanically.)

As a simple example, consider the following procedure to swap two elements of an array

```
type Index is range 1 .. 10;
type Atype is array (Index) of Integer;

procedure Swap_Elements(I, J: in Index; A: in out Atype)
--# derives A from A, I, J;
--# post A = A~[I => A~(J); J => A~(I)];
```

```
is
   Temp: Integer;
begin
   Temp := A(I);  A(I) := A(J);  A(J) := Temp;
end Swap_Elements;
```

This procedure interchanges the values of the elements with index I and J. The postcondition uses the array update notation mentioned in Section 11.2. Note carefully that it is the original value of A that is referred to on the right hand side of the postcondition and so the three instances of A are decorated with a tilde.

The verification condition produced by the Examiner makes use of the element and update operations of FDL explained in Section 11.5. We get

```
For path(s) from start to finish:

H1:    true .
       ->
C1:    update(update(a, [i], element(a, [j])), [j], element(
          a, [i])) = update(update(a, [i], element(a, [j])), [
          j], element(a, [i])) .
```

This rather indigestible mess is immediately reduced by the Simplifier to true. In fact the two expressions on either side of the = are identical but their length and layout obscure this fact.

There are several built-in rules regarding arrays such as

```
array(1): element(update(A, I, X), I) may_be_replaced_by X .
array(2): update(A, I, element(A, I)) may_be_replaced_by A .
```

and there are also built-in rules for records and aggregates involving the upf_fn, fld_fn and mk__t functions which were mentioned in Section 11.5.

Many proofs involving arrays require the concept of quantification. In mathematics we use the symbols ∀ and ∃ to mean 'for all' and 'there exists'. (These are often called the universal quantifier and the existential quantifier respectively.) Thus we might write

$$\forall\, x,\ \exists\, y,\ \text{s.t. } x + y = 0$$

which means of course that for all values $x$, there exists a value $y$ such that $x+y$ equals zero. In other words, every value has a corresponding negative (although it does not say it is unique). This can be written in the rules language as

```
for_all(X: real, for_some(Y: real, X + Y = 0))
```

Typically the universal quantifier, for_all, is omitted. Thus the rule

```
arith(3): X + 0 may_be_replaced_by X .
```

implicitly applies to all patterns X of the appropriate types (ir). Some rules apply explicitly to the quantifiers and are used for manipulating conditions involving quantifiers. For example

```
quant(1): for_all(X, Y) & not for_some(X, not Y) are_interchangeable .
```

The syntax of SPARK itself also includes quantified expressions which can be used in proof contexts such as pre- and postconditions and assertions.

As an example we might declare a function to determine whether an array has a component of a given value. The specification might be

```
subtype Index is Integer range 1 .. 10;
type Atype is array (Index) of Integer;

function Value_Present(A: Atype; X: Integer) return Boolean;
--# return for some M in Index => (A(M) = X);
```

A more elaborate example might find the index of the first such value and naturally have a precondition that asserts that the value does actually exist.

```
function Find(A: Atype; X: Integer) return Index;
--# pre for some M in Index => (A(M) = X);
--# return Z => (A(Z) = X) and
--#          (for all M in Index range Index'First .. Z–1 => (A(M) /= X));
```

We could of course use the function Value_Present in the precondition. The generated hypothesis would then contain a call of the implicit proof function rather than be the corresponding FDL quantified expression.

Another topic relating to type composition is refinement. In Section 2.8 we saw how we could have two views of the state of the package The_Stack – an external abstract view provided by the abstract variable State and an internal concrete view provided by the two variables S and Pointer. In order to develop proofs we need to map abstract conditions for the external view onto concrete conditions for the internal view. The package might become

```
package The_Stack
--# own State: Stack_Type;                    -- abstract variable
--# initializes State;
is
   --# type Stack_Type is abstract;          -- proof type

   --# function Not_Full(S: Stack_Type) return Boolean;
   --# function Append(S: Stack_Type; X: Integer) return Stack_Type;

   procedure Push(X: in Integer);
   --# global in out State;
   --# derives State from State, X;
   --# pre Not_Full(State);
   --# post State = Append(State~, X);

   ...  -- similarly Pop

end The_Stack;
```

```
package body The_Stack
--# own State is S, Pointer;                    -- refinement definition
is
   ... -- etc as in Section 2.8

   procedure Push(X: in Integer)
   --# global in out S, Pointer;
   --# derives S       from S, Pointer, X &
   --#         Pointer from Pointer;
   --# pre Pointer < Stack_Size;
   --# post Pointer = Pointer~ + 1 and
   --#      S = S~[Pointer => X];
   is
   begin
      Pointer := Pointer + 1;
      S(Pointer) := X;
   end Push;

   ...  -- similarly Pop plus initialization as in Section 2.8

end The_Stack;
```

The abstract own variable State now includes a type announcement for the proof type Stack_Type. The Examiner converts this proof type into an FDL record type having two components corresponding to the variables S and Pointer. There are also proof functions Not_Full and Append (with parameters of the proof type) which are used to give the pre- and postconditions for Push. A similar proof function Not_Empty would be given for Pop.

Three verification conditions are generated for Push – one shows that the refined precondition follows from the abstract precondition, one shows that the abstract postcondition follows from the refined postcondition and the other (the usual one) shows that the refined postcondition follows from the refined precondition. The first is

```
H1:   not_full(state) .
H2:   s = fld_s(state) .
H3:   pointer = fld_pointer(state) .
      ->
C1:   pointer < stack_size .
```

To complete the proofs we need proof rules for the proof functions in terms of the concrete variables such as

```
not_full(S) may_be_replaced_by fld_pointer(S) < stack_size .

append(S, X) may_be_replaced_by
     mk__stack_type(s := update(fld_s(S), [fld_pointer(S)+1], X),
                    pointer := fld_pointer(S)+1) .
```

Note how these rules use the FDL record selection and construction operations explained in Section 11.5. Given such rules the verification conditions can all be proved.

---

**EXERCISE 11.8**

1 Write a procedure with Ada specification

```
procedure Idarr(A: out Atype);
```

that sets each component of the array to its index value. Include proof annotations.

---

## 11.9 Run-time checks

The final topic to be discussed in this survey of the SPARK proof tools is the generation and elimination of run-time checks. This was briefly introduced in Section 3.4 when we discussed the procedure Inc and showed how to ensure that an exception would not be raised.

As noted in Section 3.1, the design of SPARK ensures that the exceptions Tasking_Error and Program_Error can never arise in a SPARK program. Moreover, space requirements can be computed statically and so Storage_Error cannot arise given an appropriate implementation. That leaves Constraint_Error which might arise as the result of a division check, index check, range check or overflow check (the other checks which might raise Constraint_Error in Ada are access check, discriminant check and tag check – none of these are possible in SPARK).

In most of our proofs we have ignored the possibility of overflow and most out of range values. Thus in developing the proof for G_C_D we explicitly ensured that M and N were not negative but did not consider any upper limit. Nor did we consider whether the computation of C **rem** D might cause overflow or whether any of the assignments might violate a range check. In this example, we are quite confident that no such checks could fail but in general we need to prove it.

Indeed we have remarked a number of times that the analysis is in terms of the mathematics of the situation and, in the normal use of the Examiner, considerations of ranges are ignored unless specific hypotheses are inserted such as N > 0 for G_C_D.

We could insert additional hypotheses and check annotations by hand at appropriate places. But inserting such annotations is tedious and prone to error and so the Examiner has a mode of operation in which appropriate checks are inserted automatically. Of course we still have to prove the resulting verification conditions.

Two levels of automatic check generation are available. The plain Run Time Checks option covers index, range and division checks whereas the RTC plus Overflow option also covers overflow checks. Note that in both cases all the usual verification conditions associated with any explicit proof statements are generated as well.

Suppose we write

```
subtype Index is Integer range 1 .. 1000;
```

```
procedure Checks(I: in Index; J: out Integer; K: out Index)
--# derives J, K from I;
is
begin
   J := I;
   K := J * J;
end Checks;
```

and apply the Run Time Checks option. The **fdl** file now includes

```
const index__last : integer = pending;
const index__first : integer = pending;
const integer__last : integer = pending;
const integer__first : integer = pending;
```

The **rls** file gives values for index__last and index__first as explained in Section 11.4 and will also give values for integer__last and integer__first provided they have been supplied in a target data file as explained in Chapter 9. Remember that the target machine might not be the same as the host on which the Examiner is running.

The **rls** file also includes a number of rules regarding relationships between the first and last attributes and the base range attributes. Thus the **rls** file commences

```
checks_rules(1): integer__first may_be_replaced_by -32768 .
checks_rules(2): integer__last may_be_replaced_by 32767 .
checks_rules(3): integer__base__first <= integer__base__last
                                               may_be_deduced .
checks_rules(4): integer__base__first <= integer__first
                                               may_be_deduced .
checks_rules(5): integer__base__last >= integer__last
                                               may_be_deduced .
```

Similar rules are given for the attributes of the subtype Index.

There are three verification conditions, two correspond to automatically generated checks and one is for the overall path – this last one is just 'true' because there is no postcondition anyway. Those for the checks correspond to the assignments to J and to K. That for J is

```
H1:   true .
H2:   i >= index__first .
H3:   i <= index__last .
      ->
C1:   i >= integer__first .
C2:   i <= integer__last .
```

Note that the Examiner inserts the hypothesis that the initial value of I satisfies the constraints of the range of Index. The conclusions then follow from the values given in the **rls** file since Index'First is greater than Integer'First and Index'Last is less than Integer'Last.

The conclusions for the path leading to the assignment to K are

```
C1:   i * i >= index__first .
C2:   i * i <= index__last .
```

but these cannot be proved and so there is the possibility of a run-time check failing and so raising an exception.

In this example, the verification conditions generated by the Run Time Checks option are identical to those which we could have obtained by hand by writing

```
procedure Checks(I: in Index; J: out Integer; K: out Index)
--# derives J, K from I;
--# pre I in Index;
is
begin
   --# check I in Integer;
   J := I;
   --# check J * J in Index;
   K := J * J;
end Checks;
```

The number of verification conditions generated may seem all rather tedious but in practice the Simplifier reduces most conclusions to true leaving only critical ones to be formally proved. Observe that the Examiner itself performs no optimizations, thus it inserts checks even when it is statically known that subtypes match and leaves it to the Simplifier to remove the trivial conclusions.

Checks are similarly inserted to ensure that array index ranges are not violated and that there is no attempt to divide by zero.

If the RTC plus Overflow option is used then additional checks are inserted to ensure that overflow does not occur when evaluating expressions. Checks are against the base range of the type for intermediate values in expressions and against the range of the type when assigning to a variable. In the case of the predefined types the base range is the same as the range but it will not be for our own types such as

```
type My_Integer is range -100_000 .. 100_000;
```

In such a case, the `rls` file will contain values for my_integer__first and my_integer__last and the values for my_integer__base__first and my_integer__base__last have to be supplied according to the target machine.

Ada allows expressions containing operations of the same precedence to be reordered by the compiler. Thus

```
I + J - K
```

could be compiled as any of

(I + J) – K   or   I + (J – K)   or   (I – K) + J   etc.

The Examiner always assumes left to right order as in the first form and issues a warning if the compiler might rearrange the expression. Of course we can always insert parentheses to ensure that rearrangement does not take place.

An important point to note is that run-time check analysis can usually be carried out without inserting any additional annotations. The only general exception to this is that assertions are required in loops in order to carry the hypotheses forward; but note that the Examiner will put dummy assertions in for us. However, in some circumstances it may be necessary to give preconditions in order to provide information not captured by the type model; this is illustrated by one of the procedures Inc in Section 3.4 where the condition X < T'Last was explicitly added. The possible need to add such extra information also applies to assert annotations.

Note that information flow analysis is not necessary in order to perform run-time check analysis – data flow analysis will suffice. However, this analysis must demonstrate the complete absence of all flow errors. For example, in the case of The_Stack of Section 2.8, it would be necessary for the variable S to be explicitly initialized even though we know that it is logically unnecessary.

We conclude with an observation on unconstrained array types. In a program as a whole, all arrays have statically known bounds. However, a subprogram may have an unconstrained array type as a formal parameter in which case the actual array supplies the bounds at run time. Such a subprogram cannot be proved correct in isolation and annotations therefore have to be inserted into the calling code where the bounds of the array are known. The Examiner warns of this situation.

# 12 Design Issues



Program design, in the overall sense of converting a set of requirements into a final program, is not an exact science. Indeed it is not really a science at all but verges onto the borders of art and craft coupled with engineering experience. Nevertheless, many methods have been devised which assist in the conversion of a set of requirements into a high level design. It would be inappropriate to attempt a comprehensive review of these methods and in any event SPARK as a language strives to remain independent of design method.

This chapter therefore concentrates on some general aspects of design which should enable the resulting program to be easier to understand, to analyse and to maintain. Many of the points made here have already been alluded to in earlier chapters; bringing them together will hopefully consolidate greater understanding.

## 12.1 Some principles

We start by surveying some of the general principles of the design of SPARK itself. The overall goal is of course to enable programs to be written which are more likely to be correct. Ideally we would like to be able to prove that a program is correct.

The techniques of the previous chapter can be used in some circumstances. But these techniques are expensive to apply and are usually only applicable to algorithms of a rather mathematical nature. We therefore often have to use various pragmatic approaches to ensure that the risks of residual errors in a program are reduced to a level which is as low as reasonably practicable (the so-called ALARP principle). These approaches revolve around understanding the program and are made much easier if the program is well structured.

Programming is typically about three things

- Communication between the program and the outside world. This can be the real outside world in the sense of physical devices such as temperature gauges, actuators, keyboards and so on. Alternatively it might be other parts of a software system.
- Algorithmic computation on data such as the determination of the value of some mathematical expression.
- The flow of information between various parts of the program.

Historically, early thoughts on programming concentrated on algorithmic aspects and external communication but it is now realized that much of the difficulty of programming lies in a proper understanding of how to organize the flow of information within a program.

The realization of how important this is has given rise to the concepts of Object Oriented Programming which in essence conceives a program as a number of objects which send messages to each other.

OOP can be seen as embracing two rather different concepts

- the abstract data type which comprises an abstract data structure plus operations (methods) upon it,
- reuse through inheritance whereby several abstract data types are related by being specializations of an overall class of types through extension.

We will return to these two aspects of OOP in a moment.

There are a number of important guiding principles that we have encountered in the design of SPARK. Some are mechanical details which greatly simplify or are even vital to the workings of the proof tools. Examples are the insistence that every subtype has a name, the restrictions on the use of exit and return statements and so on.

Another important principle is that exceptions should never arise during execution and we have seen how this demands that all space requirements be known statically. Thus recursion, arrays with dynamic bounds and dynamic storage allocation (such as through access types) have to be forbidden.

Another principle is the avoidance of hidden 'action at a distance'. Thus it is not permissible to give default initial values to record components in a type declaration because such values would be remote from the place where an object of the type was declared.

Of course, abstraction is in a sense about action at a distance. But the key thing about good abstraction is that it hides irrelevant detail and provided such detail is truly irrelevant then it does not matter. A key goal of SPARK is to ensure that all relevant information regarding abstraction is localized in some way at the point of use.

A concrete example mentioned earlier is provided by the package Go_Between in Section 2.9. Its specification was

```
--# inherit The_Stack;
package Go_Between is

   procedure Use_Stack;
   --# global in out The_Stack.State;
   --# derives The_Stack.State from The_Stack.State;

end Go_Between;
```

We noted that an inherit clause was required for the package The_Stack and that this had to be placed on the specification of Go_Between even though it was only referred to (in the Ada sense) in the body of Go_Between. The key point is that the existence of the state represented by The_Stack.State is not an irrelevant detail of the abstraction defined by The_Stack since it is changed by calls of Use_Stack as indicated by the derives annotation. Of course the fine detail is irrelevant and that is hidden by the use of refinement.

The placing of the inherit clause on the specification provides a local awareness of the effect of the action at a distance – or in other words a local statement of aspects of the information flow associated with the package.

The core annotations are all about information flow and, as we shall see in this chapter, a key property of a well designed SPARK program is that the information flow between the abstract objects of the program is clear and coherent.

Returning now to the two aspects of OOP, we see that the abstract data type concept of OOP is a cornerstone of SPARK. On the other hand, inheritance is not supported by SPARK because it has the flavour of action at a distance and would require much repetition if it were localized; indeed it might be argued that such localization is more naturally performed by type composition anyway. Moreover, the highly dynamic aspects of inheritance provided by the ability to select operations at execution time are clearly not conducive to program provability.

We might summarize these thoughts by saying that SPARK has all the benefits of the static aspects of good Object Oriented Design without the risks of the dynamic aspects of Object Oriented Programming. 

## 12.2 Program architecture

An important aspect of the design of a program is that of its overall architecture; in other words, its decomposition into program units and their relationship to each other.

A good choice of architecture is a major influence in ensuring the following important properties of a program.

- The text is clear to the human reader. Human understanding is important for informal proofs such as those provided by walkthroughs and later for program maintenance in the light of changing requirements.
- Program analysis is straightforward. A convoluted architecture will give rise to complications during information flow analysis.
- Program proof is feasible. Formal proof is not always possible but an appropriate architecture is vital in ensuring that the components are sufficiently simple to be proved.
- Testing and validation is eased. The decomposition into testable units is necessary for the purposes of validation.
- The program is stable. Changes in the implementation of one abstraction should not unnecessarily pervade the whole program.

Important aspects of the architecture are the agglomeration of state through composition and refinement, and the location of state as described by Abstract Data Types and Abstract State Machines.

The core annotations, and especially the global and derives annotations, describe the flow of information between the state components. A good choice of architecture based on a sound decomposition will lead to compact and comprehensible derives lists. A convoluted architecture, on the other hand, with complex and interacting structures will lead to large, unwieldy and incomprehensible derives lists.

Generally speaking the comprehensibility of derives lists can be taken to be a measure of the quality of the architecture.

It is interesting to observe that adding annotations to an existing program ('Sparking the Ada') often gives rise to unwieldy and repetitive derives lists. This is indicative of poor design; as mentioned in Section 1.4, such retrospective annotation should be avoided. The annotations should be treated as part of the design process and are a good guide to the quality of a design.

However, there are occasions when a program already exists and some annotations are better than none. In such cases of reverse engineering, the use of the data flow option should be considered as mentioned in Section 3.2. Using this option, it will be recalled, does not require derives annotations but only global annotations with modes. Note that verification conditions (including for run-time checks) can still be generated although path functions cannot.

SPARK encourages (virtually enforces) a hierarchical package structure within a program (actually, a partial ordering). This can be based on embedded internal packages (typically compiled as subunits) or alternatively can be based on private child packages.

In the next sections we shall see how the use of various aspects of state, such as its refinement and location, impact upon derives annotations. We noted above that derives annotations can be taken as a measure of the quality of an architecture. We shall also see that a good SPARK design leads to derives annotations which positively add value to the software by enhancing important attributes such as its testability and maintainability.

## 12.3 Location and visibility of state

Our first example concerns unnecessary state and was mentioned in Section 2.5 when we looked at the implementation of the procedure Exchange using a global variable rather than a local variable for the temporary T.

The proper implementation is

```
procedure Exchange(X, Y: in out Float)
--# derives X from Y &
--#         Y from X;
is
   T: Float;
begin
   T := X;  X := Y;  Y := T;
end Exchange;
```

and the foolish alternative is

```
T: Float;

procedure Exchange(X, Y: in out Float)
--# global out T;
--# derives X from Y &
--#         Y, T from X;
is
begin
   T := X;  X := Y;  Y := T;
end Exchange;
```

The introduction of unnecessary state can have a profound impact on the clarity of the derives annotations. In this case the symmetry between X and Y has been lost because of the intrusion of the global T.

Although the two fragments have the same apparent meaning we have to ensure in the second case that there is no information flow via T between calls of the procedure. Moreover, in the second case a succession of calls such as

```
Exchange(A, B);
Exchange(P, Q);
```

results in the following message from the Examiner

```
                Exchange(A, B);
                ^1
!!! (  1)  Flow Error           : Assignment to T is
           ineffective.
```

This is because the value of T produced by the first call of Exchange is overwritten by the second call without being used. Remember that analysis of the calls is done using only the abstract view presented by the specification and so the internal use of the value of T in the body is not relevant.

Unnecessary state should thus be avoided. Indeed, the use of unnecessary state as in this example requires a global annotation for T on the subprogram calling Exchange and a corresponding derives annotation for T and so on. The annotations therefore cascade and so the use of unnecessary state is very painful and thereby discouraged.

An appropriate use of the global annotation is in the implementation of Abstract State Machines (ASMs) such as the package The_Stack of Section 2.7. An ASM comprises state and operations that act on the state. A general template is

```
package P
--# own State;
is
   procedure Op( ... );
   --# global in out State;
   --# derives State from State;
   ...
end P;
```

An ASM package is an object in the OO sense; those at library level behave like overall global objects. It is important to note that an ASM may be implemented in terms of other ASMs.

We have seen how refinement may be used to ensure that although the existence of state in an ASM must be made visible, nevertheless the fine details are properly hidden. (We can have our abstraction cake and still eat it!)

There is an interesting analogy between abstraction through refinement and the composition of records out of components. Consider a record type defining a position in terms of *x*- and *y*-coordinates

```
type Position is
   record
      X_Coord, Y_Coord: Float;
   end record;
```

Such a record type is sensible because the two coordinates are logically related; we can then consider a value of the type Position as a single entity which can be manipulated as a whole.

Refinement allows an abstract own variable to provide an external view of a more detailed set of variables within the package. Using the analogy to records, we should only use refinement to group together naturally related items. Thus the refinement of the variable State of the package The_Stack into the variables Pointer and S is appropriate.

A bad example might be where the internal variables were really independent such as variables recording the running average of some data such as temperature and pressure. There might be subprograms to read the running average and to submit a new data point. If the variables were represented externally as a single abstract variable then rather surprising data coupling would result since the subprogram to update the temperature average would seem to affect both averages.

Thus it may well be appropriate for the internal state of a package to be represented by two or more abstract variables. Again a guideline is provided by the simplicity of the derives annotations.

Refinements can be nested. The constituents of an abstract own variable can themselves be abstract own variables of embedded packages or private child packages. The analogy with records is simply that a component of one record may itself be another record.

A variation on the Abstract State Machine is the Abstract Data Type (ADT) implemented as a package exporting a private type and operations on the type. A good example is the package Stacks of Section 2.6 which exports the type Stack and the operations Clear, Push, Pop, Is_Empty and Is_Full.

An abstract data type itself has no state and objects of the type are declared where required. If such an object is declared immediately within a package then it becomes part of the state of that package (and in the case of a private child package or an embedded package it also becomes part of the state of the parent package and so on). But of course an object declared locally in a subprogram in a package is not part of the state of the package.

The impact of changing the location of the state when using an ADT was illustrated by Exercise 2.9(**1**) which recast the example of the package Go_Between to use the ADT package Stacks rather than the ASM package The_Stack. The annotations are significantly simpler using the ADT because the state is more localized; there are also changes to the initialization mechanism which will be discussed in more detail in a moment.

## 12.4 Package hierarchy

An appropriate choice of package hierarchy is very important. As a simple example, suppose we have three packages, Voltage, Frequency and Phase, supplying interfaces to three input devices. Each package might have some local state recording perhaps the last healthy value received. A fourth package, Power, might provide the rest of the program with an abstraction of the other three.

One approach might be to make them all simple library packages thus

```
package Voltage
--# own State;
...

package Frequency
--# own State;
...

package Phase
--# own State;
...

--# inherit Voltage, Frequency, Phase;
package Power is
```

```
    procedure Read_Power( ... );
    --# global in out Voltage.State, Frequency.State, Phase.State;
    --# derives ...
    ...
end Power;
```

The problem is that the package Power is supposed to provide an abstraction of the other three packages. However, this abstraction is not enforced by Ada since it is possible to gain visibility and thus affect the state of any of the packages by suitable with and inherit clauses. Thus any new package could access, say, the package Voltage directly and circumvent the intended protocol of always using the interface provided by the package Power.

The essential violation of the abstraction is particularly apparent when we come to use a subprogram such as Read_Power. The annotations on Read_Power show quite clearly that the individual states are being accessed. User subprograms calling Read_Power will also need annotations revealing the use of the state of the low level packages even though the subprograms might always correctly use the proper protocol.

This difficulty can be overcome in two ways – either by making the packages Voltage, Frequency and Phase internal to the package Power or by making them private child packages of Power.

The embedded approach leads to

```
package Power
--# own State;
is
    procedure Read_Power( ... );
    --# global in out State;
    --# derives ...
    ...
end Power;

package body Power
--# own State is Voltage.State,
--#              Frequency.State,
--#              Phase.State;
is
    package Voltage
    --# own State;
    ...

    package Frequency
    --# own State;
    ...

    package Phase
    --# own State;
    ...

end Power;
```

With this arrangement the package Power is implemented as an ASM with three internal ASMs represented by the internal packages. The hierarchy of state is now clearly described by the refinement and the global annotation on Read_Power provides the abstract view so that the user program no longer needs to be aware of the inner structure. In practice, the bodies of the internal packages can be compiled as subunits.

The arrangement using private children is as follows

```
package Power
--# own State;
is
   procedure Read_Power( ... );
   --# global in out State;
   --# derives ...
   ...
end Power;

private package Power.Voltage
   --# own State;
   ...

private package Power.Frequency
   --# own State;
   ...

private package Power.Phase
   --# own State;
   ...

with Power.Voltage, Power.Frequency, Power.Phase;
package body Power
--# own State is Power.Voltage.State,
--#               Power.Frequency.State,
--#               Power.Phase.State;
is
   ...
end Power;
```

Remember from Chapter 7 that a parent body requires with clauses for any private children that it accesses but that inherit clauses are not required for them. Again the private children are quite invisible to the user.

One characteristic of SPARK is that any inherit clause always goes on a package specification and never on the body. The case of private children is interesting because if an inherit clause were required for private children in order for them to be used by the parent body then it would go on the parent specification, but this would lead to a contradiction since the parent specification must exist before the children.

A consequence of the general rule that any inherit clauses always go on a package specification is that packages always form a hierarchy (a partial ordering) and there are never any circular dependencies.

If the modification of the state of an object requires access to the state of another object, then the package hierarchy should be arranged so that such access is straightforward without the need to maintain a local copy of the state of the other object. Maintaining a local copy of the state of another object can result in very confusing information flow as the following example will reveal.

Suppose we have two packages Pressure and Temperature concerned with providing the values of pressure and temperature through calls of accessor functions Pressure.Value and Temperature.Value. Suppose also that the calculation of new values of the pressure and temperature are triggered by calls of subprograms Pressure.Calculate and Temperature.Calculate respectively. Given just this the specification of the packages would both look like

```
package Temperature
--# own State;
is
   function Value return Integer;
   --# global State;

   procedure Calculate;
   --# global in out State;
   --# derives State from State;

end Temperature;
```

Now suppose that the calculation of the temperature is triggered by an explicit call of Temperature.Calculate from the user and is independent of the pressure. On the other hand, suppose that the calculation of the pressure requires the value of the latest temperature and, moreover, is triggered by a call of Pressure.Calculate from some other mechanism such as a regular timer. (This asymmetric example may seem highly contrived but is typical of situations found in practice.)

The obvious solution is for Pressure.Calculate to obtain the latest temperature by calling Temperature.Value. The package Pressure becomes

```
--# inherit Temperature;
package Pressure
--# own State;
is
   function Value return Integer;
   --# global State;

   procedure Calculate;
   --# global in out State; in Temperature.State;
   --# derives State from State, Temperature.State;

end Pressure;
```

Now suppose that for some overriding reason the package hierarchy has to be such that the package Pressure precedes Temperature so that Pressure cannot have an inherit clause for Temperature. This means that Pressure. Calculate is unable to call Temperature.Value – in other words Pressure cannot read the state of Temperature. Instead we have to modify Temperature. Calculate so that it pushes a copy of the state into the package Pressure by using a procedure Put_Temp provided for this purpose. (Very peculiar, the reader might feel, but this is for illustration only.) The packages then become

```
package Pressure
--# own State;
is
   function Value return Integer;
   --# global State;

   procedure Put_Temp(T: in Integer);
   --# global in out State;
   --# derives State from State, T;

   procedure Calculate;
   --# global in out State;
   --# derives State from State;

end Pressure;

--# inherit Pressure;
package Temperature
--# own State;
is
   function Value return Integer;
   --# global State;

   procedure Calculate;
   --# global in out State, Pressure.State;
   --# derives State from State &
   --#          Pressure.State from State, Pressure.State;

end Temperature;
```

Note that Temperature now has an inherit clause for Pressure. The annotations for Temperature.Calculate show that it updates the state of package Pressure as well as the state of its own package. The state of Pressure now of course includes both the pressure (its real state) and the copy of the temperature.

Finally suppose we have a procedure PT which accesses the state of both packages through calls of the functions Value and then returns the values through out parameters. It triggers the calculation of the temperature by calling Temperature.Calculate but remember that it just reads the pressure and does not trigger the calculation of a new value of the pressure. The procedure PT is

```
procedure PT(P, T: out Integer)
--# global in out Pressure.State, Temperature.State;
--# derives P from Pressure.State &
--#          T, Temperature.State from Temperature.State &
--#          Pressure.State from Pressure.State, Temperature.State;
is
```

```
begin
   Temperature.Calculate;
   T := Temperature.Value;
   P := Pressure.Value;
end PT;
```

The procedure PT implicitly updates the state of Pressure as a consequence of the call of Temperature.Calculate and the derives annotation reflects this complexity.

The Examiner produces the following perhaps surprising message on analysing PT

```
??? (  1)  Warning            : The imported value of
           Temperature.State may be used in the derivation
           of P.
```

This reveals the hidden coupling between the apparently independent state of the packages Pressure and Temperature resulting from the call of Put_Temp and suggests that all is perhaps not well. We will return to this example in Section 12.6.

## 12.5 Refinement and initialization of state

The previous examples have shown the importance of localization and abstraction of state in obtaining good derives annotations. The choice of refinement also has a major impact on the quality of derives annotations.

There are a number of different kinds of state which can be broadly categorized as follows.

Abstract state modelling the outside world

This was introduced in Section 8.3 when we showed how interaction with the outside world could be considered as communication with sequences of values modelled as abstract state in hardware interface packages.

Essential state of an object

This is state which is the essence of an abstract state machine or object. An example is the package The_Stack with its internal state of pointer and array.

State introduced by optimization

The performance of certain functions can often be improved by introducing local state. Thus a function which computes some complex mathematical function might maintain a cache of recently computed values; this improves performance but adds state (such functions have been called memo functions). This kind of state is really a form of essential state.

Auxiliary state

This is state which is not necessary for the correct behaviour of a system but is introduced for other reasons. Good examples are test point variables (for probing with a debugger or logic analyser) and pseudo-constants (memory mapped variables which are constant so far as the program is concerned).

Local copies of state

This is state which could in principle be obtained from another package using an accessor function.

It is a useful guideline never to mix state of the above different kinds in a single abstract own variable since it can result in confusing derives annotations with unexpected coupling of data. Thus in the last example of the previous section, the abstract variable Pressure.State contained both the essential state of package Pressure and a local copy of the state of package Temperature and thereby resulted in an unexpected message from the Examiner.

Another important aspect of state is its initialization. Every object must be initialized with a meaningful value before it is used; this is checked by the Examiner as a part of data flow analysis.

Library level state can be initialized in two ways

- During package elaboration, either at the point of declaration of the variable(s) or in the initialization part of the package body. This occurs before the main subprogram is invoked. In either case an initializes annotation is required and this informs the Examiner that the state can be referenced safely.
- By calling a procedure. In this case there is no initializes annotation on the package but the annotations on the procedure instead provide the information that enables the Examiner to ensure that the state is not referenced before it is initialized.

When the main subprogram is analysed, the Examiner checks the whole system state for use before initialization. However, it can only perform this check successfully if refinement does not mix state initialized in the two different ways.

State should always be initialized with meaningful values. It is a great mistake to initialize data at elaboration with junk values in order to ensure that the whole package state is initialized. If appropriate values are not available at elaboration, it is far better to provide an initialization procedure; the Examiner can then ensure, by data flow analysis, that this procedure is called before the state is otherwise accessed. Assigning junk values at elaboration undermines the ability of the Examiner to ensure that all state is initialized to meaningful values and is potentially very dangerous.

Nevertheless, some situations are awkward. The classic stack implemented as array and pointer as in the package The_Stack of Section 2.8 is an interesting example. We know from dynamic considerations that it is only necessary to initialize the variable Pointer. However, the refinement requires initialization of the array S as well. A similar dilemma arises if an initializing procedure is used as in the implementation of the type Stack of Section 2.6. However, if only partial initialization is performed, it is better to do it in the initialization part since the error message can then be justified locally.

Similar considerations apply to local variables. They should never be initialized with junk values 'to be on the safe side' since again this undermines the ability of the Examiner to warn of the use of such variables before they have been given sensible values.

As mentioned above, mixing state which is initialized at elaboration with state initialized by a procedure call prevents the Examiner from carrying out a thorough analysis. Consider the following

```
package P
--# own State;
is
   procedure Init_B;
   --# global in out State;
   --# derives State from State;
   ...
end P;

package body P
--# own State is A, B;      -- refinement
is
   A: Integer := 1;
   B: Integer;

   procedure Init_B
   --# global out B;
   --# derives B from ;
   is
   begin
      B := 0;
   end Init_B;
   ...
end P;
```

In this example the Examiner reports that the initialization of A is not announced since there is no initializes annotation. Moreover, when analysing a subprogram Q using the package P, it cannot deduce that B has been initialized from the refined annotations on the procedure Init_B since only the annotations on the specification of Init_B are visible from outside. There is thus no requirement that Init_B is called before subprograms that read B. Even if Init_B is called first, examination of Q will report that the undefined initial value of State is used; this is because State is an import as well as an export of Init_B.

On the other hand, if an initializes annotation is added, the Examiner then reports B as uninitialized when examining P. And then, when analysing a subprogram Q using the package P, it assumes that B is indeed initialized (since B is a constituent of P.State) and so if Init_B is not called before subprograms that read B, it will not be able to report the error.

If we try to wriggle out of these difficulties by changing the annotation on Init_B so that State is just an export then we obtain an error message on the analysis of Init_B stating that the initial value of A is implicitly used in deriving the final value of State. Either way we are stuck.

This may seem all rather confusing but the overall point is that the combination of the two ways of providing an initial value within the same abstract variable State means that the initializes annotation can neither be correctly provided nor correctly omitted.

We have thus seen that an abstract own variable should only be refined into a set of variables representing the same kind of state and with the same form of initialization. Abstraction of state is an important tool for information hiding and properly used gives rise to good annotations. But the agglomeration of state of different kinds into a single abstract variable results in misleading coupling between logically unrelated entities and confusing information flow analysis. The maximum use of abstraction and refinement is not always the most effective.

## 12.6 Decoupling of state

We continue by looking in detail at techniques for avoiding unnecessary coupling of state.

Our first example concerns the use of external sequences to model interaction with the real world as discussed in Section 8.3. Consider the following package

```
package World
--# own State;
is
   procedure Read_Temp(T: out Integer);
   --# global in out State;
   --# derives T, State from State;

   procedure Write_Press(P: in Integer);
   --# global in out State;
   --# derives State from State, P;
   ...
end World;
```

This gives access to some external temperature through calls of Read_Temp and outputs a desired pressure (presumably as a setpoint of some controller) through calls of Write_Press. The total external state is encapsulated in the abstract variable State. Now suppose we write a procedure as follows

```
procedure Process(Press: in Integer; Temp: out Integer)
--# global in out World.State;
```

```
--# derives Temp from World.State &
--#         World.State from World.State, Press;
is
begin
  World.Write_Press(Press);
  World.Read_Temp(Temp);
end Process;
```

This simply writes a new value for the pressure and then reads the temperature. The derives annotations reflect our understanding of the situation but the Examiner produces the following message

```
??? (  1)  Warning          : The imported value of Press
           may be used in the derivation of Temp.
```

This message arises because the pressure and temperature data sequences have been coupled together through the one abstract variable State. The solution is to use two abstract state variables, one to represent the sequence of output values and one to represent the sequence of input values. The package World then becomes

```
package World
--# own In_State, Out_State;
is
  procedure Read_Temp(T: out Integer);
  --# global in out In_State;
  --# derives T, In_State from In_State;

  procedure Write_Press(P: in Integer);
  --# global in out Out_State;
  --# derives Out_State from Out_State, P;
  ...
end World;
```

and the annotations on Process become

```
--# global in out World.In_State, World.Out_State;
--# derives Temp, World.In_State from World.In_State &
--#         World.Out_State from World.Out_State, Press;
```

The annotations are now clearer and more symmetric and the Examiner no longer produces a warning.

It is worth noting that outside world inputs can normally be regarded as being initialized at elaboration since the sensors will have some values provided by the real world. Moreover, such external data is often processed before use and so these sequence states can often be made refinement constituents of higher level states using embedded or private child packages.

Another example of the problems caused by coupling was encountered in Section 12.4 when we discussed the impact of the hierarchy of the packages

Pressure and Temperature on the procedure PT. We noted that if the hierarchy was such that Pressure could not inherit Temperature, then it was necessary for Pressure to hold a local copy of the state of Temperature and that this gave rise to a confusing message because of the coupling thereby introduced.

Sometimes such reversal of the desired hierarchy cannot be avoided; other parts of the program may impose more severe demands on the design which cannot otherwise be met. If this is the case, so that making local copies of remote state cannot be avoided, then such copies should be kept distinct from the essential state of the package. This is an example of the guideline that different kinds of state should not be mixed up in a single refinement.

Thus the packages Pressure, Temperature and the procedure PT should be rewritten as

```
package Pressure
--# own State, Temp_Copy;
is
   function Value return Integer;
   --# global State;

   procedure Put_Temp(T: in Integer);
   --# global out Temp_Copy;
   --# derives Temp_Copy from T;

   procedure Calculate;
   --# global in out State; in Temp_Copy;
   --# derives State from State, Temp_Copy;

end Pressure;

--# inherit Pressure;
package Temperature
--# own State;
is
   function Value return Integer;
   --# global State;

   procedure Calculate;
   --# global in out State; out Pressure.Temp_Copy;
   --# derives State from State &
   --#           Pressure.Temp_Copy from State;

end Temperature;

...

procedure PT(P, T: out Integer)
--# global in Pressure.State;
--#        in out Temperature.State;
--#        out Pressure.Temp_Copy;
--# derives P from Pressure.State &
--#         T, Temperature.State from Temperature.State &
--#         Pressure.Temp_Copy from Temperature.State;
is
```

```
begin
  Temperature.Calculate;
  T := Temperature.Value;
  P := Pressure.Value;
end PT;
```

The copy of the temperature is now held in a distinct own variable Pressure.Temp_Copy and is not agglomerated with the rest of the state of Pressure. Although the procedure PT now has a longer global list, the derives annotations are slightly shorter and certainly clearer and there are no messages regarding flow errors.

Note that since only a single value has to be maintained in the local copy, it is sensible to make Temp_Copy a concrete own variable of Pressure and avoid unnecessary refinement.

In general, if the package hierarchy has been carefully chosen, the number of local copies should be small and so they might as well be concrete own variables. Of course, if there are several local copies of variables from the same package then these could be combined into a single abstract own variable but it is vital that this not be combined with the essential state of the package.

## 12.7 Read-only and write-only state

Auxiliary state is inevitably either read-only or write-only from the point of view of the program. (If a variable is both read and written then it would appear to be some other form of state such as essential state.) We will consider the two cases separately.

Read-only state can be introduced for a number of reasons. ROM data is an obvious example. Another is where some values are to be patched into the program, perhaps just prior to execution, but which appear as constant to the program.

In both cases it is usual to supply an attribute definition clause to give the address of the data thus

```
Data: T;
for Data'Address use ... ;
```

However, some implementations only permit such an attribute definition clause with variables and so although the object Data is logically a constant it appears as a variable.

The problem now arises that because such variables are really constant they should not appear in derives annotations since they do not influence information flow analysis and their presence would create confusing messages. They can be eliminated for the purpose of analysis either by using shadow packages (see Section 8.8) or by using inlined parameterless functions whose bodies are hidden from the Examiner by the hide directive (see Section 8.2).

Thus in the case of ROM we might compile

```
with System;
package ROM is
   type T is ...
   Data: T;
   for Data'Address use ... ;
end ROM;
```

and the corresponding shadow package might be

```
package ROM is
   type T is ...
   Data: constant T := ... ;
end ROM;
```

As explained in Section 8.8, the original code is compiled whereas the Examiner is presented with the shadow version. It is sensible to keep such read-only data in separate packages in order to minimize the amount of material that has to be shadowed for the purpose of analysis.

An alternative is to use parameterless functions. This has the advantage over shadow packages that the same code is presented to both the compiler and Examiner. The variables are simply replaced by functions with no parameters or global variables. Such functions are interpreted by the Examiner as returning a constant. Moreover, if the pragma Inline is used then the code of the function body will be expanded inline at the point of call so that there is minimal overhead (but the efficiency will depend upon the implementation). Thus rather than

```
package V_Const is
   type T is ... ;
   V_Data: T;
   for V_Data'Address use ... ;
end V_Const;
```

we instead write

```
package V_Const is
   type T is ... ;
   function V_Data return T;
   pragma Inline(V_Data);
end V_Const;

package body V_Const is
   --# hide V_Const;
   V_Temp: T;
   for V_Temp'Address use ... ;

   function V_Data return T is
   begin
      return V_Temp;
   end V_Data;
end V_Const;
```

The use of such a function is transparent to the remainder of the software since the syntax of a parameterless function call is identical to a reference to the original variable.

If during later development a fixed value for the constant is determined then a normal constant declaration can replace the function declaration without any impact on the rest of the program including the annotations.

Write-only state usually arises where intermediate values of calculations are made available as static (global) data in order to provide *test points* which can be interrogated by a debugger or logic analyser. Since these variables are written by the program they must appear in the information flow annotations. As mentioned earlier such state should not be mixed up with other kinds of state in one refinement.

Consider the following example

```
package C
--# own State;
is
   procedure Calibrate(Raw: in Integer; Cal: out Integer);
   --# global in out State;
   --# derives Cal, State from State, Raw;
   ...
end C;
```

The main purpose of procedure Calibrate is to convert a raw value into a calibrated value in standard engineering units. This conversion is done using some essential state inside the package C such as an interpolation table. This essential state is of course not changed by a call of Calibrate (although there are likely to be other subprograms to update this state if the characteristics of the measuring instrument are changed). However, for test purposes, we suppose that the last value computed is also remembered as a test point. The overall state of the package C thus includes the essential state required for the calibration plus the state of the test point.

Now consider a procedure which calibrates two raw pressures

```
procedure Two_Press(Raw_1, Raw_2: in Integer;
                    Cal_1, Cal_2: out integer)
--# global in out C.State;
--# derives Cal_1 from Raw_1, C.State &
--#         Cal_2 from Raw_2, C.State &
--#         C.State from Raw_1, Raw_2, C.State;
is
begin
   C.Calibrate(Raw_1, Cal_1);
   C.Calibrate(Raw_2, Cal_2);
end Two_Press;
```

The annotations on the procedure Two_Press reflect our understanding of the calibration process but the Examiner reports

```
??? (  1)  Warning            : The imported value of Raw_1
           may be used in the derivation of Cal_2.
```

This reveals an unexpected dependency of Cal_2 on Raw_1 and is another example of the now familiar problem of coupling. The solution is to separate the test point from the essential state of package C. We then have

```
package C
--# own State, Test_Point;
is
  procedure Calibrate(Raw: in Integer; Cal: out Integer);
  --# global in State; in out Test_Point;
  --# derives Cal from State, Raw &
  --#         Test_Point from Test_Point, State, Raw;
  ...
end C;

...

procedure Two_Press(Raw_1, Raw_2: in Integer;
                    Cal_1, Cal_2: out integer)
--# global in C.State; in out C.Test_Point;
--# derives Cal_1 from Raw_1, C.State &
--#         Cal_2 from Raw_2, C_State &
--#         C.Test_Point from Raw_1, Raw_2, C.State, C.Test_Point;
is
begin
  C.Calibrate(Raw_1, Cal_1);
  C.Calibrate(Raw_2, Cal_2);
end Two_Press;
```

With this arrangement there is no apparent coupling between Cal_2 and Raw_1. Separating out the test point clearly reveals that the value of the test point correctly has no impact on other variables and so does not contribute to the essential state of the system. Furthermore, the derives annotation for the test point shows precisely what contributes to the value of the test point which is useful for testing. Also, the test point annotations can be easily distinguished and thus ignored when considering the essential behaviour of the system.

Note that we have assumed that several test point values are retained in the system and therefore the state Test_Point depends upon itself. If there is only one test point which repeatedly gets overwritten, then it is still convenient to treat the test point rather like an external sequence and so leave the annotation as showing it depending upon itself. Otherwise we get flow error messages noting that the first assignment to the test point is ineffective and that the value of Raw_1 is not used in the derivation of the test point. However, as mentioned above, we could simply ignore these messages since they clearly relate just to the test point and not to the essential behaviour of the system.

Once more the overall message of this example is not to combine different kinds of state, in this case write-only state and essential state.

## 12.8 Summary of design guidelines

This chapter has discussed a number of important guidelines which should help in choosing an appropriate architecture and levels of refinement. They can be summarized as follows.

- Use refinement to hide detail but avoid combining different kinds of state or logically distinct state.
- Use embedded packages or private child packages where the state of a package is wholly a component of some higher level package.
- Avoid making local copies of state which is available by accessor functions from elsewhere in the system.
- Separate state initialized by elaboration from that initialized by explicit procedure call.
- Use shadows or hiding to eliminate pseudo-constant or read-only variables.
- Separate write-only variables, such as test points, from essential system state.
- Regard unexpected annotation growth or annotation obscurity as a warning that program structure and state location could be improved.

Using shadows or hiding is of course a 'kludge'. However, it is better to use them so that it is quite clear where analysis has been omitted rather than to distort the program and perhaps have a mass of incomprehensible annotations or have to sift through overwhelming messages from the Examiner.

Good derives annotations are the heart of a well designed SPARK program. As well as being essential in enabling the Examiner to perform information flow analysis, clear derives annotations provide a number of less tangible but important benefits. For example

They promote understanding of the behaviour of the program. If the architectural design of the program is good and hence the derives annotations are clear, then they provide useful insight into how the code behaves. For example, they can be scanned in order to identify the absence of some expected dependency or the presence of an unexpected dependency. Annotations are particularly helpful in code reviews – simply asking 'does this annotation make sense?' is a straightforward and fruitful line of approach.

They can highlight non-standard cases. It often happens that there are groups of similar subprograms which, if the program is well designed, should have similar patterns of annotations. If a particular subprogram of a group has a different pattern then this is a sign of a need for further investigation.

They are an aid to navigation. Derives annotations provide significant assistance when navigating unfamiliar code; this is particularly important during program maintenance. When reading unfamiliar code, with the intention of updating it, the ability to identify all its interactions with the rest of the system is extremely useful.

They are an aid to testing. Derives annotations can assist in constructing unit tests. For example, if annotations indicate independence between certain imports and exports, then there is no point in devising tests to investigate their relationship.

But remember that only a good design has good derives annotations. The quality of annotations is a measure of the quality of the design and provides practical guidance during the design process.

It is very important not to add annotations late in the coding process. The annotations should be written as part of the process of designing the overall program architecture and writing package and subprogram specifications. The annotations will then assist in the coding process by detecting errors before unit testing. If they are added late in the coding process, it is likely that a poor architecture will have already been established and much of the benefit of SPARK will have been lost.

## 12.9 Coding style

A chapter on design would not be complete without a few remarks on coding style. A number of aspects of good style are automatically imposed by the use of SPARK anyway. Trivial examples are the prohibition of the goto statement and deeply nested exit statements.

The sensible use of constructions generally helps with program analysis and proof and a few specific points are worth emphasizing.

- Avoid unrelated collections of objects and subprograms; they give rise to confusing annotations.
- Avoid the declaration of variables in package specifications; they obscure opportunities for data abstraction. But the declaration of constants in package specifications is encouraged where appropriate.
- Use subtypes with range constraints where appropriate; this simplifies run-time check analysis.
- Use for statements in preference to while statements; for statements always terminate and avoid the risk that a proof is only partial.
- Use loop statements with exit statements in preference to while statements since the exit condition in relation to any assert annotation is clearer.
- Assign entire arrays wherever possible in order to avoid creating spurious self-dependencies.

It would be inappropriate to consider further details of the general issue of good coding style because this is admirably discussed at length in *Ada 95 Quality and Style* published by the Software Productivity Consortium [SPC, 1995].

# 13 Case Studies



This final chapter contains a few longer examples which illustrate various aspects of the use of SPARK. Full scale programs are inevitably far too long to include in a book of this nature so even these case studies are somewhat incomplete.

There are three examples, a lift controller, an autopilot and a sorting algorithm. The first two illustrate the use of structure and interaction with external state but no proof is attempted. The lift controller is fully annotated and information flow analysis is performed. The autopilot has a more elaborate structure and illustrates the use of refinement using private child packages; for illustration, this example omits derives annotations and so only the simpler data flow analysis is possible. The sorting algorithm shows the use of proof techniques with a larger example than has been treated in earlier chapters.

## 13.1 A lift controller

This example shows how SPARK can be helpful in the conceptual decomposition of a program into a number of interrelated components (objects) each with its own state. The annotations on the individual components indicate their interrelationships in a formal manner which can be checked by the

Examiner at an early stage in the design. This can be done long before the code is written and also before any private parts are completed.

Suppose we have a building with four floors and a lift (elevator). There are doors in the usual way on each floor but the lift itself has no doors (as in many small European hotels). There are buttons in the lift and on each floor which are illuminated when pressed. The rules are

- The lift has a set of buttons, one for each floor. These illuminate when pressed and cause the lift to visit the corresponding floor. The illumination is cancelled when the lift visits the floor (when it stops at it).
- Each floor has two buttons (except ground and top), one to request upward travel and one for downward travel. These illuminate when pressed. The illumination is cancelled when the lift visits the floor and is either going in the desired direction or visiting the floor with no requests outstanding to continue in the same direction. In the former case, if both buttons are illuminated, only one should be cancelled.
- All requests must eventually be serviced.
- When there are no requests outstanding, the lift should remain at its last destination with the door closed.

The controller can command the following actions

- Move the lift to a floor; this can only be acted upon when the lift is stationary and all the doors are closed.
- Open and close the door on a specified floor; this can only be acted upon when the lift is at that floor and is stationary.
- Clear the latch for a given button; this turns out the light.

The program is split into three packages representing the building, the lift and the buttons. The main subprogram is then a procedure which accesses the state of the packages and issues commands to the building (to move the doors), to the lift (to go to a floor) and to the buttons (to turn off their illumination). The overall design is thus

```
package Building
--# own Door_History;
is
   type Direction_Type is (Up, Down);
   type Floor_Type is (Floor_0, Floor_1, Floor_2, Floor_3);
   ...
end Building;

with Building;
--# inherit Building;
package Lift
--# own State;
is
   ...
end Lift;
```

```
with Building;
--# inherit Building;
package Buttons
--# own Button_History;
--# initializes Button_History;
is
   ...
end Buttons;

with Building, Buttons, Lift;
--# inherit Building, Buttons, Lift;
--# main_program;
procedure Lift_Control
--# global in out Buttons.Button_History;
--#        out Building.Door_History, Lift.State;
--# derives Building.Door_History, Buttons.Button_History, Lift.State
--#              from Buttons.Button_History;
is
   --# hide Lift_Control;
end Lift_Control;
```

The overall structure is typical of a controller which interacts with external processes. Note that the states of the lift, the building and the buttons are represented by own variables of the packages. The Button_History state is initialized during elaboration and thus before the main subprogram is called but the others are not (as we shall see they are initialized by explicit calls from within the main subprogram). As a consequence the derives annotation for the main subprogram shows the states as depending only on the previous Button_History.

One can pontificate on the philosophy of situations such as this; one point is that the main subprogram never terminates anyway. Moreover, the buttons are certainly in charge and so it is appropriate for the ongoing outcome to depend on the button state.

The Button_History can be seen as representing the sequence of values of a vector giving the states of all the individual buttons; similarly for Door_History. However, Lift.State is more of a single value.

Various alternatives are possible. For example, one might consider it more appropriate for the doors to be modelled as Door.State. Whether the state is perceived as a sequence or a single value depends very much on how it is represented in the software. If there is no state in the software but rather an interface to external devices (which could be achieved by memory-mapped local variables which do not appear in annotations) then we would model this interface by a history of values written to the hardware. The initializing procedure might then send a code to the hardware to ensure that all doors are initially shut and we can view this as initializing the external sequence.

Alternatively, the software system might maintain state recording the state of each of the doors in the lift system – this state then mirrors the hardware state and enables the software to ensure that only one door is open at a time.

A minor point is that we have chosen to declare the various enumeration types in the package Building; this is why the other packages have with and inherit clauses for the package Building. The types could perhaps go in a distinct types package.

This simple outline design is worthwhile in that it allows us to discuss and capture some of the relationships between the objects at a very early stage in a form which the Examiner can check. Actually the Examiner has little to say except that the only code is hidden and that the package Buttons requires a body (this is because of the initializes annotation).

We can now flesh out the specifications of the three packages to include various subprograms. The specification of the package Building is

```
package Building
--# own Door_History;
is
   type Direction_Type is (Up, Down);
   type Floor_Type is (Floor_0, Floor_1, Floor_2, Floor_3);

   procedure Initialize_Door_States;
   --# global out Door_History;
   --# derives Door_History from ;
   --    postcondition: all doors closed;

   procedure Open_Door(Floor: in Floor_Type);
   --# global in out Door_History;
   --# derives Door_History from Door_History, Floor;

   procedure Close_Door(Floor: in Floor_Type);
   --# global in out Door_History;
   --# derives Door_History from Door_History, Floor;

end Building;
```

This is much as expected. Note the comment hinting at a postcondition. In order to develop such annotations and proofs, we would need to be more explicit about the state of the doors since we clearly need to be able to say that all the doors are closed or that just one is open and so on. In order to do this we would need to introduce annotations relating to the Door_History in more detail. However, the object Door_History has not yet been declared nor have we yet declared its type; in such circumstances the own annotation would need a type announcement as mentioned in Section 11.2.

The specification of the package Lift is

```
with Building;
--# inherit Building;
package Lift
--# own State;
is
   function Present_Floor return Building.Floor_Type;
   --# global State;

   procedure Initialize_Lift_State;
   --# global out State;
   --# derives State from ;
```

```
      procedure Move(Next_Stop: in Building.Floor_Type);
      --# global out State;
      --# derives State from Next_Stop;

   end Lift;
```

Note that the procedure Move simply moves the lift to the given floor so that the State does not depend upon its previous value.

The specification of the package Buttons is

```
   with Building;
   --# inherit Building;
   package Buttons
   --# own Button_History;
   --# initializes Button_History;
   is
      procedure Inspect_Floor_Button(Direction: in Building.Direction_Type;
                                     Floor: in Building.Floor_Type;
                                     Call_Found: out Boolean);
      --# global in out Button_History;
      --# derives Call_Found from Direction, Floor, Button_History &
      --#         Button_History from Button_History;

      procedure Inspect_Lift_Button(Floor: in Building.Floor_Type;
                                    Call_Found: out Boolean);
      --# global in out Button_History;
      --# derives Call_Found from Floor, Button_History &
      --#         Button_History from Button_History;

      procedure Clear_Floor_Button(Direction: in Building.Direction_Type;
                                   Floor: in Building.Floor_Type);
      --# global in out Button_History;
      --# derives Button_History from Direction, Floor, Button_History;

      procedure Clear_Lift_Button(Floor: in Building.Floor_Type);
      --# global in out Button_History;
      --# derives Button_History from Floor, Button_History;

   end Buttons;
```

The bodies of the three packages are not given here but are left to the imagination of the reader. Many of the subprograms require communication with the external world using the interfacing techniques introduced in Chapter 8.

---

## EXERCISE 13.1

1 Rewrite the specification of the package Building with appropriate proof annotations on the three procedures. Model the own variable Door_History as an array with index Floor_Type and components indicating whether the individual doors are open or closed. Ensure that the actual variable Door_History remains hidden.

---

## 13.2 Lift controller main program

We now consider the coding of the controller itself. The essence of the approach is to traverse up and down the floors looking for the next destination. The lift does not reverse direction unless it finds no request in its current direction or it reaches the ground or top floor. So a first refinement of the main subprogram is

```
with Building, Buttons, Lift;
--# inherit Building, Buttons, Lift;
--# main_program;
procedure Lift_Control
--# global in out Buttons.Button_History;
--#            out Building.Door_History, Lift.State;
--# derives Building.Door_History, Buttons.Button_History, Lift.State
--#                  from Buttons.Button_History;
is

   procedure Traverse(Direction: in Building.Direction_Type)
   --# global in out Building.Door_History, Buttons.Button_History,
   --#                  Lift.State;
   --# derives Building.Door_History,
   --#            Buttons.Button_History,
   --#            Lift.State
   --#                from *, Direction, Buttons.Button_History, Lift.State;
   is separate;

begin   -- Lift_Control
   Building.Initialize_Door_States;
   Lift.Initialize_Lift_State;
   while True loop
      Traverse(Building.Up);
      Traverse(Building.Down);
   end loop;
end Lift_Control;
```

The main procedure initializes the door and lift states by calling the appropriate procedures and then calls **Traverse** to go up and down alternately within an endless loop. The Examiner comments that the loop is stable of index zero as expected.

The procedure **Traverse** has been made separate so that it can be compiled as a subunit. This is a useful technique for the functional decomposition of subprograms. Note also the use of * in the derives annotation. The subunit is

```
separate (Lift_Control)
procedure Traverse(Direction: in Building.Direction_Type) is
   Lift_Called: Boolean;
   Next_Stop: Building.Floor_Type;

   procedure Poll(Direction: in Building.Direction_Type;
```

```
                          Lift_Called: out Boolean;
                          Next_Stop: out Building.Floor_Type)
      --# global in Lift.State;
      --#        in out Buttons.Button_History;
      --# derives Lift_Called, Next_Stop, Buttons.Button_History
      --#                from Direction, Buttons.Button_History, Lift.State;
      is separate;

   begin   -- Traverse
      loop
         Poll(Direction, Lift_Called, Next_Stop);
         exit when not Lift_Called;
         Lift.Move(Next_Stop);
         Building.Open_Door(Lift.Present_Floor);
         Building.Close_Door(Lift.Present_Floor);
         Buttons.Clear_Lift_Button(Lift.Present_Floor);
         Buttons.Clear_Floor_Button(Direction, Lift.Present_Floor);
      end loop;
      Buttons.Clear_Floor_Button(Building.Up, Lift.Present_Floor);
      Buttons.Clear_Floor_Button(Building.Down, Lift.Present_Floor);
   end Traverse;
```

This uses an internal procedure Poll which looks for the next stop in the current direction. If there are no calls outstanding in that direction then Lift_Called is set to False and this causes the traversal to be terminated. The procedure Poll is again conveniently written as a subunit.

The text of Poll is

```
   with Building; use type Building.Floor_Type;
   separate (Lift_Control.Traverse)
   procedure Poll(Direction: in Building.Direction_Type;
                  Lift_Called: out Boolean;
                  Next_Stop: out Building.Floor_Type) is

      Requested: Boolean;
      Final_Floor, Inspected_Floor: Building.Floor_Type;
      Reverse_Direction: Building.Direction_Type;

      function Next_Floor(Current_Floor: Building.Floor_Type;
                          Direction: Building.Direction_Type)
                                               return Building.Floor_Type
      is
         Next_Floor_Value: Building.Floor_Type;
      begin   -- Next_Floor;
         case Direction is
            when Building.Up =>
               Next_Floor_Value := Building.Floor_Type'Succ(Current_Floor);
            when Building.Down =>
               Next_Floor_Value := Building.Floor_Type'Pred(Current_Floor);
         end case;
```

```
      return Next_Floor_Value;
    end Next_Floor;

  begin    -- Poll
    case Direction is
      when Building.Up =>
        Final_Floor := Building.Floor_Type'Last;
        Reverse_Direction := Building.Down;
      when Building.Down =>
        Final_Floor := Building.Floor_Type'First;
        Reverse_Direction := Building.Up;
    end case;
    Requested := False;
    Inspected_Floor := Lift.Present_Floor;
    loop
      Buttons.Inspect_Floor_Button(Direction,
                                    Inspected_Floor, Requested);
      exit when Requested;
      exit when Inspected_Floor = Final_Floor;
      Inspected_Floor := Next_Floor(Inspected_Floor, Direction);
      Buttons.Inspect_Lift_Button(Inspected_Floor, Requested);
      exit when Requested;
    end loop;
    if not Requested then
      loop
        exit when Inspected_Floor = Lift.Present_Floor;
        Buttons.Inspect_Floor_Button(Reverse_Direction,
                                      Inspected_Floor, Requested);
        exit when Requested;
        Inspected_Floor := Next_Floor(Inspected_Floor,
                                       Reverse_Direction);
      end loop;
    end if;
    Lift_Called := Requested;
    Next_Stop := Inspected_Floor;
  end Poll;
```

Note the use type clause which enables equality tests to be carried out for checking the floor values. Remember that a use type clause must be in a context clause which contains a preceding with clause for the package containing the declaration of the type. Hence we have to provide a with clause for the subunit even though the package Building is already available to the subunit. (The use type clause could alternatively be placed in the context clause for the main procedure Lift_Control.)

The cognoscenti of lift controllers will recognize that the algorithm is not ideal. For example, once the lift has decided on its destination, it flashes past anyone who meanwhile presses a button at an intermediate floor. Very typical of small hotels. It also seems to leave no time for actual people to enter and leave the lift since it closes the doors immediately after opening them. The reader might like to consider how the algorithm could be improved.

**EXERCISE 13.2**

1 The lift stops with its doors closed when it has nothing to do. How can we tell this without looking at the code of Poll?

## 13.3 An autopilot

Our next example considers the control system of an autopilot controlling both altitude and heading of an aircraft. The altitude is controlled by manipulating the elevators and the heading is controlled by manipulating the ailerons and rudder. We will sketch the general structure and then look at the altitude part in more detail.

The autopilot has a control panel with three switches each of which has two positions – on and off. The switches are

- the master switch; the autopilot is completely inactive if this is off,
- the altitude switch; the autopilot controls the altitude if this is on,
- the heading switch; the autopilot controls the heading if this is on.

For reasons which will become clear in a moment, we declare the package providing access to the switches as a private child of the main autopilot package AP. A suitable package specification is

```
private package AP.Controls
--# own Master_Switch, Altitude_Switch, Heading_Switch;
--# initializes Master_Switch, Altitude_Switch, Heading_Switch;
is
   type Switch is (On, Off);

   procedure Read_Master_Switch(Position: out Switch);
   --# global in out Master_Switch;

   procedure Read_Altitude_Switch(Position: out Switch);
   --# global in out Altitude_Switch;

   procedure Read_Heading_Switch(Position: out Switch);
   --# global in out Heading_Switch;

end AP.Controls;
```

This specification takes a familiar form. The three switches are treated as external sequences since they are manipulated by the pilot and so the global annotations on the procedures have mode in out. The derives annotations, if given, would be

```
--# derives Position, Master_Switch from Master_Switch;
```

for the procedure Read_Master_Switch and similarly for the others.

The autopilot reads various instruments as follows

- the altimeter giving the height in feet,
- the bank indicator giving the angle at which the aircraft is banked in degrees,
- the compass giving the heading in degrees,
- the heading bug giving the heading to the destination in degrees,
- the vertical speed indicator (VSI) giving the rate of climb in feet per minute,
- the Mach indicator giving the airspeed as a Mach number,
- the pitch indicator giving the upward pitch in degrees,
- the slip indicator giving the angle of slip in degrees.

The units chosen represent typical commercial practice.

There is a difference in the way in which the target altitude and target heading are indicated. The target altitude is the current altitude when the altitude switch is turned to On (much as the cruise control in a car selects the target speed to be the current speed when it is first engaged). The target heading on the other hand is obtained by reading the instrument known as the heading bug which is set by the human pilot.

The package specification giving access to the instruments is

```
package Instruments
--# own Altitude         : Feet;
--#     Bank             : Bankangle;
--#     Heading          : Headdegree;
--#     Heading_Bug      : Headdegree;
--#     Mach             : Machnumber;
--#     Pitch            : Pitchangle;
--#     Rate_Of_Climb    : Feetpermin;
--#     Slip             : Slipangle;
--# initializes Altitude, Bank, Heading, Heading_Bug,
--#             Mach, Pitch, Rate_Of_Climb, Slip;
is
  type Feet is range 0 .. 50_000;
  type Bankangle is range -45 .. 45;
  type Headdegree is range 0 .. 359;
  type Feetpermin is range -6000 .. 6000;
  type Machnumber is range 0 .. 100;
  type Pitchangle is range -10 .. 20;
  type Slipangle is range -25 .. 25;

  procedure Read_Altimeter(Present_Altitude: out Feet);
  --# global in out Altitude;

  procedure Read_Bank_Indicator(Present_Bank: out Bankangle);
  --# global in out Bank;
```

```
   procedure Read_Compass(Present_Heading: out Headdegree);
   --# global in out Heading;

   procedure Read_Heading_Bug(Target_Heading: out Headdegree);
   --# global in out Heading_Bug;

   procedure Read_Mach_Indicator(Present_Mach: out Machnumber);
   --# global in out Mach;

   procedure Read_Pitch_Indicator(Present_Pitch: out Pitchangle);
   --# global in out Pitch;

   procedure Read_VSI(Present_Rate_Of_Climb: out Feetpermin);
   --# global in out Rate_Of_Climb;

   procedure Read_Slip_Indicator(Present_Slip: out Slipangle);
   --# global in out Slip;

end Instruments;
```

Largely for the convenience of the reader, the own variables announce their type (this facility is primarily intended for use with proof and was described in Section 11.2). The various types are then declared and use a style in which the type identifier indicates the units. This introduces some strong typing which prevents certain errors. The types are all integer types which are easier to deal with if proof of run-time errors is to be attempted. The ranges reflect the values encountered by typical commercial aircraft. Mach numbers are given as a percentage of the speed of sound. The various procedures enable the instruments to be read and have the expected global annotations.

Remember that the own variables represent external sequences and are abstract; there is no corresponding refinement since the package body will be hidden from the Examiner as explained in Section 8.3. There are no Ada variables called Altitude, Bank and so on. The same applies to the package AP.Controls.

Finally, there are the control surfaces which the autopilot manipulates. These are the elevators, the ailerons and the rudder. They are conveniently accessed through the following package

```
package Surfaces
--# own Elevators, Ailerons, Rudder;
--# initializes Elevators, Ailerons, Rudder;
is
   type Controlangle is range -45 .. 45;

   procedure Move_Elevators(Position: in Controlangle);
   --# global in out Elevators;

   procedure Move_Ailerons(Position: in Controlangle);
   --# global in out Ailerons;

   procedure Move_Rudder(Position: in Controlangle);
   --# global in out Rudder;

end Surfaces;
```

This is very straightforward. We have used the same type for all three control surfaces for simplicity. In these cases, the derives annotations, if given, would be

```
--# derives Elevators from Elevators, Position;
```

and so on.

The packages Instruments and Surfaces are declared as public library packages and so the existence of their state is globally visible. This is in contrast to the package AP.Controls which is private to the autopilot and not visible to the outside world. The argument is that the autopilot switches are a matter of concern only to the autopilot but the other instruments and the control surfaces are of global concern.

## 13.4 Autopilot main program

The autopilot itself is represented by a package AP. It contains a procedure Control which performs a single control cycle of the autopilot. The main subprogram then calls AP.Control repeatedly. We use this package structure rather than the simple procedural decomposition of the lift controller so that the state of the autopilot can be refined. (The main loop could have been in the procedure AP.Control but for the purposes of proof it is better to have a subprogram that represents a single control cycle.)

The specification of the package representing the autopilot is

```
--# inherit Surfaces, Instruments;
package AP
--# own State;
--# initializes State;
is
   procedure Control;
   --# global in out State,
   --#                Surfaces.Elevators, Surfaces.Ailerons,
   --#                                              Surfaces.Rudder,
   --#                Instruments.Altitude, Instruments.Bank, ... ;
end AP;
```

The overall internal state of the autopilot is represented by the variable State and this is manipulated by the procedure Control.

The main subprogram is

```
with AP;
--# inherit Surfaces, Instruments, AP;
--# main_program;
procedure Main
```

```
   --# global in out AP.State,
   --#               Surfaces.Elevators, Surfaces.Ailerons,
   --#                                              Surfaces.Rudder,
   --#               Instruments.Altitude, Instruments.Bank, ... ;
is
begin
   while True loop
      AP.Control;
   end loop;
end Main;
```

The essence of the procedure Control is to read the switches in order to determine whether altitude or heading or both are to be controlled and then to read all the instruments and finally to call the two internal parts of the autopilot, one for controlling the altitude and the other for controlling the heading.

The altitude and heading controllers are represented by private child packages AP.Altitude and AP.Heading. They both have a procedure Maintain with parameters passing relevant information. For example, the specification of the package AP.Altitude is

```
with AP.Controls, Instruments, Surfaces;
--# inherit AP.Controls, Instruments, Surfaces;
private package AP.Altitude
--# own State;
--# initializes State;
is
   procedure Maintain(Switch_Pressed: in Controls.Switch;
                      Present_Altitude: in Instruments.Feet;
                      Mach: in Instruments.Machnumber;
                      Climb_Rate: in Instruments.Feetpermin;
                      The_Pitch: in Instruments.Pitchangle);
   --# global in out State, Surfaces.Elevators;

end AP.Altitude;
```

Note that the internal state of the altitude controller is represented by an abstract own variable State whose details we will look at in the next section. The heading controller similarly has an abstract own variable State.

We are now in a position to look at the body of the package AP which is

```
with Instruments;
with AP.Controls, AP.Altitude, AP.Heading;
package body AP
--# own State is AP.Controls.Master_Switch,
--#              AP.Controls.Altitude_Switch,
--#              AP.Controls.Heading_Switch,
--#              AP.Altitude.State,
--#              AP.Heading.State;
is
```

```
procedure Control
--# global in out Controls.Master_Switch, ... ,
--#               Altitude.State, Heading.State,
--#               Surfaces.Elevators, Surfaces.Ailerons,
--#                                          Surfaces.Rudder,
--#               Instruments.Altitude, Instruments.Bank, ... ;
is
  Master_Switch, Altitude_Switch, Heading_Switch,
    Altitude_Selected, Heading_Selected: Controls.Switch;
  Present_Altitude     : Instruments.Feet;
  Bank                 : Instruments.Bankangle;
  Present_Heading      : Instruments.Headdegree;
  Target_Heading       : Instruments.Headdegree;
  Mach                 : Instruments.Machnumber;
  Pitch                : Instruments.Pitchangle;
  Rate_Of_Climb        : Instruments.Feetpermin;
  Slip                 : Instruments.Slipangle;
begin
  Controls.Read_Master_Switch(Master_Switch);
  Controls.Read_Altitude_Switch(Altitude_Switch);
  Controls.Read_Heading_Switch(Heading_Switch);

  case Master_Switch is
    when Controls.On =>
      Altitude_Selected := Altitude_Switch;
      Heading_Selected := Heading_Switch;
    when Controls.Off =>
      Altitude_Selected := Controls.Off;
      Heading_Selected := Controls.Off;
  end case;

  Instruments.Read_Altimeter(Present_Altitude);
  ...                                    -- read all instruments
  Instruments.Read_Slip_Indicator(Slip);

  Altitude.Maintain(Altitude_Selected, Present_Altitude, Mach,
                    Rate_Of_Climb, Pitch);
  Heading.Maintain(Heading_Selected, Mach, Present_Heading,
                   Target_Heading, Bank, Slip);
end Control;

end AP;
```

The abstract own variable State of the package AP is refined into the state of the three switches in the package AP.Control plus the internal states of the individual controllers AP.Altitude and AP.Heading. These three packages are private child packages and so their state is not visible outside the package AP.

Since the state is refined, the annotations on the procedure Control are also refined. Every global variable has mode **in out** which is typical of such procedures but is not very revealing. Derives annotations would have revealed the individual couplings; for example that for Altitude.State would be

```
--# derives Altitude.State from Altitude.State,
--#                            Controls.Master_Switch,
--#                            Controls.Altitude_Switch,
--#                            Instruments.Altitude,
--#                            Instruments.Rate_Of_Climb,
--#                            Instruments.Pitch;
```

This is much as expected; we would be surprised if the altitude state depended upon the heading or angle of bank for example. Perhaps surprisingly, Altitude.State does not depend upon Mach even though this is also a parameter of Maintain. In fact it is only Surfaces.Elevators that depends upon Mach. As we shall see, the Mach number is used to determine the elevator movement after having determined the pitch change required – the faster the speed the less movement required.

A practical variation might be to introduce an intermediary procedure Read_Instruments to read all the instruments at the same time. This procedure would then be called by the procedure AP.Control. This is good practice and ensures that the controllers are working on a consistent set of data. If we wanted to do this then we should restructure the system so that AP.Control cannot read the individual instruments at all. The simplest way to do this is just to make the individual procedures local to the body of Instruments so that it becomes

```
package Instruments
--# own Altitude, ... ;
--# initializes Altitude, ... ;
is
   type Feet is range 0 .. 50_000;
   ...

   procedure Read_Instruments(Present_Altitude: out Feet; ... );
   --# global in out Altitude, ... ;

end Instruments;

package body Instruments is
--# hide Instruments;

   procedure Read_Altimeter(Present_Altitude: out Feet) is
   begin
      ...
   end;
   ...

   procedure Read_Instruments(Present_Altitude: out Feet; ... ) is
   begin
      Read_Altimeter(Present_Altitude);
      ...
      Read_Slip_Indicator(Slip);
   end;

end Instruments;
```

Note that we have hidden the body of the package in the style shown in Section 8.3. If we do not hide the package body as a whole then its own variables must be concrete Ada variables declared somewhere in which case the body could be written as

```
package body Instruments is
   Altitude: Feet;
   ...
   procedure Read_Altimeter(Present_Altitude: out Feet)
   --# global in out Altitude;
   is
   --# hide Read_Altimeter;
   begin ... end Read_Altimeter;
   ...
   procedure Read_Instruments(Present_Altitude: out Feet; ... )
   --# global in out Altitude, ... ;
   is
   begin
      Read_Altimeter(Present_Altitude);
      ...
      Read_Slip_Indicator(Slip);
   end Read_Instruments;

begin
   --# hide Instruments;
end Instruments;
```

In this arrangement we hide the bodies of the individual procedures such as Read_Altimeter since no doubt they read the actual instruments using some low level technique (or we could use pragma Import as discussed in Section 8.1). We also have to persuade the Examiner that the variables are initialized; we can do that by providing a hidden initialization part as shown. A curious feature of this example is that the Ada variables Altitude and so on are never actually used but only exist in order to discuss their hypothetical state.

A further variation might be to declare the individual procedures in a private child package. The Ada variables can then be declared in the private part of Instruments so that they can be seen by the private package and yet be hidden from the external system. We would then have

```
package Instruments
--# own Altitude, ... ;
--# initializes Altitude, ... ;
is
   ...
private
   Altitude: Feet;
   ...
end Instruments;
```

```
--# inherit Instruments;
private package Instruments.Single is

   procedure Read_Altimeter(Present_Altitude: out Feet);
   --# global in out Altitude;
   ...

end Instruments.Single;

with Instruments.Single;
package body Instruments is

   procedure Read_Instruments(Present_Altitude: out Feet; ... )
   --# global in out Altitude, ... ;
   is
   begin
      Single.Read_Altimeter(Present_Altitude);
      ...
      Single.Read_Slip_Indicator(Present_Slip);
   end Read_Instruments;

begin
   --# hide Instruments;
end Instruments;
```

Note the with and inherit clauses. The specification of Instruments.Single has an inherit clause for its parent but does not need a with clause since a child package never needs a with clause for its parent. However, the body of the package Instruments has a with clause for Instruments.Single but does not need an inherit clause. Remember that a private child is similar to a package embedded within the body of its parent as explained in Section 7.2 and so the parent body never needs an inherit clause for a private child.

Yet another variation would be for the individual procedures to actually update the local state of Instruments directly in order to avoid a double layer of parameter passing.

## 13.5 Altitude and heading controllers

When the altitude switch is first moved to On, the altitude controller notes the altitude and then maintains it by adjusting the pitch as necessary. If the altitude subsequently falls below the desired target then the autopilot increases the pitch (by pulling back on the stick) and if it climbs above then it decreases the pitch (by pushing forward on the stick).

The pitch is itself controlled by the internal pitch autopilot which adjusts the elevators. It is important that the rate of change of pitch is not excessive since this is uncomfortable for the passengers and is likely to tip over their gin. The pitch autopilot is in turn defined by a private child (AP.Altitude.Pitch) of the altitude controller and itself has internal state. The specification of the pitch autopilot is

```
--# inherit Surfaces, Instruments;
private package AP.Altitude.Pitch
--# own State;
--# initializes State;
is
   procedure Pitch_AP(Present_Altitude: in Instruments.Feet;
                      Target_Altitude: in Instruments.Feet;
                      Mach: in Instruments.Machnumber;
                      Climb_Rate: in Instruments.Feetpermin;
                      The_Pitch: in Instruments.Pitchangle);
   --# global in out State, Surfaces.Elevators;

end AP.Altitude.Pitch;
```

Observe that the parameters of Pitch_AP are similar to those of the procedure Maintain of the package AP.Altitude which calls it. The difference is that the target altitude is explicitly passed and so the local information of AP.Altitude concerning the state of the switch is no longer required. We will return to the pitch autopilot in a moment.

The state needed for the altitude controller is the target altitude and the last state of the switch (so that it can tell when the switch is moved) plus of course the internal state of the pitch autopilot.

So the body of AP.Altitude is

```
with AP.Altitude.Pitch;
package body AP.Altitude
--# own State is Target_Altitude, Switch_Pressed_Before,
--#              AP.Altitude.Pitch.State;
is
   Target_Altitude: Instruments.Feet := 0;
   Switch_Pressed_Before: Controls.Switch := Controls.Off;

   procedure Maintain(Switch_Pressed: in Controls.Switch;
                      Present_Altitude: in Instruments.Feet;
                      Mach: in Instruments.Machnumber;
                      Climb_Rate: in Instruments.Feetpermin;
                      The_Pitch: in Instruments.Pitchangle)
   --# global in out Target_Altitude, Switch_Pressed_Before,
   --#               Pitch_State, Surfaces.Elevators;
   is
   begin
      case Switch_Pressed is
         when Controls.On =>
            case Switch_Pressed_Before is
               when Controls.Off =>
                  Target_Altitude := Present_Altitude;
               when Controls.On =>
                  null;
            end case;
```

```
            Pitch.Pitch_AP(Present_Altitude,
                           Target_Altitude, Mach, Climb_Rate, The_Pitch);
         when Controls.Off => null;
      end case;
      Switch_Pressed_Before := Switch_Pressed;
   end Maintain;

end AP.Altitude;
```

The body of the procedure Maintain is as expected. Note that the internal state has to be initialized because the abstract variable Altitude.State was announced as initialized. The logic does not actually require this for the target altitude and so the value of 0 is arbitrary. However, we recall from Section 12.5 that it is bad to mix state that does need initializing with state that does not. So really the state should be separated out. Indeed code with a potential target altitude of zero is positively worrying and we need to do flow analysis to show that the target altitude is properly set.

We now return to the pitch autopilot. As mentioned earlier it is important that the rate of change of pitch or pitch rate is not excessive. The pitch autopilot first uses the current altitude and target altitude to determine the target rate of climb; this is done by multiplying their difference by 10 and is then limited to plus or minus 1000 feet per minute. The target rate of climb and current rate of climb are then used to determine the target pitch rate; this is done by dividing their difference by 10 and is then limited to 10 degrees per second – remember the gin.

The current pitch rate is not given by an instrument but has to be computed from current and previous measurements of the pitch angle; this involves retaining knowledge of the pitch history. This historical information and the calculation of the pitch rate are encapsulated in a subsidiary private child package AP.Altitude.Pitch.Rate whose specification is

```
--# inherit Instruments;
private package AP.Altitude.Pitch.Rate
--# own Pitch_History;
--# initializes Pitch_History;
is
   type Degreespersec is range -180 .. 180;

   procedure Calc_Pitchrate(Pitch: in Instruments.Pitchangle;
                            Present_Pitchrate: out Degreespersec);
   --# global in out Pitch_History;

end AP.Altitude.Pitch.Rate;
```

The procedure Calc_Pitchrate uses the current pitch angle and the state represented by the abstract own variable Pitch_History to compute Present_Pitchrate. The details of the body are omitted.

The current pitch rate and the target pitch rate are then used to compute the desired elevator movement. This also uses other factors such as the Mach number. These actions are performed by the body of AP.Altitude.Pitch which is

```
with Instruments;
  use type Instruments.Feet, Instruments.Feetpermin;
with AP.Altitude.Pitch.Rate;
  use type AP.Altitude.Pitch.Rate.Degreespersec;
package body AP.Altitude.Pitch
--# own State is AP.Altitude.Pitch.Rate.Pitch_History;
is
  procedure Calc_Pitchrate(Pitch: in Instruments.Pitchangle;
      Present_Pitchrate: out Rate.Degreespersec)
                                    renames Rate.Calc_Pitchrate;
  subtype Degreespersec is Rate.Degreespersec;

  function Target_ROC(Present_Altitude: Instruments.Feet;
                      Target_Altitude: Instruments.Feet)
                                return Instruments.Feetpermin is
    Result: Instruments.Feetpermin;
  begin
    Result := Instruments.Feetpermin(
                      (Target_Altitude - Present_Altitude) * 10);
    if Result > 1000 then
      Result := 1000;
    elsif Result < -1000 then
      Result := -1000;
    end if;
    return Result;
  end Target_ROC;

  function Target_Rate(Present_Altitude: Instruments.Feet;
                       Target_Altitude: Instruments.Feet;
                       Climb_Rate: Instruments.Feetpermin)
                                        return Degreespersec is
    Target_Climb_Rate: Instruments.Feetpermin;
    Result: Degreespersec;
  begin
    Target_Climb_Rate := Target_ROC(Present_Altitude,
                                           Target_Altitude);
    Result := Degreespersec((Target_Climb_Rate - Climb_Rate)/10);
    if Result > 10 then
      Result := 10;
    elsif Result < -10 then
      Result := -10;
    end if;
    return Result;
  end Target_Rate;

  function Calc_Elevator_Move(Present_Pitchrate: Degreespersec;
                              Target_Pitchrate: Degreespersec;
                              Mach: Instruments.Machnumber)
                                  return Surfaces.Controlangle is
```

```
      --# hide Calc_Elevator_Move;
    begin
      ...
    end Calc_Elevator_Move;

    procedure Pitch_AP(Present_Altitude: in Instruments.Feet;
                       Target_Altitude: in Instruments.Feet;
                       Mach: in Instruments.Machnumber;
                       Climb_Rate: in Instruments.Feetpermin;
                       The_Pitch: in Instruments.Pitchangle)
    --# global in out Rate.Pitch_History,
    --#               Surfaces.Elevators;
    is
      Present_Pitchrate: Degreespersec;
      Target_Pitchrate: Degreespersec;
      Elevator_Movement: Surfaces.Controlangle;
    begin
      Calc_Pitchrate(The_Pitch, Present_Pitchrate);
      Target_Pitchrate := Target_Rate(Present_Altitude,
                                      Target_Altitude, Climb_Rate);
      Elevator_Movement := Calc_Elevator_Move(Present_Pitchrate,
                                              Target_Pitchrate, Mach);
      Surfaces.Move_Elevators(Elevator_Movement);
    end Pitch_AP;

  end AP.Altitude.Pitch;
```

This is all quite straightforward. We do not need a with clause for the package Control because the context clause for a parent applies also to its children and the context clause on AP.Altitude has a with clause for Control. However, we have to repeat the with clause for Instruments so that we can write a use type clause for the types Feet and Feetpermin.

Note also the declaration of the subtype Degreespersec which is essentially a renaming of that from the child package AP.Altitude.Pitch.Rate. By way of illustration we also have a renaming of the procedure Calc_Pitchrate from that package so that it can be called with just its direct name. Unfortunately the syntax requires the renaming first so that it cannot have the benefit of the subtype.

We conclude with a few remarks on the heading controller. This is similar to the altitude controller except that two subsidiary autopilots are required, one to control roll and one to control yaw. The roll autopilot adjusts roll to maintain the heading by moving the ailerons and the yaw autopilot then corrects any slip by moving the rudder. These are implemented as two private child packages AP.Heading.Roll and AP.Heading.Yaw. The body of the package AP.Heading is somewhat simpler than that for the altitude because the target heading is obtained from the heading bug.

The control principles are also similar and involve establishing and controlling desired roll and yaw rates. The calculation of these rates can similarly be factored out into two child packages AP.Heading.Roll.Rate and AP.Heading.Yaw.Rate.

The final overall decomposition into hierarchical library units may be summarized as follows

```
Instruments
   Instruments.Single
Surfaces
AP
   AP.Controls
   AP.Altitude
      AP.Altitude.Pitch
         AP.Altitude.Pitch.Rate
   AP.Heading
      AP.Heading.Roll
         AP.Heading.Roll.Rate
      AP.Heading.Yaw
         AP.Heading.Yaw.Rate
Main
```

This example has shown the value of private child packages in decomposing a system while maintaining integrity of state and allowing separate compilation of both specifications and bodies. Remember that although decomposition can be done using embedded packages and subunits, the specifications of embedded packages cannot be compiled separately.

---

**EXERCISE 13.5**

1 Write the package AP.Heading by analogy with AP.Altitude. The roll autopilot needs the Mach number, present and target headings and the angle of bank. The yaw autopilot just needs the Mach number and the angle of slip. Note that the target heading is passed as an explicit parameter as can be seen from the body of the package AP.

---

## 13.6 A sorting algorithm

This final example illustrates the use of proof techniques with arrays in a bit more detail. It consists of a procedure Sort declared together with a few related types in a package Array_Utilities (which in practice might contain other subprograms operating on arrays as well). The package specification is

```
package Array_Utilities is

   Max_Table_Size: constant := 100;
   type Base_Index_Type is range 0 .. Max_Table_Size;
```

```
    subtype Index_Type is Base_Index_Type
                                        range 1 .. Max_Table_Size;
    type Contents_Type is range -1000 .. 1000;
    type Array_Type is array (Index_Type) of Contents_Type;

    --# function Ordered(A: Array_Type; L, U: Index_Type)
    --#                                         return Boolean;
    --# function Perm(A, B: Array_Type) return Boolean;

    procedure Sort(Table: in out Array_Type);
    --# derives Table from Table;
    --# post Ordered(Table, 1, Max_Table_Size) and
    --#      Perm(Table, Table~);

  end Array_Utilities;
```

The various type declarations are straightforward but note that for the purpose of this exercise the array type is constrained to a fixed length which is Max_Table_Size.

The postcondition on Sort uses two proof functions. The function Ordered is true if the part of the array from L to U is in ascending order. The function Perm is true if the set of values of the two array parameters are the same set with identical duplications if any. The array is then sorted if all the elements are in order and the final array is a permutation of the original array.

The point about duplication is often overlooked. It is all too easy to assume for example that an array is sorted if every value in the original array is also present in the final array and that they are ordered; but this can fail if duplications occur.

The package body is

```
  package body Array_Utilities is

    --# function Partitioned(A: Array_Type; L, M, U: Index_Type)
    --#                                         return Boolean;

    procedure Sort(Table: in out Array_Type) is
      Key: Index_Type;

      --# function The_Smallest(A: Array_Type; L, U: Index_Type)
      --#                                       return Index_Type;

      function Find_Smallest(Arr: Array_Type; L, U: Index_Type)
                                              return Index_Type
      --# pre 1 <= L and L <= U and U <= Max_Table_Size;
      --# return The_Smallest(Arr, L, U);
      is
        K: Index_Type;
      begin
        K := L;
        for I in Index_Type range L+1 .. U loop
          if Arr(I) < Arr(K) then
            K := I;
          end if;
```

```
            --# assert 1 <= L and L+1 <= I and
            --#            I <= U and U <= Max_Table_Size and
            --#            K in Index_Type and
            --#            K = The_Smallest(Arr, L, I);
          end loop;
          return K;
        end Find_Smallest;

        procedure Swap_Elements(T: in out Array_Type;
                                I, J: in Index_Type)
        --# derives T from T, I, J;
        --# post T = T~[I => T~(J); J => T~(I)] and Perm(T, T~);
        is
          Temp: Contents_Type;
        begin
          Temp := T(I);  T(I) := T(J);  T(J) := Temp;
        end Swap_Elements;

      begin   -- Sort
        for Low in Index_Type range 1 .. Max_Table_Size-1 loop
          Key := Find_Smallest(Table, Low, Max_Table_Size);
          if Key /= Low then
            Swap_Elements(Table, Low, Key);
          end if;
          --# assert 1 <= Low and Low <= Max_Table_Size-1 and
          --#            Ordered(Table, 1, Low) and
          --#            Partitioned(Table, 1, Low, Max_Table_Size) and
          --#            Perm(Table, Table~);
        end loop;
      end Sort;

    end Array_Utilities;
```

The algorithm is very straightforward but not the fastest. At any time the array is partitioned into two parts – the first part already sorted and the second part not yet sorted. It repeatedly scans the (diminishing) second part, finds the least element (which because of previous scans is not less than any element of the previously sorted part) and then swaps it so that it is now the last element of the sorted part. Incidentally, this algorithm is a version of the so-called bubble sort.

The procedure Sort contains two internal subprograms Find_Smallest and Swap_Elements. It is an interesting stylistic point as to whether these are best declared inside or alongside Sort. Logically one might argue that they belong inside because they are not needed outside. However, some prefer a flatter style and placing them alongside does not make them globally visible because they are in the package body. Moreover, the absence of global annotations shows that they can be moved without difficulty – an important benefit of global annotations. A possible practical advantage of declaring all three subprograms at the same level is that all the verification conditions would then be generated in the same directory.

The function Find_Smallest returns the index of the smallest element of the part of the array from L to U. It uses the corresponding proof function The_Smallest in its return annotation and also in the assert statement within its loop. This loop scans the array keeping a note of the index of the smallest element found so far in the variable Key. The assert statement assures that the loop parameter is within appropriate bounds and that Key does indeed denote the smallest element found so far.

The procedure Swap_Elements is similar to that discussed in Section 11.8. Note that the postcondition also includes Perm(T, T~); this is actually implied by the other part of the postcondition but is provided in order to simplify the proof of the loop in the procedure Sort which calls Swap_Elements.

The procedure Sort is now quite straightforward. The key to the proof is of course the assert annotation in the loop. This uses an additional proof function Partitioned which is true if all elements in the first part of the array (from 1 to Low) are less than or equal to all elements in the second part of the array (from Low+1 to Max_Table_Size). The assertion uses Ordered to ensure that the first part is sorted and Perm to ensure that all the elements are still there. The general idea is that when the loop exits all the elements are in the first part of the array and so are sorted.

There are several sets of verification conditions generated for the three subprograms – there are six for Find_Smallest (one from start to finish bypassing the loop, a pair from the start to the assert, a pair around the loop and one from the assert to the end (the pairs arise from the if statement)), there are eight for Sort (much as Find_Smallest but extra paths are introduced by the checks for the call of Find_Smallest) and one for Swap_Elements.

In order to prove these we need various rules for the proof functions which we will now consider in turn.

The rule defining Ordered is

```
rule_family ord: ordered(A, L, U) requires [A: any, L: i, U: i] .

ord(1): ordered(A, L, U) may_be_replaced_by
                for_all(o: integer, L <= o and o < U ->
                        element(A, [o]) <= element(A, [o+1])) .
```

This simply says that an array is ordered means that each element is less than or equal to the next one.

The rule defining Partitioned is

```
rule_family part: partitioned(A, L, M, U) requires [A: any, L: i, M: i, U: i] .

part(1): partitioned(A, L, M, U) may_be_replaced_by
                for_all(p: integer, L <= p and p <= M ->
                        for_all(q: integer, M+1 <= q and q <= U ->
                                element(A, [p]) <= element(A, [q]))) .
```

This has nested universal quantifiers but again is simple. It says that an array is partitioned means that every element in the first part of the array (from L to M) is less than or equal to every element in the second part of the array (from M+1 to U).

The rules for Perm are

```
rule family perm: perm(X, Y) requires [X: any, Y: any] .

perm(1): perm(update(update(A, [I], X), [J], Y), B)
                may_be_deduced_from
                     [ perm(update(update(A, [I], Y), [J], X), B) ] .

perm(2): perm(A, A) may_be_deduced .

perm(3): perm(A, B) may_be_replaced_by perm(B, A) .
```

The first rule says that if an array A with elements A[I] and A[J] equal to X and Y respectively is a permutation of some array B, then it follows that the same array with elements A[I] and A[J] interchanged is also a permutation of B. The second rule is self-evident. The third rule is not actually required for this exercise but is given for completeness.

The rules for The_Smallest are

```
rule_family smallest: X = Y requires [X: i, Y: i] .

smallest(1): X = the_smallest(A, L, U) may_be_replaced_by
                  for_all(w: integer, L <= w and w <= U ->
                        element(A, [X]) <= element(A, [w])) and
                              L <= X and X <= U
                        if [1 <= L, L <= U, U <= max_table_size] .
```

This daunting rule says X is the smallest means that A(X) is less than or equal to all other elements of the array with index in the range from L to U. It also asserts that the index X is also in the range L to U. Note the condition that L and U themselves have appropriate values.

Finally we have rules for the implicitly declared proof function corresponding to Find_Smallest which is used in the verification conditions for Sort. The rules are

```
rule_family small: X = Y  requires [X: i, Y: i] &
                   X <= Y requires [X: i, Y: i] &
                   for_all (X, Y) requires [X: any, Y: any] .

small(1): X = find_smallest(A, L, U) may_be_replaced_by
                 for_all(w: integer, L <= w and w <= U ->
                       element(A, [X]) <= element(A, [w])) and
                             L <= X and X <= U
                       if [1 <= L, L <= U, U <= max_table_size] .

small(2): for_all(w: integer, L <= w and w <= U ->
               element(A, [find_smallest(A, L, U)]) <= element(A, [w]))
                    may_be_deduced_from
                         [1 <= L, L <= U, U <= max_table_size] .

small(3): L <= find_smallest(A, L, U) may_be_deduced_from
                         [1 <= L, L <= U, U <= max_table_size] .
```

```
small(4): find_smallest(A, L, U) <= U may_be_deduced_from
                              [1 <= L, L <= U, U <= max_table_size] .
```

The first rule repeats the rule for the explicit proof function The_Smallest. It could therefore have been expressed as

```
small(1): X = find_smallest(A, L, U) may_be_replaced_by
                              X = the_smallest(A, L, U) .
```

The other rules (which we can consider to be theorems rather than definitions) are essentially the first rule taken apart. Each part of the consequence of the first rule has X replaced by find_smallest(A, L, U) and the three consequences are then stated as three separate rules.

---

**EXERCISE 13.6**

1 One of the conclusions of the verification condition for Swap_Elements is

```
C2:   perm(update(update(t, [i], element(t, [j])), [j], element(t, [i])), t) .
```

Show that this is true using the rules perm(1), array(2) and perm(2). The rule array(2) was given in Section 11.8 and is

```
array(2): update(A, I, element(A, I)) may_be_replaced_by A .
```

---

## 13.7 Proof of sorting algorithm

We now turn to considering the verification conditions. There are too many to consider them all in detail and so we will just consider a few.

The procedure Swap_Elements has just one path and the verification condition is

```
H1:   true .
      ->
C1:   update(update(t, [i], element(t, [j])), [j], element(t, [i])) =
              update(update(t, [i], element(t, [j])), [j], element(t, [i])) .
C2:   perm(update(update(t, [i], element(t, [j])), [j], element(t, [i])), t) .
```

The conclusion C1 is a tautology and occurred previously in Section 11.8; the Simplifier reduces it to true. The conclusion C2 relates to the postcondition Perm(Table, Table~) and was proved in Exercise 13.6(**1**).

The function Find_Smallest has six paths as mentioned in the previous section. Four of these are in two pairs because of the two paths through the if statement. There is a pair of paths from the start to the assert, a pair of paths from the assert around the loop to the assert, one path from the assert to the end and one path from start to finish. The path from start to finish can never be taken and that from the assert to the end is trivial. The most interesting paths are those around the loop; they are similar and we will look at the one corresponding to the if statement being obeyed.

Most of the hypotheses and conclusions are straightforward but the interesting ones are

```
H7:   k = the_smallest(arr, l, i) .
H9:   element(arr, [i + 1]) < element(arr, [k]) .
      ->
C7:   i + 1 = the_smallest(arr, l, i + 1) .
```

(Note that the verification conditions produced actually have loop__1__i rather than i for reasons explained in the answer to Exercise 11.3(**1**); for clarity we just use i.)

The approach is to use rule smallest(1) to express H7 and C7 as quantified expressions which are similar but have different ranges and then to use H9 to extend the range of H7 to give that of C7. Intuitively this is obvious and can be done with the Proof Checker in a few steps although the details take us outside the scope of this book.

The procedure Sort has eight paths. Several of these are rather boring but nevertheless are very important because it is all too easy to make an error in boundary conditions in this sort of application. As in the case of Find_Smallest, the path from start to finish can never be taken; in this example the Simplifier spots this and reports the contradiction in the hypotheses. The interesting paths are around the loop and from the assert to the end.

The path from the assert to the end is often trivial in this type of example but it is not trivial in this particular case. The reason is that the algorithm in a sense omits its last iteration. This is because at the end of the iteration with Low equal to Max_Table_Size-1 the unsorted partition only has one element and a single element does not need to be sorted! The verification condition for this final path is (writing low rather than loop__1__low)

```
For path(s) from assertion to finish:

H1:   1 <= low .
H2:   low <= max_table_size - 1 .
H3:   ordered(table, 1, low) .
H4:   partitioned(table, 1, low, max_table_size) .
H5:   perm(table, table~) .
H6:   low = max_table_size - 1 .
      ->
C1:   ordered(table, 1, max_table_size) .
C2:   perm(table, table~) .
```

The conclusion C2 is the same as H5 and so can be dismissed. Substituting for low using H6, and abbreviating max_table_size to m, (the Simplifier replaces it by 100 of course), the essence becomes as follows

```
H3:   ordered(table, 1, m-1) .
H4:   partitioned(table, 1, m-1, m) .
      ->
C1:   ordered(table, 1, m) .
```

The first step is to use the rule part(1) and to note that the range in the second quantification has just a single element. Making the appropriate substitutions we get

```
H4:  for_all(p: integer, 1 <= p and p <= m-1 ->
                element(table, [p]) <= element(table, [m])) .
```

In fact all we really need is to consider the highest value of p so we have

```
element(table, [m-1]) <= element(table, [m])
```

If we now expand H3 and C1 using the rule ord(1) we get

```
H3:  for_all(o: integer, 1 <= o and o < m-1 ->
                element(table, [o]) <= element(table, [o+1])) .
```

the known hypothesis, and

```
C1:  for_all(o: integer, 1 <= o and o < m ->
                element(table, [o]) <= element(table, [o+1])) .
```

which we have to prove. Now C1 is the same as H3 except that the range of the quantification has an extra value; but the case of this extra value is covered by the relationship between the last two elements which we have just deduced from H4. So C1 is proved.

The paths around the loop can be proved in a similar manner although a little further manipulation is required especially in the case when the if statement is executed.

And finally of course, we must also prove termination; however, using for statements makes this easy since for statements always terminate!

Space precludes any further discussion but the general principles used should be clear. The full set of verification conditions will be found on the CD that accompanies this book together with a listing of an audit showing the details of all proofs using the Proof Checker. A discussion of an extended form of this example showing how to prove that it is free of run-time errors will also be found on the CD.

# Appendix 1

# Syntax

This appendix gives the full syntax of SPARK using the same BNF notation as for Ada. Syntactic categories are represented by lower case names; some of these contain embedded underlines to increase readability. A category is defined in terms of other categories by a production consisting of the name being defined followed by the special symbol ::= and its defining sequence. Some categories are atomic and cannot be decomposed further – these are known as terminal symbols. Other symbols used are

- [ ] square brackets enclose optional items,
- { } braces enclose optional items which may be omitted, appear once or be repeated many times,
- | a vertical bar separates alternatives.

In some cases the name of a category is prefixed by a word in italics. Such a prefix is intended to convey some semantic information and can be treated as a form of comment as far as the context free syntax is concerned.

Many productions are exactly the same in Ada and SPARK. Some are altered but have the same category name – these are prefixed with an asterisk (*). Some are additional and are prefixed with a plus sign (+).

## A1.1 Syntax of core SPARK language

This section includes the core annotations but not those for proof contexts.

*Chapter 4*

graphic_character ::=
    identifier_letter | digit | space_character | special_character

character ::=
    graphic_character | format_effector | other_control_function

identifier ::= identifier_letter {[underline] letter_or_digit}

letter_or_digit ::= identifier_letter | digit

numeric_literal ::= decimal_literal | based_literal

decimal_literal ::= numeral [. numeral] [exponent]

numeral ::= digit {[underline] digit}

exponent ::= E [+] numeral | E – numeral

* based_literal ::= base # based_numeral # [exponent]

base ::= numeral

based_numeral ::= extended_digit {[underline] extended_digit}

extended_digit ::= digit | A | B | C | D | E | F

character_literal ::= 'graphic_character'

string_literal ::= "{string_element}"

string_element ::= "" | *non_quotation_mark*_graphic_character

comment ::= -- {*non_end_of_line*_character}

pragma ::= **pragma** identifier [(pragma_argument_association
{, pragma_argument_association})];

pragma_argument_association ::=
[*pragma_argument*_identifier =>] name
| [*pragma_argument*_identifier =>] expression

*Chapter 5*

* object_declaration ::= defining_identifier_list :
[**constant**] subtype_mark [:= *constant*_expression];

defining_identifier_list ::= defining_identifier {, defining_identifier}

defining_identifier ::= identifier

* type_declaration ::= full_type_declaration | private_type_declaration

* full_type_declaration ::= **type** defining_identifier **is** type_definition;

* type_definition ::=
enumeration_type_definition | integer_type_definition
| real_type_definition | array_type_definition
| record_type_definition

subtype_declaration ::=
**subtype** defining_identifier **is** subtype_indication;

subtype_indication ::= subtype_mark [constraint]

subtype_mark ::= *subtype*_name

constraint ::= scalar_constraint | composite_constraint

* scalar_constraint ::= range_constraint

* composite_constraint ::= index_constraint

* range_constraint ::= **range** *static*_range

range ::= range_attribute_reference
| simple_expression .. simple_expression

* enumeration_type_definition ::=
(defining_identifier {, defining_identifier})

* integer_type_definition ::=
**range** *static*_simple_expression .. *static*_simple_expression

real_type_definition ::=
floating_point_definition | fixed_point_definition

* floating_point_definition ::=
**digits** *static*_simple_expression [real_range_specification]

real_range_specification ::=
**range** *static*_simple_expression .. *static*_simple_expression

* fixed_point_definition ::= ordinary_fixed_point_definition

* ordinary_fixed_point_definition ::=
**delta** *static*_simple_expression real_range_specification

* record_type_definition ::=
**record**
component_list
**end record**;

* component_list ::= component_declaration {component_declaration}

* component_declaration ::=
defining_identifier_list : component_definition;

* component_definition ::= subtype_mark

array_type_definition ::=
unconstrained_array_definition | constrained_array_definition

unconstrained_array_definition ::=
**array** (index_subtype_definition
{, index_subtype_definition}) **of** component_definition

index_subtype_definition ::= subtype_mark **range <>**

constrained_array_definition ::=
**array** (discrete_subtype_definition
{, discrete_subtype_definition}) **of** component_definition

* discrete_subtype_definition ::= *discrete*_subtype_mark

* index_constraint ::=
(*discrete*_subtype_mark {, *discrete*_subtype_mark})

* aggregate ::= record_aggregate | array_aggregate

* record_aggregate ::=
positional_record_aggregate | named_record_aggregate

\+ positional_record_aggregate ::= (expression {, expression})

\+ named_record_aggregate ::=
(record_component_association {, record_component_association})

* record_component_association ::=
*component_*selector_name => expression

array_aggregate ::=
positional_array_aggregate | named_array_aggregate

* positional_array_aggregate ::=
(aggregate_item , aggregate_item {, aggregate_item})
| (aggregate_item {, aggregate_item} , **others** => aggregate_item)

\+ aggregate_item ::= aggregate | expression

* named_array_aggregate ::=
(array_component_association {, array_component_association}
[, **others** => aggregate_item])
| (**others** => aggregate_item)

* array_component_association ::=
discrete_choice_list => aggregate_item

discrete_choice_list ::= discrete_choice { | discrete_choice}

* discrete_choice ::= *static_*simple_expression | discrete_range

* discrete_range ::= *discrete_*subtype_indication | *static_*range

* name ::= direct_name | indexed_component | selected_component
| attribute_reference | function_call

* direct_name ::= identifier

* prefix ::= name

indexed_component ::= prefix (expression {, expression})

selected_component ::= prefix . selector_name

* selector_name ::= identifier

attribute_reference ::= prefix ' attribute_designator

range_attribute_reference ::= prefix ' range_attribute_designator

* attribute_designator ::= identifier [(*static_*expression)] | Delta | Digits

range_attribute_designator ::= Range [(*static_*expression)]

expression ::=
relation {**and** relation } | relation {**and then** relation}
| relation {**or** relation } | relation {**or else** relation}
| relation {**xor** relation}

```
relation ::=
        simple_expression [relational_operator simple_expression]
      | simple_expression [not] in range
      | simple_expression [not] in subtype_mark

simple_expression ::=
      [unary_adding_operator] term {binary_adding_operator term}

term ::= factor {multiplying_operator factor}

factor ::= primary [** primary] | abs primary | not primary

* primary ::= numeric_literal | character_literal | string_literal
      | name | type_conversion | qualified_expression | (expression)

logical_operator ::= and | or | xor

relational_operator ::= = | /= | < | <= | > | >=

binary_adding_operator ::= + | - | &

unary_adding_operator ::= + | -

multiplying_operator ::= * | / | mod | rem

highest_precedence_operator ::= ** | abs | not

* type_conversion ::= subtype_mark (expression)

qualified_expression ::=
      subtype_mark ' (expression) | subtype_mark ' aggregate

number_declaration ::=
      defining_identifier_list : constant := static_expression;
```

*Chapter 6*

```
sequence_of_statements ::= statement {statement}

* statement ::= simple_statement | compound_statement

* simple_statement ::= null_statement
      | assignment_statement | procedure_call_statement
      | exit_statement | return_statement

* compound_statement ::= if_statement | case_statement | loop_statement

null_statement ::= null;

assignment_statement ::= variable_name := expression;

if_statement ::=
       if condition then
          sequence_of_statements
      {elsif condition then
          sequence_of_statements}
      [else
          sequence_of_statements]
       end if;
```

```
  condition ::= boolean_expression

* case_statement ::=
          case expression is
             case_statement_alternative
            {case_statement_alternative}
            [when others => sequence_of_statements]
          end case;

  case_statement_alternative ::=
          when discrete_choice_list => sequence_of_statements

  loop_statement ::= [loop_statement_identifier :]
          [iteration_scheme] loop
              sequence_of_statements
           end loop [loop_identifier];

  statement_identifier ::= direct_name

  iteration_scheme ::=
          while condition | for loop_parameter_specification

* loop_parameter_specification ::=
    defining_identifier in [reverse] discrete_subtype_mark [range range]

* exit_statement ::= exit [when condition];

* return_statement ::= return expression;

* subprogram_declaration ::=
            procedure_specification ; procedure_annotation
          | function_specification ; function_annotation

+ procedure_specification ::=
          procedure defining_identifier parameter_profile

+ function_specification ::=
          function defining_designator parameter_and_result_profile

* defining_designator ::= defining_identifier

  parameter_profile ::= [formal_part]

  parameter_and_result_profile ::= [formal_part] return subtype_mark

  formal_part ::= (parameter_specification {; parameter_specification})

* parameter_specification ::=
          defining_identifier_list : mode subtype_mark

  mode ::= [in] | in out | out

+ procedure_annotation ::=
          [global_definition | moded_global_definition]
          [dependency_relation]

+ function_annotation ::=
          [global_definition]
```

+ global_definition ::= --# **global** entire_variable_list;

+ entire_variable_list ::= entire_variable {, entire_variable}

+ entire_variable ::= [*package*_name .] direct_name

+ moded_global_definition ::=
    --# **global** global_mode entire_variable_list;
        {global_mode entire_variable_list;}

+ global_mode ::= **in** | **in out** | **out**

+ dependency_relation ::=
    --# **derives** [dependency_clause {& dependency_clause}];

+ dependency_clause ::=
    entire_variable_list **from** imported_variable_list

+ imported_variable_list ::= [*] | [* ,] entire_variable_list

* subprogram_body ::=
    procedure_specification [procedure_annotation] **is**
        subprogram_implementation
    | function_specification [function_annotation] **is**
        subprogram_implementation

+ subprogram_implementation ::=
        declarative_part
    **begin**
        sequence_of_statements
    **end** designator;

* designator ::= identifier

* procedure_call_statement ::= *procedure*_name [actual_parameter_part];

* function_call ::= *function*_name [actual_parameter_part]

* actual_parameter_part ::= (parameter_association_list)

+ parameter_association_list ::=
    named_parameter_association_list
    | positional_parameter_association_list

+ named_parameter_association_list ::=
    *formal_parameter*_selector_name => explicit_actual_parameter
    {, *formal_parameter*_selector_name => explicit_actual_parameter}

+ positional_parameter_association_list ::=
    explicit_actual_parameter {, explicit_actual_parameter}

explicit_actual_parameter ::= expression | *variable*_name

*Chapter 7*

* basic_declaration ::= object_declaration | number_declaration
    | type_declaration | subtype_declaration

```
* declarative_part ::=
          {renaming_declaration}
          {declarative_item | embedded_package_declaration
                              | external_subprogram_declaration}

* basic_declarative_item ::= basic_declaration | representation_clause

  declarative_item ::= basic_declarative_item | body

  body ::= proper_body | body_stub

* proper_body ::= subprogram_body | package_body

+ embedded_package_declaration ::=
          package_declaration {renaming_declaration}

+ external_subprogram_declaration ::=
          subprogram_declaration
          pragma Import(pragma_argument_association,
                        pragma_argument_association,
                        {pragma_argument_association});

  package_declaration ::= package_specification;

* package_specification ::=
          [inherit_clause]
          package defining_program_unit_name
             package_annotation
          is
            {renaming_declaration}
            {package_declarative_item}
          [private
            {renaming_declaration}
            {package_declarative_item}]
          end [parent_unit_name .] identifier;

+ package_declarative_item ::= basic_declarative_item
          | subprogram_declaration | external_subprogram_declaration

* package_body ::=
          package body defining_program_unit_name
          [refinement_definition]
          is
             declarative_part
          [begin
             sequence_of_statements]
          end [parent_unit_name .] identifier;

  defining_program_unit_name ::=
          [parent_unit_name .] defining_identifier

  parent_unit_name ::= name

+ inherit_clause ::=
          --# inherit package_name {, package_name};
```

\+ package_annotation ::=
  [own_variable_clause [initialization_specification]]

\+ own_variable_clause ::= **--# own** own_variable_list;

\+ own_variable_list ::= own_variable {, own_variable}

\+ own_variable ::= direct_name

\+ refinement_definition ::=
  **--# own** refinement_clause {& refinement_clause};

\+ refinement_clause ::= subject **is** constituent_list

\+ subject ::= direct_name

\+ constituent_list ::= constituent {, constituent}

\+ constituent ::= [*package*_name .] direct_name

\+ initialization_specification ::= **--# initializes** own_variable_list;

* private_type_declaration ::=
  **type** defining_identifier **is** [**limited**] **private**;

use_type_clause ::= **use type** subtype_mark {, subtype_mark};

* renaming_declaration ::=
  **function** defining_operator_symbol formal_part **return** subtype_mark
    **renames** *package*_name . operator_symbol;
  | function_specification
    **renames** *package*_name . *function*_direct_name;
  | procedure_specification
    **renames** *package*_name . *procedure*_direct_name;

defining_operator_symbol ::= operator_symbol

operator_symbol ::= string_literal

compilation ::= {compilation_unit}

compilation_unit ::=
  context_clause library_item | context_clause subunit

* library_item ::=
  [**private**] package_declaration | package_body | main_subprogram

\+ main_subprogram ::=
  [inherit_clause]
  main_subprogram_annotation
  subprogram_body

\+ main_subprogram_annotation ::= **--# main_program**;

context_clause ::= {context_item}

* context_item ::= with_clause | use_type_clause

* with_clause ::=
  **with** *library_package*_name {, *library_package*_name};

* body_stub ::= subprogram_body_stub | package_body_stub

* subprogram_body_stub ::=
    procedure_specification [procedure_annotation] **is separate**;
  | function_specification [function_annotation] **is separate**;

package_body_stub ::= **package body** defining_identifier **is separate**;

subunit ::= **separate** (parent_unit_name) proper_body

*Chapter 8*

representation_clause ::=
    attribute_definition_clause
  | enumeration_representation_clause
  | record_representation_clause
  | at_clause

local_name ::= direct_name | direct_name ' attribute_designator
  | *library_unit*_name

attribute_definition_clause ::=
    **for** local_name ' attribute_designator **use** expression;
  | **for** local_name ' attribute_designator **use** name;

enumeration_representation_clause ::=
  **for** *first_subtype*_local_name **use** enumeration_aggregate;

enumeration_aggregate ::= array_aggregate

record_representation_clause ::=
  **for** *first_subtype*_local_name **use**
    **record** [mod_clause]
      {component_clause}
    **end record**;

mod_clause ::= **at mod** *static*_expression;

component_clause ::=
  *component*_local_name **at** position **range** first_bit .. last_bit;

position ::= *static*_expression

first_bit ::= *static*_simple_expression

last_bit ::= *static*_simple_expression

at_clause ::= **for** direct_name **use at** expression;

In the production for discrete_choice_list the vertical bar stands for itself and is not a metasymbol.

Note that the above does not capture the fact that annotations may be extended over several lines by repeating --# at the start of successive lines.

The syntax for representation_clause is identical to that for Ada 95 and is included for completeness. Note that the forms mod_clause and at_clause are considered obsolescent in Ada 95.

## A1.2 Syntax of proof contexts

The following changes and additions to the above productions show the location and form of proof annotations.

* statement ::=
    simple_statement | compound_statement | proof_statement

\+ proof_statement ::=
    assert_statement | check_statement

* loop_statement ::= [*loop*_statement_identifier :]
    [iteration_scheme [loop_invariant]] **loop**
        sequence_of_statements
    **end loop** [*loop*_identifier];

\+ loop_invariant ::= assert_statement

\+ assert_statement ::= **--# assert** predicate;

\+ check_statement ::= **--# check** predicate;

\+ procedure_annotation ::=
    [global_definition | moded_global_definition]
    [dependency_relation]
    [precondition]
    [postcondition]

\+ function_annotation ::=
    [global_definition]
    [precondition]
    [return_annotation]

\+ precondition ::= **--# pre** predicate;

\+ postcondition ::= **--# post** predicate;

\+ return_annotation ::=
    **--# return** expression;
    | **--# return** identifier => predicate;

\+ predicate ::= *boolean*_expression

* expression ::=
    quantified_expression
    | relation -> relation
    | relation {**and** relation }
    | relation {**or** relation }
    | relation {**xor** relation}
    | relation <-> relation
    | relation {**and then** relation}
    | relation {**or else** relation}

\+ quantified_expression ::= quantifier_kind
    defining_identifier **in** *discrete*_subtype_mark [**range** range]
        => (predicate);

\+ quantifier_kind ::= **for all** | **for some**

```
* name ::= direct_name [~]
        | indexed_component | selected_component [~]
        | attribute_reference | function_call
        | record_update | array_update

+ record_update ::= prefix [ selector_name => expression
                              {; selector_name => expression} ]

+ array_update ::= prefix [ index_list => expression
                              {; index_list => expression} ]

+ index_list ::= expression {, expression}

* basic_declarative_item ::= basic_declaration | representation_clause
        | proof_function_declaration | basic_proof_declaration

+ proof_function_declaration ::= --# function_specification;

+ basic_proof_declaration ::= proof_type_declaration

+ proof_type_declaration ::=
        --# type defining_identifier is proof_type_definition;

+ proof_type_definition ::= abstract

+ own_variable_clause ::= --# own own_variable_specification
                              {own_variable_specification}

+ own_variable_specification ::= own_variable_list [: subtype_mark];
```

In the productions for record_update and array_update the square brackets stand for themselves and are not metasymbols.

Appendix 2

# Words, Attributes and Characters

This appendix lists the reserved words and attributes of SPARK. It also gives the names of all the constants in the package Ada.Characters.Latin_1.

The reserved words come in three categories. First there are the reserved words of Ada 95. In addition, certain other words are reserved for use in annotations. These two categories comprise the reserved words of the SPARK language itself. Finally, further words are used in FDL and these should also be avoided in programs for which verification conditions and path functions are to be produced.

## A2.1 SPARK words

The following words may not be used as identifiers in any SPARK program.

**abort**
**abs**
**abstract**
**accept**
**access**
**aliased**
**all**
**and**
**array**
**assert***
**at**

**begin**
**body**

**case**
**check***
**constant**

**declare**
**delay**
**delta**
**derives***
**digits**
**do**

**else**
**elsif**
**end**
**entry**
**exception**
**exit**

**for**
**from***
**function**

**generic**
**global***
**goto**

**hide***
**hold***

**if**
**in**
**inherit***
**initializes***
**invariant***
**is**

**limited**
**loop**

**main_program***
**mod**

**new**
**not**
**null**

**of**
**or**
**others**
**out**
**own***

**package**
**post***
**pragma**
**pre***
**private**
**procedure**
**protected**

**raise**
**range**
**record**
**rem**
**renames**
**requeue**
**return**
**reverse**

**select**
**separate**
**some***
**subtype**

**tagged**
**task**
**terminate**
**then**
**type**

**until**
**use**

**when**
**while**
**with**

**xor**

The words **hold** and **invariant** are reserved for historical reasons or possible future extensions. The words that are not reserved in Ada 95 are marked with an asterisk.

## A2.2 FDL words

The following words should be avoided as identifiers in any program for which verification conditions or path functions are to be generated. In addition, all identifiers commencing with Fld_ or Upf_ should be avoided as explained in Chapter 11.

**are_interchangeable**
**as**
**assume**

**const**

**div**

**element**

**finish**
**first**
**for_all**
**for_some**

**goal**

**last**

**may_be_deduced**
**may_be_deduced_from**
**may_be_replaced_by**

**nonfirst**
**nonlast**
**not_in**

**odd**

**pending**
**pred**
**proof**

**requires**

**save**
**sequence**
**set**
**sqr**
**start**
**strict_subset_of**
**subset_of**
**succ**

**update**

**var**

**where**

Note that the list includes First and Last which are also used as attributes in Ada. This is not a problem since attributes such as Range already use reserved words in Ada anyway.

## A2.3 Attributes

The following attributes of Ada 95 are permitted in SPARK.

Adjacent
Aft

Base

Ceiling
Component_Size
Compose
Copy_Sign

Delta
Denorm
Digits

Exponent

First
Floor
Fore
Fraction

Last
Leading_Part
Length

Machine
Machine_Emax
Machine_Emin
Machine_Mantissa
Machine_Overflows
Machine_Radix
Machine_Rounds
Max
Min
Model
Model_Emin
Model_Epsilon
Model_Mantissa
Model_Small

Pos
Pred

Range
Remainder
Rounding

Safe_First
Safe_Last
Scaling
Signed_Zeros
Size
Small
Succ

Truncation

Unbiased_Rounding

Val
Valid

Many of these attributes are described in the body of this book but a number of specialized ones such as those for use with floating point types or concerning representation are not discussed. For details of their meaning consult the *ARM* [ISO, 1995] or a textbook such as [Barnes, 1998].

## A2.4 Character names

The various characters in the Latin-1 set may be referred to by using the names of constants in the package Ada.Characters.Latin_1 whose specification has the following form

```
package Ada.Characters.Latin_1 is
   NUL              : constant Character := Character'Val(0);
   ...
   Space            : constant Character := ' ';
   Exclamation      : constant Character := '!';
   ...
   LC_Y_Diaeresis   : constant Character := 'ÿ';
end Ada.Characters.Latin_1;
```

All nongraphic characters and most graphic characters can thus be referred to using the names of the various constants. For example, the exclamation mark

**Table A2.1** The Latin-1 names.

| 0.. 15 | NUL, SOH, STX, ETX, | EOT, ENQ, ACK, BEL, | BS, HT, LF, VT, | FF, CR, SO, SI |
|---|---|---|---|---|
| 16.. 31 | DLE, DC1, DC2, DC3, | DC4, NAK, SYN, ETB, | CAN, EM, SUB, ESC, | FS, GS, RS, US |
| 32.. 35 | Space, | Exclamation, | Quotation, | Number_Sign |
| 36.. 39 | Dollar_Sign, | Percent_Sign, | Ampersand, | Apostrophe |
| 40.. 43 | Left_Parenthesis, | Right_Parenthesis, | Asterisk, | Plus_Sign |
| 44.. 47 | Comma, | Hyphen, | Full_Stop, | Solidus |
| 48.. 57 | (the digits 0 to 9 are not named) | | | |
| 58.. 61 | Colon, | Semicolon, | Less_Than_Sign, | Equals_Sign |
| 62.. 64 | Greater_Than_Sign, | Question, | Commercial_At | |
| 65.. 90 | (the upper case letters A to Z are not named) | | | |
| 91.. 94 | Left_Square_Bracket, | Reverse_Solidus, | Right_Square_Bracket, | Circumflex |
| 95..122 | Low_Line, | Grave, | LC_A, LC_B, ... | LC_Z |
| 123..126 | Left_Curly_Bracket, | Vertical_Line, | Right_Curly_Bracket, | Tilde |
| 127..130 | DEL, | Reserved_128, | Reserved_129, | BPH |
| 131..140 | NBH, | Reserved_132, | NEL, SSA, ESA, HTS, | HTJ, VTS, PLD, PLU |
| 141..153 | RI, SS2, SS3, DCS, | PU1, PU2, STS, CCH, | MW, SPA, EPA, SOS, | Reserved_153 |
| 154..161 | SCI, CSI, ST, OSC, | PM, APC, | No_Break_Space, | Inverted_Exclamation |
| 162..165 | Cent_Sign, | Pound_Sign, | Currency_Sign, | Yen_Sign |
| 166..169 | Broken_Bar, | Section_Sign, | Diaeresis, | Copyright_Sign |
| 170..173 | Feminine_Ordinal_Indicator, | Left_Angle_Quotation, | Not_Sign, | Soft_Hyphen |
| 174..177 | Registered_Trade_Mark_Sign, | Macron, | Degree_Sign, | Plus_Minus_Sign |
| 178..181 | Superscript_Two, | Superscript_Three, | Acute, | Micro_Sign |
| 182..185 | Pilcrow_Sign, | Middle_Dot, | Cedilla, | Superscript_One |
| 186..188 | Masculine_Ordinal_Indicator, | | Right_Angle_Quotation, | Fraction_One_Quarter |
| 189..191 | Fraction_One_Half, | Fraction_Three_Quarters, | | Inverted_Question |
| 192..195 | UC_A_Grave, | UC_A_Acute, | UC_A_Circumflex, | UC_A_Tilde |
| 196..199 | UC_A_Diaeresis, | UC_A_Ring, | UC_AE_Diphthong, | UC_C_Cedilla |
| 200..203 | UC_E_Grave, | UC_E_Acute, | UC_E_Circumflex, | UC_E_Diaeresis |
| 204..207 | UC_I_Grave, | UC_I_Acute, | UC_I_Circumflex, | UC_I_Diaeresis |
| 208..211 | UC_Icelandic_Eth, | UC_N_Tilde, | UC_O_Grave, | UC_O_Acute |
| 212..215 | UC_O_Circumflex, | UC_O_Tilde, | UC_O_Diaeresis, | Multiplication_Sign |
| 216..219 | UC_O_Oblique_Strike, | UC_U_Grave, | UC_U_Acute, | UC_U_Circumflex |
| 220..223 | UC_U_Diaeresis, | UC_Y_Acute, | UC_Icelandic_Thorn, | LC_German_Sharp_S |
| 224..227 | LC_A_Grave, | LC_A_Acute, | LC_A_Circumflex, | LC_A_Tilde |
| 228..231 | LC_A_Diaeresis, | LC_A_Ring, | LC_AE_Diphthong, | LC_C_Cedilla |
| 232..235 | LC_E_Grave, | LC_E_Acute, | LC_E_Circumflex, | LC_E_Diaeresis |
| 236..239 | LC_I_Grave, | LC_I_Acute, | LC_I_Circumflex, | LC_I_Diaeresis |
| 240..243 | LC_Icelandic_Eth, | LC_N_Tilde, | LC_O_Grave, | LC_O_Acute |
| 244..247 | LC_O_Circumflex, | LC_O_Tilde, | LC_O_Diaeresis, | Division_Sign |
| 248..251 | LC_O_Oblique_Strike, | LC_U_Grave, | LC_U_Acute, | LC_U_Circumflex |
| 252..255 | LC_U_Diaeresis, | LC_Y_Acute, | LC_Icelandic_Thorn, | LC_Y_Diaeresis |

can be referred to as Ada.Characters.Latin_1.Exclamation. For convenience, all the names are given in Table A2.1 which is taken from [Barnes, 1998].

There are also a number of alternative names for certain characters. They include: Minus_Sign for Hyphen, NBSP for No_Break_Space, Ring_Above for Degree_Sign and Paragraph_Sign for Pilcrow_Sign. (These alternatives are introduced by renamings in full Ada, but the SPARK version simply declares additional constants – the effect is the same.)

Appendix 3

# Changes from SPARK 83

For the convenience of those familiar with earlier versions of SPARK based on Ada 83 (and thus referred to as SPARK 83), this appendix summarizes the main differences between SPARK 83 and SPARK 95.

Parameters of mode **out** can be read in SPARK 95 (as in Ada 95). This removes a number of awkward anomalies and permits a more sensible match between the modes and the rules of access to parameters. As a consequence an **in out** parameter must now be both imported and exported; this was not required in SPARK 83 for nonscalar parameters.

Global annotations did not have modes in SPARK 83. They were introduced largely to permit just data flow analysis in which the derives annotation is not required. Moreover, the change to the rules for **out** parameters permits greater symmetry between parameters and globals and gives additional opportunities for consistency checks if information flow analysis is required.

If information flow analysis is required (and thus derives annotations must be provided), then modes may be omitted from global annotations. This is not recommended but provides backward compatibility with SPARK 83.

Use type clauses are new in SPARK 95. Renaming of operators should now be considered obsolescent.

The floating point equality operation is permitted in SPARK 95 but gives rise to a warning; it was forbidden in early versions of SPARK 83 but this caused problems with abstraction and private types.

Rounding from floating point types to integer types is now fully specified for values that lie midway between two integers – the value always rounds away from zero.

Literals do not need to be qualified in fixed point expressions but qualification is otherwise still needed in intermediate expressions although it is not in Ada 95.

There are no reduced accuracy subtypes for fixed and floating point types in SPARK 95. This odd feature of Ada 83 is deemed obsolescent in Ada 95.

The ordering of declarations required by Ada 83 (some declarations such as those of variables had to precede the declarations of bodies) do not apply in Ada 95 and are similarly not required by SPARK 95.

An enumeration type is permitted to have only one literal in SPARK 95; this was not allowed in SPARK 83.

The type Character corresponds to Latin-1 and thus has 256 values whereas in SPARK 83 it corresponded to the ASCII set and had 128 values. Thus Character'Pos(Character'Last) is now 255.

Static expressions are much more liberal in SPARK 95 and include membership tests, short circuit forms, type conversions and array attributes provided all constituents are themselves static. Named numbers are also permitted. Moreover, an expression that has the form of a static expression is always evaluated statically even when it occurs in a context that does not demand a static expression.

Both public and private child packages are introduced although there are some additional visibility rules compared with full Ada. Thus a public child cannot see a private sibling and vice versa. Moreover, a parent cannot see its public children.

A private part can now contain the declarations of any objects and types (and not just those of types declared as private in the visible part). It can also contain renaming and subprogram declarations. Also a deferred constant can be of any type.

There are a number of additional reserved words. These are the reserved words of Ada 95 that were not reserved in Ada 83. They are **abstract**, **aliased**, **protected**, **requeue**, **tagged** and **until**. However, none of these are used by the subset of Ada that is the kernel of SPARK.

The attributes accepted by SPARK 95 are somewhat different to those accepted by SPARK 83. These reflect differences between Ada 83 and Ada 95. Note in particular that Base only applies to scalar types in SPARK 95.

The syntax for specifying certain aspects of representation clauses has been changed; the old forms are still available but considered obsolescent.

The pragma Interface is replaced by the pragma Import to match the similar change to Ada. The pragma Elaborate_Body is now required for library packages that have a body but do not require one in order to satisfy Ada language rules.

The type File_Mode of the package Spark_IO now has the third literal value Append_File to match the corresponding change to Text_IO. This mode enables items to be appended to the end of an existing file.

## Appendix 4

# Using the CD

The CD accompanying this book contains the following tools, documentation and examples.

### *Tools*

There are three distinct items.

| | |
|---|---|
| The Examiner | The version provided is intended for demonstration use. |
| The Simplifier | This is also a demonstration version. |
| The Interface | This is the Windows Interface to the tools. |

The Examiner and Simplifier run under the Windows Interface as described in Chapter 9 and Section 11.6 respectively. The Examiner has a number of capacity and other limitations which are described in the associated help files. The Simplifier similarly has a fixed heap size in this demonstration version.

The user should be aware that the Examiner and Simplifier are based on well-established programs written using mature tools and techniques and can be expected to be very reliable. However, the Interface has been crafted in Visual Basic and may prove to be less robust. If in difficulty the Examiner can always be run directly from DOS as described in the documentation.

### *Documentation*

The Windows Interface includes help files. In addition, the following documents are provided in Adobe Acrobat format and are accessible through the help files.

Examiner Manual.

Simplifier Manual.

Further material on run-time check analysis.

Adobe Acrobat reader software is included on the CD.

### Examples

All significant examples in this book will be found on the CD under the directory **\examples** in local directories **\chap2**, **\chap3** etc. In the case of those chapters with many examples the files are further grouped by section in subdirectories giving the section number; thus the examples for Section 9.1 are in **\examples\chap9\9_1**.

For ease of recognition the file names of most examples reflect the section in which they are first introduced. Thus the file **ex0204a.ada** contains the first example of Section 4 of Chapter 2. Succeeding examples or variations have final letter **b**, **c** etc. Examples relating to exercises and their answers have the exercise number instead of the final letter. Thus the answer to Exercise 2.9(**1**) is in file **ex02091.ada**. Each file also includes Ada comments giving more details of the example, any related files and the use of the Examiner; these comments also indicate whether verification conditions are to be generated and the Simplifier applied to the results.

The examples in Chapter 9 (most of which use multiple files) use the file names as described in that chapter.

There is also a subdirectory **\sparkio** which contains the specification and body of Spark_IO.

The directory **\results** mirrors the directory **\examples**. As well as containing all the examples it also contains the files resulting from running the examples using the Examiner and Simplifier as appropriate.

### Installation

The CD is installed by inserting it into an appropriate drive and running **setup.exe**. This gives the option of running the tools directly from the CD or of installing them on the hard disk.

The system is typically installed on the hard disk under a directory such as **\winspark**. Within this directory are three text files, **licence.txt**, **readme.txt** and **filelist.txt**. The first contains essential information regarding the licence for the use of the demonstration system. The second contains additional information regarding the configuration. The third lists the various files.

Within **\winspark** are five local directories as follows

**\gui** This contains the Interface software.

**\examiner** This contains the Examiner, **dosspark.exe**.

**\simplify** This contains the Simplifier, **simp.exe** and associated files.

**\examples** This contains the source of the examples as explained above.

**\results** This also contains the results of running all the examples.

Note that this is the normal structure. However, it is possible to use other structures provided appropriate changes are made using the General options dialogue box as explained in Chapter 9.

# Answers to Exercises

## Answers 2

*Exercise 2.5*

1
```
procedure Inner(K: in Integer)
--# global in out I;
--# derives I from I, K;
is
   J: Integer;
begin
   J := K + I;
   I := J + 2;
end Inner;
```

2
```
procedure Start
--# global out Seed;
--# derives Seed from ;
is
begin
   Seed := 12345;
end Start;
```

3 The mode must be **out**. Although Exchange does read T, nevertheless the initial value of T has no impact on the final value of any exported variable.

*Exercise 2.9*

1 The package Stacks can be declared as a library unit.

```
package Stacks is
   ...
end Stacks;
```

```
--# inherit Stacks;
package Go_Between
--# own A_Stack;
is
   procedure Use_Stack;
   --# global out A_Stack;
   --# derives A_Stack from ;

end Go_Between;

with Stacks;
package body Go_Between is

   A_Stack: Stacks.Stack;

   procedure Use_Stack is
      A: Integer;
   begin
      ...
      Stacks.Clear(A_Stack);
      ...
      Stacks.Push(A_Stack, 55);
      ...
      Stacks.Pop(A_Stack, A);
      ...
   end Use_Stack;

end Go_Between;

with Go_Between;
--# inherit Go_Between;
--# main_program;
procedure Main
--# global out Go_Between.A_Stack;
--# derives Go_Between.A_Stack from ;
is
begin
   ...
   Go_Between.Use_Stack;
   ...
end Main;
```

Note that the procedure Main no longer needs an inherit clause for the package Stacks. This is because Stacks has no global state; the state is all in the variable A_Stack internal to Go_Between. Moreover, because the state is explicitly given a first value by the call of Clear which occurs after the procedure Main has been entered, it follows that the global annotation on Main shows that A_Stack is global of mode **out** and the derives annotation confirms that its initial value is not used. The same applies to the annotation on Use_Stack.

It is interesting to observe that the inherit clause always goes on the specification even though there may be situations where neither the

SPARK annotations nor the Ada code of the specification refer to the package concerned. Thus, in this example, Go_Between requires an inherit clause for Stacks on its specification even though Stacks is only referred to in its body.

## Answers 3

*Exercise 3.4*

1

```
procedure Solve(A, B, C, D: in Integer; P, Q: in Float; X, Y: out Float);
--# derives X, Y from A, B, C, D, P, Q;
--# pre A * D /= B * C;
--# post Float(A) * X + Float(B) * Y = P and
--#      Float(C) * X + Float(D) * Y = Q;
```

However, there is considerable difficulty in modelling floating point values for the purposes of proof, especially since we have omitted any accuracy criterion. As noted in Section 5.4, the Examiner issues a warning whenever floating point equality is used.

## Answers 4

*Exercise 4.3*

1 There are three main errors:

(1) a real literal cannot be in based notation;
(2) Check is a reserved word and so cannot be used as an identifier;
(3) an annotation cannot be broken by an Ada comment – it has to be a SPARK comment thus

```
--#   -- note that B only depends upon F
--#   -- and not on Stop and Start
```

In addition, Start is a reserved word of FDL and so should be avoided if verification conditions or path functions are to be generated.

## Answers 5

*Exercise 5.6*

1

```
Zero: constant Complex := Complex'(Re => 0.0, Im => 0.0);
...
Z: Complex := Zero;
```

2

```
Stack'(Stack_Vector => Vector'(Index_Range => 0),
       Stack_Pointer => 0)
```

# Answers 6

*Exercise 6.3*

1

```
My_Loop:
for I in Integer range 1 .. 100 loop
   A(I) := A(I) + 1;
   if A(I) = 10 then
      exit;
   end if;
   A(I+1) := 0;
end loop My_Loop;
```

*Exercise 6.6*

1

```
procedure Clear(S: out Stack) is
begin
   S := Stack'(Vector'(Index_Range => 0), 0);
end Clear;
```

Remember that the derives annotation is not repeated in the body. Note that since flow analysis of records is in terms of the individual components, it is also acceptable to make individual assignments to the two components S.Stack_Vector and S.Stack_Pointer thus

```
begin
   S.Stack_Vector := Vector'(Index_Range => 0);
   S.Stack_Pointer := 0;
end Clear;
```

2 In logical terms the derives annotation is correct. However, because flow analysis of arrays is always in terms of entire variables, the assignment in the first double loop is seen as changing just part of Z and so overall it looks as if the initial (and undefined) value of Z is used to provide the final value. The solution is to assign a complete aggregate to Z thus

```
Z := Matrix'(Matrix_Index => (Matrix_Index => 0));
```

3 In the case of Write there is only one possible derives annotation

```
--# derives S from S, X;
```

However, in the case of Read there are three possibilities

```
--# derives S, X from S;

--# derives S from S &
--#         X from ;

--# derives S from   &
--#         X from S;
```

The first is typically the correct one.

4 There are nine possibilities

```
--# derives X from   & Y from X, Y;
--# derives X from X & Y from Y;
--# derives X from X & Y from X, Y;
--# derives X from Y & Y from X;
--# derives X from Y & Y from X, Y;
--# derives X from X, Y & Y from ;
--# derives X from X, Y & Y from X;
--# derives X from X, Y & Y from Y;
--# derives X from X, Y & Y from X, Y;
```

If there is more than one export (the solution is unique in the case of only one export) then the number of possibilities escalates rapidly with increasing numbers of imports and exports. The insomniac reader might contemplate the general solution when there are $p$ imports and $q$ exports.

# Answers 8

*Exercise 8.3*

1

```
with Input_Port, Output_Port, The_Stack;
--# inherit Input_Port, Output_Port, The_Stack;
--# main_program;
procedure Copy
--# global in out The_Stack.State,
--#               Input_Port.Input_Sequence,
--#               Output_Port.Output_Sequence;
--# derives The_Stack.State from *, Input_Port.Input_Sequence &
--#         Input_Port.Input_Sequence from * &
--#         Output_Port.Output_Sequence
--#           from *, Input_Port.Input_Sequence, The_Stack.State;
is
  Value: Integer;
begin
  loop
    Input_Port.Read_From_Port(Value);
    The_Stack.Push(Value);
    exit when Value = 0;
  end loop;
  loop
    The_Stack.Pop(Value);
    Output_Port.Write_To_Port(Value);
    exit when Value = 0;
  end loop;
end Copy;
```

2
```
with Input_Port, Output_Port, Stacks;
--# inherit Input_Port, Output_Port, Stacks;
--# main_program;
procedure Copy
--# global in out Input_Port.Input_Sequence,
--#               Output_Port.Output_Sequence;
--# derives Input_Port.Input_Sequence from * &
--#         Output_Port.Output_Sequence
--#            from *, Input_Port.Input_Sequence;
is
   The_Stack: Stacks.Stack;
   Value: Integer;
begin
   Stacks.Clear(The_Stack);
   loop
      Input_Port.Read_From_Port(Value);
      Stacks.Push(The_Stack, Value);
      exit when Input_Port.End_Of_Input_Sequence;
   end loop;
   loop
      Stacks.Pop(The_Stack, Value);
      Output_Port.Write_To_Port(Value);
      exit when Stacks.Is_Empty(The_Stack);
   end loop;
end Copy;
```

## Answers 10

*Exercise 10.1*

1 In the first example we get

```
X = Y~ and T + 1 = X~      -- replacing Y by T + 1
Y = Y~ and T + 1 = X~      -- replacing X by Y
Y = Y~ and X + 1 = X~      -- replacing T by X
```

and in the second

```
X = Y~ and X = X~          -- replacing Y by X
Y = Y~ and Y = X~          -- replacing X by Y
Y = Y~ and Y = X~          -- replacing T by X
```

*Exercise 10.3*

1 The matrices for the individual statements are

$$L_1 = \begin{array}{c} \\ w \\ x \\ y \\ z \end{array} \overset{\begin{array}{cc} 1 & 2 \end{array}}{\begin{pmatrix} 0 & 0 \\ 0 & 0 \\ 1 & 0 \\ 1 & 0 \end{pmatrix}} \qquad M_1 = \begin{array}{c} 1 \\ 2 \end{array} \overset{\begin{array}{cccc} w & x & y & z \end{array}}{\begin{pmatrix} 0 & 1 & 0 & 0 \\ 0 & 0 & 0 & 0 \end{pmatrix}} \qquad R_1 = \begin{array}{c} w \\ x \\ y \\ z \end{array} \overset{\begin{array}{cccc} w & x & y & z \end{array}}{\begin{pmatrix} 1 & 0 & 0 & 0 \\ 0 & 0 & 0 & 0 \\ 0 & 1 & 1 & 0 \\ 0 & 1 & 0 & 1 \end{pmatrix}}$$

$$L_2 = \begin{array}{c|cc} & 1 & 2 \\ \hline w & 0 & 0 \\ x & 0 & 1 \\ y & 0 & 0 \\ z & 0 & 0 \end{array} \qquad M_2 = \begin{array}{c|cccc} & w & x & y & z \\ \hline 1 & 0 & 0 & 0 & 0 \\ 2 & 1 & 0 & 0 & 0 \end{array} \qquad R_2 = \begin{array}{c|cccc} & w & x & y & z \\ \hline w & 0 & 0 & 0 & 0 \\ x & 1 & 1 & 0 & 0 \\ y & 0 & 0 & 1 & 0 \\ z & 0 & 0 & 0 & 1 \end{array}$$

It is then seen that $R_1R_2$ equals $R$ for the sequence.

**2** We have

$$L = \begin{pmatrix} 0 & 0 \\ 0 & 0 \\ 1 & 1 \\ 1 & 1 \end{pmatrix} \qquad M = \begin{pmatrix} 1 & 1 & 0 & 0 \\ 1 & 0 & 0 & 0 \end{pmatrix} \qquad LM = \begin{pmatrix} 0 & 0 & 0 & 0 \\ 0 & 0 & 0 & 0 \\ 1 & 1 & 0 & 0 \\ 1 & 1 & 0 & 0 \end{pmatrix}$$

The result then follows.

**3** $D$ is the null matrix of order $V_n$;
$L$ and $M$ are null matrices of orders $(V_n \times E_n)$ and $(E_n \times V_n)$ respectively;
$P$ and $R$ are unit matrices of order $V_n$.

*Exercise 10.5*

**1** The matrix $R$ reveals that the initial value of Y is not used at all and this results in

```
!!! (  2)  Flow Error          : Importation of the initial
           value of variable Y is ineffective.
```

Checking the matrix $R$ against the derives annotation results in three messages

```
!!! (  4)  Flow Error          : The imported value of Y is
           not used in the derivation of X.

??? (  5)  Warning             : The imported value of X may
           be used in the derivation of X.

!!! (  6)  Flow Error          : The imported value of X is
           not used in the derivation of Y.
```

*Exercise 10.6*

**1** The $R$ matrices for the two calls are now

$$R_1 = \begin{array}{c|ccc} & a & b & c \\ \hline a & 0 & 1 & 0 \\ b & 1 & 0 & 0 \\ c & 0 & 0 & 1 \end{array} \qquad R_2 = \begin{array}{c|ccc} & a & b & c \\ \hline a & 1 & 0 & 0 \\ b & 0 & 0 & 1 \\ c & 0 & 1 & 0 \end{array}$$

The matrix for the procedure as a whole is $R_1R_2$ which is

$$R = \begin{array}{c|ccc} & a & b & c \\ \hline a & 0 & 0 & 1 \\ b & 1 & 0 & 0 \\ c & 0 & 1 & 0 \end{array}$$

All six elements off the diagonal are incorrect and therefore result in six messages from the Examiner as follows

```
!!! (  1)  Flow Error         : The imported value of C is
           not used in the derivation of A.

??? (  2)  Warning            : The imported value of B may
           be used in the derivation of A.

!!! (  3)  Flow Error         : The imported value of A is
           not used in the derivation of B.

??? (  4)  Warning            : The imported value of C may
           be used in the derivation of B.

!!! (  5)  Flow Error         : The imported value of B is
           not used in the derivation of C.

??? (  6)  Warning            : The imported value of A may
           be used in the derivation of C.
```

**2** The matrices are

$$L = \begin{array}{c} \\ a \\ b \\ c \end{array}\begin{array}{c} \begin{array}{cccc} 1 & 2 & 3 & 4 \end{array} \\ \begin{pmatrix} 0 & 1 & 1 & 0 \\ 1 & 0 & 0 & 1 \\ 0 & 0 & 0 & 0 \end{pmatrix} \end{array} \quad M = \begin{array}{c} \\ 1 \\ 2 \\ 3 \\ 4 \end{array}\begin{array}{c} \begin{array}{ccc} a & b & c \end{array} \\ \begin{pmatrix} 0 & 1 & 0 \\ 1 & 0 & 0 \\ 1 & 0 & 0 \\ 0 & 1 & 0 \end{pmatrix} \end{array} \quad R = \begin{array}{c} \\ a \\ b \\ c \end{array}\begin{array}{c} \begin{array}{ccc} a & b & c \end{array} \\ \begin{pmatrix} 1 & 0 & 0 \\ 0 & 1 & 0 \\ 0 & 0 & 1 \end{pmatrix} \end{array}$$

The overall checks that variables are used or set somewhere reveal that C is neither read nor updated. This results in the following two messages

```
!!! (  1)  Flow Error         : Importation of the initial
           value of variable C is ineffective.

!!! (  2)  Flow Error         : The variable C is exported
           but not (internally) defined.
```

Note that this is a slightly different situation to that in Sections 11.4 and 11.5 where the messages related to misuse of the local variable T. In this case they relate to the parameter C which passes through without being read or updated. This is considered undesirable and an **in out** parameter must always be updated on some path. The fact that the parameter C passes through unused and unchanged can also be deduced by noting that the C row of the *L* matrix and the C column of the *M* matrix are both null.

There are six mismatches in comparing the matrix *R* with the derives annotation. However no message is issued to the effect that C may be used to compute itself because the anomalies in C have been covered by the two previous messages.

```
!!! (  3)  Flow Error         : The imported value of C is
           not used in the derivation of A.

??? (  4)  Warning            : The imported value of A may
           be used in the derivation of A.
```

```
!!! (  5)  Flow Error         : The imported value of A is
           not used in the derivation of B.

??? (  6)  Warning            : The imported value of B may
           be used in the derivation of B.

!!! (  7)  Flow Error         : The imported value of B is
           not used in the derivation of C.
```

*Exercise 10.7*

**1** The matrices are

$$L = \begin{array}{c} \\ w \\ x \\ y \\ z \end{array} \begin{array}{c} \begin{matrix} 1 & 2 & 3 \end{matrix} \\ \begin{pmatrix} 1 & 0 & 0 \\ 0 & 0 & 0 \\ 0 & 1 & 0 \\ 0 & 1 & 0 \end{pmatrix} \end{array} \qquad M = \begin{array}{c} \\ 1 \\ 2 \\ 3 \end{array} \begin{array}{c} \begin{matrix} w & x & y & z \end{matrix} \\ \begin{pmatrix} 0 & 1 & 0 & 1 \\ 0 & 1 & 0 & 0 \\ 0 & 0 & 0 & 1 \end{pmatrix} \end{array} \qquad R = \begin{array}{c} \\ w \\ x \\ y \\ z \end{array} \begin{array}{c} \begin{matrix} w & x & y & z \end{matrix} \\ \begin{pmatrix} 1 & 1 & 0 & 1 \\ 0 & 1 & 0 & 0 \\ 0 & 1 & 1 & 0 \\ 0 & 1 & 0 & 1 \end{pmatrix} \end{array}$$

*Exercise 10.8*

**1** The flow graph for the loop now is

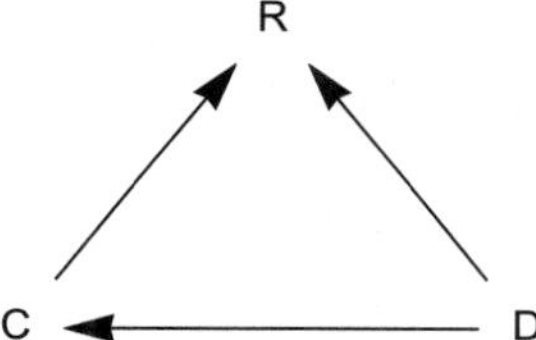


There are no cycles and so all the variables are stable. D has index 0, C has index 1 and R has index 2. The loop condition which depends only upon D is therefore also stable and has index 1. The Examiner accordingly reports

```
!!! (  1)  Flow Error         : Exit condition is stable, of
           index 1.
```

**2** Following the technique used to compute $L$ in the text, we have

$R = L_e M_e D_A$ **or** $R_1$ **or** $I$    using formula for the conditional statement
$\quad = L_e M_e D_A$ **or** $R_A R$ **or** $I$    using formula for A followed by the loop

and then using the transitive closure to remove $R$ from the RHS, we finally get

$R = R_A^*(L_e M_e D_A$ **or** $I)$

The multi-exit loop statement can be treated in exactly the same way. Thus the loop

**loop**
  **exit when** $e_1$;

```
    S1;
    ...
    exit when en;
    Sn;
  end loop;
```

can be rewritten as nested conditional statements

```
if not e1 then
  S1;
  if not e2 then
    S2;
    ...
      ...
      if not en then
        Sn;
        S;
      end if;
    ...
  end if;
end if;
```

where S represents the loop itself.

We then just keep applying the formulae for the conditional statement and sequence in a nested manner. It is convenient to write $Q_i = L_{e_i} M_{e_i} D_i$ and we get

$$R = Q_1 \textbf{ or } I \textbf{ or } R_1(Q_2 \textbf{ or } I \textbf{ or } R_2(Q_3 \textbf{ or } I \textbf{ or } \ldots R_{n-1}(Q_n \textbf{ or } I \textbf{ or } R_n R) \ldots))$$
$$= Q_1 \textbf{ or } I \textbf{ or } X_1(Q_2 \textbf{ or } I) \textbf{ or } X_2(Q_3 \textbf{ or } I) \textbf{ or } \ldots X_{n-1}(Q_n \textbf{ or } I) \textbf{ or } X_n R$$

where $X_i \doteq R_1 R_2 \ldots R_i$. We then use the transitive closure to remove $R$ from the RHS and finally get

$$R = X_n^*(Q_1 \textbf{ or } I \textbf{ or } X_1(Q_2 \textbf{ or } I) \textbf{ or } X_2(Q_3 \textbf{ or } I) \textbf{ or } \ldots X_{n-1}(Q_n \textbf{ or } I))$$

# Answers 11

*Exercise 11.2*

**1** The function Max becomes

```
function Max(X, Y: Integer) return Integer
--# return M => (X > Y -> M = X) and
--#             (Y > X -> M = Y) and
--#             (X > Y or Y > X);
is
  Result: Integer;
begin
  if X > Y then
    Result := X;
  elsif Y > X then
```

```
      Result := Y;
   else
      Result := 210;
   end if;
   return Result;
end Max;
```

The verification condition for the third path is now

```
function_max_3.
H1:    true .
H2:    not (x > y) .
H3:    not (y > x) .
       ->
C1:    (x > y) -> (210 = x) .
C2:    (y > x) -> (210 = y) .
C3:    (x > y) or (y > x) .
```

Conclusion C3 cannot be proved.

As an aside note that the form

```
(A -> P) and (B -> Q) and (C -> R) and (A or B or C)
```

is logically equivalent to

```
(A and P) or (B and Q) or (C and R)
```

The Simplifier is more likely to be able to prove the first form whereas the second often more naturally occurs when writing formal specifications.

2 As SPARK text, the function is clearly self-consistent. However, it is presumably not what the programmer had in mind. There is obviously a danger in cutting-and-pasting a result into the return annotation (it should really be vice versa) as might happen in such a trivial example. In practice, of course, the return annotation will present a different view of the activity of the function. But ultimately nothing can prevent us from solving the wrong problem.

*Exercise 11.3*

1 A possible solution using a for statement is as follows

```
package body P is

   --# function Fact(N: Natural) return Natural;

   function Factorial(N: Natural) return Natural
   --# pre N >= 0;
   --# return Fact(N);
   is
      Result: Natural := 1;
   begin
      for Term in Integer range 1 .. N loop
```

```
      Result := Result * Term;
      --# assert Term > 0 and Result = Fact(Term);
    end loop;
    return Result;
  end Factorial;

end P;
```

It is important that the condition for leaving the loop is precise otherwise the exit path will be harder to prove. Thus writing **while** Term < N **loop** is unfruitful.

There are four paths and the verification conditions are as follows

```
For path(s) from start to assertion:

H1:    n >= 0 .
H2:    1 <= n .
       ->
C1:    1 > 0 .
C2:    1 * 1 = fact(1) .

For path(s) from assertion to assertion:

H1:    loop__1__term > 0 .
H2:    result = fact(loop__1__term) .
H3:    not (loop__1__term = n) .
       ->
C1:    loop__1__term + 1 > 0 .
C2:    result * (loop__1__term + 1) = fact(loop__1__term + 1) .

For path(s) from start to finish:

H1:    n >= 0 .
H2:    not (1 <= n) .
       ->
C1:    1 = fact(n) .

For path(s) from assertion to finish:

H1:    loop__1__term > 0 .
H2:    result = fact(loop__1__term) .
H3:    loop__1__term = n .
       ->
C1:    result = fact(n) .
```

These are all easy to prove given the theorems

$$\text{fact}(n) = n \times \text{fact}(n-1) \qquad n > 0$$
$$\text{fact}(0) = 1$$

Note that it is important to include Term > 0 in the assertion because otherwise the condition $n > 0$ in the first theorem will not be satisfied. Remember that an assertion resets all hypotheses and so the fact that Term must have been greater than zero is forgotten.

Note also the use of the identifier loop__1__term to correspond to the

SPARK identifier Term (note the double underlines). This is necessary in general because loop parameters are implicitly declared and several in a subprogram could have the same identifier. If a loop is named such as

```
My_Loop: for Parameter in ...
```

then the generated identifier would be My_Loop__Parameter.

*Exercise 11.4*

1

```
rule_family fact:
   fact(X) requires [X : i] .

fact(1): fact(N) may_be_replaced_by N * fact(N-1) if [N > 0] .
fact(2): fact(0) may_be_replaced_by 1 .
```

2 The function does not terminate in the case when the parameter N is zero.

*Exercise 11.8*

1

```
subtype Index is Integer range 1 .. 10;
type Atype is array (Index) of Integer;

procedure Idarr(A: out Atype)
--# derives A from ;
--# post for all M in Index => (A(M) = M);
is
begin
   for I in Index loop
      A(I) := I;
      --# assert I in Index and
      --#          (for all M in Index range Index'First .. I => (A(M) = M));
   end loop;
end Idarr;
```

It is important to remember to include the condition I **in** Index in the assert. Note also that there is no precondition because there are no in parameters.

# Answers 13

*Exercise 13.1*

1

```
package Building
--# own Door_History: Doors_State_Type;     -- type announcement
is
   type Direction_Type is (Up, Down);
   type Floor_Type is (Floor_0, Floor_1, Floor_2, Floor_3);
   type Door_Position is (Open, Closed);
   type Doors_State_Type is array (Floor_Type) of Door_Position;
```

```
   procedure Initialize_Door_States;
   --# global out Door_History;
   --# derives Door_History from ;
   --# post Door_History = Doors_State_Type'(Floor_Type => Closed);

   procedure Open_Door(Floor: in Floor_Type);
   --# global in out Door_History;
   --# derives Door_History from Door_History, Floor;
   --# pre Door_History(Floor) = Closed;
   --# post Door_History = Door_History~[Floor => Open];

   procedure Close_Door(Floor: in Floor_Type);
   --# global in out Door_History;
   --# derives Door_History from Door_History, Floor;
   --# pre Door_History(Floor) = Open;
   --# post Door_History = Door_History~[Floor => Closed];

end Building;
```

It might be better to change the precondition for Open_Door to ensure that all the doors are closed before opening one of them. A further improvement would be to couple the conditions with the state of the lift to ensure that a door can only be opened if the lift is at the floor concerned.

*Exercise 13.2*

1 The body of Poll cannot change the state of the doors since the annotations on Poll do not mention Building.Door_State. Looking at the body of Traverse and Lift_Control, we see that the only call of Open_Door is immediately followed by a call of Close_Door. It follows that the doors are closed when the lift is quiescent.

*Exercise 13.5*

1 The package AP.Heading might be

```
with AP.Controls, Instruments, Surfaces;
--# inherit AP.Controls, Instruments, Surfaces;
private package AP.Heading
--# own State;
--# initializes State;
is
   procedure Maintain(Switch_Pressed: in Controls.Switch;
                      Mach: in Instruments.Machnumber;
                      Present_Heading: in Instruments.Headdegree;
                      Target_Heading: in Instruments.Headdegree;
                      Bank: in Instruments.Bankangle;
                      Slip: in Instruments.Slipangle);
   --# global in out State, Surfaces.Ailerons, Surfaces.Rudder;

end AP.Heading;
```

```
with AP.Heading.Roll, AP.Heading.Yaw;
package body AP.Heading
--# own State is AP.Heading.Roll.State, AP.Heading.Yaw.State;
is
  procedure Maintain(Switch_Pressed: in Controls.Switch;
                     Mach: in Instruments.Machnumber;
                     Present_Heading: in Instruments.Headdegree;
                     Target_Heading: in Instruments.Headdegree;
                     Bank: in Instruments.Bankangle;
                     Slip: in Instruments.Slipangle)
  --# global in out Roll.State, Yaw.State,
  --#               Surfaces.Ailerons, Surfaces.Rudder;
  is
  begin
    case Switch_Pressed is
      when Controls.On =>
        Roll.Roll_AP(Mach, Present_Heading, Target_Heading, Bank);
        Yaw.Yaw_AP(Mach, Slip);
      when Controls.Off => null;
    end case;
  end Maintain;

end AP.Heading;
```

*Exercise 13.6*

1 Take the rule perm(1) and replace I, J, X, Y, A and B as follows

```
I => i
J => j
X => element(t, [j])
Y => element(t, [i])
A => t
B => t
```

The first part of perm(1) is then precisely the required conclusion C2 and the second part becomes

```
perm(update(update(t, [i], element(t, [i])), [j], element(t, [j])), t)
```

This can be transformed as follows

```
= perm(update(t, [j], element(t, [j])), t)     -- using array(2)
= perm(t, t)                                   -- using array(2) again
= true                                         -- by perm(2)
```

and so the original conclusion C2 then follows. This straightforward but rather laborious process is easily done with the aid of the Proof Checker.

# Bibliography

The following items are referred to in the body of the text.

[Barnes, 1998] J. G. P. Barnes, *Programming in Ada 95*, 2nd edn, Addison-Wesley, Harlow, 1998.

[Bergeretti and Carré, 1985] J.-F. Bergeretti and B. A. Carré, Information-Flow and Data-Flow Analysis of while-Programs, *ACM Transactions on Programming Languages and Systems*, ACM, New York, Vol. 7, pp. 37–61, Jan. 1985.

[Böhm and Jacopini, 1966] C. Böhm and G. Jacopini, Flow Diagrams, Turing Machines, and Languages with Only Two Formation Rules, *Communications of the ACM*, ACM, New York, Vol. 19, no. 5, May 1966.

[Carré and Jennings, 1988] B. A. Carré and T. J. Jennings, *SPARK – The SPADE Ada Kernel*, Department of Electronics and Computer Science, University of Southampton, 1988.

[Farrow, Kennedy and Zucconi, 1975] R. Farrow, K. Kennedy and L. Zucconi, Graph Grammars and Global Program Flow Analysis, *Proceedings of 17th IEEE Symposium on Foundations of Computer Science*, pp. 42–56, IEEE, New York, 1975.

[Finnie, 1997] G. Finnie, *SPARK – The SPADE Ada Kernel*, Edition 3.3, Praxis Critical Systems Limited, 1997.

[ISO, 1995] International Standards Organization, *Reference Manual for the Ada Programming Language*, ISO/IEC 8652: 1995.

[ISO, 2000] International Standards Organization, *Guide for the Use of the Ada Programming Language in High Integrity Systems*, ISO/IEC TR 15942: 2000.

[Marsh and O'Neill, 1994] D. W. R. Marsh and I. M. O'Neill, *The Formal Semantics of SPARK*, Program Validation Ltd, Southampton, 1994.

[SPC, 1995] The Software Productivity Consortium, *Ada 95 Quality and Style*, SPC, Herndon, Virginia, 1995.

[Warshall, 1962] S. Warshall, A Theorem on Boolean Matrices, *Journal of the ACM*, Vol. 9, pp. 11–13, Jan. 1962.

The following papers give additional information on SPARK and its tools.

B. A. Carré and J. R. Garnsworthy, SPARK – An Annotated Ada Subset for Safety-Critical Programming, *Proceedings of TRI-Ada '90*, ACM, New York, 1990.

B. A. Carré and D. W. R. Marsh, Designing Out Verification and Validation Costs, *Proceedings of 1992 Avionics Conference*, London, ERA Technology Ltd, Leatherhead, England, 1992.

B. A. Carré, I. M. O'Neill, D. L. Clutterbuck and C. W. Debney, SPADE – the Southampton Program Analysis and Development Environment, in *Software Engineering Environments*, I. Sommerville (ed.), Peter Peregrinus, 1986.

R. Chapman and A. Burns, Combining Worst-Case Timing Analysis and Program Proof, *Real-Time Systems*, Vol. 11, pp. 145–171, 1996.

M. Croxford and J. M. Sutton, Breaking Through the V & V Bottleneck, *Ada in Europe 1995*, LNCS 1031, Springer-Verlag, Berlin, 1995.

J. R. Garnsworthy, I. M. O'Neill and B. A. Carré, Automatic Proof of the Absence of Run-Time Errors, in *Ada: Towards Maturity*, L. Collingbourne (ed.), IOS Press, Amsterdam, 1993.

I. M. O'Neill, D. L. Clutterbuck, P. F. Farrow, P. G. Summers and W. C. Dolman, The Formal Verification of Safety-Critical Assembly Code, *Proceedings of SAFECOMP '88*, Pergamon Press, Oxford, 1988.

I. M. O'Neill, Industrial Report on Applications of Prolog in Software Validation and Verification Tools, *Proceedings of Practical Applications of Prolog Conference (PAP '95)*, Paris, 1995.

J. M. Sutton and B. A. Carré, Ada – The Cheapest Way to Build a Line of Business, *Proceedings of TRI-Ada '95*, pp. 320–330, ACM, New York, 1995.

The following books provide more general background reading.

R. C. Backhouse, *Program Construction and Verification*, Prentice-Hall International, Englewood Cliffs, New Jersey, 1986.

D. Gries, *The Science of Programming*, Springer-Verlag, Berlin, 1981.

S. S. Muchnik and N. D. Jones (eds), *Program Flow Analysis*, Prentice-Hall International, Englewood Cliffs, New Jersey, 1981.

C. T. Sennett (ed.), *High-integrity Software*, Pitman, London, 1989.

M. K. Smith, *The AVA Reference Manual*, Technical Report 64, Computational Logic Inc., Austin, Texas, 1992.

J. Woodcock and M. Loomes, *Software Engineering Mathematics*, Pitman, London, 1988; and Addison-Wesley, Reading, Massachussetts, 1989.

# Index